Understanding Bereaved Parents and Siblings

Understanding Bereaved Parents and Siblings is based on lived experiences and provides insight, ideas, and inspiration on how to support the bereaved, how to talk to them about their experience, and how to help people manage their own shock or grief.

Part I of the book contains ten stories from parents and six from siblings sharing their experiences. Each narrator discusses their relationship with the person who died; what led up to the death; the impact of the loss on the speaker; as well as what helped and what hindered them in their grief. Part II is aimed at professionals and draws on various topics such as grief and bereavement models, transgenerational loss, resilience, protection, and creative ways of working with grief.

The book will be an essential read for the bereaved and the professionals, family, and friends who are supporting them.

Cathy McQuaid is a bereaved mother. She is also a researcher, psychotherapy supervisor, and trainer. She decided to use her skills to undertake a research project to help her understand her own grief and the responses and behaviours of those around her. This book is the outcome of that research.

Understanding Bereaved Parents and Siblings

A Handbook for Professionals, Family, and Friends

Cathy McQuaid

Routledge
Taylor & Francis Group

LONDON AND NEW YORK

First published 2021
by Routledge
2 Park Square, Milton Park, Abingdon, Oxon OX14 4RN

and by Routledge
605 Third Avenue, New York, NY 10158

Routledge is an imprint of the Taylor & Francis Group, an informa business

© 2021 Cathy McQuaid

The right of Cathy McQuaid to be identified as author of this work has been asserted by her in accordance with sections 77 and 78 of the Copyright, Designs and Patents Act 1988.

All rights reserved. No part of this book may be reprinted or reproduced or utilised in any form or by any electronic, mechanical, or other means, now known or hereafter invented, including photocopying and recording, or in any information storage or retrieval system, without permission in writing from the publishers.

Trademark notice: Product or corporate names may be trademarks or registered trademarks, and are used only for identification and explanation without intent to infringe.

British Library Cataloguing-in-Publication Data
A catalogue record for this book is available from the British Library

Library of Congress Cataloging-in-Publication Data
Names: McQuaid, Cathy, author.
Title: Understanding bereaved parents and siblings : a handbook for
   professionals, family and friends / Cathy McQuaid.
Description: Abingdon, Oxon ; New York, NY : Routledge, 2021. |
   Includes bibliographical references and index.
Identifiers: LCCN 2020053490 (print) | LCCN 2020053491 (ebook) |
   ISBN 9780367702984 (hardback) | ISBN 9780367702960
   (paperback) | ISBN 9781003145547 (ebook)
Subjects: LCSH: Parental grief. | Grief in children. | Bereavement—
   Case studies. | Bereavement in children—Case studies.
Classification: LCC BF575.G7 M438 2021 (print) | LCC BF575.G7
   (ebook) | DDC 155.9/37—dc23
LC record available at https://lccn.loc.gov/2020053490
LC ebook record available at https://lccn.loc.gov/2020053491

ISBN: 978-0-367-70298-4 (hbk)
ISBN: 978-0-367-70296-0 (pbk)
ISBN: 978-1-003-14554-7 (ebk)

Typeset in Baskerville
by Apex CoVantage, LLC

To Vikki – you opened my eyes to a whole new world, thank you.

To Michael, Chris, and Jenni, thank you for all your love and support and for accompanying me on this journey. Without you my world would be a much smaller and darker place.

To all the children and siblings whose stories are contained in this book, including:

Andrew Brian Slack

David Bryn Cripps

Ebony Matthews

Emilie-Rose Bowers

Harry Patrick Davis

James

Jamie P.

Jason Clarke

Matthew Lee Evans

Michael

Polly

Rose

Tariq Hussain

Tom

Finally, to Sally, with love.

Contents

List of Figures/Tables   xi
Foreword   xii
Acknowledgements   xiii

Introduction   1

PART I   7

1. We are forever changed by this experience   9

2. "Stillbirth is such a taboo subject": Claire's story remembering her daughter Emilie   17

3. "How many children do you have? It's just something I hate": John's story remembering his daughter Emilie   28

4. "There was this crowd of women all wailing": Elisa's story remembering her daughter Ellen   40

5. "Nobody foresaw that she would die so quickly": Joanne's story remembering her daughter Rebecca   54

6. "Goodbye, have a good evening, take care": Julia's story remembering her daughter Pippa   67

7. "I'm sorry to say he's dead": Steffy's story remembering her son Jason and her brother Matthew   80

8. "They laughed at me and said, you've got to be joking": Nancy's story remembering her daughter Angel   92

viii *Contents*

9 "I think I was in shock for a year": Carol's story
  remembering her son David   99

10 "Tell mum not to worry. I'm going to the pure land":
   Susan's story remembering her son Michael   113

11 "What more could we have done?": Wilf and Kath's story
   remembering their son Michael   120

12 "Her horror penetrated me": John's story remembering
   his brother Jamie   130

13 "They're just living in their lovely little bubble and my
   bubble burst": Rose's story remembering her older sister Lizzie   138

14 "Everything was coming together for him": Shireen's story
   remembering her brother Tariq   148

15 "Don't judge my life on the chapter that you came in on":
   Beth's story remembering her brother Jim   156

16 "Jacky was my most significant security base":
   Edward's story remembering his brother Jacky   169

17 "I think you have a sister": Sally's story remembering
   her sister Rose   180

18 The ABC of grief   185
   Aftermath 185
   Bonds 187
   Rupture and reconnecting bonds 187
   Hostage bonds 189
   Challenging existing bonds 190
   Continuing bonds and developing resilience 191
   Compassion 192

19 Living with loss   193
   Maslow's Hierarchy of Needs 193
   Self-care 198
   Anniversaries 199
   Acceptance 200

20 Transformational loss 203
  1. *A disorienting dilemma 203*
  2. *Self-examination with feelings of guilt or shame 204*
  3. *A critical assessment of epistemic, socio-cultural, or psychic assumptions 205*
  4. *Recognition that one's discontent and the process of transformation are shared and that others have negotiated a similar change 206*
  5. *Exploration of options for new roles, relationships, and actions 207*
  6. *Planning of a course of action 207*
  7. *Acquisition of knowledge and skills for implementing one's plans 208*
  8. *Provisional trying of new roles 208*
  9. *Building of competence and self-confidence in new roles and relationships 209*
  10. *A reintegration into one's life on the basis of conditions dictated by one's new perspective 209*

PART II 213

21 Models of grief and bereavement 215
Staged models 215
Visual models 216
Task models 218
Meaning making 223

22 Transgenerational loss and Family Constellations 228
Transgenerational trauma and epigenetics 228
Systemic Family Constellations and the Orders of Love 229
Other options 231

23 Resilience, grief, and grief disorder 234
What is resilience? 234
Factors that affect resilience 234
Measuring resilience 235
The physiological impact of grief 236
When does normal grief turn into a disorder? 237
Medication or therapy 239
Assessment tools 240

24 Protection and self-knowledge 245
Protection 245
Boundaries 245

The Drama Triangle 246
The Awareness ARENA 248
Assertiveness 250
Self-care 251
Compassion and compassion fatigue 253
Identifying personal processes 254
Attunement 256

25 Creative ways of working with loss 258
ATTEND 258
Creative techniques 260
Mindfulness 264
The CIRCLE of compassion 265

Appendix 1: questions and activities 268
Appendix 2: sources of help and support 273
Index 278

Figures/Tables

Figures

I.1	Number of UK deaths registered for under 25s for 2008–2018	2
I.2	Number of deaths registered for people aged 50 and under, 2008–2018	3
19.1	Maslow's Hierarchy of Needs original five-stage model (1987)	194
20.1	The snakes and arrows of transformational grief	210
21.1	The Waterfall of Bereavement	217
21.2	The Dual Process Model	223
24.1	The Drama Triangle	247
24.2	The Awareness ARENA	248

Tables

21.1	Summary of Worden's Task/Mediator Model	219
23.1	Diagnostic criteria for ICD-11 Prolonged Grief Disorder	238

Foreword

In my opinion there is no right or wrong way of coping with grief.

The truth is the trauma of loss and grief is profoundly realistic depending on whom you have lost.

However, I do believe there are different types of grief, and I am not undermining any of them. But, having lost my beautiful daughter, Caron, at 41 after battling breast cancer for seven years, I really believe that losing a child takes you to a level in the 'black hole of living' that one can never believe actually exists.

Trying to cope with Caron's passing turned out to be a long, lonely path – I did not seem to be able to take on anyone else's grief within the family.

For example, I just did not seem to have the capability to take on and fully understand my two sons' feelings of loss. Of course, I knew they were truly devastated about their sister, but there was something about 'them' also worrying about how I would survive which added another level of deep anxiety.

However, I was lucky to receive thousands of letters, many of which came from parents who had lost a child.

One of them told me about how one day she was running out of the house, her son put his hand out and stopped her and said, "Mum, I am your child as well," which was a huge awakening to get me away from what I call in hindsight 'the selfish grief.'

Since Caron died in 2004 I have had many lessons to learn and discover new paths of living, but to quote one of those letters I had from parents who had lost a child, "You never get over the loss but eventually you do learn to live in and around it."

Dr Cathy McQuaid has written a most comprehensive book with many coping strategies and many ways to best remember our loved ones. I know you will gain strength from reading her book.

Gloria Hunniford OBE.

Acknowledgements

This book would not have been possible without the generosity of the research participants. I want to thank each of them for their courage and willingness to share their story, not only with me but also for allowing them to be published in this book.

My heartfelt thanks go to friends and family, especially to Enid Welford and Jean Lancashire for their unwavering support and encouragement, for reading through draft chapters and making wise and perceptive comments. Thanks too to Andrew Reeves, Kathy Raffles, and Robin Hobbes who generously gave their time to read the manuscript and to write endorsements.

Finally, thank you to Gloria Hunniford for writing the Foreword.

Introduction

This book is not concerned with the age of the child or sibling at death. Everyone is someone's child; it is more concerned about the experience of that death and the impact on those left behind. Therefore, these stories concern children/siblings of varying ages, from a stillborn baby to someone in their sixties. The grief isn't any easier or more difficult the older or younger the child or sibling, but it is different.

The death of a child or sibling, no matter what age, has a significant impact on those left behind, even on later generations. This book contains the lived experiences of such a death and the aftermath on those who are grieving. The book is for parents and siblings who want to know how others have been impacted by the death of a son or daughter, brother or sister, and what has helped or hindered them. It is for professionals who want to understand the phenomenological experience of bereaved parents and siblings, and to appreciate how they can best support those with whom they are working. Finally, this book is for the family and friends of bereaved parents or siblings; here you will find information to help you understand the depth of the grief involved when a parent loses a child or a sibling, a brother or sister, how it permeates the rest of their life and what you can do to help and support them.

Context

In the UK we live in a relatively peaceful and, excepting the 2020 Covid-19 pandemic, healthy environment and expect that we, and future generations, will live long and healthy lives. However, this has been the case only since the late 1940s. Prior to that, in the late 19th century and the early 20th century, the loss of a child was common from the effects of such diseases as typhoid, smallpox, cholera, tuberculosis, scarlet fever, and other air, water, or foodborne infections. Later, the loss of 882,000[1] people as a result of World War I and 454,000[2] during World War II meant that few families remained unscathed by the loss of a child or sibling.

In Georgian and Victorian times the public displays of mourning could be rather lavish, with strict rules about what someone could wear, what

2 *Introduction*

activities they were allowed to engage in, and how they were meant to behave.[3] People understood there was a collective reason to grieve and there were correct ways to do so. This waned in the late 19th and early 20th centuries, and after the First World War people were expected to be stoical in the face of loss, managing their grief with spirit, happily accepting a deceased's war medal.[4] Indeed, some people report that any public display of mourning, e.g. wearing black clothing, was viewed as unpatriotic and that the only recognition should be at specified times, e.g. Armistice Day. This development of the 'stiff upper lip' for women, now emulating the men, continued and was reinforced during and after the Second World War.[5] As a result, many people were unable to fully express their grief; this has led to a decline in later generations knowing how to grieve or mourn, and so they often feel more isolated.

Since the end of the Second World War, the general population has enjoyed better nutrition and housing which, along with the introduction of the National Health Service in the UK in 1948 providing access to free medical care and vaccinations, means we enjoy longer and healthier lives. It is now unusual for a parent to experience the death of their child. Figure I.1 shows the male and female death registrations for people aged 25 and under for 2008 to 2018.[6]

Although the total number of deaths of children and young people have reduced, from 8940 in 2008 to 6869 in 2018, they have remained fairly steady over the last five years. In 2018 the UK population was 66.4 million,[7] so 6869 people aged 25 or under dying in that year represents 0.01% of the

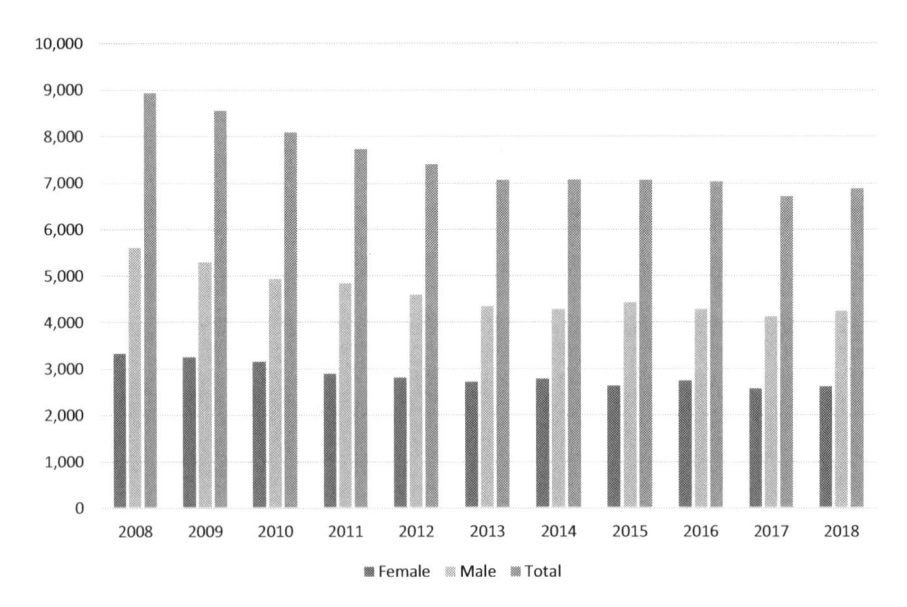

Figure I.1 Number of UK deaths registered for under 25s for 2008–2018

population, nearly 19 people per day. If we take into account that there may be two parents, four grandparents, and, say, one other sibling in the family then that is 48,083 people (nearly two and a half times the capacity of the O2 arena in London),[8] just over 0.07% of the population, who have been impacted by the death of a child, grandchild, or sibling. If we extend this to include people who died aged 50 and under (see Figure I.2),[9] this increases to 34,559 deaths, 94 people per day.

Assuming two grandparents, both parents, and one sibling are still alive, this now means over 172,795 people, over 0.26% of the population, are impacted by the death of a child, grandchild, or sibling.

Despite the significance of these numbers, the death of a child appears to be the ultimate taboo. Some people cross the street so they don't have to look at you or, even worse, speak to you. Several even treat you as if the death is somehow contagious. A few will say something that is shocking or clumsy. Only a handful will be there to listen to the hurt and distress and sometimes say just the right thing. If you are a sibling who has lost a brother or sister, then you can be worse off, often forgotten, or expected to look after your grieving parents.

The death of a child is something that probably all parents fear the most and few siblings will even think about until it happens. Only a handful of

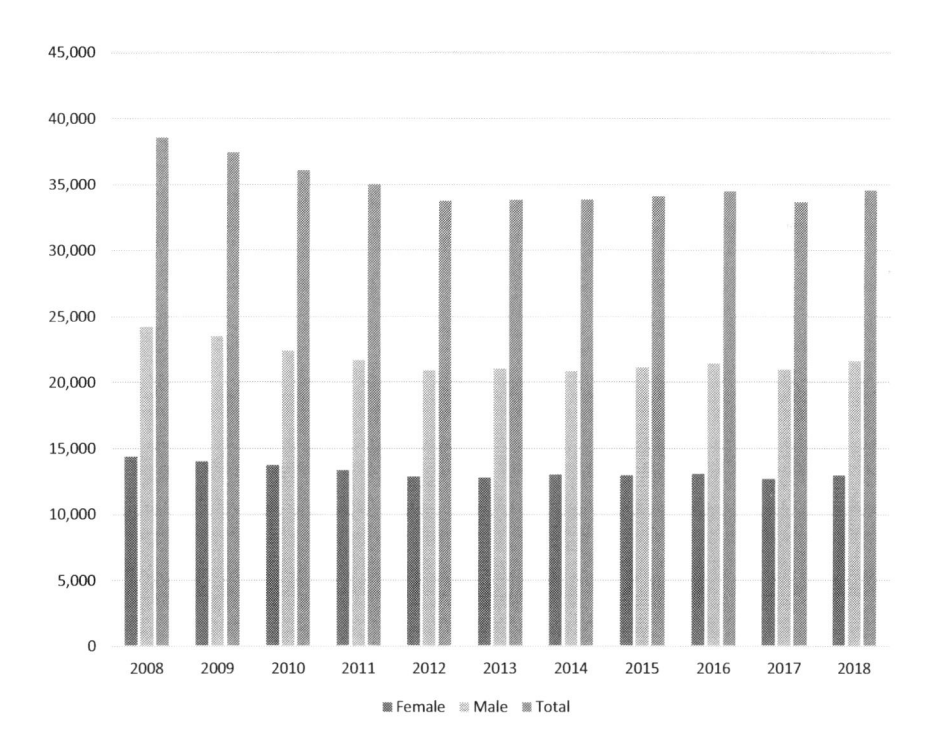

Figure I.2 Number of deaths registered for people aged 50 and under, 2008–2018

professionals have the necessary experience to fully appreciate the stress and distress caused by such a loss and the impact others can have, for good or ill. Others, along with family and friends, may shy away. People may feel helpless and may not know what to say or do. How do they support those who have lost a child or sibling? What is helpful, and what is not?

Grief is such a unique encounter; no two people will have the same experience, and this is especially true for the parents who suffer the death of their child and for any surviving siblings. This is not a grief that will ever be 'got over'; rather, it is one that the bereaved have to learn to accept and live with for the rest of their lives.

This book contains ten stories from parents and six from siblings who have been bereaved. Some contain real names, other use pseudonyms according to the participant's wishes. The narratives provide you with each person's raw and heartfelt experience. Some of the stories may come across as disjointed or repetitive; this captures the process and experience of the participant at the time of the interview and accurately reflects how their grief impacts on them. For those of you who are bereaved, I hope you will find some comfort or reassurance and, through the accounts, find a way to understand, manage, and even transform your loss. For those of you who are professionals, family, or friends, I hope you find something to help you in your support of a bereaved parent, sibling, or family.

The book is in two parts. Part I starts with my story of loss and how the research and book came about. This is followed by 16 chapters, one from each of the research participants. Chapter 18 contains what I call the ABC of Grief, which looks at how the bereaved person relates to themselves and others after such a loss, how bonds are ruptured, reconnected, and continued throughout life, and how compassion can influence someone's experience of grief. Chapter 19 focusses on living with loss and includes ideas about how to manage anniversaries and promote resilience and self-care. Part I concludes with Chapter 20, which describes how the phases of transformational learning can be applied to the grief experienced by the participants and to the ways they changed and adjusted to their loss.

Part II is primarily aimed at professionals who work with bereaved parents, siblings, or families. There are five chapters.

Chapter 21 focusses on an overview of a number of grief and bereavement models and how they can be used with those who are mourning. Chapter 22 provides a basic understanding of transgenerational loss and epigenetics and describes how the use of Family Constellations work can be useful in helping someone deal with unprocessed loss or trauma. Chapter 23 considers resilience, why some people may appear to be more able than others in dealing with their loss. This is followed by a discussion on what is viewed as normal grief and when this is perceived to become a disorder. Models and assessment tools are offered to help the professional in assessing and working with their clients. Chapter 24 focusses on the necessary protection needed when working with bereaved people. A range of questions and activities are provided that can be used by the professional to understand their own personal process, increasing self-knowledge and identifying any training needs. Chapter 25 provides the reader with a range of creative ways of working with grief and loss.

Questions and activities for trainees and professionals who are learning or wish to develop their self-reflective practice are contained in Appendix 1. Finally, sources of help and support that the reader may find useful are contained within Appendix 2.

Notes

1 G. Thompson, O. Hawkins, A. Dar, M. Taylor, N. Battley, A. Mellows-Facer, C. Rhodes, D. Harari, D. Webb, F. McGuinness, G. Berman, G. Allen, L. Booth, L. Maer, M. Keep, N. Broughton, P. Bolton, R. Harker, R. Cracknell, R. McInnes and Rutherford (2012). *Olympic Britain: Social and Economic Change since the 1908 and 1948 London Games.* London: House of Commons Library, UK Parliament, p. 155.
2 Ibid.
3 Anon. (1769). *The Town and Country Magazine, Or Universal Repository of Knowledge, Instruction, and Entertainment,* Vol. 1. London: A. Hamilton, p. 639.
4 A. Hetherington (2018). *British Widows of the First World War.* Barnsley: Pen and Sword Books.
5 L. Noakes (2015). Gender, Grief, and Bereavement in Second World War Britain. *Journal of War & Culture Studies,* 8(1), pp. 72–85. DOI: 10.1179/1752628014Y.0000000016.
6 Source: Office for National Statistics Licensed under the Open Government Licence. Available from: www.ons.gov.uk/peoplepopulationandcommunity/births deathsandmarriages/deaths/datasets/deathregistrationssummarytablesengland andwalesdeathsbysingleyearofagetables [Accessed 4 April 2020].
7 Source: Office for National Statistics Licensed under the Open Government Licence. Available from: www.ons.gov.uk/peoplepopulationandcommunity/pop ulationandmigration/populationestimates/timeseries/ukpop/pop [Accessed 22 March 2020].
8 AEG. (2019). *O2 Brochure.* Available at: www.theo2.co.uk/assets/doc/The-O2-Deck-2019-91215e4112.pdf [Accessed 23 March 2020].
9 Source: Office for National Statistics Licensed under the Open Government Licence. Available from: www.ons.gov.uk/peoplepopulationandcommunity/births deathsandmarriages/deaths/datasets/deathregistrationssummarytablesengland andwalesdeathsbysingleyearofagetables [Accessed 4 April 2020].

Part I

1 We are forever changed by this experience

Vikki, my eldest daughter, died seven years ago. I found her dead in her bed after taking too many painkillers. She was 20 years of age and had so much potential. Her death knocked me sideways. My whole life changed, and I found myself on a rather surreal journey that I would say is still ongoing. For me the landscape of life changed overnight. I had been running a therapy centre and was busy working as a psychotherapist, and although I still needed to work to pay the mortgage and bills, I no longer felt particularly competent to undertake the client work. I was concerned that I might be so absorbed in my own process that I would not be sufficiently available for my clients. Thankfully, my clinical practice had already been significantly reduced as I'd been writing a book about counselling and psychotherapy training,[1] so few clients were impacted by my decision to stop that aspect of my work. I did feel able to continue with my supervision practice and to undertake some training workshops. This work helped me to have a focus that was outside of me and helped me to still feel useful but without the responsibility of my own clients. In addition, I ended up taking on voluntary work for an organization I belonged to and spent a lot of time getting deeply involved in dealing with the various tasks that needed attention. I also had a family to support.

I've always worked, and I started my first job a month after my 16th birthday. I've had a number of careers working in a bank, the emergency services, and then as a counsellor and psychotherapist, supervisor, trainer, and researcher. I had a strong work ethic, and much of my identity was tied up in my job. Throughout my adult life I've used my various work roles as a way of coping and of distracting myself from the impact past events have had on me. Although that worked well for a long time, it was not sustainable, and in my late 30s, I was diagnosed with post-traumatic stress disorder (PTSD). Thankfully, with the help of the therapy, many of the PTSD symptoms reduced.

With Vikki's death, many of the symptoms I had before came back with increased intensity. I jumped at the slightest noise or touch. I was hypervigilant, watching others like a hawk. I wanted and needed to know where my family were, who they were with, and what they were doing. Sleep was the only time I got any respite from the intrusive thoughts and images; thankfully, I was so tired that sleep came fairly easily to me. During the day, pictures would flash through my mind of finding my daughter dead in her bed. I couldn't recall any good memories; only times when we had disagreed or argued. I believed I was the worst possible mother, blaming myself for her death. I would imagine all sorts of horrors of what was going to happen to me and my family. At times it was so bad, I thought it would be best if we all died; I believed no one would notice or mind. It was a real struggle to stay alive, to go shopping, to prepare and cook meals for us all. Often it took all my concentration to read the most insignificant of things. I could manage only in short bursts of time and would need to read and reread the same paragraph before the content might sink in.

Physically for the first few months, I had a constant pain in my chest which eventually subsided into a dull ache. I often had back pain, as I have a residual back injury and whenever I am stressed, the tension goes to that part of my back. The arthritis I have in my knees also flared up, meaning at times I could barely walk. Despite this, I knew I had to carry on, to get up in the morning and deal with whatever the day had to throw at me.

Over the next few years after Vikki's death, life carried on. I continued with the voluntary work and looking after my family. After an incident concerning some of the voluntary work, I began to question what I was doing, and realized that I was burnt out. It came as a shock to me, but probably not to those who knew me well. I gave up some of that work which was an immediate relief. But it brought up the familiar questions of "What am I going to do now?" And "Who am I?" I decided to take a step back and to review what was going on in my life.

I am naturally very curious and began wondering whether what I was experiencing was normal. And what was normal anyway? I certainly understood my reaction to Vikki dying and those first few days, weeks, and months when nothing is the same, but everything is the same. I was fascinated about the behaviour of others towards me and especially towards my other two children. I was perplexed as to why some people completely blanked me, would change the subject if I mentioned Vikki, or seemed to be so focussed on themselves and their current achievements, I wondered why they had bothered visiting. A number seemed to use her death as a means of idle gossip: "Have you heard . . ." Several made up stories about her, some of which were posted on Facebook, or made out that they were her best friend, when I knew she really didn't like them or even know them. All without any apparent thought for the hell we were already going through or what impact their rumour-mongering would have on us when we heard about it, which we did.

I am a relatively reserved person, and as a family we are very private. I did not appreciate being the centre of attention or being made the focus of others' speculation. I hated people knowing or thinking that they knew what had happened to Vikki. I was shocked at the things some people wrote – e.g. she'd died in a car crash, she'd taken a heroin overdose, she'd died from alcohol poisoning, or that her boyfriend had killed her – and it made me wonder why they would do such a thing. They seemed like a wake of vultures around a corpse trying to see what titbits they could get and then brag about later with some made-up story with them as the centre of attention. I remember feeling angry and very protective of my family, especially as mainly my children got to hear some of the horrible stuff before I did. Such is the influence of social media, so I needed to find a way to help them to manage not only their grief but also the actions of others.

I read whatever books on grief and the loss of a child that I could find and that my concentration would allow. I wanted to find out what research had been done into the impact of the death of a child on parents and siblings, and although some things were helpful, nothing I read seemed to speak to me in a way that really worked. So, I decided to do my own research. This book is the story of that research, and I invite you, the reader, to embark on a similar adventure into an exploration of the impact of the death of a significant person in your life.

My initial plan was to undertake a series of semi-structured interviews, as many as I could, and to analyse the transcripts to find themes. I intended then to write a couple of academic papers and that would probably have been it, although I had mooted the idea of writing a book. I was keen that the project would be an organic process and wanted to follow wherever the research took me.

I interviewed my first participant, Julia, two years ago. I'd known her for about 15 years, and she'd been incredibly helpful to me after Vikki died. I knew some of her story and that of her daughter Pippa. Despite knowing aspects of this narrative when I interviewed Julia, I was struck by the pain and trauma that she was still carrying 21 years after Pippa died, of how some things had stayed with her and other things that we'd talked about in the past did not arise. Whilst she was talking, I could identify with some aspects of her tale and not with others. At times I felt relief that some aspects of my experience had been similar, or indeed quite different, and at other times felt a strange sort of envy. I wondered how my reactions might influence the research.

As I continued to interview people, I realized that the idea of analysing the transcripts and using themes was rather missing the point. I felt that the themes reduced such powerful and emotional experiences into categories that in many respects devalued it. What I appreciated was hearing the whole story of who the person was that died, how they had lived and been loved as well as how they had died, and what had happened to the storyteller subsequently. I became increasingly aware of my own reactions to the stories and the people I interviewed. For example, after one interview I came away feeling disheartened, detached, and quite depressed. After another I came away feeling excited and that I'd met someone with whom I could identify in a number of ways.

Following my desire for the process to be organic, the project then changed to be more of a heuristic inquiry.[2] Which, according to Moustakas, is

> a process that begins with a question or problem which the researcher seeks to illuminate or answer. The question is one that has been a personal challenge and puzzlement in the search to understand oneself and the world. The heuristic process is autobiographic, yet with virtually every question that matters personally there is also a social – and perhaps universal – significance.[3]

I knew that the research was autobiographical. I wanted to know if my experience was similar to that of other people. I wanted to understand what helped them get through their loss. To ascertain if they had experienced some of the challenges that I had faced as a consequence of another's behaviour and what effect that had on their grief. I was keen to find out how they supported any surviving children and what impact the loss had on them.

I realized that at times I felt angry on another's behalf about how they had been treated by a member of their family or someone they thought of as a friend. I also felt, possibly irrationally, incensed with people who I thought 'should know better,' mainly other professionals, who had blundered their way into someone else's grief, creating havoc along the way.

I recognized that a few of the things that some people did or said I may have done or said. Only now, being on the receiving end or hearing the impact, could I fully appreciate how crass or unthinking those words or actions could appear, despite some of them coming from a place of care or good intent. I knew this would be a valuable learning experience for me.

I remembered a caveat I'd be given when I first became a researcher, which was that one of the challenges of undertaking research was that I might learn something that I did not want to know; that any hypothesis might be disproven; in other words, that I might be wrong in any assumptions I held. Although I did not have an existing hypothesis that I was hoping to prove, I did wonder what other assumptions I might have been holding. After each interview, I reflected on how I felt about what I'd heard, what I'd been thinking, what judgements I had made, what themes I noticed, where our stories reflected each other and where they did not. I also noticed my reaction to the storyteller and how they told the story.

One of the themes that arose for me concerned how I interacted with the person I was interviewing. Whether I interrupted the speaker's flow or allowed them to talk continuously. I felt there were pros and cons. To disturb their flow might mean I lose some valuable aspect of their story. To allow them to speak without retaining the focus may mean colluding in some form of avoidance. I realized that in my work as a psychotherapist, I tend to be quite direct. If a client is repeatedly telling a version of the same story, I will often stop them and invite them to focus on the key issue(s) that we are meant to be dealing with in our one-hour time slot. Having the luxury of more time in the interviews meant that it was possible to hear some of the twists and turns that fleshed out the narrative. I was aware too that sometimes people talk as a way of distracting themselves and others from what is really causing them difficulties. I understood that although I wanted to give people the time and space to tell their story, I also needed to help us to stay focussed.

Furthermore, I know from my psychotherapy work that when someone suffers a trauma, they may need to tell their story repeatedly. This can be a double-edged sword. On the one hand, this could help them to share their experience with an attuned other, to help them to put the events into words, and to begin to process what has happened. On the other hand, it may reinforce their suffering and distress, especially if the listener was not really engaged. I was reminded of times when I've heard a client's story and could tell that it was something that had been told many times to such a degree that it seemed rehearsed and that the client was in some way detached from the story. When working with clients like this, I would bring them back to themselves by saying something like "What are you feeling now as you tell me what happened to you?" Sometimes this worked, but occasionally it did not, and I'd hear more about the story. I knew then that I needed to hear the narrative in full, and only once it had been completely told could I then start to work with the client.

I decided to continue facilitating the participants to tell their story with any twists and turns and to ask questions to help clarify their meaning or to further the telling of their story. I knew I needed to trust in the process of the research, that I would get the relevant information.

Another theme that arose for me was my energy levels. These would fluctuate; I would move in and out of the research, at times being wholly immersed and at other times feeling almost disinterested. In those indifferent times, I wondered why I was doing this project. What was I going to learn? Would any findings be of use to anyone else? This alternating process has continued through the research and writing of this book. When I was talking with a good friend about this, she asked if I'd heard of the Dual Process Model[4] (see Chapter 21 and Figure 21.3) of coping with bereavement; I hadn't. She emailed me a paper that I read and at once understood what was happening to me.

In this model, I appreciated how the authors indicated that the bereaved person shifts their focus from avoidance to confrontation of the impact of their loss; this was my experience. The authors refer to loss-oriented coping (processing the loss of the person, e.g. grief, dealing with the loss of the planned future, avoidance of taking on new roles or adapting to the changes) to restoration-oriented coping (the secondary stressors that arise as a consequence of the loss, e.g. having to learn a new skill that the dead person did on our behalf, rebuilding a new future without the deceased person, avoidance of the grief).

I appreciated how the process of coping with a bereavement is not shown as a staged or task-focussed progression with which some of us may be more familiar (see Chapter 21). Rather, the authors discuss how someone's grief is influenced by their attachment style, and that this in turn affects the bereaved person's continuing bond with the deceased person, in summary that:

> (a) different coping styles are adopted by, and are differentially efficacious for, bereaved people according to their style of attachment; (b) bereaved people's ways of continuing bonds differ according to their attachment style; and (c) grief complications are associated with insecure attachment styles. The authors conclude that it is better for some bereaved individuals to work toward retaining ties and for others to work toward loosening ties.[5]

This model helped me to understand further why some participants needed to spend more time telling their story, retaining the ties they needed to hold, whereas a few seemed to be more detached, and several quite focussed in their storytelling.

As I continued to complete the interviews, I was able to appreciate the uniqueness of each story. Even if some had similar themes, how the participant was impacted by their grief varied. The process of listening to the narratives, of reflecting upon how the story impacted me; what I felt connected to and what I did not; being honest about what I was thinking during the interview and afterwards, for example whether I felt sorrow, anger, fear, or relief; whether my thinking of the other's story was one of understanding, judgement, surprise, or disgust; or if I felt dismissive or overwhelmed at their experience; all took time and energy. Being with and understanding the effect on me was crucial in helping me to start processing my own grief, as I found a way to locate and piece together my own story in a wider and broader context. It seemed like each interview contained pieces of my own jigsaw; it was a truly remarkable and unexpected gift.

I continued to question my life and my purpose. I became increasingly disinterested in the voluntary work I was still doing and in my role as a supervisor and trainer. It took all my willpower to complete the tasks I had agreed to do. I decided to stop all the voluntary work and to take two months off over the summer. As I started my two-month break, I realized I could not face resuming in September. I had constant arguments with myself: "I don't want to work" versus "You have to work, what about all the people who are relying on you?" "I need to stop and rest" versus "If you stop then who are you?" "I need to grieve" versus "You'll fall apart, then what will happen?" These dilemmas kept me feeling stuck, and I seemed incapable of resolving them despite my best efforts.

Then, in the days leading up to the sixth anniversary of Vikki's death, I began to toy with what it would be like to let people know I was going to stop work. Again, my mind was full of predicaments. In my heart I wanted to stop work altogether, but my head wanted me to continue. Strangely, but not uniquely as I discovered in the research, the days leading up to the anniversary are far worse than the day itself. I was in turmoil, and then on the anniversary morning, I knew what I was going to do. I would take a year off on sabbatical so I could complete the interviews and write this book. Then I would decide what I would do next. The relief I felt was palpable, and I felt excited. The process of telling all those with whom I'd been working was not so easy. Many were accepting of my decision, some reluctantly, and a couple were understandably angry or disappointed. It was hard to keep a handle on my delight at stopping work for an extended period to focus on what was important to me whilst also managing others' thoughts and feelings towards me during those final sessions.

Eventually, the first day of my sabbatical arrived. I had lots of plans to complete the interviews that were already scheduled and to work on the transcripts of those that had already been completed. In my imagination I thought a few months would have it all completed. As with many things in life, reality did not turn out quite like that.

I had realized by this point that what I wanted to do was to convert the transcripts into stories. I knew the previous idea of a thematic analysis didn't work for me and the amount of work needed for the conversion was significant. I also needed to contact each participant again to ask for their permission to do this, I was concerned they might not agree, and all the work done thus far would have been in vain. It all felt too much.

I went into a period of depression; I just couldn't be bothered with anything to do with the research, and should I get an email about anything work related, my heart would sink. I realized the burnout that I'd experienced a couple of years beforehand was still evident. I kept going to the gym and to some exercise classes and, although I felt energized afterwards, this energy dissipated quite quickly once I was back home. Thankfully, as there was no real time restriction, I allowed myself to stay with my process.

This period lasted for about three months. Then I saw two participants in a fairly short period of time, and their interviews spurred me on. After each of them I realized I felt a real connection, for different reasons, to the participant. They were both very positive women and were active in understanding and processing their loss; they saw the value in what I was doing, and they liked the idea of stories rather than themes.

I began to feel energized and started with the first story. It took hours, and at times I wondered if I was doing the right thing. Eventually, I was happy and sent it off to the participant for them to read and edit further as they wished. Completing one spurred me on to do more. Most of the participants were happy to continue with the new format of a book with stories, but understandably, not all wanted their experience to be told in this way.

I began to get feedback from the participants. Overall, they felt the story that I'd sent to them accurately reflected their experience, but reading it had been a shock and a surprise. This was useful information. From then on, when I sent out the stories, I informed the participants that they may be shocked or surprised by the narrative and so to take that into consideration when thinking about when and where they were going to read it.

What I have learned

The loss of a child or sibling is probably one of the most traumatic events that can happen in someone's life. We are forever changed by this experience. I am changed. I am not the same person I was before Vikki died. I have certainly found out who I can rely on and who really cares about me and my family. But I ended some friendships, and I think I now know why. I have met some truly inspirational people, some of whom have listened to me, others who have told me their stories. In each I have learned that I am not alone in my experience. I have learned what works for me and what does not.

The future

My view on work is changing. I had thought that I would not return to my role as a supervisor and trainer, but I now think I will. I have often used more creative ways of working, and I think this will be at the centre of any workshops for bereaved parents and siblings as well as professionals. I will work in short bursts so I can still take time out to keep processing my loss and to take much-needed breaks. I have plans to travel and to fulfil those dreams on my bucket list. In the meantime, Vikki stays with me; I have a tattoo of a butterfly on my right arm. She may not be here in person, but she is certainly still very much alive in my heart.

Notes

1 C. McQuaid (2014). *What You Really Need to Know about Counselling and Psychotherapy Training: An Essential Guide*. Hove: Routledge.
2 C.E. Moustakas (1990). *Heuristic Research: Design, Methodology, and Applications*. Newbury Park, CA: Sage.
3 Ibid., p. 15.
4 M.S. Stroebe, H.A.W. Schut and W. Stroebe (2005). Attachment in Coping with Bereavement: A Theoretical Integration. *Review of General Psychology*, 9(1), pp. 48–66. DOI: 10.1037/1089-2680.9.1.48.
5 Ibid., p. 48. APA, reprinted with permission.

2 "Stillbirth is such a taboo subject"
Claire's story remembering her daughter Emilie

Emilie died seven and a bit years ago. She was stillborn; she was very much wanted. We've suffered from infertility, so when we first decided to start trying for a family, we were under the impression it was going to take a very long time, and the chances were, I wouldn't be able to get pregnant. I got pregnant with Sam very quickly, and the pregnancy didn't go especially well. I was seriously ill, and Sam stopped growing at 27 weeks. They delivered him at 33 weeks; he was the size of a 28-weeker, and he was really poorly. They then did a lot of tests and found out that the placenta had died off quite early in the pregnancy due to blood clotting.

They weren't entirely sure what had happened. They said the chances of it happening again were probably about 10%. If I got pregnant again, it would be a high-risk pregnancy. I was told I'd be very well looked after with lots of precautions in place. This time it did take us a long time to conceive. We decided to start trying when Sam was about one. I got pregnant when he was two and a bit. In the grand scheme of things, with what's happened since, that doesn't sound like a long time, but at the time it felt like a very long time to be able to conceive again.

The pregnancy started off okay. I had horrific morning sickness and was very, very ill again, but we expected that. Again, she wasn't growing especially well, but they were monitoring her closely and thought that her slow growth was just because of my history. Then, at 32 weeks, I hadn't been feeling very well for a week or so. I went to the doctor's, and he basically said, "You're 32 weeks pregnant. You have a toddler. You're going to be tired." He didn't take my blood pressure, he didn't check on anything. A few days later, I noticed reduced movement, so I went into the hospital. They scanned and realized that Emilie had died. The normal procedure would be to send me home, but they realized that my preeclampsia was really severe and my blood pressure was very high, so they induced her. She was born the following morning. They couldn't find anything wrong with her and realized again it was due to the clotting. It was pretty horrific. I think the thing I've always struggled with is the fact that both my children were born at 32 and 33 weeks. Actually, no one said this to me, but I'm always fearful that people are going to think because that wasn't full term that it didn't matter as much; but actually we'd since been told that 33 weeks was as far as I would ever get in a pregnancy, so that's full term for me. I carried her for the whole time.

Some people have said things like, "I had a miscarriage as well." Even my mum said to me, "I had a couple of late miscarriages. They were kind of at 16 weeks." I thought, "It's not really the same." Well, it's not the same. She should've survived. Sam survived. I probably worry about what other people are going to think or what they're going to say. Stillbirth is such a taboo subject. As soon as you say to people, "I've lost a child; my daughter died," the first question is, "How old were they?" You kind of go, "Well, actually they were stillborn." You can see the absolute look of horror on people's faces that that still happens in this day and age. Actually, it's really quite common. A lot more common than people think. It's horrific, really awful.

The day we found out she had died, I think, had to be the worst day of my life, and Samuel was with us; in hindsight, we could've left him with a friend. But we did not expect her to have died. Because of my history with Sam, I thought they were going to deliver her there and then, so I packed my overnight bag including some makeup for photos afterwards. It was the last thing I expected.

I remember being in the room where they were scanning, and a midwife scanned me, I could see she was looking worried. Then she brought my consultant in who happened to be on call that day. Thankfully, we didn't have to see someone I didn't know. They brought her in, and she scanned me. I think it was then when she said Emilie had died. I just started screaming. It was like an out-of-body experience. Because I'm quite a people pleaser, I have been worried about the effect it must've had other people in the other cubicles to hear it all going on. We were whisked off down the corridor to the bereavement suite. It felt like something out of a television drama or just something really horrific.

You see videos on television about people being told their children had died. The reaction that mothers have. Obviously, you don't ever think, "How would I react?" because it's not something that you possibly want to think about. You just don't know how you're going to react in that situation. I think I was shocked at my reaction at the time. Since then, that's probably been the thing that's shocked me the most, is just the horror. It's just the violence of it, I suppose. It's quite a primal thing, I think. It's just horrific. Just absolutely awful. Then the aftermath was just absolutely terrible.

Waking up each morning, I'd have fantasies that we'd get a phone call from the hospital saying that she'd woken up and things were okay, and "We've never experienced this before," and "Come in and get her," and "She's in special care." Obviously, it didn't happen. One really horrific moment was when we went to register her death. You register the deaths and the births in the same place. We were sat in the waiting room with couples who'd just had their baby and had brought them down from delivery and were registering their birth as we sat there registering Emilie's death. That was awful. That same day, there were two young porters, they can't have been even 20, we could hear them talking about their porter lives and everything else. One of them said to the other one, "That's nothing. I had to wheel a dead baby down here the other day." They just were laughing about it; just how surreal it was for them. John, my husband, actually made a complaint about it. The manager at the hospital said it would never have been their job to do that. They were lying and fantasizing and sensationalizing everything. He said, "I'm so sorry that you had to hear that. Please know that the person in question will be disciplined for it." That was absolutely devastating because whether it was Emilie or not, we'll never know. But the thought of a baby being treated with so little respect was just horrific. The whole thing was just the worst experience of my life.

When they whisked us to the bereavement suite, I've always thought it might have been to protect the other people in the cubicles, but I think probably if I'm normalizing it, they just wanted to get us into the suite as quickly as they possibly could and once we were there, the care was outstanding. But we'd waited about an hour and a half in the hospital before they even saw us, so I've always had in the back of my mind, what if she wasn't dead at that point? Could they have saved her? It's just really awful. I do remember people staring at us as we were taken off down the corridor. They took Sam away from me as well; he had the best day of his life. I think he does remember it, because he really struggles with separating now. They blew up gloves, painted them with faces and gave him balloons, and he was plied with biscuits for the whole day until my friend could come and pick him up. He absolutely loved it; he thought it was wonderful. Then he got taken to my friend's house, spoiled rotten, and spent the night with them. He just loved it, but now he struggles with separation. It obviously had an impact on him as well, the whole situation.

The care we received after we found out Emilie had died was absolutely outstanding. I'm certain that questions were raised from things that have been said since, some things that my midwife hinted at and I think questions about the care and questions about the GP who saw me in the week leading up to it, all these things have been raised, so I've just left it alone. I thought, it's a hornet's nest and I'd rather not kick it, to be completely honest.

We decided not to have a post-mortem. Mainly because my consultant was pretty certain on the day that the same thing happened with Emilie as happened with Sam. They took the placenta to histopathology and did umpteen tests which brought back all of the information that we needed to know. It showed that in pregnancy I have something called absent end-diastolic flow, which means that the blood goes through only one part of the umbilical cord, so the baby gets starved of nutrients and blood and everything else, and it's caused by clotting. They did a full newborn screen of Emilie, and she seemed absolutely fine. That sounds ridiculous because she was dead, but she was perfect; there was nothing wrong with her. The cord hadn't been wrapped around, she had no obstruction to her passages or anything else. It was just purely down to my body. That is something that I've always struggled with.

I initially blamed myself, but I don't so much anymore. At the time I had a lot of support from my consultant and from other professionals and my therapist, Carol. She was saying that there was nothing I could have done, and I wasn't responsible, but I spent hours on Google. Google's my worst enemy, reading up on anything that I could have possibly done. Because she'd also suffered a placental abruption, which is when the placenta comes away from the wall of the uterus. It can be fatal to both the mother and the baby unless they catch it in time.

The placental abruption was caused by the placenta just dying off, so it naturally came away, but a lot of the time placental abruption can be caused by trauma. I'd taken Sam to a soft play centre a few days before and had been crawling around with him in there. I spent ages thinking, "Is it because I've done that or is it because I was not eating properly?" I had Hyperemesis gravidarum, which is really severe morning sickness, I couldn't eat very well. I tried my best to be eating properly. It's all those questions that would come up and I'd think, "Was it the morning sickness? Was it this? Was it just not caring for myself?" I was working, I worked all the way up until her death as well, so there's all those questions.

When Sam was born, the consultants and staff treated him as this miracle baby. Everybody was absolutely amazed at the lack of life support that he needed. He was in there for a while but just feeding and growing. I was shocked by everybody's amazement because I saw other 33-weekers coming in and going home within about five days, which is the norm for that gestation, but Sam was in for five weeks. My thinking was, "33 weeks, it can't actually be that bad," but it was a fact that he had all of this growth retardation and all of the clotting. We found out when Emilie died that she'd had a number of strokes in utero, and looking at Sam's reports, he'd had a number of strokes in utero as well. It really shocked me as to how Sam possibly survived. Then I suddenly realized why everybody saw him as this amazing miracle baby.

He's fine now, but it was a bit scary seeing how serious it actually was with Sam, because of course, they don't really tell you that. They want to keep you calm and try and let them take the stress, but with Emilie, we realized just how serious the situation was, and the fact that my life was at risk as well was something that I completely discounted at the start. It wasn't until I went on to have two miscarriages following Emilie that the seriousness of that actually hit me, because it's very hard when your child dies and people say to you, "You're lucky to be alive." It's very hard to see it as lucky because I actually thought, "I really don't see that at the moment. I'd much rather be dead if I'm completely honest." So, I discounted how lucky I was to have survived placental abruption, preeclampsia, hypertension (because my child was dead) as that was all I could see at the time.

I was so glad that my consultant was on call that day. That was just unbelievable, I wouldn't have trusted anyone else to be with us. I'm not entirely sure how I would have taken the news from anybody else. She was the one who delivered the news Emilie had died, and she was with us the whole day and came back the following day. She was just so incredibly supportive. I think if we'd had to be supported by someone we didn't know, in that moment, I'm not sure how I would have coped with it. She was just wonderful. She'd supported us all through Sam's pregnancy as well, so we knew her very well. We could see that she'd been upset, we could see that she'd been in tears herself. She was saying things like, "I don't understand how this has happened. I really don't understand it." For some reason, that was quite helpful. There was no clinical coldness. We could see her grief in it as well and the devastation that it had happened. She wasn't removed from the situation; she was fully in it with us.

On the day, John called my mum who was actually quite helpful, well, over the phone, which was a bit of a shock because in the past she's been horrific. He called his parents, but their reaction was not good at all. John's dad just cried on the phone and passed the phone over to John's mum and then she came out with something along the lines of "Oh, but we had such a wonderful day with you yesterday." Which was just irrelevant. They weren't helpful on the day, and they weren't helpful in the coming months or years actually, to be completely honest.

John's mum tried to cheer us up but, you can't really be cheered up, and his dad has never spoken Emilie's name. I think he's so caught up in his own grief that he just doesn't see us in it. They've got a lodge in the lakes and we went to see them in between Emilie dying and her funeral and again, Emilie wasn't mentioned at all. Once when walking down to a play area, I saw a lady with a pram. I just lost it and had a panic attack, and they just carried on regardless. They didn't stop to see if I was okay or if I could breathe or anything. John supported me, but they just carried on walking, it just felt really discounting, really. It was awful, actually, but they have tried. That's their way of trying. She has been better since then. She read a book that I wrote about my experience, and she bought it for a friend whose daughter had had a similar experience. I can see that she's tried; there's just no emotional support.

It's been friends who've got us through it. On the day, Carol, my therapist, was with us; she was with us for the whole day, and she was with us the following day as well. She came and met Emilie and held her. The leaders of our church came to be with us, and again they were there on the day and the following day after I delivered her as well. They came and treated her like a newborn baby. Because I could barely touch her, to start off with, to see them treating her as she deserved to be treated, really helped me. It was almost modelling to me what I needed to do. That was really helpful.

We had an unusual experience. A midwife came into the room and she came over and she looked in the crib and she went, "Oh, isn't she beautiful?" She said, "She looks just like you," and I went, "You know she's dead, don't you?" In hindsight, it was what I needed to hear. I needed her to be treated like a human, but it just really threw me because it was said with such compassion and seeing her as a beautiful baby who just looked like she was asleep. She looked like she was a normal baby. It baffled me a little bit at the time, but she was really gracious with it. She said, "Yes, I do. I'm really sorry but she is, she's beautiful and she looks just like you. Would you like a cup of tea? Here's a tissue." Then off she went again. The hospital staff were incredible. Our friends generally were wonderful, although we lost our closest friends through the experience which was just another awful loss.

They were the first people whose house we went to after Emilie died because they were our best friends and we just needed to be with them. This was a few days later, and they had a very young baby. She opened the door to me and the first thing she said was, "Oh, breastfeeding is horrible." I don't know what I said. I thought I don't know because I've had one premature baby who was tube fed and a dead baby so, actually, I have no idea whether breastfeeding is awful or not. We went in and it was a very surreal experience. We tried to carry on seeing them and we tried to keep the friendship going. We went for days out, we went for coffees and she came around here. Then one day just before Christmas, about three months after Emilie died, Peter called my husband John and asked if they could meet up for a drink, which they did. Peter said to him, "We're happy to carry on seeing you but only if you don't mention Emilie because Jane has taken on all of the grief of Emilie and none of the joy of Thomas. We can carry on a relationship, but you can't speak about Emilie."

John came home and told me, and I just lost the plot. I don't think I've ever been so angry in my life as I was in that moment. We then didn't see them again for about nine months, and they moved away. They have apologized now, but they actually blamed us for moving away as well. They said that too much had happened up here and they needed a new start, so they moved away. We have seen them again and it's been okay, but it's not the same friendship as it used to be, so we lost that as well. I understand, from reading other people's accounts and speaking to other people who've lost children, it is very common to lose friendships and to lose relationships. It was a bit of a shock. It completely changed our world. Thankfully, other friends stepped in and were very supportive. One of them arranged a meal plan for us. We had meals cooked for us for five weeks. Others would come and take Sam off our hands. I needed Sam with me a lot of the time, but they would do things like take him to playgroup, things that I couldn't do because I couldn't bear to see other babies for a few weeks.

When I started going back to the playgroups, they would just stand with me; they were just there, it was that presence again, no one tried to make us feel better. No one tried to rationalize it, they were just there with us. They clubbed together and sent us out for a meal. Someone once said to me, "I wanted to come and speak to you but your friends were like a force field around you, so I didn't really want to penetrate that." They were like this protective screen, that's what it felt like. I didn't get bombarded with stupid people saying stupid things when my friends were there because they were quite protective of me. They have continued to be so since; they talk about Emilie, they acknowledge her. There's no discomfort there at all. They talk to their children about her. They've been wonderful really. My 30th birthday was six months after Emilie died, and I really didn't want to do anything. One group of friends arranged a tea party in the park for me, they didn't invite anyone else; and they bought me 30 presents, just little bits and pieces. They bought five each and put them into a big bag, so I had things to open, things that they've made themselves or books that they'd bought second-hand, just little things that really meant so much. One of them was a jewellery-making kit so that I could have something to occupy my time. They were wonderful.

Something I found unhelpful is that I've never really like platitudes like "everything happens for a reason," that sort of thing. That's just a ridiculous thing to say. Also something I found hard was if I was telling someone what had happened and they started to cry, I would end up feeling like I needed to comfort them. It was almost in a, "You've upset me by telling me this." I had one woman who said to me, "Oh, I don't want to hear any horror stories." I was a bit taken aback. I thought, "Oh, well it's my horror story. I'm trying to tell you about my daughter." Actually, there's loads of unhelpful things. Other things are people who share their birth stories but then don't want to hear my birth story, and my birth story for both of my children is actually quite important to me. I want to be able to talk about that. I don't know what it's like to give birth to a live baby because Sam was C-section, and actually he was resuscitated at birth. I don't know what it's like, but it still doesn't make my birth stories any less important than other people's. I struggle with people who want to share their "horror" birth stories – which, to me, are not horrific, if I'm completely honest – but then don't want to hear mine because mine ends in a stillbirth and not a live birth. It's just a massive taboo; child loss is a massive taboo, stillbirth really is. People don't want to hear about it.

I didn't do the whole support group thing because it's just not me. I met people online. The people I've met online have been some of the best support actually, people we met in forums. One of them was a lady who'd written a book on stillbirth, and I contacted her. I'm still in touch with these people now, and you have that bond. Three years ago, a friend of a friend had a neonatal death. I sent over a memory box that I'd put together and a card and some things like that and a copy of my book. I finally met her for the first time recently and it was just incredible, really, to finally get to meet her. Someone you've never spoken to, don't even know what she looks like, but you have that connection with her, because they've experienced the same thing that you've experienced. It was really lovely to meet her. We were both quite emotional with that. It helps to meet other people who've experienced the death of a baby.

My Christian faith was tested. I was thinking that because something horrific had already happened to us, it couldn't possibly happen again, and then we went on to have the miscarriages and infertility. That's when I became really angry at God. I was thinking, there's a verse in the Bible that says God will give us the desires of our hearts, and I was saying, "This is the desire of my heart, the desire of my heart is to have a live baby." It just didn't happen, and I couldn't possibly understand that, and I couldn't link that up with what I believed. It was all very contradictory, but at the same time, having my faith, and having an eternal perspective, is what got me through it. There were lots of questions, an awful lot of questions that I don't think will ever be answered at all, but it did really help me, and Church really helped me as well. Having that, and having people to stand with us. Having something to cling to that I believed in as well was really comforting. Emilie's death didn't feel futile in any way. I genuinely believe that we'll see her again, and that's one of the things that's kept me going. I think when you have a faith, there's less finality with death than there is without one, possibly.

The first year after Emilie died was horrific. We had a miscarriage four months after she died. We had another miscarriage exactly a year after she died. At that time, we were having fertility treatment, which in hindsight probably wasn't the best idea, but it's what I needed to do at the time. Things got easier after that, but I don't feel like the grief went away. I don't feel like the grief has ever gone away. I feel like our lives have changed around it – I suppose, grown around it. I don't think it's ever going to go away. Each anniversary is really hard but becomes a little bit easier in some respects as well. Although there'll be times when I find myself straight back into the grief. We scattered her ashes this September, so seven years after she died. We hadn't been able to bring ourselves to do it before. We only did it because we had a letter from the funeral directors asking us what we wanted to do with them.

I had a ring made, with some of her ashes in, and when the ring arrived a couple of weeks ago, it was far too big. The jeweller had sized it wrong, and in that moment, it felt like she'd died all over again. It was just awful. Things affect me a lot more than they used to affect me, but I think the main thing is that our lives have just changed. Our lives are completely unrecognizable from what they were prior to her death, and in some ways, they're a lot better, actually, because we make different choices, we have a different perspective on things. I don't stay in friendships because I feel it's the right thing to do. I stay in friendships that edify me, because I get something out of it, and I please other people less.

I have so much more appreciation for our family unit than I possibly could have done before Emilie died, but then in the same respect, there are other things that are really hard. I still struggle to think that if I put our son to bed if he's poorly, that he'll still be alive the following morning. There's a fear there that something catastrophic is going to happen to him, or to our daughter Sophie, who we adopted a few years after Emilie died, although she doesn't really get ill. That's something I can't help, but I feel like the innocence has completely been taken away.

One of the things a lot of people have said was, "I can't possibly imagine what you're going through." The thing is, now I know what it feels like to lose a child. People don't like to think that their child might die, but I know exactly what it's like, so that's what the fear is, that something would happen to one of my children. I end up thinking I don't know how I'd cope with that again. The memory of just the trauma, and the horror of exactly what it's like. I couldn't do that again, and a lot of my friends, they wouldn't even entertain that thought, because it's so uncomfortable and it's such a horrific thing to think that it just wouldn't be within their frame of reference, but for me, it is. I do fear about something happening to him, and I have to be really careful that I don't pass that on to him, and that's one of the hardest things.

Sam was nearly three when Emilie died, he has always been a very clever, intuitive little boy, and he would say, "I miss Emilie," and I would find that really hard. "Why did Emilie die? Why did Emilie die in your tummy?" and all of these questions. That happened for a long time after she died, and still he asks, but I think he understands as much as he can. I think the biggest impact it's had on him is the separation. I'm not entirely sure. I don't know if this has come from a combination of Emilie or the fact that he will have some attachment problems because he's an incubator baby and everything that comes with that. I couldn't imagine, for example, ever leaving him in the house on his own, even for a short period of time, because he will get so panicked if he thinks I'm not coming back. The panic that he feels is really awful. I went to pick Sophie up from Rainbows a couple of months ago; it's only down the road. He asked to stay in the car on his iPad. I was going to be a few minutes. I got back to the car and he was having a full-blown panic attack. Last week I was working late and I didn't get to the after-school club till 25 past five, he knew I was going to be later, but he'd had another panic attack in there, and he was absolutely livid by the time I went to get him. It's quite frustrating for me, but then when I think about the fact that he has had some pretty traumatic separation from me, I can see exactly where it comes from.

He had some therapy last year, which made a difference, and I don't know if he could do with it again. He has quite a lot of pent-up anger; the innocence has been taken away, and he knows it has. Four years ago, one of my best friends went into labour and we had her children overnight. We all went to bed, and by the following morning we hadn't heard anything, and Sam thought she'd died. Her two children were there, and we're having this conversation at the breakfast table. There was a moment when I thought, "We need to whisk Sam upstairs and just have this conversation upstairs because this isn't an appropriate conversation to have in front of her children." His understanding of situations has changed completely because he knows the worst things can happen.

Every year on the anniversary of Emilie's death, we go away to a working farm. The kids help out with farm tasks there. The first couple of years we were a bit zombified, and it was somewhere we would go to occupy us a for a couple of days and to get out of the city, but now we really enjoy it. We love going, and the kids really enjoy it, and we make a cake and we take that. This year, we scattered Emilie's ashes at the farm because it's such a special place to us. One year when we got back from the farm, my friends had let themselves into the garden and had filled the garden with helium balloons and dragonflies. Dragonflies are my big thing, and it was just lovely to get home to and see that and realize that Emilie meant something to them as well. A friend had been round and got people to write little notes. There were dozens of them all round the garden. I've kept them in her memory box. We were given a book called *Waterbugs and Dragonflies*;[1] it's by the Alder Centre, who support bereaved parents. It's a great book.

The other books I've read all seem to have a happy ending of another child being born or of everything being okay ultimately, and actually, that's not our experience at all. We adopted Sophie, but we never had another birth child. Grief is really messy. I wanted the books to be a bit messy; that sounds really strange to say. My book ends with us adopting Sophie, which I suppose could be seen as a kind of happy ending, but actually she's a child with autism; it meant that we couldn't have another birth child. We adore her, but there were a lot of implications and a lot more grief for us to deal with. There was no new, fluffy newborn baby to make everything okay. It's not going to happen. I know that you need to be given hope and I really completely understand that, but I think there also needs to be a sense of reality as well, of reality testing.

I'm actually the only person I know who hasn't had another baby after having a stillbirth. I know there are other people around, but they just don't share their stories. Even with Sophie, she's obsessed with weddings at the moment. She's convinced she's going to marry Prince George. That's what's going on in the house at the moment you know, aim high, and there's grief there too; I don't know if she will ever leave us, I don't know if she will get married. I don't know if she will be okay to have an adult relationship, and then I'm thinking, would Emilie have been? It's very strange. Grief is a very, very strange thing.

What I think is needed is some honesty and saying grief is horrible, it's a really crap situation, but nothing's actually going to make it okay. I think that's genuinely what I want books to say, which sounds awfully negative, but we need to support people in their grief and let the grief be okay, not wrap it all up and move it on with unrealistic expectations.

Note

1 D. Stickney (2004). *Water Bugs and Dragonfiles: Explaining Death to Young Children*. Cleveland, OH: The Pilgrim Press.

3 "How many children do you have? It's just something I hate"

John's story remembering his daughter Emilie

John is Claire's (Chapter 2) husband, and this is his view of what happened.

To set that kind of context, to Emilie, it's important to talk about our firstborn Samuel's birth. We'd been forewarned prior to getting married, Claire might struggle to conceive; but at that point we weren't too concerned about that. Then, when we decided to start trying for Samuel, we miraculously conceived instantly. The pregnancy didn't progress smoothly. Everything was fine at the 12-week scan. Then, I think just before 20-week midwife check, it was identified that the bump was smaller than it probably ought to be, so they were a little bit concerned, and referred us to the maternity hospital. Based on that, they identified the blood flow through the placenta was restricted. They were not concerned too much, but concerned enough to know they needed to keep an eye on things.

We started with fortnightly checks at the hospital which then, after a while, went to weekly, then daily. The consultant we had explained to us some of the issues, and the dangers of what was going on. In particular, some of the warning signs they were looking for in particular were with the blood flow through the placenta which, obviously, nourishes the baby. They could see he was developing okay, if just a little bit smaller as a result. They were particularly looking for the internal organs starting to suffer, and they said the baby develops in a very clever way in that they look after the brain as a priority, so if there isn't enough coming in, it concentrates on the brain and perhaps the stomach and other organs will suffer a little bit, which they said they were less concerned about. It's obviously when the brain starts to suffer, they really have to intervene.

That was what they were looking out for, so we ended up having daily checks. At 32 weeks, they said they would deliver within the next two weeks. We saw the consultant the following week; she did the scan, then went away and had a little chat. When she came back, she said, "Okay, have we thought about delivery options?" Claire likes to do her own research into everything so she can have informed discussions. She said, "I've heard for very small babies that natural birth can be very traumatic and quite high risk, so probably a C-section." The consultant went, "Well, that's good, because

I thought was going to have to convince you because I booked you in for the morning."

That was all a bit of a roller coaster. He was in special care for a month, just basically while he bulked up, because he was born at 2 pounds, 13, so pretty small. He was born at 33 weeks and was the size of a 28-week baby. That was all quite traumatic. We had always said we wanted more than one child, I think at that point, we were both kind of set on two. I was probably leaning towards three. It took us a while to build up the courage, really, for Claire to get pregnant again. We'd had a little bit of post-birth liaison with the consultants. They said it was difficult to predict the likelihood of it re-occurring; they guessed that 10%, but then, they said they'd treat it as a high-risk pregnancy and give us extra monitoring anyway.

We were excited. It took a bit longer to conceive that time, but we got pregnant, and the 12-week scan was good. Then, from that point onwards we had two weekly checks with the consultant. She kept an eye on the placenta and the blood flow. Everything was fine, so we had quite a few of these fortnightly checks. Then one Saturday night, Claire wasn't feeling particularly well. She had an early night, and then on the Sunday when she woke up, she wasn't feeling any better. Her hands were a bit puffy and she hadn't really felt much movement during the night. She was quite concerned, so we went to the Women's Hospital to have a basic activity scan. We had to go into a waiting room, which we knew like the back of our hands because of the amount of time we'd spent waiting in there. Then, we were called through into where they do the sound heart machine, so they scanned around the stomach to find the baby's heartbeat. We were with a nurse who found what sounded like the heartbeat, but she knew straight away that was Claire's, not the baby's. She moved around for a different position and said, "This happens. Don't worry." Then, after a few more moments, again she found Claire's heartbeat, but not the baby's.

At this point, I could see that her hands were shaking as she was trying to do this. You start to think, okay, it could be a bit concerning. I can't remember how long, but I'm sure she had a look for a good few minutes before she very politely and calmly excused herself and said she just needed to go and check with a colleague. Then, thankfully, and it was pure chance, our consultant who'd supported us with Sam was just passing. She came in with two other nurses. I remember thinking, "This doesn't look particularly good." She took over the scan. The two nurses were going to take care of Sam, so they took him away. I'd say that after another few more moments of not being able to find anything, she said that Emilie had died. One of the delivery rooms at the Women's Hospital is set aside for stillbirths and baby deaths. We were whisked away down there. I have very clear memories of that walk down the corridor; both Claire and I were literally just wailing. Different people passing by in my periphery, but I was just completely lost in the trauma of what we'd just heard. We were taken through to this room where Claire had a panic attack and was screaming desperately that she wanted Sam. I remember the nurse and the consultant saying, "Let's just calm down." She said, "John, get me Sam." I said, "No, I think actually they're right here. Sam doesn't need to be witnessing this." She just wanted to be able to cling to Sam.

Then, the rest of that day unfolded. It was pretty horrific, really. The next conscious thought was that Claire still had Emilie inside her, and that needed to change. Claire had been concerned about having a natural birth anyway, and was very much undecided. We had a big discussion about it. The consultant, quite rightly, was saying she really wouldn't advise a C-section. I remember I had a word away from Claire about it and just explained how determined she was. Then, when we went back in to see Claire, she was actually quite willing to have a natural birth – partly, in a way, because it was the last part of the pregnancy that we were going to have. I think, in a way, she wanted that. That still came with a problem: the normal standard procedure would be that they would give Claire drugs to induce the birth, send us home for 24 to 48 hours, and then we'd go back when the labour started. I think the idea of going home in that state certainly wasn't appealing for Claire; it was too much to consider having to face.

I was flitting between trying to look after Claire and protecting her and the remaining part of her wishes, as best as I could. Then, there was all of the practical stuff to take care of, like making phone calls to our parents. I remember that didn't go particularly well. The staff then realized that they hadn't done Claire's blood pressure, and it turned out it was very high. She had preeclampsia, so at that point, it ruled out any option of sending her home. That was something slightly going in our favour. So, then, I was liaising with friends to get Sam picked up, to get an overnight bag, things like that.

Our consultant was very keen they did as much as they could to make it as easy as possible. She said, given that Claire had to stay in now, there may be something different that they could do with the drug plan to enable us to stay in for that waiting period. She was able to speak to the pharmacy department, and they came up with a way of giving the induction medicine that allowed her to both be in hospital for the preeclampsia but also accelerate the birth. They still said it could take 24 to 48 hours. I think after about 20 hours or so, the labour started. That, in particular, I remember being very difficult and being an outsider to it. Sam was a C-section, so neither of us had experienced a normal birth before. Obviously, the pains of birth without the anticipated joy at the end is pretty horrendous to sit and watch, really. Especially as most of it was through the night. I think it started at about half ten, eleven pm. I think she was born about six or seven in the morning.

I remember flitting between wanting to do whatever little I could do for Claire, but also just wanting to lie down and sleep through it all. In that waiting period, we had some of the leaders from our church with us; that was very useful. Also Carol, who Claire had been seeing for therapy, and who

I incidentally met the first time the week before. She came, and it was really useful, having her there with us.

Once we finally came home, I remember again, being split between trying to make any sense of all the emotions myself, but also then very consciously looking after Claire. Obviously she'd gone through the birth and had all the hormones and all of that, so I was trying to prioritize her needs. She was completely not interested in eating for the first day or so, which was normal but, again, hard to see. I would say, fortunately, we had a lot of friends who were able to help us. We joked that Sam had a whale of a time at the unit, the nurses had given him some blue gloves they'd blown up, tied a knot in and drawn a face on, he kept that around with him for weeks after. It just didn't go down. He loved his little balloon. He was taken away by some friends and had a sleepover and had a really nice time there.

I think the first night when we were home, some of our friends from church who live around the corner came around, and we actually had some laughs that evening. It was just nice having a distraction, really. A different couple came around who'd lost a son, a stillbirth, about two and a half years before us, so that was really useful. I remember one of the first things they said was something about how they were really struggling six months later. I just remember those words and of not being able to comprehend feeling this awful for that length of time. They were saying that even now, several years later, it was still painful. The enormity of it just stretching out seemingly for endless days felt overwhelming. It was something that was such a shock to hear. But, I think it was certainly useful to have that expectation almost handed to me right from the outset.

Over the next few mornings, we'd wake up and have those few sleepy moments of not remembering. Having Sam was the main motivation to get up and keep going with everything after the reality set back in. He was coming up to two, he was fully aware of having a baby sister coming and everything. He was very excited about it as well. Obviously, with someone that young as well, we were kind of conscious about how we delivered the news to him. Mainly, if his attention wasn't on Emilie, then it probably wouldn't make any sense to him. We made the decision that we'd wait for him to ask either about Emilie or what had been going on. We both wanted to be there to support each other through telling him, but he didn't ask anything. Apparently, he asked at bedtime when Claire put him to bed. I wasn't there, so Claire had to explain. I think for him at that age, I suppose he perhaps saw it a bit more matter of fact. On the surface of it, initially, he was okay. We got him a kitten, mainly to give him a little bit of a distraction and also a distraction from our grief as well. He really loved that cat, and he would play with it, we would just sit and watch.

Emilie's death has had a definite effect on him, though. We had a meal plan from friends for four or five weeks, where every night they cooked our food and brought it round to us, which was amazing. Sam was really excited about "who's cooking for us and what's it going to be." As soon as that stopped, Sam stopped eating pretty much, which wasn't unheard of for him. Having been in special care, he had developed some feeding aversions initially with milk. Then, I suppose, on the face of it, kind of fussy eating. He'd been under a dietician, previously, for making sure he was able to keep putting on weight. In the end, once he reverted back to food not being a novelty event of someone different bringing it round, he went back to, at best, picking at one thing on his plate, and at worst, not eating anything really at tea times. It's obviously all related to his process of grief; he ended up back under a dietician for a little while.

Those months that followed were obviously not nice, really. I think if there was any goodness there, it was the fact that Claire and I were very much in it together. I went for grief counselling at Alder Hey; they did a free service there, that was useful, in externalizing my thoughts. I'd never had any counselling or therapy before that. I would never do any self-checks of, "What am I feeling? What am I thinking about that? Or what do I feel about that?" One of the things I found most useful about the whole process was being asked those questions explicitly; it started me thinking and then having an hour a week, or whatever it was, set aside to then discuss those points and externalize them. That really helped, I think.

I suppose it was a bit of a can-do attitude for both of us. We wanted to come through this. We didn't want to be forever held back by this grief and trauma, as much as you can be, I suppose. There is always a loss; a phrase we've used a lot lately is "the new normal." It's not particularly a phrase we wanted to introduce into our language, but everything changed at that point. So it was a case of, okay, what is the new normal? What does it look like, and how can we ultimately make the best of that?

We were still determined to have more children. That's where things start to get all the more complicated, really, with then trying again to conceive. Which then resulted in extended bouts of infertility; with Sam we conceived straightaway, and Emilie was relatively quick too. We went through the longest period of trying to conceive. Then we did, and that was our first miscarriage; it came at a time just when we'd started to get a feel for what the new normal might look like, and then we thought, "well if we can get pregnant soon, that would be OK." The age gap between Sam and the next child was always a big issue in our minds. Originally, we wanted two years, and to have that taken away with Emilie's death, and then the struggle of conceiving, got us quite worried. I suppose, in a way, that was just a distraction for the fact that we weren't conceiving and we still had so much grief. We had some fertility treatment, but the miscarriage confused me quite a lot in terms of the grief.

I think this is one of the things I discussed in therapy. Losing Emilie, I kind of understood how I felt about it. I understood the enormity of it. Then, to have the miscarriage, I think I couldn't really distinguish the two. Miscarriage and stillbirth, perhaps, in a lot of people's minds, get grouped together, when they're really quite different. Emilie was born at 32 weeks, just one week difference to Sam, and effectively the same weight as him. The whole expectation through that pregnancy was that we weren't going to make it past 34 weeks. If we got to 33, it would be good. Even though everything had been going well, no one really expected the full term to be at 40 weeks. For us, Emilie was born pretty much at full term. She was a baby. We held her for two days, so that was very different to a miscarriage, although the miscarriage was horrible.

I think in a way, I was trying to separate the feelings of the two. I wanted other people to appreciate the difference of the two, and we still didn't have a baby we wanted. It was another life, and it was lost. I don't think there was the same kind of sledgehammer, the whole world has rocked, feeling. With Emilie the world took on a frozen effect. With the miscarriage I think we were still in the grief with Emilie. Everything was numbed anyway. If we hadn't had the stillbirth, then the news of the miscarriage would probably have hit us a lot harder. When you have a miscarriage, at that point, you haven't met the child. I figured afterwards that with any kind of pregnancy loss, the longer the pregnancy goes on, the more bonding there is, and therefore, the bigger the impact of when it happens. We were back to square one. I think that was the hard part of it, back to unpicking a lot of our expectations and hopes around it all, really.

We're both Christians, so when Sam was born, I said, "It was miraculous." We were told before we were married that we'd probably need have some fertility treatment to conceive. We went to Claire's GP, who's also a Christian at our church, he prayed that we would be pregnant in two weeks, and a stranger from our church, who we barely knew, came over to us that same week and said, "This is weird. I barely know you, but God's told me to pray for you to have a baby, conceive a baby, in two weeks." To then conceive within two weeks, that made the whole process of Sam's difficult pregnancy a lot easier to trust that everything was going to be okay. To then roll our mindset on to Emilie, and then conceive, I think we had a default go-to of 'everything will be fine.' I had a lot of prayer about it being fine, but if I look back honestly on what we prayed and what we felt God said to those prayers, it was always us asking God to protect our baby, but never in the same way as with Samuel did we get promises back from God that the baby would be protected.

Frankly, the Bible doesn't teach of life on earth being perfect and without drama. It was a reflection of the way we'd set our mindset on one side of the conversation with God, rather than perhaps the totality in trying to see that, unfortunately, terrible things do happen and certainly, God didn't want it to happen, but it did happen. I think I found it useful because I didn't have a church background as such when I was young. I came to church not long after I met Claire, so I think because I discovered my faith at a nice, stable point in life, I made conscious and mature decisions that I believed the way of the Bible. I found comfort, and I knew I made those decisions about my faith then. That's not to say it made much of it any easier in terms of the disappointment and the suffering. I think the overarching thing was, unfortunately, bad things do happen. I don't think it's right to blame any of it on God.

What happened certainly affected my faith, and probably, my overall prayer life has been less than it was, but that could be other factors as well. The faith itself was a constant, and having that constant certainly helped. This 'shit happens' thing is true, so if I hadn't had faith that God was bigger than that, then I think it would have been a lot more challenging.

I was still very cross with God, particularly when Claire was going through the labour, and I remember praying very angry prayers about just wanting it to be quick and wanting it to be done. One of things we did speak about with the church leaders when they were there was that we believe that God wants to know us individually and he can understand that we're cross. He's not going to particularly hold it against me that I was cross with him, in that moment.

We went on the fertility treatment later on. Unfortunately, there was another miscarriage. At that point, we were starting to get a bit sick and tired of it all. I think in a way we counted from September to September. Emilie was born in September, and then we had a miscarriage in the early new year. Then, another miscarriage that following September, so in that 12-month period, we had three babies die on us. I think at that point we were worn out, especially with the fertility treatment as well, having an effect. In a way, at that point, we knew, we'd given it a lot, and perhaps we needed a rest.

I remember that period was just generally horrible of physically having just Sam, and feeling so, so desperate for a second child. We'd had a second child, which no one could see. I remember things like going to the park, and it was hard only having Sam. The bedroom for Emilie, we'd had it all decorated. It was her room. The door stayed shut for a long time. We didn't even really know how to refer to it. Is it Emilie's room? Is it the spare room? That sounded even worse. I suppose we had a mixed experience with how family and certain pockets of friends who had supported us before but were not supporting us through all of this as well; that added to all the issues quite a bit.

Some of the most useful things people did were practical things. The meal plan was brilliant. I'd say there was no way we could have worked out what we were going to eat and gone to the shops and buy it. Natural thought processes just seem to disappear. I had three weeks off work; that was useful. We did what we called the "grief tour" of coffee shops of South Liverpool. Sam must have been at pre-school at some points of the day, and we didn't want to just sit in the house all the time, so trying to be slightly creative about what the two of us could do, we used to go out for coffees. We didn't specifically plan this, but we started off with coffee shops where we knew we wouldn't see people we knew and then started to build up to ones where we were perhaps more likely to see friends.

It helped to build our confidence a little bit so that was one of the ways we kind of tried to get out and about. I remember some people saying, "If you wanna chat, let me know." It's like, "Nah I don't really want to, I'd rather sit with Claire and make sure she's okay." One night someone just came and knocked on the door and said, "Fancy a cup of tea?" I remember I just gave him a hug on the step and cried because yes, I really did. If someone had asked me, I would have said no, but it's someone just taking that initiative, really, and then I said yes. There were other friends who said, "Let us know if we can do this, let us know if this will be useful." But it's like you don't have a thought process to think that would be useful. So, you don't take them up on it, whereas if they said "We will do this, or we will come and do that, or we will come and take Sam for a bit," that worked much better for us.

The very mundane points you do not have any kind of mind capacity for. Then the overall mindset was just horrible that the rest of the world is carrying on without you. I'd say that was probably one of the reasons why we were keen to get out of the house a little bit, as well as to stop ourselves from going stir crazy. Everything stopped for us that day in September, whereas unfortunately everything else was going on around us, and at some point you have to start being aware of that, I suppose.

I remember my parents weren't able, either then or since, to really understand. Right from that first phone call, when we were in the hospital and I called and my dad answered. I said, "We're in the hospital, unfortunately, the baby's died." I think my dad wailed and went silent or something, so then my mum picked up the phone and went, "What's going on, what's going on?" So I had to explain again to her and she was going, "What? What?" In the end, I said "just speak to Dad" and hung up. It's like, "you're not really making this process very easy for me." They came to see us a couple of days later, the first thing my dad said to me was, "Are you starting to get over it yet?" They were there for a few hours, and then when they left, they said, "Okay, we'll see you at the funeral. Hopefully, you can get some closure there." And I was like, "Really?" At the funeral we arranged things so that we would sit with a couple of specific friends rather than being surrounded by family, so that helped a lot. Ever since, my family just don't speak about Emilie; they'll change the subject if it's even veering in that direction. So that's not ideal.

I know it's very tough because your parents are your parents, and you expect support when you need it. My family, typically, were never particularly good at talking about emotions and that side of things. Perhaps on some level I was not overly surprised that there was a limit to how much I could have expected to get in terms of that kind of support. But, probably the biggest values growing up from my mum and dad were very much "family is the main thing, we look after our family, we invest in family time." All those real core values. Another was my dad had been married before he met my mum and had a child, Chris; it was agreed that he'd walk away and leave them to it. So, he'd had an experience of what it's like to have no contact with a baby. Also my dad's brother died when he was 21, so again he has a conception of what grief is and what it feels like. So with these values and experiences I thought they'd be able to understand. They ought to put more effort into actually facing the fact that Emilie died. They'd happily mention Chris, who I only really got to know after Emilie died, but if its anything related to Emilie, they don't mention it.

Chris is much more in tune with emotions. I got a letter in the post from his wife; she'd managed to get my address and written to say, "Listen, Chris would really like to reach out to you." I said, "Okay, we're going through this at the moment, so I do want to meet but it will be in a little while." I think they've known us from that point onwards and there's been a lot more understanding about everything. So that has affected our relationship with mum and dad a little bit, I think, because it feels like that value of 'family first' seems a little bit disingenuous in a way. Coupled with the fact that for many years whilst we were carrying that heavy grief we were getting absolutely nothing from them. It was quite obvious they didn't ask us how we're feeling or anything like that because they didn't want to go anywhere near it themselves. When we went to see them, there was a bit of it that was nice but at the same time we felt we were being forced to hide our emotions for a few hours, and we wondered, "Is that really what we want? Is this particularly helpful for us?" That's been a huge challenge.

As the years moved on, we decided to have a break from the fertility treatment, and we switched our focus to fostering which is something we'd wanted to do long term anyway. That's when Sophie came to live with us. At that point, we hadn't completely ruled out having another baby at some stage but were getting fairly close to it. So we then started to explore adoption a little bit as well. Let's say the two paths collided in a way in that Sophie was meant to be a six-month placement with us but that had just extended naturally anyway because there was a lot of paperwork and some of her issues were becoming more pronounced. We were the first family she'd made an actual and emotional bond with, so they were concerned about moving her on especially given that she had so many placements already and hadn't really connected.

So, we were then effectively given a choice by the social workers: Would we want to adopt Sophie? At that point she'd been with us probably six or eight months. It was quite an easy decision for us to make. It took quite a long time for the adoption to go through, but that was really healthy for us as a family. We'd decided, mainly due to the risk of disappointment and the risks to Claire's health, we wouldn't pursue pregnancy anymore.

Then, fast forward a few years, I think I was suffering from depression and again had some psychotherapy in relation to this. If I had to sum up the whole thing, I'd probably had depression for a year or so at that point. I'd been really struggling, and I came to a point where I was very short and snappy and had a complete apathy, really, for a lot of things, always thinking about what might be next and having very little enjoyment or excitement about current life. The therapy I had was useful; we talked about what had happened and dealt with my emotions. I realized all my energy had gone into dealing with the grief with Emilie and the miscarriages, in supporting Claire as well through that process, coping with the way my family responded with things. The friends who'd literally walked away from us, as well as other friends who have been supportive but had to move away. All of those additional aspects that had been too much to process. I got to a point where I felt more acceptance of the situation and the new normal and everything else.

Life now is good. Sophie in some ways couldn't be further apart from Sam in that she's got additional needs and attachment disorders and autism and a lot of things that are challenging. Academically, she's at the opposite end of the spectrum to our Sam, but she's extremely loving. She and Sam have a real sibling relationship. They'll spend a few days of being inseparable, and the next minute they'll be screaming and fighting with each other. I think it's certainly helped Sam in being able to be that brother figure he's waited a long time to be. I think he's very loving and very proud of her.

I think at times there has still been a desire to have three children, certainly for me perhaps more than Claire. Claire kind of flicked with it for a while. With Sophie's needs it would be impractical. I think we're very accepting of that; we wouldn't change anything. It does mean some weeks everything's going great, and then let's say we have a few meltdowns and whatnot. I think we are comfortable with being able to talk about and remember Emilie. I think she's remained an important part of the family.

I think going back to that family who'd experienced it all before us, one of the tips they gave us was always do something to mark her birthday. That's been really nice. We found a very nice family-run farm, we go and stay, and it's really special going away in that week in September, and from being very young the kids knew why we were there, knew who we were remembering. Even if Sophie keeps on getting the name wrong. She keeps on calling Emilie baby Annabel, which is a doll she got last Christmas. But, it's good, and this year we crossed another milestone with scattering of Emilie's ashes, something again we'd put off for quite a while but, that was a really nice time. The kids really got involved because we did it at the farm. We did a little walk around and chose special places where we thought would be good to scatter some ashes. I think with our grief now being less than it was, it's easier to integrate or liaise with family. We still know we're not going to get support, but the need for that support isn't as much, so that makes it easier as well.

I suppose one area that is still difficult, not from an emotional point of view but from a social point of view, is the inevitable questions about "How many children do you have?" It's just something I hate. Even with the people I worked with, it's a question that I don't particularly like answering because "Is it two? Is it three? Is it five?" I can't give an answer. Given I work from home, I don't see my work colleagues that often; there's a very real chance they don't remember what happened seven years ago. That's difficult, but then it's more so at a conference or something and you're sat around a table with people you don't really know and these questions start coming up again, "Well. How many children do you have?" It's, "Do I want to take this conversation in that direction?" A lot of the time you just try push that question off, change the subject in a way because I can talk about it in that context without getting upset myself, but it adds a weight to the conversation that probably the other person wasn't really prepared for, and you're never really sure how people are going to respond. Some people go very quiet and as they look at me might as well hold up a flag of "Get me out of here." Some people engage and can be empathetic about it. Then other people probably misjudge it in a way and either try and be helpful and say something cruel for want of the better way of putting it, "oh you can have more," or almost try, not to joke it off, but to get out of the conversation in a way that just comes across as very inappropriate.

I don't think I've had any particular horrors. The main thing is when people brush it aside. I met a taxi driver once, it was six months to the day since Emilie died, and so I wasn't particularly in a gleeful mood when the taxi picked me up at 6:00 a.m. or something to go and get a flight. The taxi driver was chatting away and I just sat down and said, "It's six months since my daughter died in stillbirth." He said, "Okay," then just completely carried on rabbiting away. I was like, "Just leave me alone." He made me feel worse. I'd just explained the situation, and he just completely ignored it.

That was probably one of the worst reactions in that complete non-reaction. One of the lasting memories of a good reaction in a way was with someone else at church. This was probably one of the first days we'd been in church after Emilie died. I didn't know him particularly well, I've got to know him quite a bit more since then. He literally just came over to Claire and I, put his hand on my shoulder, gave me a little shoulder cuddle and said, "I'm thinking of you. I'm sorry, but that's all I've got." That was really poignant because it showed that he was acknowledging what had happened, acknowledging what we're going through as best as they can, but at the same time he knew he was not the person to say, "Let's talk it through. Let's cry it out." Rather it was, "I'm standing with you. I can't actually do anything, but I'm here." Much better than people who plough ahead anyway and dig themselves a hole or simply steer clear.

During the grief counselling I found their explanations reassuring, especially when they told us that, as a couple, going through the same event together, it doesn't necessarily mean we're going to do it in the same way. I think fortunately for us, we did go through it in a similar way, at a similar pace. But again, it's just that reassurance that that might not be the case. That one person might not want to be talking about it, that they might be feeling good about different things and using that as their coping mechanisms, just as long as they are moving on a journey of dealing with the grief rather just completely shutting away, then that's fine. You have to respect and acknowledge that with each other, not try and force them to feel how you're feeling or feel bad because you're not feeling the way they are feeling on that particular day. I think it's important to acknowledge early the significance of the event and know it's going to be with you for the rest of your life ultimately, and also that real heartbreak grief is going to last a long time in itself. You won't get closure at the funeral.

We were both quite sold on getting counselling and therapeutic support and seeing the benefits of that, particularly for me as a person who would normally internalize things and who's probably at risk of bottling things up if I hadn't had those outlets. Then also, having the grief process explained to you and that you do go through peaks and troughs.

I've always found that the anticipation of an event is worse than the event itself. We mark Emilie's birthday every year, the lead up to them initially was pretty horrific. But on the actual day, deliberately trying to do something as a family to mark it has been good; it's also a distraction, and we've had some good times and good memories.

I think with the anniversaries, it's important to mark them as much as you can, celebrate them with friends. It's good to recognize which friends can give you that support, whether it's in the early days when you need more practical support, such as who is going to walk your dog for you or a regular basis, or who is good for when you do need to sit and chat. Who to avoid sitting and chatting to, because they're just going to dig themselves a hole and make you both feel awful at the end of it.

4 "There was this crowd of women all wailing"

Elisa's story remembering her daughter Ellen

The story seems very short because Ellen's life was very short. I was pregnant in a country in southern Africa, and we came back at 37 weeks to have the baby because we wanted to have the delivery in the UK in case something went wrong. When she was three weeks old, we went back to Africa. Everything seemed fine until one day when I was in the market on a Saturday morning shopping with my husband. I was carrying her in one of those across-the-body slings. She'd just had a feed and I thought she was sleeping. Then I just thought something was a bit funny; she had some fluid coming from her nose, and I realized she wasn't breathing. I pulled her up and she was floppy, I called my husband and we ran through the market doing CPR to get to our car.

He sat in the passenger seat doing CPR whilst I drove to the hospital where we both worked, which was five minutes away. We ran directly onto the ITU through a back door (we actually kicked through the glass on the door and replaced it later on), and a doctor who was doing his rounds resuscitated her. They were able to get her heartbeat back, which was amazing because it had been 20 minutes later with no heartbeat, and by that point it is medically very unlikely. However, the next morning when they tried to wean her off the ventilator, she had a lot of seizures. I knew immediately that this meant she had suffered some brain damage, although the medical team tried to be reassuring. They evacuated Ellen and I down to South Africa because that was the nearest paediatric intensive care unit. My husband followed the next day. Then about two days after that, she suffered severe brain swelling. At first, we were told that she was brain dead and that just a few final tests were needed to confirm that. These tests showed flickers of activity, but from then on, she was really disabled. She was quadriplegic, epileptic, blind and deaf and couldn't even make a sound. Because she couldn't swallow properly or cough, she kept getting pneumonias, and we had to suction her airways several times a day to try and remove secretions. They did a small operation to place a feeding tube directly into her stomach, but she died of pneumonia shortly after that. That is our story, and there isn't much more to say about Ellen's life.

When we were in South Africa, we asked if they would try and see if there was any syndrome or genetic problem that we should be watching for should we have another baby. However, all tests showed that everything was fine and there was no reason that explained why the cardiac arrest had happened. They said it was most likely that she died from Sudden Infant Death Syndrome (SIDS). If she'd been at home in her cot, and I hadn't been holding her at the point when she stopped breathing, we would have just found her dead. In the medical literature, there is a case series of these near SIDS, and they're all the same, they all do badly. They either die or they're so disabled that their life is really difficult. We think it was a near sudden infant death and unexplained really. That was really what happened in a nutshell; she was just 15 weeks old when she died. She only lived three months. It seemed long, but you know, I look back now and it was very short.

My husband took unpaid leave. He just told his head of department, "I'll be back whenever I'm back." His department were totally understanding of the complex and unpredictable situation we were in and were fully supportive. We were together in a city where we knew nobody, at first. That was actually very helpful because it meant we could do an awful lot of that working through things without interference from well-meaning but intrusive visitors. We had quite a few people that got in touch with us, though.

There was no parents' accommodation at the hospital. We had nowhere to stay; we were sleeping in corners, on floors or in chairs and things. After about a week, I fainted on the ITU and the doctors were getting worried that I was not okay. I wasn't okay at all, but I really did not want to leave the hospital for even a few minutes. Then some friends that were friends of friends, a family with five children, living about two miles from the hospital, invited us to stay with them. We were quite uncertain about this, "You sure? We are strangers." They said, "No, come and stay." Then they said, "By the way, our brother has got a car that he's not using at the moment, and he says you can use that." Then somebody else, the sister-in-law of one of my friends, whose husband works at the Bible College out there, came up to visit quite a lot. Before we knew it, we were surrounded by this network of people, but we had known none of them before.

In some ways, that also really helped in a way, because people just took us as we were. We had lots of space. I spent the first three weeks hoping that she would recover, praying that she'd recover. Then, when it became so clear how bad the disabilities were, it was really obvious she was never going to walk, talk, communicate in any way. It became evident that her life expectancy was very limited, and I started to pray that she would not suffer long. One of the most helpful comments was made by a neurologist we saw at the specialist hospital. He explained that a lot of our feelings were to be expected, and that it might help to remember that each person is made up of body, soul, and spirit. Just because the body is broken, badly broken, it does not change the essence of who the child is. That was simple but profound and changed my perspective greatly. As the years have gone by, I remember these words very clearly and have used them myself when talking with families in similar situations.

When she died, we brought her body back to England and we buried her there. Having the funeral in our hometown in England was also a bit strange. Nobody had known I was pregnant until we arrived back a few weeks before the birth, because I hadn't actually told anyone in the UK; it was a surprise. The reason for this was that I've got a genetic syndrome. It affects my connective tissue and makes me very flexible, but I also get injured very easily and have had lots of different surgeries to correct some of the problems. I had been told that I might not be able to carry a child to term – the biggest risk would be a late miscarriage or stillbirth because of a problem with my cervix. Because we were in living in Africa, I didn't want to tell people that I was pregnant because I didn't want people back home to be worried when there would have been nothing they could do to change the outcome.

By the time we felt safe to tell people, I was about seven months, and by this point we thought we might as well just go home for the delivery and surprise people. That was fine. But because people hadn't really adjusted to the fact I was pregnant, they didn't really associate us with a baby, as being parents. I came in heavily pregnant, had the baby, disappeared again, then the next thing we were back to bury the baby, all within a very short time span. It must have been really surreal for other people. Once the funeral was over, we spent another week or so in the UK, and then went back to Africa. Our lives and our work were out there, and we wanted to try and get back to some kind of normality.

That's where it gets interesting, because at that point, in the town where I was living, one in eight children died under the age of five, and most women had at least four children. That basically meant that one in two women in my town had a child die under the age of five. When I went back to work, my nurse said, "Oh, I remember when my child died," and I would think, "I never knew you had a child die." It was almost like everybody around me had had a child die and had lived through the pain but adjusted and gone on living. I think that really helped us.

I felt that I couldn't go to pieces or fall apart because it was actually a normal experience. The women supported me very much. The only thing that was really strange was that one day, I was walking between two parts of the hospital and I met a nurse who was a Rwandese refugee that had been through an awful situation during the genocide. She was working with us, and she asked me, "How's the baby?" I responded, "Oh, you don't know, do you?" She said, "Know what?" I said, "The baby died." She threw up her hands and then, before I knew it, there was this crowd of women all wailing in this kind of way the African women wail. It's really difficult to explain. It got bigger and bigger and I was standing in the middle. I just didn't know what to do. I was thinking, "Help, get me out of here! This is really awkward."

Then the next day, I was talking to a British paediatrician, and I told him, "You wouldn't believe what happened yesterday." He said to me, "Yes, but do you not think that's actually a lot more appropriate than a British person who would just say, "I am terribly sorry to hear that?" Looking back, I completely agree with that. In Africa, sadly, the whole experience of the death of a child is more normal. But there is also a lot more expression of grief and solidarity of women standing together. This is not the case for the men, though; bereaved fathers are often neglected in every context, and in many African settings, it is only the women who attend the funerals of babies and express their grief in this context.

The different cultural expressions of grief meant that when I came back to the UK a year later to have my next child, it was almost like I had to go through the grieving again in my own culture. This was interesting although painful, because it felt almost like it had just happened, and it felt really raw. I think this is because the death of a child is seen as shocking in the UK. It's seen as an unusual experience, and it's still a bit shocking, and dramatic, even though we know many people in that position. Although it had felt like a long time to be parents without children, I was pregnant again relatively quickly. The due date of the next child was basically three days off the anniversary of my daughter's death. She died on May the 26th, and the next baby was born on May 29th the following year.

Again, we wanted to come back to the UK to have a safe delivery. My husband found a three-month locum job up in a Scottish city, where we knew nobody. As we had done with our daughter's birth, we arrived kind of homeless in a completely new city. I was about 35 weeks pregnant at this point, and people would ask, "Is it your first baby?" I would reply, "No, I had another last year and she died." People would gasp. I don't know if people thought that I was being mentally not quite with it, a bit detached or something. It became quite awkward at times. I almost didn't know what to say because people used to get more upset than I did.

I wasn't really detached and unemotional; it was just that I had learned to see my experience as normal, and so I would be matter of fact about it. But it certainly affected me! I think around about the time our baby son was at that nine-week-old stage, I used to sometimes think he was not breathing. I'd be in the car, and I'd have to stop the car and prod him, and I used to hate it when he was sleeping. I know a lot of this is quite normal because he was the same age that Ellen had been at when she became unwell. I was just so scared, and I didn't know that what I was feeling was normal given the circumstances.

That was quite a hard time. I don't know, it just felt really weird because I felt like I should be over it by now because it was a year ago, and yet, it's all really fresh. I remember my midwife sent me to see a perinatal psychiatrist. I thought, "Okay, whatever." I couldn't work out if I was depressed or not because you just don't know. He was quite clear: "You're completely not depressed." He said, "it's just really interesting because you almost grieved in a couple of completely different cultures, and you've moved around so many times that you're having to face things afresh." He was very good actually, and he just said, "No, you're not depressed." I can't remember what else he said, but we had a very interesting discussion about grief in different cultural contexts. After that, I think things became better with time and as my son grew.

I felt when I was in Africa that it wasn't okay to cry, it wasn't okay to accept that it was actually a bad thing that had happened. Rather, we were quite accepting of it as in these things happen for a reason, and we were at that time aware of how common our experience was. The truth was, we were all right, but it was still desperately sad, and yet, the other thing I felt was that many of our friends were scared because they didn't know what to say. I don't mean our local friends, who stood with us in a quiet, unspoken, but deeply understanding way, but rather the expat community with whom we worked; they didn't know what to do, or what to say, or what to think. Some people that I expected to be there in a supportive way really backed off.

I felt like I had to spend a long time and make a lot of effort to reassure people that we were okay. We are quite strong Christians, and it felt as though we spent a lot of time having to counsel people in the church and say, "No, God hasn't made a mistake, and this is why." Sometimes I felt that it should be the other way around. Our church leaders and fellow church members should surely be the one bringing us the comfort and encouragement, but it was almost the other way around. It was as though if I was going to fall apart, and if I really needed to just have a good cry or talk to someone, there wasn't anybody that fitted that role. I often felt quite lonely and wished that I could talk things over with somebody. That was extremely hard, looking back.

We were on our own really with that aspect of the experience. In some ways it helped, because I had some friends a couple of years later who had a child die in the UK. They were almost given so much support, having so many people tiptoeing around them and saying, "Gosh, it's so hard for them." Actually, that probably put them into a category of "those poor people whose child died." Even now, years later it is almost part of their identity, as in, "They're the ones whose child died. Oh, it was awful." We never wanted to be in that category.

I felt that if I'd been offered lots and lots of counselling and so forth, it might have made me worse, because in some ways, she was dead, and nobody was going to bring her back, and talking about it wasn't going to change that. I just had to move on with living, and talking about how I felt maybe didn't matter so much. I don't know. It was just very different to how it would have been handled if I'd been in the UK, but not necessarily worse.

Two people said to me, not long after Ellen died, "I'm really glad it was your baby that died, and not your friend's, because, well, you're doctors and you know what to do with these kind of things, and she wouldn't have coped." I remember thinking. "That's an interesting way of looking at things."

A few months before Ellen was born, I'd been looking at a paper on outcomes after out-of-hospital cardiac arrest in children. The big debate was along the lines of, "Should you even bother resuscitating?" Because the outcomes are dreadful, the child either dies or they're so badly disabled that you may almost find yourself asking, "Did I do the right thing?" When her arrest happened, I felt very clear that there was no point in resuscitating. I just felt sure that she had died. Why resuscitate her? She's dead. My husband was doing the CPR, and so I thought, "Just go along with it." Because of this, I felt completely calm driving to the hospital whilst my husband did mouth-to-mouth resuscitation and CPR from the passenger seat because I felt like, "Well, she's died. He can do that if he wants, if he feels that helps, but I don't think it's going to." It was that medical awareness of futility that made me calm. I felt that we would not be able to improve the outcome.

We weren't particularly traumatized by the ITU. Whereas I know some other parents who have had children die on ITU, and they talk a lot about the trauma of it all and almost like post-traumatic stress from that. There was nothing that scared us about it. But it was still upsetting and distressing because it was our baby.

As a doctor, it was much easier to accept. I think that helped, but perhaps what didn't help is two things. One, we are trained to adopt a calm, rational, problem-solving approach to the most difficult life-and-death situations. It's not that you're being false with people, but you spend so much of your life in a role that it's very difficult to talk about how you are if you're not okay. So that made things tough. Second, some people almost felt like it didn't affect us as much because we were doctors, or "it must have been easier for you." So many people said that to me, "It must have been so much easier for you because you know all about hospitals." I felt like responding, "Yes, but actually, that didn't really make it easier. It maybe made it faster for us to accept that it was futile. It doesn't make the sorrow of having a child die any less." That was quite hard to explain to people, and also because neither my husband nor I are particularly given to displays of emotion.

Our Christian faith would be the thing that helped us the most. Even before I was pregnant, there are sections in the Psalms where it talks about how God knows you even before you're made. It talks about how we are fearfully wonderfully made. There's one line, and it's actually on Ellen's gravestone, that says, "All the days ordained for me were written in your book before one of them came to be" (Psalm 139, verse 16). We very much have this feeling of, we don't know how long our lives are, but God does, and nothing's a mistake. Nothing's beyond what is meant to be. The other thing – this is going to sound really weird – when I had Ellen I was midway through my PhD, there were times when it wasn't going beautifully. When she was about eight weeks old, so about a week before she got sick, I think I was doing some emails and she was on the floor near me. I was daydreaming, so definitely I wasn't asleep. I was thinking, about how when people write up their PhD and they put some dedication at the front like,

"To my husband who stood by me," something like that. I saw her name and I saw her date of birth and a date of death. I didn't see what the date was, but I saw clearly date of birth and date of death. There's a verse in Job (chapter 1, verse 21) that says, "The Lord gives and the Lord takes away. Blessed be the name of the Lord." I saw it so clearly and I'd written underneath, "This thesis is dedicated to my daughter, who was with us for such a short time," but she was perfectly healthy at that point. I metaphorically slapped myself on the cheek, and I thought maybe it's like some postnatal depression, or something like that. I don't know. I just thought, "That's a weird thought," and I went and got a cup of tea and didn't really think about it again.

When her heart stopped, that verse was immediately in my mind. I'm not one of those Christians that's always having "messages" – some people believe that God will speak to them daily in a very direct and obvious manner. That doesn't happen to me, but it did on that occasion. That bothered me for a long time because it was out of keeping with what is normal from my experience. Then somebody said to me, "Yes, but did that help you understand that it was kind of meant to be?" It did help me make sense of something so sudden and shocking, and it kept me very calm at the start because I felt that what was going to happen, was somehow meant to happen. I was being sort of warned. That might sound odd, but it helped. I suppose the other thing is that she didn't obviously suffer; I think that really helped.

Sometimes when I talk to other parents, if they've got a child that's going through chemo, and they're really distressed and having to have loads of drips and procedures done, that must be very hard. For Ellen, things didn't go on for that long for her, either. It felt long, but compared to, say, two, three years of chemo, and all the "they're in remission" or "no, they're not" rollercoaster that some of my other friends have gone through, for us it was short.

After Ellen died, we talked about anything we felt guilty or worried about and drew a line under it, so that in the future, if things start to come up in our minds, we can say "No." For example, I was worried that I might somehow have caused her to suffocate through how I had been carrying her in the market, or because of the type of baby sling I was using. I spoke to a few paediatricians and staff, I explained how I had been holding her, and they reassured me, Actually, as time has gone by, and I've seen other babies being carried in similar positions, I think that's exactly how I was holding her. The fact that we did nothing wrong, there was no feeling of, "If only we had done this, if only we hadn't done that." It was no one's fault. It was short, it was painless, and the fact that together we both saw what happened, I think all those things helped.

There was one girl at my workplace in Africa, she was an Australian girl, an atheist, rather different in her worldview to me, but a very good friend. She used to come to my desk most mornings and just say, "How are you?" One day I was like, "Not okay." She was like, "Right, let's go for coffee." We left the building and had some coffee and a chat. Afterwards I said to her,

"I'm so sorry, I've wasted your whole morning." She said, "If I didn't want to know how you were, I wouldn't ask." She was not scared of how I might be, and that helped a huge amount.

There were a few things that got in the way for me, in terms of grieving. For example, some people in the family that can't cope with things that they can't 'fix.' I would never have expected anybody to fix things, and if there was an easy answer, I am sure we would have been able to work it out ourselves. Although I am a Christian and my church community are always very important to me, it felt like some Christians were sometimes the worst. It was as though they felt they had to have the right, neatly packaged theological answer, and they couldn't cope with uncertainty. Whereas sometimes people that don't have any faith, or they have multiple faiths, seem happier with uncertainty. Sometimes we just wanted somebody to say something like, "That was bad, and it hurt, and I care about you. I don't need to have a rationale for why it happened. I'm just going to support you through it."

The relationship with some of the people in the church changed. Some backed off; they didn't know what to say. They wouldn't ask, and it just felt like at the time when we could have really valued some of the spiritual support they might be able to offer, it was just not there. I lost a bit of respect for some people. I think that was hard. I remember it being very painful. I was thinking, "Why can't you guys just pop around and see how we are? Just ask how we are and accept us how we are, not because you feel sorry for us, but just because you care," but that didn't happen. Whereas people that were going through more minor stuff would often get a lot more support. I think it's because people can support others within their comfort zone. Sometimes when somebody has a baby and they're healthy, everyone at church makes meals for a few weeks and does all these things, because that's what they do. That's probably more of a normal lived experience that people are comfortable dealing with, and they know what to say.

Then this year, it was ten years since Ellen died, and somehow, I was finding it harder; I don't know why. I had to go to South Africa, and my husband said, "Would it help you to spend an extra day on the way back and just go stay with those guys that knew you at that time? Who knew her, who were actually there?" I was like, "Yes, it would help." So, I stayed with them. That was really helpful because they've just been there, and I didn't have to say anything. I stay in touch with them, we send them flowers every May at the time when she died, and we're still in touch with their children who were teenagers at the time, and they're all growing up now. I think we'll probably be friends for life.

I think we probably gained more real friendships than lost. That was the thing that was amazing, because there we were in South Africa, and we'd get these occasional emails from people saying, "You guys, are you okay?" I'm like, "Seriously, we have a house, we have a car, we're getting fed. We've got visitors, we had everything we physically needed." I remember one day, somebody gave my husband an envelope containing cash, and we felt a bit awkward. He said, "Just for incidentals." I remember thinking, "What's an incidental?" Then something happened, I can't remember what it was, but we actually needed the money that day. We said to him afterwards, "That was amazing because we felt really uncomfortable because it's money and we're British and we really needed it. If you hadn't have given it, we'd probably have had to ask you anyway."

People just came around us, and that was actually quite incredible. I suppose it does give you faith for humanity. I like to think I would do the same for somebody else. After you've been through something like that, you think, if there's someone else in that position, you'd want to go the extra mile for them. The friendships that we had were really deep. We had every second we could have with Ellen. Sometimes I look back – life is so hectic now, there is barely time to really think. But at the time when we needed it most, we had that precious gift of time. Now, perhaps even more so as the years go by, I see there was something really precious about those days, even though it was the darkest time.

We sometimes look back on those six weeks as being like the richest in our lives in many ways. I think that's probably quite common. I think sometimes when you talk to people that have gone through some trial or suffering, they say something similar that the things that really matter are there and you realize what really matters, and you don't worry about silly small stuff anymore, and that's a good thing. I find it's really hard sometimes when people are complaining about stuff and you think, "Seriously? Life is short; get over it." I feel impatient with certain people but then feel guilty because I think that's not very kind.

After Ellen's death I had another two months off. The week I went back to work, I was looking after the part of the ward where the patients with meningitis were being looked after. There were six women under my care; they were all postpartum, and they were unconscious. The guardians (the friend or relative who needs to stay with a patient in an African hospital to provide basic nursing care and provide food) used to put the babies on their breasts to feed them, because even if you're unconscious, your pituitary and everything still works, so you can still lactate. Eventually, all of these mothers died. I remember thinking, "Who would look after these babies?" People would just say, "Somebody will somehow. Maybe there is a sister or somebody who can take the baby." It never seemed clear. Prior to this, we had thought about adopting a baby, but I suppose, to be honest, I'd worried about some of the relatively small things, such as issues arising from adopting a baby of a different race. Suddenly now, things were clear: "These are babies and they need mothers. I'm a mother, and currently I don't have a baby. Is this not a simple equation?" When you are faced with matters so complicated as life and death, who cares about small things like skin colour? My husband, who had been even more convinced about adoption before this happened, just said, "Well, why don't we adopt a baby?" Almost as soon as we had discussed this, I was pregnant – you know, before I blinked.

He said, "Why don't we adopt a baby at the same time, and we can raise the two like twins?" I found this a bit much: "Don't be so silly. Let's just have the baby make sure I'm okay."

We went to Scotland, had that baby, and then went back to Africa and we registered to adopt. By the time our new baby was 10 months old, we were matched by the social workers with a four-month-old baby from an orphanage. I've got these two sons that are six months apart, and I know that if Ellen hadn't died, I might not have got to the point where I'd definitely have adopted. We may have done it; who knows? Over the years that followed, I had another boy biologically, and we adopted an African girl in the country where we now live. Life hasn't been straightforward though. My third child, he had sepsis when he was about five months old and nearly died. I had taken him to the clinic every day for about a week and kept getting fobbed off by doctors until he was nearly dead. By the time we were taken seriously, he required resuscitation. If he'd died, I would have felt really guilty that I hadn't pushed harder. He's fine now.

These days I meet people who don't even know I had a daughter; I always say I have five children. My other four move so quickly that it probably looks like I have about 12! Often people don't notice that there's only four with me. But it is such a common question, when you meet people for the first time, "How many children do you have?" Sometimes you have to explain.

I think that lot of the grief that comes when a young baby dies is about potential, it's a loss of hopes and a loss of dreams of what you thought the future would be. We know, rationally, that we wouldn't have the family we have if Ellen had lived. I suppose, day to day being busy with four young children running around, travelling all over the world, you don't often have long to stop. But I often think about her. We have a photobook. Each of my children has a first-year-of-life photobook. For my second child it starts with the ultrasound that my husband did when we thought I might be pregnant. The next boy's starts in the orphanage when we met him. Ellen has hers, pictures of her when she was born. Then, even pictures when she was sick as well. We've put some simple explanations that the other children can understand. We always talk about her. My boys are very happy they've got a big sister that's already in heaven. They'll say things like, "When we get to heaven, she's going to have to play with us for twice as long because of all the time she's not playing with us now." They just talk about her casually, as she is a normal part of their lives. Last year, the baby boy of one of our friends died. We knew it was coming as he had been unwell for a while. One of the boys, who was eight at the time, said, "That's wonderful. He's with our sister. He's no longer disabled. He can dance now." He had been so disabled, that wee boy. My children seemed to have a clear understanding, "He's free now. He's with our sister; they'll be together." They just accept that death happens. Having had a sister makes this a very real experience for them; it changes their outlook. We're a Christian household, and we talk about heaven and things. It makes it much more real to them, because it's the reality. It's not just a faith that, as soon as something goes wrong, will get wiped away. They talk about her a lot. They ask questions sometimes. To them, it's just normal. So, it's not like they're going to discover at some point, "I had a big sister." They've got her photobook, but they can look at it when they want. They sometimes show it to visitors. Or, they'll show theirs and say, "Would you want to see my big sister's?" It's just normal.

Part of Ellen's photobook is from her time in ITU. She had tubes everywhere, for breathing, for medicine, for feeding, and she's lying under a knitted blanket. I find it helpful having the photobooks because they tell the story. Sometimes, there are things you don't have to explain. People can look at it and they can ask questions if they want. Sometimes I think people wonder, "Do I talk to you about her or not?" My response would always be, "Please talk about her." I actually wish people talked about her more. I feel like if at least we're showing that it's okay to talk, if we are clear that it is okay to ask questions, maybe they will.

You hear of people that lose their faith through things like this. If anything, that's the only thing we didn't lose. It felt like the whole of our life was potentially just changed entirely in the blink of an eye. The only thing we were left with was our faith. That was interesting to me because it was the opposite of what I might have feared. With religion there is a lot of miscommunication, misperceptions, so some people do struggle with their faith when bad things happen. Often that is because they haven't really looked at what the Bible says about life, eternity, and the reasons for it. We spend quite a lot of time talking with people who are going through something like a severe illness or a bereavement. We try and show them how we think it all falls together. I don't always know if that helps or not. I think it sort of does because we've been through it, sometimes people say, "Actually, that makes a lot of sense the way you're expressing that." It really is okay to doubt. I don't think that's wrong. It was just for us; we didn't. I know sometimes, people said to me things like, "It's okay to doubt. It's okay to shout. It's okay to get angry, and scream and say, 'Why?' " But I think, we never wanted to. It was really strange. We just felt really content that this somehow was meant to be.

I find it impossible to explain, and it sounds kind of crazy to those who might not understand our faith, but it wasn't that we weren't sad. Deeply sad, we were. There were times we felt we had been ripped in two so that it was hard even to breathe. Because we hadn't lost our faith and our marriage wasn't on the rocks and we were not abusing alcohol, I don't know whatever else you might do. Because we weren't doing any of those things, I think some people felt we didn't need any support or encouragement. Perhaps, if we'd been more, obviously falling apart or going off the rails, maybe people would have felt, "Oh actually, they need a bit of support." I don't know.

I've got an older sister, and I think she was affected by Ellen's death. This was her first niece. She doesn't often talk about it because I think she feels that if she talks about it, she might upset me when actually, in some ways, I'd prefer it if she did. She's very happy that I've got lots more children. I think she feels like, "You've got more children, so it's okay." Everybody was so relieved when I got pregnant for the second time. It was like, "Thank goodness she's having another baby. Everything's going to be okay." Of course, it helps. When the others were little, when I had three boys under the age of three, I couldn't spend a lot of time moping around because there was just so much activity. It helps in a way, it's a distraction, but it doesn't take away the fact that you've lost a child. I think some people don't understand that. Even if I had 10 children, there would be one missing, wouldn't there? But I also appreciate that there are things other people go through that I'm probably not the most perceptive about, and I probably say stupid things to them in that respect.

You don't get over it. It's actually more precious when someone talks about Ellen now after all this time because I think that nobody would, unless they really cared. Occasionally, I get an email from somebody that maybe I passed in one of these random places where we have lived, that will talk to me about her and how the story of her life had an impact on them. That's just lovely when it happens, because it makes me feel that sometimes she's living on through somebody else's lived experiences somehow, and that helps.

As for what I've learned, a few things really. Firstly, it took me a long time to work that out that grief and faith weren't opposite, that you could be deeply sorrowful but completely trusting in your faith or completely hopeful or completely accepting, that you can be both. The second is that grief is not linear. It's not that you have shock, anger, denial, guilt, acceptance. You have those, but you can have them all at once. You can go backwards several steps. That there isn't a right or wrong way to be. So, maybe there were times when my husband really didn't want to talk about it. He'd be like, "My baby died, talking about her is not going to bring her back." He was, in some ways, probably more devastated emotionally than I was. His response would be, "There's no point in talking." Sometimes, people would try and approach him and see how he was, and he'd be like, "I'm fine, thanks." Just like, "What's the point in talking about it? My baby died. How do you think I am?" That was hard.

Sometimes I wanted to talk it over again and again, even though I knew it couldn't change anything. Neither of us was wrong. Maybe if you're in a marriage, you can't always be the main support for the other person, and that's not failing. Sometimes you might need to grieve in slightly different ways. I wish I had known that before.

I wish I had known about things like triggers. The obvious ones you can cope with. So, like going back to the same hospital where Ellen was born for my booking in visit with the next child. That was horrible, and that was probably because the midwife was so awful. I think health services are often stretched, but she seemed to have no idea what it felt like to have all the hopes of expecting a new baby, but even more fears than before because of what had happened with Ellen.

It's the unexpected triggers that are harder. Where you're just randomly out and about somewhere and say you see a family that have a child the same age as Ellen might have been. Even at church, there was a family and their oldest daughter had the same name and she was 10. I just said, "When was your birthday?." She was like, "February." I realized that she was, within a few days, the same age as Ellen and shared her name. I'm like, "Oh gosh is that what she would have been like now?"

I suppose the first year or so after your child has died, most people know what's happened. They almost expect you to break into tears randomly from time to time. But 10 years later, when you're living in a completely different country, and so much time has gone by, if you have a random wobbly moment for no apparent reason, it can be difficult to know what to do, and whether to try and explain anything. Actually, it happens less and less as time goes by, but I wish maybe somebody had warned me about that.

Our experience has totally changed our life. But I don't think that has to be a bad thing. I think it becomes part of who you are, but you can channel your grief into positive ways. For us, it's been through adoption, we're involved in setting up an NGO to handle adoption out here and through our work and through working with other people in the same journey that can channel that grief into something positive. I think also if I'd known ahead of time, what would happen. I would have thought, "No way would I ever cope through that," and you do sometimes get enough strength when you need it. Sometimes it's from random places. There were some friendships that definitely got stronger. There were some people that perhaps I hadn't known so well before that really came alongside.

I think it's important to not to be disappointed with other people, because maybe there's good reasons why somebody feels they don't know what to do. The other thing is, nobody means to say anything stupid or hurtful, they really don't. For us, we were very thankful we had a sense of humour. Actually, I would 100 times rather someone said something stupid than said nothing. I think it's the saying nothing that's really hard. I wish somebody had just asked how our marriage was because although it's been fine, we've been married 20 years, but we have our ups and downs like everyone. I know the statistics about divorce rates. I used to tell everyone I see, "Did you know that basically one in two couples who have a child die will get divorced." I don't know if people felt it was too personal a question, but it would just be nice if somebody asked. I'd almost want to write a list entitled, 'if your best friend's baby has just died, here's what should you do.' Things like, do mention their name, do ask about them. If Ellen had a terrible accident, that I felt really guilty about, maybe I wouldn't want people to talk about it. So, maybe if it's your friends who have been bereaved, you should ask them what they want. Does it help you to talk about her or not? Because most people are pretty clear when saying they don't want to talk. If somebody said to me, "Does it help you to talk about her?" I would be like, "Yes, a million times yes." Someone else might say, "Actually, no, I find it too painful." Don't be afraid to ask. Also, you can change your mind. You could say no initially and then later find it would be really helpful and vice versa.

I remember when my son was a few months old, I met a friend in Scotland, and I think my son was just beyond the age that Ellen had been when she died. She picked him up and she just looked at me, she said, "This must be so hard for you." I cried, and she was concerned and said, "I didn't mean to upset you." My response was the opposite: "No, you're the first person that's actually acknowledged that it must be hard." I felt it was because people didn't care, but I would advise people that if your friend cries, it might be because you said the *right* thing rather than because you said anything wrong. You have to take into account how diverse we all are, there's so many complex factors. That's okay, and it's tangled and it's muddy and it's messy, and that's also okay. It's not a pass or fail. It's not like an exam. Oh, you grieved well, or you didn't grieve well. What does that mean? Never, ever say to somebody they're doing so well, when you haven't asked them how they're doing, because that's really insensitive and among the most hurtful things. When people come up to you and say, "You're doing so well," how do you know? You haven't seen me cry myself to sleep every night for the last month. How do you know I'm doing well? People don't mean it, they mean to encourage you, but sometimes it can come across as a bit much.

5 "Nobody foresaw that she would die so quickly"

Joanne's story remembering her daughter Rebecca

I'm the youngest of five children and am married to Tony. We live in the West Country. Rebecca is my eldest daughter; she was born in 1994. I liked the thought of having a girl first. Well, Rebecca, she's just a lovely little girl, really. Into lots of things but particularly always loved trains, from the word go.

She was an avid Thomas the Tank collector and loved trains and train tracks. My dad was an engineer. So, he and Rebecca used to love drawing together, drawing trains and working out, quite factually, how steam trains are put together and stuff like that. She just loved animals too. Her sister, Jill, came along when she was almost three. They just loved each other from the word go, were very close, always bathed together, slept together, that sort of thing.

We lived in the centre of a town and the nearest school when we went to look around, Rebecca didn't like, which surprised us. We started to look around at other schools and fell in love with a school on the other side of town. I don't drive, so we decided to move so that we could walk to school. It's quite difficult to get into that area, but we managed to find a house very close to her school. She just adored it, adored her teacher, even asked if she could sleep over there! I think she thought her teacher stayed overnight as well.

She always had lots of friends. She went in with a couple of her best friends and just loved it. She was very active, and she started learning karate too. The school that we chose is very creative and they did a play every year. Each year group did their own play, and of course reception always got the nativity story. She was a star and part of a little choir that sang. There was a tummy bug going around the school. Looking back, there's different times when I look at pictures and think she looked tired. A couple of days before Christmas, she went down with this tummy bug and wasn't well. On Christmas Day, we were at my parents and she was sick and blood came up. That was the first time she went to see a doctor.

She probably saw about six different doctors over a period of two weeks. But by January the 6th, she was dead. That was 21 years ago, and it still gets to me when I tell that story. She never seemed to get better from the tummy bug. She kept being sick. Each doctor would say, "Oh, give it a few more days. Give it a few more days." The Monday before she died on the Wednesday, I called the doctor out because she got to a stage where she wasn't really drinking, and I was just worried about her and she said, "Give it another couple of days. She'll probably get better," but she didn't come and see her. On the Tuesday, a friend of mine who's a nurse popped in. She's the mum of one of Rebecca's good friends and she'd heard she wasn't well. She just took one look and said, "You have to call a doctor out Joanne." Luckily that doctor, although he didn't know what was wrong with Rebecca, referred her to hospital. If he hadn't referred her, she would have died at home, I don't think I could have coped with that.

We arrived at hospital at about two o'clock. By four o'clock, she'd been diagnosed with leukaemia. They just seemed to know when we got into hospital that things weren't right. They did say afterwards that a general practitioner rarely sees a form of childhood leukaemia. Sadly, her form of leukaemia was an adult variety and very aggressive, and she died the next day. They think she'd only had leukaemia for possibly four or five days. The consultants were shocked; they hadn't seen such an aggressive form. Apparently, they had a couple of meetings afterwards where they looked at whether they could have picked it up earlier. Of course, they thought once they'd diagnosed it that they'd have time for treatment to start, but it was that aggressive. It was very sudden and really quite horrible. I think we just went into a bit of numbness at the time.

The doctors thought that leukaemia could be triggered at key ages when people go into a new bug environment, which is why leukaemia is often triggered at the ages of 4, 11, 18 and 40. Apparently, of course, you can get leukaemia at other times. But there seem to be key ages, and they think that was what happened; she'd started school with all the new bugs that she'd have been exposed to with all the other children. The tummy bug was the final straw, that her immune system just crashed at that point with too much coming at her. It might even have been a couple of bugs coming at her. I mean, what we learned with our other two was that there are certain forms of tummy bugs that they build an immunity to. The first time they get it quite badly, then the next time, less so. I think everybody was just very shocked. I don't know why it was such a rare form of leukaemia.

I've now got my theories, having spoken to other parents and stuff like that. It was very shocking for everyone because she'd started off in our local hospital. When they diagnosed it as leukaemia, we were introduced to the consultants there. They said, "You'll go to Bristol Children's Hospital for the first few weeks, they'll start treatment. Then, you'll come back and be under us. We just thought we'd introduce ourselves." We really thought it would be a normal course and you know, if you can have a normal course for a horrible treatment like that. Nobody foresaw that she would die so quickly.

After she died, we had a card from the ambulance that took us down because they'd seen her and talked to her. I think when a child dies, there can be ripples that go out and to suddenly find yourself talking to people that you never would have done or getting cards from people that wouldn't normally send cards. You suddenly enter this new world.

Rebecca was almost five when she died. She was four and three quarters, and a day. Age at that point, it's important to them isn't it? "I'm four and a half," or "I'm four and three quarters." Yes, she was four and three quarters. Jill was almost two.

I saw my mum not coping at all well. Her sister died when she was four and my mum was six, and she'd never been allowed to talk about it. My mum was born in 1926, and there's such a legacy of the two wars so you don't talk about things, but suddenly my mum was talking about her sister. My mum had been looking after Jill, and I realized she wasn't coping and had gone into a little bit of a shock. We had to go back to Bristol to start looking after Rebecca's body and sorting things out. So, I had to get some friends to look after Jill. Just seeing the pain of all the family, really was tough. We've never really done feelings as a family. I think my mum has always been a bit shut down partly because of her sister, partly because my dad was quite an angry person. My dad didn't quite know how to cope with it all. He asked the doctor for Valium or something to get through Rebecca's funeral, but the doctor wouldn't give it to him, which I thought was a bit sad.

My dad had been an alcoholic but had come through that and didn't use that as a prop when Rebecca died. Feelings are a bit tricky for him as well. Telling family at a distance, like my husband's family, was hard. Looking after Jill was hard. It's shocking how quickly news spreads. I think that's what shocked me. Rebecca died at two o'clock, but about four o'clock my childminder had a knock on the door from somebody she didn't know very well who said, "You look after Rebecca, don't you?" Then they told her, rather than me being able to tell her. I think that shocked me a bit as well. It's almost as if something is bigger than you and you're not in control of it. Of course, we felt so out of control anyway.

I think our town's not a big community, but realizing how quickly news goes around was quite shocking, especially because she'd been ill over Christmas and everybody is so busy. That's one reason why she didn't see a consistent doctor. Another impact was that the doctor we normally saw actually went off with depression. Apparently, he blamed himself that he hadn't seen Rebecca, hadn't been able to help her. We'd seen a variety of doctors; there was no consistency. The one doctor we saw two or three times, I didn't rate. She came around the day after Rebecca died, but it felt as if she was checking out to see if we were going to complain about her, rather than any sympathy or anything. You end up feeling that you're looking after a whole range of people rather than actually being able to go through your own process. That's how it felt for me. I was looking after a whole range of people and trying to do things right rather than necessarily expressing what I actually felt.

Somebody along our street popped in, and there's another mother whose son died when he was six from leukaemia. I had known her but not that closely. I got to know her better after Rebecca died. Only a couple of days after Rebecca died, somebody I knew called in and she said, "When so and so died, I crossed the street to avoid her." She said, "So, I'm not going to avoid you," but she came out with strange stuff as well. She believed in Steiner, and she said, "Well, you will meet Rebecca again, but it might be in your next life and she might be your mother." You just have these things said to you. I didn't want to get cross about it because I knew it was brave of her to come and see me when she'd avoided this other mum, but it's just bonkers. You look back and say, "Gosh, that was bonkers. I really didn't need that." I know it's their belief, but I didn't need that. You are just kind at the time and get on with it.

It felt there was quite a bit of that. I had a phone call from somebody whose baby had died. She said, "I had to call you because I know what you're going through." I really was quite angry because I didn't feel she knew what I was going through, and she felt she could just ring me up when I didn't know her. Again, I was just polite. She said, "Please do call me anytime," and I didn't call back. There was a lot to wade through, and it felt really intrusive and sometimes strange. We'd only just bought the house because we'd moved to be near the school, and the estate agent left a bottle of wine outside. I got that he didn't want to knock, but he wanted to acknowledge what has happened. But yes, that was strange.

We decided we didn't want Jill to be an only child, but it took me a while to conceive. In the greater scheme, it wasn't that long, but Rebecca was born on the fifth of April and our son Richard was born on the following year on the second of April. Sadly, it felt quite hard that he was being born at the same time as Rebecca's birthday. I got so many flowers from people I didn't necessarily know; that I found really hard because they thought it was a new beginning or they could be positive about a birth rather than supportive of a death. That's how it felt. It put me off flowers a bit. I love flowers but at the time, it was too much. It's a really strange time that you work through.

I think if we hadn't been in the hospital, Rebecca wouldn't have had support, and she probably would have died at home. That would have been unbearable to me if I had woken up and found her dead. We were transferred to Bristol Children's Hospital, and into the leukaemia ward. During the night, she fitted, they were keeping a close eye on her, and they woke me in the night because she wouldn't wake to take medicine. They moved her down to the intensive care ward where they always have two nurses to each child. They decided probably about midday that she wasn't going to survive, so they asked if we wanted anybody else there. We got various people there. We were with her when she died, which is great, we had to be really. Luckily, we could be because otherwise that would have been unbearable. She died on the Wednesday. On the Monday before, my husband had started a new job and had been away on the induction. On the second day, I called him back to join me when we moved Rebecca into hospital. His company luckily were very good because he'd only been there a day, really.

We were both there, thank goodness. My mum and dad were able to come in. The first person we saw as we came out was our vicar, because we'd been active in the church and he'd always been special to us. He was great, just very pragmatic and supported us for quite a while, in his own way. It was great that we saw him first, actually. It was very tricky, and I don't think we knew what to ask for, I don't think we knew what support we needed. My husband and I, we are relational, we didn't necessarily shut down.

The day after Rebecca died was the anniversary of my husband's dad's death. He'd had a heart attack over breakfast and died in my husband's arms on the seventh of January several years previously. Tony was still very raw from that. It was too much happening for him and he actually had a panic attack whilst he was driving me and Jill, and we ended up just arriving at our local hospital and they took him in because he thought he was having a heart attack.

I kind of went into doing mode and just sorting everything, the funeral, and working everything out. My husband couldn't cope; he didn't read any cards that arrived, or letters, so I took on acknowledging those, and then coping with everything, really. After about two and a half weeks, I did make him go back to work because I didn't think he'd go back otherwise. I felt a bit cruel doing that, but I don't think he'd have gone back. I was self-employed, and a colleague helped me get back to work probably about a month later because, again, she thought I wouldn't go back if I didn't and she'd said, "I need help with this piece of work, Joanne. Only you can do it," which wasn't true, but she got me back to work, and it helped, really. It's so hard to find meaning and purpose at a time like this. So that did help. I was doing a lot of training at that point. You kind of put on your identity and go in and it helped to have a little bit of normality.

I realized very quickly after Rebecca died that if I didn't take Jill back to groups, I wouldn't go. I did shock people because two or three days after Rebecca died, I was taking Jill back to nursery group and the church had a group that met once a week, and we went there too. A few friends helped me do that because it was hard facing everyone. The vicar at the time, a different vicar to the one who came to visit us in the hospital, but the vicar who'd run the church groups had obviously been going to do a session about Rebecca, and it really threw him that I was there. He didn't handle that very well and he took me to the side, and he said, "I would understand if you completely lost your faith through all of this." I didn't need to hear stuff like that at the time. I kind of wanted people to stand a little bit firmer for me and just say, "There's no answers, there's no reasons, take it day by day" sort of thing.

It is easier to look after others in lots of ways. I think there's so much avoidance, really, as well that people don't know quite what to say to you. If you don't know what to say for yourself, then it kind of goes unsaid. I feel I didn't really know what I needed for probably a couple of years, actually. Then I realized I really needed people just to step in and kind of lead me through it. My family, they don't do feelings, and they didn't even acknowledge the first anniversary. I had no phone calls, no cards from them on that day. It's not that I necessarily wanted cards, but I definitely wanted them to acknowledge it. The first year we had a few family occasions, and nobody really wanted to acknowledge that Rebecca wasn't there. I found that so hard. What I appreciated was my brother-in-law, for the first three weeks, did come up and visit and to take us out for walks; that helped. Then, of course, he needed to be at work. One or two friends did just be beside me, and that really helped. It's not that you want people to necessarily say anything in particular, in fact there's nothing to say but to not avoid you, just to stand by you that really helped me.

I didn't feel I was beginning to live again or be alive for about six years. I mean, I worked and had our children. We did lots of trips out, and we appeared as a normally functioning family, I think. I had a great outer face that I'm okay, getting on with stuff and I worked. I can remember beginning to feel a bit alive again about six years after Rebecca died. I don't know that you trust life again. Even now, if my husband's late driving back, I panic or I still think I'm going to lose another child; it's hard.

We've done loads. I think the lesson we learned from Rebecca was to live in the now. I think some of my family think that we've had too many holidays, but holidays have been really important to us and to experience things with the kids. Not necessarily big holidays, but like a week in Wales or camping or going up to Scotland. Holidays have always been important and to have experiences and memories, rather than necessarily having things.

In saying that, we have got a lovely house that we both worked hard for, we're both self-employed now, and my husband became self-employed five years ago. We've worked hard, but there's something about trying to be in the now, and I think his dad dying and Rebecca dying, you never know. People seem to go so suddenly. My dad died suddenly in the night, and so it's very much about trying to live.

I was very angry with my family for a number of years, and I feel it's probably only since I've done lots of my own personal therapy that I've begun to understand them or mellow with them more and not be angry, to see us all as a product of our upbringing and my parents' upbringing. I was so angry for quite a while, I felt so abandoned by my sisters in particular, really. One of my sisters is very intelligent, but she just doesn't get feelings, she still doesn't get stuff. That can be so hurtful when people don't realize. I did go through an angry phase and said things to them. They did start calling on her anniversary but then, it felt a bit mechanistic because they think they should. There are so many painful bits.

When I had Richard, I was still in the maternity hospital, and it was Rebecca's birthday and I was crying. I hadn't told people until the midwife and this woman said, "Now, come on. Pull yourself together, there's no need to cry." I think she just thought it's a normal birth. I thought it would be written all over my notes and that people would understand. I realized I needed to overtly tell people. That was a bit of a shock. I've realized since as well that it's been a bit of a journey for Jill too. When she was little and had her first tummy bug, she asked to go and see the doctor in Bristol because she thought she was going to die like Rebecca and needed to be checked out. When she was four, on her fourth birthday, she was in nursery and they sang happy birthday to her. The first thing she said was, "Rebecca's in heaven." It wasn't until I walked her home I said, "You know, love, why did you say that?" She goes, "Well, I'm going to die now, aren't I?"

I hadn't realized there's so much that's unsaid. I had actually worked really quite hard to be really open with both of them and talk about stuff and their relationship with Rebecca, but I hadn't realized that she thought she was going to die. When she was 11, she suddenly had this lump on her forehead. We took her to various consultants. The first consultant though she'd had it from birth and we just hadn't noticed. I went to check with my friend, who'd always cut our hair. She said, "Joanne, I would have seen that." We took her to another consultant who thought it was a dermal cyst and wanted to operate straight away and in front of Jill, talked about how she'd be shaved, they'd cut the head open, and so on. It was awful for Jill, really awful.

We had an MRI scan, which showed that it was an infected sinus in her forehead and luckily, the lump had pushed out her forehead rather than pushing out her eye or going into her brain. She was very lucky it had pushed out. We were referred on to a much more practical ear, nose, and throat bloke who was great, and it was resolved without operating although she had a soft forehead for a few years. That was a bit of a scary time. I don't think I've been over-vigilant because I don't feel people would understand. I realized, every time I went to the doctor, if it was a different doctor, they didn't understand unless I overtly told them. Then, I felt as if I'd be judged as an overprotective mum. There were two doctors that knew our history, so I tried to see them because then, I'd feel a bit more understood.

I feel so much guilt about Rebecca. I've always felt that I wanted to say sorry for not understanding or getting her support earlier. Whether she'd have survived, because she would have had horrendous treatments, but I guess I have always felt I just wanted her to know that she was so loved and that we tried our best. I guess I'd want to hear back that she felt that we did too. We did take her to see a number of doctors, but perhaps we should have pushed more. We saw a doctor on the Sunday who said, "There's no point referring you to hospital because it will be shut, and you'd have to wait until the Monday." I was saying if she'd gone on the Sunday and started the treatments on the Monday, would that have helped saved her? She was so young, really. Four and three quarters. The consultant said that if she'd survived, she could have been brain damaged. She'd definitely have been infertile. Her form of leukaemia gathered in big lumps. It gathered first of all, in her organs, and then she died when it gathered in her head, in big lumps. The thought of her not being herself, the Rebecca I knew because she was bright and kind. I don't know that I'd have cared for a disabled child very well. But who knows until you're put through it?

After Rebecca died, we had an undertaker pick her up. I think she was two days in Bristol. I wanted her back home. On the Thursday, I spoke to the undertaker who organized collecting her body. We met with the undertakers on the Friday and were able to go and visit her every day until the day before her funeral when they felt that her body, because she'd had so much medication, they thought her body was deteriorating. My dad visited her. He was the only person who wanted to, one sister and my brother-in-law saw her in Bristol Hospital. We didn't take Jill to see her because she was quite little. I wanted all of Rebecca's friends to be at the funeral, but I said it was up to the parents. They could make that decision if they wanted them to be there or not.

I felt I needed space at the funeral, Jill would have stayed with me, so I decided that she wouldn't go. I do feel children should be allowed to go and to be part of it and to understand. The funeral was at two o'clock on Wednesday, so a lot of my friends came without their children. We'd planned it a lot. We had big frames full of pictures of her. I had one or two people come up to us, one friend who's a bit blunt, he's a bit of a funny person. He goes, "I'm surprised this is a celebration, Joanne." I said to him, "What else could we do but celebrate?" Certain friends came and joined the service. I didn't really want to talk, but I welcomed everybody into the church, which shocked a lot of people. They didn't necessarily want to talk to me, but I knew quite a few people had travelled and I just wanted to thank them for coming. I think that did shock a few people. They didn't have to talk to me. I didn't make them. I did talk to quite a few people who came.

The vicar who came to see us in the hospital led the service, which is what I wanted. It wasn't his church, he'd recently moved and he'd got his own church in another area, but I wanted him to do the service, and the local vicar allowed it. He did a lovely eulogy and talk. We got through it. Our aim was just to get through it, to be honest.

A few days before the funeral, when we were sitting with Rebecca's body, this beautiful light came through the window. Because it was January, it was grey, but this beautiful sunshine came through and just rested on the three of us. Tony and I sat either side of the coffin. We felt that Rebecca went then and that the funeral was just looking after her body, really, taking it onto the crematorium, because we had her cremated. We got through it, and different people helped.

After the service some of my local friends did teas and coffees and cake in the church. We, just the family, went on to the crematorium. Then we went back to my mum's house. The day after the funeral was the worst. That's when I collapsed a little bit. I just kept going until then, I think.

I was crying because I lived near to Rebecca's school, and just watching them all go to school was so painful because she wasn't there, and life was just carrying on. That was a tough day, and Tony went and collected her ashes that day. It was hard. We kept her ashes with us for about six years. To begin with, I even took them on holiday when we were camping. She just stayed with us for a while. We did have a holiday abroad with my mum and dad a few months after. We just wanted some warmth, we just had to take lots of pictures of her with us. My dad died three years later; he had wanted his ashes to be scattered, but he said to Tony that, actually, he'd like to be buried with Rebecca.

We got approval for a family plot at a nearby church. It wasn't our church, but we can see it from our house. My dad was interred first, and then a couple of years afterwards, three years afterwards, I was ready to put Rebecca in. The vicar who did the service came across and did that for us. It was just Tony, and I, and the vicar, and the undertaker. My mum died in 2017, so she's in the plot as well. There's room for Tony and me, and for Jill and Richard, if they want that.

After Rebecca died, I do feel that the world stopped, it was just a day at a time that got me through. Jill really helped in terms of I had to keep going for her. Our way of coping for a few months was to get a huge pile of books and to sit and read them all, and she'd get me tissues. It became a joke that she'd always get me tissues like on anniversaries. Even now at leaving assemblies, she'll always have a pack of tissues for me. She'll be 24 soon, and I know she'll probably carry that on for quite a while. I think Jill really helped me. She was very distressed for a couple of days, and she slept in with us the first few nights.

One night I woke up and Jill was sitting up in bed talking to Rebecca, and she kissed the air. After that, she was fine. She was really calm. It was very, very strange. Rebecca's best friend had a dream about her. Her mum rang me and said, "Charlie came down and told me all this. Actually, Charlie said Rebecca's fine." Charlie was okay after that. It's very strange. A few people had dreams about Rebecca. I sadly didn't. It was just very strange seeing Jill, and she was just talking and kissed the air and then became very calm after that. She just said it was Rebecca. I think there's so much that, whether you have faith or not, there's so many strange things around that time that we couldn't explain, but it was reassuring. Even now, at strange times, we hear train whistles and it just feels like it's a soothing sign. When we put Rebecca's ashes in, it was mid-afternoon, and a train whistle blew. People might say, well, it's bound to because whatever time train was going through, but it just helps you get through stuff.

I guess what's helped me get through the years was the sense that she's close. Even though I haven't necessarily had a dream, I've had people from a local spiritualist church come and give me messages, which I found a bit strange, and part of me is thinking, "Why don't I get a message from her?" It does feel as if there's a spiritual world that is close and she's looked after. We find white feathers at funny times, and that soothes us. It's like an angel's near or something. They just turn up in really funny places. The day after Rebecca died, I was sat, cuddling Jill, and I had a feather on my shoulder. I kept brushing it off, and every time I looked, it was back on me. It was when I said to a friend about it and she said, "Well, you know some people believe that white feathers are angels."

A couple of times I rang Compassionate Friends locally to get some help, I left messages on the answer phone, but nobody called me back. Because I didn't hear, I just folded in a bit. It was a number of years later before I had counselling about Rebecca. At the time I think there was a general lack of support. We had a local charity that supported bereaved children. I rang up to get support for Jill. They said, "No, no, she's too young. We'll be able to help her when she's about six or seven." Two days later, they were in Rebecca's school, helping the school. I just felt so alone. I couldn't get support. I couldn't find support for Jill. That charity, a few years later, actually apologized because a friend of mine got angry with one of their workers and said, "Do you realize this is how you treated my friend?" At the time, they didn't have an understanding of early bereavement. Richard was actually part of their pilot for preschool years' bereavement support. It kind of worked through in the end, but I did feel very isolated for quite a time.

Tony and I had support from the social worker from Bristol Hospital, who came out a few times, and she really helped. The first thing she said to us is, "Do realize that you two will grieve differently. Don't judge each other if one cries and the other doesn't." That so helped, because, again, I had somebody, within the first few days of Rebecca dying, say, "Oh you do realize 70% of couples split up when their child dies?" It was like, "Oh, thank you, so I have to deal with that too?"

I think there's a lot more awareness now and a lot more support. I still don't think we talk enough about bereavement, and I don't think there's enough support out there. We do understand how to support children's bereavement more, though.

I think I moved into counselling because of Rebecca. Not in the obvious way, but when Richard was about two, I noticed some local parenting courses and signed up. They were really good, and I got Tony to go as well, and it really helped us as parents. They were looking for trainers, just on a sessional basis. They had a course called "Helping Children through Change and Loss." I thought, "Well, perhaps that will give me some meaning if I run that for parents," because it's so hard to find any meaning out of my loss.

I've done some running to raise money for different charities. I started doing training for this parenting charity and then just got to do a bit more, and then the funding changed. We started working with more and more vulnerable families and I thought, "I need to get more skills here." I did the counselling diploma and then, of course, the diploma took me in a different direction as it does. I never meant to be a counsellor but kind of ended up doing that. Sometimes, I think, it does give meaning and purpose; it's a hugely meaningful job. There are times, with certain clients, I feel as if I was meant to work with them.

We used to be very active with our church, but we haven't been for probably about eight years now. We have a faith. We still believe in God, but for both of us our faith shifted in different ways. I think we definitely get restored by nature, and it is actually important for us to be in nature and with nature. I don't know that the organized church appeals to us at the moment. I wouldn't say that losing Rebecca changed our faith. I think it reinforced it in different ways that didn't necessarily mean that we found support from the church.

Winston's Wish is an amazing charity. When she was about six, Jill went through the camp for kids and we did the parents' camp. That was a turning point actually for Tony, because they allocated a male support worker to us. That was huge for Tony because he'd only met women, like the social worker from the hospital. To have a male alongside really helped him, and this bloke was just brilliant and would challenge me and help me to see the stages of grief that Jill went through and different things. When she was about seven or eight, she'd suddenly start coming home, sick from school. Actually, she was just checking that I was okay, and she needed that reassurance. I started giving her things to hold or to keep that she'd give back at the end of the day and reassuring her I was okay. Then she was fine. She kind of moved on again.

I realized to a greater degree how people can grieve differently. I cry, but Tony's very private. I know men who cry and women who don't. Any expression of grief is okay even if it's hard to talk. I felt a bit hijacked by my anger, a bit out of control for a while. My family pattern is not asking for help, so that's the main reason that I didn't ask for help. If I'd pushed, I'd like to have found the wisdom that what you're experiencing is normal or it's okay to express it this way. A lot of people tried to shut down my tears, a lot of my friends couldn't cope with me crying, and so I learned to hide it. That silent scream inside, that just sat there and got released when I was on my own. I think the support I needed was to have somebody just to walk with me.

My doctor offered me counselling, but I wasn't ready for counselling given my background and that we didn't talk as a family. But to have somebody just visit perhaps and say, "No, that's normal, that's okay," or "Come, let's go out for a walk now," that would've helped because, to me, the talking came later. I think that's why I call it kind of wisdom. It's kind of just gentle things that can help because they're such tough times. No wonder couples split up, because it's unbearable. The pain and the missing. It's unbearable for grandparents as well. I couldn't get close to my parents about it. We kind of all had to be separate. It was just the way my family was.

I think the grief will always be there, and Rebecca will always be in my heart. I think the one thing that, again, really hit me at the time was a couple of elderly women in my church came up and said, "You'll never get over this, but you will learn to live with it," and they'd lost children. Again, that really helped, just to know that I will always miss her, and I'll always be upset; 21 years on, I'm still crying. But actually, it stops very quickly, I will always miss her and the what ifs and those big occasions like her 18th birthday, 21st. That did help, some of those gentler supportive messages, really.

In the early days on the anniversary of Rebecca's death, we would always release helium balloons with messages tied on, but there came a time when the kids didn't want to join in. We only did helium balloons for a few years. Tony and I always go for a long walk on the day of her death. Just head out. It always helps us. We always take up flowers around the time of her death and put them on the grave.

For a number of years, on her birthday, we used to do days out with the kids. It's close to Richard's birthday, but we would always mark it. Tony travels quite a bit with his work, and he was asked recently to be travelling on Rebecca's birthday. He said, "No," because he just can't bear the thought of that. Only once have I done a bit of work on the anniversary of Rebecca's death, and it just felt completely wrong. It's so close after Christmas that it is just easy to feel the pressure getting back to work.

Walking has always really helped us, nature has. We've had a dog for 12 years, and the dog has really helped all of us. I light candles all through Christmas, which helps. We still love Christmas. Some people said to us, "You must hate Christmas." But Rebecca loved Christmas and it is a family time. Because of Christmas, she did see everybody, all my family and Tony's family, even though she wasn't well.

The mum of one of Rebecca's friends asked where the ashes had been buried because she wanted somewhere to take her daughter because she thought she needed somewhere to go. I did feel bad that we didn't have a grave for a number of years. There is something about having somewhere to go, and to mark, and to just remember somebody. I couldn't bear the thought of scattering her ashes. I've heard some people have some really bad experiences where the wind blows them in everyone's faces, and it can be quite traumatic. It did feel right to put her in a grave and to mark it, but everyone's different in that.

When he was about four or five, Richard wanted to be an undertaker. He's always been a bit fascinated with dead bodies and mummies and Egypt, but he said that he wanted to be an undertaker to make funerals happier. I kind of got where he was coming from. He's now grown up and gone in a different direction!

I did discover a joy in bottle banks, smashing bottles and not having to clear it up. I still love to do that. All the recycling is collected in the house. We have a bottle bank near to where we live, and I love taking bottles and smashing them. Just that release is great.

Much later, my elder sister died. I think the difference with losing my sister is there's so much I wish I could talk to her about. It's the sadness of not being able to talk to her especially with mum dying. My sister was very much the head of the family, really, and its hard that she is not here now.

My parents were a bit tricky, so we'd had different relationships with mum and dad. My sister had already left home when I was about 18 months old, but I just regret not being able to talk to her about things and not spending enough time with her. We always lived across different sides of the country, but I felt so sad seeing her adult children go through the loss because she was only 66. I'm nine years older than her oldest son. I think I have a lot more awareness of watching the process, possibly because of my counsellor training. I just felt there was so much I was watching; my sister decided every single aspect of her funeral, and I did find that a bit strange. There were bits I didn't get. I feel in some ways, it's so important for the people left to also have input to put into the funeral because it's about them missing that person and celebrating. I kind of wish that my sister had done half of it but allowed her family to do other bits as well.

I can't remember who wrote the eulogy for my sister, but I think she wanted to be involved. She had a very strong faith, my sister, so there were six vicars at her funeral and a few people involved. During the service, a butterfly came into the church and was just hovering above her husband and sons and their families and it was just beautiful to see that. I've seen a few butterflies at funerals. My neighbour's daughter died, she was 20 and again there was a beautiful butterfly all through her funeral.

There are some things we can't always understand. I think I'd have felt very differently about my sister's death if it was my first or second family bereavement. I think I felt a lot more aware of and prepared for the funeral. I think if I hadn't lost Rebecca, I'd have been in a very different place, a bit more shocked by it or saddened.

6 "Goodbye, have a good evening, take care"

Julia's story remembering her daughter Pippa

Pippa was our second child, the second of four children. She was born in a local cottage hospital. It was very quick with no medication or intervention. Her birth was incredibly easy. I think I stayed in the hospital for maybe a day or so afterwards.

We were not living in our own home when she was born because we were having some major work done on our house, so we'd moved out and were staying in our friend's house. Although that probably didn't affect Pippa so much, it did affect her older sister, who was 15 months older and, understandably, found the move from home and adjusting to a new sibling upsetting. I really enjoyed the night feeds because I could pay attention to Pippa. I was very aware of my older daughter needing to be reassured and told that she's still loved as much.

Pippa was an incredibly easy baby. As she grew up, she was just so quick. She was so bright and so attuned to me, I think. When we'd go shopping, she'd be about four at the time, she'd be the one who I could ask to go and get the cornflakes.

Pippa was just there. She was everywhere. She was brilliant. She loved animals. She had lots of rabbits. She had a pony. She helped with all the animals we had. If we found an injured pigeon on the road, she'd have to stop and pick it up and take it home and look after it, until it could fly or die. She was very healthy, never went into hospital. She didn't have any accidents apart from falling off a pony. It was a really idyllic childhood. We had a smallholding. My husband, her dad, worked from home so was around to help with the kids and animals. The children went to a free school[1] which we were involved with. Looking back, it felt absolutely idyllic. They were all at the free school which was wonderful. It was small and intimate, and we were very involved.

I think it was probably about one year before she went to comprehensive school that the free school folded, and they went to a primary school in a village near us. Pippa had very short hair and was quite a tomboy. I remember when she first went, she was upset because somebody had thought that she was a boy; that seemed to upset her quite a lot. However, she did very well, she was very bright. She wrote the most amazing poems.

Then puberty kicked in, and she suddenly started to worry about peer groups, peer acceptance. She thought her legs were too long; indeed, there was just so much about her that was wrong, or so she thought, it became very difficult to communicate with her. She always read avidly and would read three books a week from the library, I think that was a bit of escapism for her.

She suddenly got to a period in her life where she wasn't happy in her own skin. I think that was a puberty, hormonal, adolescent thing and also that shift between being part of the family, belonging in a family, then suddenly you're moving out into a peer group, and she didn't have the confidence. I don't know why, because she was so good at everything. She played the clarinet beautifully, she swam, she was into running, she was a brilliant runner.

I do remember when she'd done some long-distance running, immediately the PE person said she wanted her to join the running club and do training. She was very good, even doing some County competitions. But she was absolutely terrified. I think when any pressure was put on her, she couldn't deal with it, she would go, "Oh, no, back off."

I remember going to a running competition with her and all the other runners were wearing Lycra. She had baggy shorts and a baggy T-shirt. She looked quite different to everybody else. She was as white as a sheet and felt so sick. She couldn't do it at all. It was a confidence thing. I don't know when that started really, or how that started, because I don't know whether that was something to do with peer group not accepting her, or not feeling accepted, or maybe somebody said something that I don't know about. I don't know whether being at a very small school and then having to go to a big school was difficult to adjust; I know my eldest daughter found that very difficult. That was massive for her, but Pippa did have a couple of years at a primary school. She had two very good friends there. I think it was in adapting to there being more people to be friends with.

Pippa's relationship with her older sister completely changed as they grew up. They got close, although they were very different. Pippa was really into ponies and sport, whereas her sister was much more musical. They didn't have the same friends and they didn't socialize together with their friends, but there was no problem between them.

A couple of times when she did a French exchange through school, Pippa was absolutely miserable. I've got little notes that say how miserable and awful it was to be there. She didn't like going away; she just wanted to get home. She was so unhappy. I can't quite understand why she had this lack of confidence or low self-esteem. When I had a sense of that being there it was a really difficult time, she would have been probably 11 or 12 starting from there, really, I felt frightened. I felt she wasn't attached enough. I think she was moving away from us. But, we had a lot in common. We had a lot of unspoken understandings. She was more like me I think than the other children were.

I'd just read *Women Who Run with the Wolves*, and I was talking to her about it and the wild woman thing. We'd sit and talk about these things. I think, in a way, some of her understandings were beyond her maturity, her emotional maturity. Other people have said that she was an old soul and there was some spiritual understanding that was ahead of her emotional maturity to process and manage herself in the world. She would go off riding on the moor on her own; she loved that. There was a very free spirit in her; she read a lot of Margaret Atwood, *The Robber Bride* and *Cat's Eyes*, they are quite edgy. But I think she hadn't quite caught up with herself; something else in her was more developed than the rest of her.

Pippa found it very difficult to talk to people about things. She was always there to talk to other people, to stand up for people if they had been teased or bullied. I remember dropping her off to meet a friend who was upset and wanted to talk to Pippa, but her friends said she would never talk to anybody if she was upset. I remember one of them saying there was one night when Pippa just disappeared. She'd gone off on her own. They knew when something was a problem because she'd go off on her own. She wouldn't tell even her friends, about any problem she had, she kept it all to herself.

She certainly didn't tell us anything. I can remember asking friends of the family, friends of hers, good friends of ours who used to come and stay and visit; trying to get them to talk to her. I could tell there was something wrong. She was moody, but so many teenagers are, aren't they? It's the essence of angst. Sometimes I'd say something and she'd shout, "It's my life," and storm off.

She left a note. She didn't leave it for me and her dad, she left it for her two friends that she had been with that night. She said in her note, "I'm beyond help. I can't help myself," which is like saying "If I can't help myself, nobody else can help me," which is so wrong, isn't it? It's such a fundamental flaw in understanding, in knowing what can help.

I remember when she was younger, she had two rabbits that she kept in one of the animal pens. She was trying to put up wire because the pigeons kept getting in to eat the food. She was really struggling with this wire netting and pliers. She'd got scratches all up her arms. I tried to help, and she wouldn't let me. She said, "I'll do it myself. I can do it myself. Don't need any help." I think because she'd found things easier when she was younger, she found it more difficult when she couldn't do something later and she believed there was something wrong with her. Because we were a busy family, I don't know if she was overlooked in some way. We had always been very close because of the horses; we used to do a lot with them. But then I just felt separate, kept away, and helpless. I was observing and not able to be effective in the struggle she appeared to be going through. I wasn't able to fix it, I suppose, or not even fix it but to share it even.

Pippa was always very aware of the injustices in the world. She paid into the World Wildlife Fund and sent money to other organizations that addressed inequalities. She was very sensitive about things not being right. Sometimes we used to talk about these things. After she died, I blamed myself for not making life look wonderful enough. Because I think the year before she died, in the family we had quite a difficult year.

Pippa's brother had a tumour in the head of his femur, so we had to go to Birmingham orthopaedic hospital. He was very ill that year. Also their dad had a bit of a breakdown, really, I don't know whether it was at the beginning of his illness, he had this terrible headache. His mum, who was also a very big support to us and lived just down the road, needed to have a big operation because she'd broken her hip, so she was in hospital too.

I had to take our son to Birmingham because my husband was too ill. He couldn't get out of bed. He was completely sick, shut down from us all and it was a really, really tough year. That probably didn't feel like life was great, because all of this horrible stuff was going on. Also, Pippa and her older sister were doing their mock exams.

I knew it was coming up for a difficult time when they had their exams, and I was up in Birmingham, and they were at home. Pippa was very close to her brother. When he came back from the hospital (he had to have the operation done twice because it didn't work the first time), she said, "He's changed, he's not the same anymore." He was on crutches for three months and needed more of our time. Also, probably he got a bit more attention, people did nice things for him, so maybe she was a bit jealous. One thing Pippa did say to me which was very, very telling, I think, was that there was nothing special about her. Her older sister was special because she was the oldest. Her brother was the only boy, so he was special. Pippa's younger sister was special because she was the little one. There was nothing special about Pippa because she was in the middle, which is often something middle children talk about, isn't it?

There was stuff brewing, because I can remember she had written an essay about a child self-harming and being very distressed. I think, now, I should have talked to her more about that. It was an expression of something which I could have got a hold of, though I doubt whether she would have talked to me about it. To be honest, I think you don't want to even go down that road, do you? Your child might be in that kind of suicidal state, perhaps I just didn't want to go there. I would now. I certainly would now.

I remember at the end of that year thinking, "New Year's Day, it's another year, it can't be as bad as this last one." It was a hard and difficult year; we didn't have much money then because my husband wasn't working. Life didn't look great. It didn't look like we were all having a great time. We weren't; we were really struggling.

Just before Pippa died, I was doing my first psychotherapy training. We'd got on to Donald Winnicott and the idea of being 'a good enough mother.'[2] This was one thing I struggled with enormously after she died, as it meant that I was not a good enough mother. Winnicott talks about adolescence and helping our children to become autonomous. Well, that's the ultimate of being autonomous, isn't it? Killing yourself. You've reared this autonomous being who can go ahead and do something like that.

But at her age, I don't believe that that was the right decision, her right decision. I think she was mistaken in getting to that place without having tried getting help. She could at least have given it a go.

Pippa died round about midnight between the 8th and 9th of March. She was just in her first year of A levels. There was another French exchange coming up which she was absolutely dreading because she would have to work in a school. I think that was really, really scary for her. We didn't really know that she was that worried about it. She'd just done a work placement at the Monkey Sanctuary and absolutely loved that. She was in her element there. If she could have stayed there, she'd be here today. She loved the people there, the whole non-judgemental atmosphere, the monkeys, and the people; she just loved it. I noticed a difference in her, so I guess there must have been something before that was not quite right that she was struggling with. She went there and when she came back, she was just serene. I remember saying, "That sounds so marvellous. We ought to be able to bottle that feeling. Keep it, so you can go back to it at any time." So that was just wonderful, really good. She had a really good experience there.

That was only a few weeks before she died. Then, the day she died; she had her friends Zoe and Isabel round. I remember they were watching something like *Mamma Mia* and dancing and just messing about. Then they'd arranged to go into the nearby town to a party that one of the boys from school was having. I dropped them off, I said "Goodbye, have a good evening, take care," something that I'd usually do. At the party, Pippa had a small amount of vodka and she'd been sliding down a bannister and she'd fallen off at the end and broken a pane of glass in a glass door in the house. The boy's parents were away and didn't know he was having a party; he was apparently furious and told her to go. When I heard that from someone who was at the party, I can remember thinking, "Oh, God, I can just imagine what that must have felt like to her," with this whole thing about being part of a peer group and being accepted. So, she left the party, the two friends that she was with had planned to come back to our house to sleep in the barn which was separate to the house.

Zoe was quite drunk, apparently, but Isabel wasn't. Pippa was saying, "I'm going home. I want to go home." Isabel wanted to go with her, but Pippa apparently said, "No, you stay, look after Zoe," because she'd had too much to drink. If Isabel had gone back with her, things might have been different.

I think the incident at the party would have been just the last straw. Amongst this group of people she so needed to feel accepted in order to validate herself. Somehow, that transition between being part of home and part of out there, that peer group was a process she struggled with. I think she felt really secure at home because the notes she wrote, when she was in France, said "Can't wait to get home, feel very homesick." It may not have been us. It may have been the animals that rooted her. I think she hadn't really found a place 'out there.' She didn't make that transition successfully. If she'd stayed longer, I'm sure she would have done, but she didn't.

She was still trying to be part of that group, with boyfriends. She didn't have a boyfriend. There were boys who wanted to go out with her, and one she fancied, but she couldn't really get into that relationship because, I suppose, she didn't feel good enough, herself.

Pippa got a taxi back, she must have been in the barn a couple of hours or so before she hung herself. We were just feet away across the yard. We were woken up in the night because her two friends had come back from the party and found her. They came tearing into the house. I can remember hearing bang, bang, bang, up the stairs, and burst into our room, "I think Pippa's hung herself." It was like "Oh," just bang, like that, in the middle of the night, they were in a state of complete terror.

We ran over, and there she was. I don't want to go into that bit, but it was just bizarre, crazy, really real craziness because we also had Pippa's brother and younger sister at home. I had to go and phone the police and ambulance. My husband stayed with her. I also had to go and get a knife so he could cut her down. It's like I didn't know where the knives were, I didn't know which knife. I thought "I can't do this." Don't know where the two girls were, they were probably just hugging each other somewhere in a corner. Then I was trying to tell people on the phone where we lived, and I couldn't tell them where we were, I didn't know my address, I just couldn't get any words out.

The police came as well. I can't go into the actual moments of that, it was just awful because none of it made any sense. I can just remember howling; I was with her for quite a time before the paramedics came. It was like you can't imagine. I couldn't see if she was dead or alive or what was going on. Then when the paramedics came, they tried to resuscitate her. I went out at that point because our children had woken up with all the noise. Then I think I made tea for everybody, I thought they had to have a cup of tea. Somebody kicked over the tea on the carpet. I can remember getting a cloth and spending a long time cleaning the carpet.

The police were there, then the paramedics, and then the GP had to come, a GP who we knew, to certify the death. They took her in the ambulance. My immediate thought was that I must go with her in the ambulance because whenever the children have had an accident or something, you go in the ambulance with them, don't you? I had to go in the ambulance with her. Someone said, "No, no, you don't go in the ambulance with her." It was so crazy.

Then I rang up a friend who runs a sort of spiritual, hospital place and offers counselling. We'd had quite a lot of contact with him before. He came over. He was brilliant. This was all about two o'clock in the morning. Then the two girls had to phone up their mum and dad to come over and pick them up. We were looking after our children. I didn't really talk to the policeman. One of the things that my husband said was how awful it was talking to the police. He had to write out a label to put on her foot, hang onto her foot or he had to approve it, or something, which he found absolutely horrendous.

He'd had a harder time, if there is a harder or easier time, than I think I did. Our friend took over, really; he took charge, and he was great. He said, "You must go back to bed now." It was three o'clock, or something like that. He went back to his place and kept a vigil for the rest of that night. We all slept in the same room. He came back about seven o'clock in the morning. He went up, and we cleansed the room where Pippa had died. We all went up there. Then we had to go down and tell my husband's mum that she had died. His sister had died at a young age too, so my mother-in-law had lost her daughter and now her granddaughter, so it was really, really hard for her.

We had to let our eldest daughter know, who was up at Uni. She had to be told. We had to arrange how to get her home. I rang up and asked to speak to her best friend first, which was a hard thing for her to have to manage. Then told her what had happened, so that she could be there for her when we told our daughter. Then we arranged for my husband's brother to go and pick her up and bring her home. It was so hard to make decisions about how to manage everything.

There were things that had to be sorted out. Our friend went and told our neighbours down the road who had children the same age; they're great friends. We had to then phone some people up. A wonderful, wonderful friend, as soon as she found out, just got in the car and came straight down with a big, enormous shepherd's pie and stayed for about a week, and did everything. She took all the phone calls. She did everything, put the washing out, cooked, she looked after us. She was wonderful.

We had a lot of people coming to the house and bringing food. It was really weird, actually. We had a big kitchen then and a big table, and there were always lots of people around the table. There were lots of people in the house always. Then my brother and sister came and stayed. During that week, ten days, or however long it was, we had a lot of people in the house which was really important for me. I know not everybody would want that. It was like we were being held in this big bowl. It was extraordinary. I don't know how we fed everybody, but we had massive meals. I don't know how that happened.

I was completely out of it, really, just like some headless chicken mainly. Another friend, who is a counsellor, used to come over every morning about 8:30 or 9 a.m., and we'd sit in the kitchen. I don't know how long after this was. I'd be standing up against the Rayburn because I was always so cold, and we'd talk. We'd just talk. It wasn't exactly counselling. She'd just come, and then we'd talk. I knew she'd come. Our youngest child would sit in the chair next to me, she was about 11 then. She just used to listen. She would never say anything, but she needed to listen to us talking. Also the local vicar, we don't go to church, but he was a good guy, he used to ring up every morning at 9:15, "How are you? Are you okay? Still here? I'm here," and that was all it was, just a little check-in thing, which was really important, those little things.

It was like our community, both in terms of geography, but also our family, all pulled together to support us in that awful time. I don't know what would have happened if I hadn't had that. We had a lot of people come and stay, came down from all over the place. Pippa's friends used to come too, which was lovely. The pain felt shared; we didn't have to do it all on our own.

I remember when my brother and sister left, went back to their home, which must have been two or three weeks after Pippa died, suddenly, it was terrifying because we were on our own. There were still people around, local people who would still pop in; that certainly helped.

Since Pippa died, it's 21 years ago now, the shock and pain is still in me. I think of events as either happening before Pippa died, or after Pippa died. But over those years, I can see a progression. To begin with, I was doing a lot with Papyrus[3] and with Healthy Schools. It was before any sense of emotional well-being came into peoples' minds, and any of the young people services had happened. You went straight from child to adult mental health services; there was nothing to cover that adolescent period. I really felt so strongly that that was a period of so much change going on and when young people are so vulnerable. For Papyrus I'd put on talks and create display boards with a lot of information I got from numerous mental health charities. It was a full-time thing, really, and I was totally invested in it, travelling around a bit, especially in Cornwall. We went and talked to the people who were setting up Healthy Schools and someone else who was setting up a counselling service for young people. I was quite involved with all of that. I was also doing an art therapy training and I applied to do a post-graduate course, but that all fell through for various reasons, mainly because I didn't feel I wanted to go away from home. I didn't think it was safe to go away. I needed to be there to make sure everyone stayed alive.

I believe though that I very much absconded from being a mother. I can remember thinking, "I can't, I can't. It's too painful. I can't be a mother." I could be a parent, but I couldn't be a mother. I think that certainly did affect my youngest daughter. I've talked to her quite a bit since then about things. We talk a lot about what things were like then. I just felt, "I can't do that. I can't do it because I'm rubbish at it, it's too painful. I can't bear that. I can't bear to have that much pain, so I'm not going to be a mother anymore."

I think I shut down something. There was a book written a few years later, I think, and I was given a copy for a Christmas present called *The Lovely Bones*.[4] It was about a family in the USA where the daughter was murdered, and the mother had to leave the family and go away; she just couldn't bear it. I felt very much like that, "I'd like to just go, not be there."

I did think about killing myself, I went up to the moor and thought, "I just can't do this. I can't bear this. I can't make everything right. I can't make it right. I'd better die," and I heard Pippa's voice saying, "It's okay mum. It's okay mum." Like that, very strongly. It was reassuring and comforting, "It's okay mum, you'll be all right."

There were other times too. I remember when I was cleaning out the freezer, and I found this pot of blackcurrant sorbet that I'd made with Pippa, and I'd never made sorbet before, or ice cream, or anything like that, so it must have been quite special, and I can remember Pippa wanted to have it, and I said, "No, no. You've got to keep it for something special. You can't eat it." When I cleaned out the freezer, many months later, I found this box of sorbet and I had voices then in my head saying, "You're just so mean, so tight, so –" like blaming me for being mean, horrible, tight about not having the sorbet. "You're a miserable person, no wonder Pippa died." I would often beat up on myself.

Soon after Pippa died, I remember being visited by the GP at home about there being a post-mortem. I went into state of panic. I refused. I wanted to refuse for there to be a post-mortem. I hated the idea of her being cut up. I can remember being really upset about the idea. I thought, "What's the need? She was there. She's left a note. It's absolutely cut and dried. You don't need a post-mortem," but apparently there had to be. I can remember a friend happened to phone up at that time to see how I was. I was in floods of tears and going on about the GP saying we've got to have a post-mortem. Why do we have post-mortem? I remember her just saying, "I think you just have to agree with that. I think you just have to go along with that. I think you just do." I think I needed to be told what to do, my friend seemed to take control for a moment.

None of the family went to the inquest. I didn't want to. I didn't want to understand that this happened and that happened and then this happened. I didn't need to know that. I needed to know *why* something had happened, not *how* it had happened.

I heard of the verdict from the newspaper. We had quite a lot of newspaper reporting. That was just awful. I remember when the local paper had it on the headline on the front page. Big headline: "Pippa's Death Stuns College." One of the campaigns I have been involved in with Papyrus is to limit the reporting of suicide.

The rest of the family were suffering too. Our youngest daughter became very rebellious at school; she got into a lot of trouble. At one point, she was sent to the time-out room because of something that she'd done. She'd punched somebody. I was furious that they'd do that to her when she was suffering and grieving. It was pointed out that what she needed was to be treated like normal, and I can see that now. But it felt dreadful for me at the time, and I was furious. She was wanting to go out and do things in town, and I was terrified of her doing that. I was just overprotective, not in a nice way but in sort of a policeman-type way. She was pushing me away the whole time. Thank goodness she was, because she needed to be telling me not to interfere.

We got some counselling for her from a school counsellor. She didn't have that many sessions with her, and it didn't really help. I think it was too soon or she wasn't ready for it, but I just felt desperate because she wouldn't let me anywhere near her, and I needed to be sure she was going to be safe.

Our son would just go off up to the coast and camp up there on the beach with his friends surfing. He didn't seem to have any big reaction, except that he didn't want to be at home, basically. Well, that's a reaction. It was more fun surfing with his mates and sleeping up there. That was quite frightening because I didn't know where he was, whether he was safe or not. I had a friend whose husband was a special constable, I remember asking if could he just keep an eye on these people sleeping on the dunes, so that someone was looking out for them. He has since talked about his fear of having a child because they can die or take their own life. I'm relieved now that we can share these fears.

Our eldest daughter went back to university. She changed courses after a year or so; she had a major collapse. She got very thin, then she went to Australia and travelled around for a bit. Maybe that was her way of avoiding the pain; it was hard not to know if she was safe.

I think a thread has been, which I'm beginning to be able to let go of, the need to understand. I think that if I hadn't been involved in some sort of psychotherapy or counselling training, I don't know if I would have felt the same, I don't know.

I think I was always on a bit of a quest to find an answer as to why Pippa had ended her life. I've done quite a lot of different suicide awareness training sessions with different people, working with suicidal clients, and ultimately, we don't know, do we? The only person who knows, really, is the person who's died.

After quite a long time I got to a point when I was thinking, "I can leave this now. I'm not going to know. It's an unknown." Then, of course, it all comes up again. I start off again. At one point I thought I was probably depressed because I was not feeling motivated, I felt very un-energetic and flattened and thinking, "Well, perhaps I'm depressed." At other times I would feel fine, I'd feel quite happy. I would think, "Right now I'm quite happy," but on a broader spectrum it's all sort of flat. Then I thought, "Well perhaps I'm not depressed, perhaps I'm just peaceful and settled and as long as I get pleasure and enjoyment in the present moment, it really doesn't matter about what else is out there. I don't have to feel particularly driven by anything, so I then thought, "Maybe I'm not depressed, maybe I'm just settled," so that's quite useful.

If I could have a conversation with Pippa, I might be quite cross with her, but I don't want to be cross with her. I think I would want to ask her why she couldn't ask for help, why didn't she ask for help? Why did she think she had to do everything on her own? I'd also want her to know that I miss her, I want her back, every day. Still.

We used to talk about my spiritual beliefs, and I often think I perhaps made it sound too glamorous, the spiritual side of things. I used to think – I don't know if I still believe this – that we are souls or spirits first, and embodied secondly, a secondary function. That we come down into this life to learn and to learn from other people and to affect other people, and then we get released and we go back to being a spirit, and we used to talk about that.

After Pippa died, I thought, "Maybe I made it sound like so much better out there than it is here. Maybe I didn't –" That was another blame thing. I don't know now. One thing I noticed after she died is that I felt, "She'll never leave me again." I'll never lose her again and that was reassuring, it was comforting, because she still is very much within me, very much. I can't lose her again. I don't know what happens after you die, whether I'll have another experience of her. She's very much still part of our family, very much talked about and included in things we do, and it's not difficult to feel that, and I'm sure the others do too. During one of my therapeutic journeys I worked a lot with visualizations. I developed a place where I could meet Pippa. Eventually, she left the place and went into the moon. Now at night when I see the moon, I say hello.

We did get a few cards and letters from people who had also lost their children. That was nice, it was good. That was personal; it felt like a very personal conversation. I think we might have written back. It's something that I did. I remember one person whose son had died soon after Pippa, I contacted her, we became good friends.

There was another woman locally whose son died. I contacted her as well, because I think that's what helped me. I had contacted Compassionate Friends,[5] someone came around, and it was helpful for me just sitting there, knowing that actually 12 years ago, this has happened to her and she's still here. People say "I don't know how you get through. I don't know how you bear it." You just do. You have to. Well, if you've got children, you have to. If you are all on your own, you might find it more difficult.

We also had a few people back off; some people didn't know quite what to say. There is nothing to say. They don't even want to give you a hug, which was what I needed. Because I was still in the same village, I know there are people who know who I am because of Pippa's death, but I don't know them. That slightly sort of unbalances something.

I miss Pippa not being here. I miss not having her in an older relationship because I think it would've gotten easier, but there is a sort of huge brick wall, and that's not going to happen. It's something that I'd love to have happen. I would love to have her back, and it's not going to happen, can't happen. It's the only certainty isn't it? It's a hard thing to have keep coming up against.

Having friends and family initially all descend upon us and support us as a family was really supportive. Later, my drawing was amazingly helpful.

That was the way I did it, I think, making images of that sort of pain, which really expressed it. I needed to express it, and it helped me for sure. I need a lot of time out in the wild, in nature. I can't bear to be with lots of people most of the time. So being in nature was also very helpful.

I think, probably, still working in mental health and working as a therapist was hard. At one point I might have felt that I couldn't help Pippa so I couldn't help someone else I was talking with. But at other times I thought if I can help someone else, then that would be good. But it was quite hard. I remember when I was working with an art therapist, there was a woman who used to come off the ward into the group, who was very suicidal, very self-destructive, and I used to think, "Why, why are you still here and Pippa's not, and Pippa just went off and did it. You haven't done it." I couldn't understand how Pippa could have done that so thoroughly. I still feel like that sometimes.

At other times, when I hear of awful stories of a client's childhood and I think they have survived and found ways of managing, I wonder if maybe some of that might be because they have had some struggle. They have grown up struggling. Maybe, they haven't had enough help, but they've struggled from a very early age and created a sort of survival, strategic survival.

One of the most difficult things after Pippa's death was my husband dying. I was at times angry with him because he'd gone off and left me for good. This is something we were going to survive. We were going to get through together, and then suddenly we weren't. We both struggled in our grief. We weren't together in our grief, because I don't think you are. We grieved very individually, very personally. It was not very compatible at times, but it was something that we shared, this huge burden if you like, or huge cloud, or weight. We shared it. Then when he died it felt, not immediately, but felt like he'd opted out. He left me with a sense of responsibility to stay for the children.

I can remember when I was diagnosed with cancer. Just before I was going into the operation, the children were very lovely. They came right down to the theatre door, literally. And I was on my own in the room for a little while and suddenly, I got terribly tearful. I said, "I'm not going to die. I can't die. I absolutely can't die because I've got to be here for them." I think, now, they are my reason to be here. Really.

I read loads of books. I've got loads of books. One book that was called *Stronger than Death*;[6] it was written by a psychiatrist whose son had killed himself. I found quite a lot of comfort from that because what she was saying was that people might actually choose this. Make those choices, and you can only put on as much on one end of the scale as you can, you don't know where the balance is going to be.

If somebody wants to kill themselves, there's nothing you can do to stop them. I really do believe that, and that has a shred of comfort about it, but I do think that Pippa, although she said in her note that she'd been thinking about doing this for a long time, it just felt that this was now the right time. But I don't think it was – I think, it was spontaneous on that night. If I'd heard her come back or gone in or made some contact, it might have been different. Whereas some people will plan it down to the nth degree. Pippa's wasn't planned in that way. She must have thought about what she'd do because she managed to kill herself, to hang herself off the beam. She must have at some point thought about that.

It's funny, isn't it, how your mind gets so convoluted after that kind of trauma. I can remember our son wanted to have a room over in another part of the barn as his room. I remember thinking, "It's okay because there are no beams, so it's all right for him to have that room." It's just doesn't make sense, does it? Well it does make sense in some ways. Another time I remember, soon after Pippa died, we didn't really have much money then, because my husband had not been working and we were worried about paying for her driving lessons. We'd given her older sister driving lessons, and you've got to be fair. I remember I was in the shower and I thought, "Oh, at least we won't have to pay for driving lessons," and I caught myself and thought, "Oh, God. Where did that come from? That's awful." The mind is really bizarre. It's the trauma thing.

The journey through this loss is still so current. Today I heard someone on the radio say "Grief for someone so close can cause you to ditch the love that you have for them because it is just too painful." I realize that I haven't been able to feel the love I had and have now for Pippa and I haven't said in this piece that I loved and still love Pippa. I will say it now: I love you, Pippa.

Thank you for allowing me this time, because it's been helpful to me.

Notes

1 A non-profit making, independent school not controlled by a local authority.
2 D.W. Winnicott (1971). *Playing and Reality*. London: Tavistock Publications.
3 https://papyrus-uk.org
4 A. Sebold (2003). *The Lovely Bones*. London. Picador.
5 www.tcf.org.uk
6 Sue Chance (1992). *Stronger than Death: When Suicide Touches Your Life – a Mother's Story*. New York: W.W. Norton & Company.

7 "I'm sorry to say he's dead"
Steffy's story remembering her son Jason and her brother Matthew

Jason was my first son. I was 16 when I got pregnant and was 17 when I had him. I'm one of six kids in my family. Our mum left us when my brothers and sisters were little, so I was one of the main carers for a while. As the mothering part of me was already switched on, I was able to mother him and be a mum. I was a single mum for a while because my relationship with his father didn't work out. He was quite violent, and we lived in different places at different times. As a result, there was no continuity in his life. Then I met Stacey's dad Robert. We got married and lived in a council house, and I had my second son, Stacey, when I was 23 years old. Unbeknown to me, he historically had a drug problem and he started to use again, so we split up. I left him and moved away with the kids. I was a single mother for a while again. That wasn't such a bad time. I was living in Norfolk then. Jason had had a very unstable early life, really, because I was in and out of relationships that were just destructive, I felt so responsible for that.

Then we met Rick. He was amazing, and I married him. We had a really nice life. But he was obsessive compulsive and very schizoid (in his head), so it was really hard to be with him. It suited me because he was stable, solid, and reliable. I think our relationship fell apart after Jason died because he just didn't connect with me about it or even talk about it. I needed someone to be with me and see how devastated I was. We just fell apart, really. At the time when Jason died, he was quite a challenging teenager. He was one of those kids who did everything you could possibly think of. I remember going to a festival with him and Stacey, who was about two or three, and Stacey's dad. We were putting up our tent, I think it was the Green Man Festival because I was a bit 'right on' and hippyish in those days. We were having a fabulous time, and then I lost Jason. I absolutely panicked. I couldn't find him anywhere. Somebody said, "I've just seen your Jason. He was selling hippy socks and bonce bouncers."[1] He was nine or ten years old at the time. This is the sort of kid he was, I found him because I could hear him shouting, "Bonce bouncers, llama knitted socks, bonce bouncers," and shouting whatever the cost was.

When we got there, he was asking for money and we hadn't got any, I said, "Jase, stop asking for money, sweetheart. We've got enough to have a nice time but we haven't got any for extras." So, he'd gone and got a job. That's the kind of kid he was. He used to get into everything, absolutely everything. He was just full on, and I loved him for that. He was such a character at school and everybody knew him; he was very athletic too. They used to put him into everything because he always did well. I remember Rick used to make his sandwiches, and we used to send him off with a half a loaf of bread because he was always so hungry!

He'd have a Pyrex dish full of cereal in the morning. We'd never have anything in the cupboard because the minute I bought it, it would go. The memories I've got of him were of him always eating, always rushing, running, doing, getting involved. Every summer holiday, I just signed him up for as much as I could. He learned how to sail and joined a sailing club; he was really good at that. I bought him a bike, and he cycled everywhere. I think he might have had ADHD, actually; it runs in the family, but I didn't know about that then. He was a really full-on kid. Then he got in with the wrong crowd and started to get involved in drugs and started to steal money from us.

He did awful things like nick his brother's bank book and take all money out of it. It got very difficult. He got in trouble with the police, he got arrested for stealing a bike. I suppose you could say he was antisocial in lots of ways. He just lived life on the edge. In the end, Rick said, "I can't have him here, he's got to go." So he chucked him out. I didn't want that, but I just felt powerless and very bad about it. But he managed to get himself somewhere to live and he got himself a life in Norwich. He met a girl who was a heroin addict; that was the beginning of the end of his life, because he just got involved with the wrong crowd. I didn't really know very much about his life. But after he died, someone told me what had happened. Jason's girlfriend was in hospital because she had taken an overdose. He had gone to visit her and met another friend of hers there, who said to Jason, "I'm going to score. Do you want to come with me?" They went to score. They got some heroin that was stolen from a pharmacy, the pure stuff. Now, they probably don't keep it there anymore, but in those days, they did. So, they both took an overdose and went into a coma. Jason fell forward and vomited and choked on his vomit. That's how he died. It was quite horrific, an awful way to end your life when you were somebody who was so full of it. He wasn't an addict, but he was on the fringes, he was dabbling.

That was the most – I can't explain it. I can't give you words for it, but only to say it just sucker-punched me, and I felt like there was something missing from my life, something precious had been taken, ripped away. It was horrible. When I found out about it, I was at home and the policeman knocked on the door, and he asked me if my son was called Jason, I said "Yes." He said, "I'm sorry to say he's dead." I said, "Oh my God. He can't be. I've only just seen him." He'd only just visited me two days before. I had to say, "Will you come in and tell me what happened?" He came in and said, "I don't have any details." So, I said, "Where is he?" He said, "He's in the morgue in Norwich Hospital. Is there anybody I can ring?" It was just awful. I said, "No, thank you. Thanks for coming."

That period of time was a bit of a haze, but I remember ringing a friend. She came over, she was pregnant and was distressed, and I thought, it was probably a bad move to ask her to be here. Then Rick came home, and he rang everybody. He found it difficult, because what a job it was to ring and say to all my family, "I'm ringing to let you know that Jason's dead." He had an awful job, and he found that very difficult. I couldn't do it. Then I had to tell Stacey, who was devastated. It's when something like that happens, you know who your friends are, isn't it? I had a friend, her name was Sue; lovely, lovely woman, who stayed friends with me right up until she died. She was much older than me, an American woman, she did what the Americans do. She came around with a casserole and a chicken. Every day she came around to my house and was there for me.

We didn't have very much money, I remember that. It's awful, because you have to find so much money out of nowhere for a funeral. It's so expensive, isn't it? We managed to get some money. Rick borrowed some money from his mum for the funeral, but we couldn't afford a funeral car. We just had a coffin bearer. We had the funeral, and all my family came, but they were just hopeless. My mum got upset for herself, my dad said, "We knew you had difficulty with him. We had actually thought to offer you at one point for us to have him to bring him up." Internally, I thought, "God, that's an awful thing to say." Not only have I lost my son, but you are now saying he might not have died if you'd have had him, that I'm a bad mother. They did not support me. I don't think they knew what to do, really. None of my brothers and sisters rang me to see how I was or what was happening with me. I didn't expect any more.

I was doing a social work course at the time, and bless them, every single person in my course wrote to me. I kept those letters because they were so comforting. They all wrote to tell me how sad they were about what had happened. Some of them recalled their own experiences and told me things about how they managed it, and I just was so filled up by that. They contacted me, rang me, sent me intermediary support, sent cards to say, "We did this at college today. We just thought we'd tell you because we knew you'd have a laugh." Because obviously there was only the landline in those days, there wasn't the stuff you could have these days. They were brilliant.

Some people from my work were really good. My boss was fantastic, because I was a children's social worker. I sometimes used to be on call, and I spent a couple of Christmases visiting parents whose children had died, because I worked with children with disabilities, so children dying was something I was very used to but never thought it would happen to me. He said, "You're quids in, just have the time you need." He gave me a whole month. It's such a total experience. You just don't feel like you can function in any way. Even going to the supermarket, I felt like I wasn't really me. I was just this person who was partly shut down from the world to cope with what's happening with me, so I felt like I'd got a barrier around myself. I'd have to make myself pick something up to check what it was I was buying to put in my basket. I made myself do it because I thought, I've eventually got to get back into the world.

When Jason died, they offered for us to go and visit him at the funeral parlour. I said, "Yes, I do. I want to go. I want to say goodbye." Actually, it was really quite strange and comforting in some ways. He didn't look like the Jason I knew; it was like the mechanics that kept him alive, were gone. It was just the shell. His energy – his life force – had gone. In some ways it was comforting, because I think what would have been harder for me was if I'd seen him and he was looking like he was asleep, I would just have to say, "Wake up." Stacey came; he didn't say very much, but I think it was good for him to see his brother as well. He didn't come to the funeral. I gave him the choice and he said, "No, I don't want to do that." I'm glad he didn't, actually, because it was horrendous. Jason's girlfriend came, and when I reached the crematorium, all I could hear was her wailing, really loud-pitched wailing, until the ceremony started. That was a bit surreal.

There were loads of people at the funeral I didn't expect to be there. His headmaster from the school came. Lots of kids that knew him came. A lot of my friends came that I knew outside of my work life, and some of the people from work came. The crematorium was full, and a lot of his anarchistic mates came, they put an anarchy wreath on his coffin. I wanted the ceremony to be a celebration, because I think funerals are for the living and not for the dead. I wanted it to be for me, but also to commemorate his life. I asked somebody to stand up and say something from Kahlil Gibran's book on being a parent.[2] I don't know what the book's called, but it was lovely. It's about us being parents and that we don't own our children. It's our job to let them be in the world and learn how to be in the world, and then I had the song "Let It Be" by John Lennon played, and also "Forever Young" by Bob Dylan. It was just like a very Jason-type funeral, really.

That was a really good process, I felt. A good goodbye process. He was cremated, and I got permission from the vicar of the church of Stacey's grandparents for his ashes to be buried there, because Jason used to go and help his granddad put the books out in the church on Sundays when he was a church warden. Both Jason and Stacey played in that graveyard, so that's where I put him to rest because I thought he'd love that idea, which is in Shouldham Thorpe in Kings Lynn. I don't get to go there often, but I don't feel like I need to because he is with me anyway, really. I've done things like I've put a cherry tree in the garden which in the spring blossoms and reminds me of him, and we talk about him a lot. To keep him alive.

Since Jason died, I've changed quite a lot, because it made me realize how tenuous life is. I'm less focussed on the minutiae and the crap that I used to be focussed on. He only had 18 years, and some of that time I didn't feel good about myself because I wasn't a very good mum. I was the mum that I was because of my own history. I learned to forgive myself for that, because if I could have done anything different, I would have. That process made me realize so much more about myself. I decided not to linger on things that are not important. If there was anything to come from it, I've become a better person. I trained to be a psychotherapist, and I love that work. I'm more a sort of person that will do something because I want to do it and not because I have to. I think I'm more positive, actually. Life's too short to worry about stuff that can make you feel miserable, so I am really much more positive, weirdly.

I had many shit things happen to me in my life before Jason died, which really affected me, and I made many bad decisions because I wasn't really being true to myself or authentic. I was doing stuff to avoid being in the world, to fully feel the world. I decided I'd go into therapy when he died and to get my shit together, which I did.

I have had conversations with Jason quite a few times since he died. If I could really talk with him I'd say, "I know I wasn't always a great mum but I really loved you deeply. I learned a lot from you, from being a mum and I'm proud of your achievements and I'm sad that you weren't able to see your brother's kids because I think you would have made a good dad and to meet your sister because you two would have become great friends because you're both really quirky. I miss you." If he could respond, he would probably say, "I love you too, mum," then he would have done something really daft, like the gorilla walk. Because he was good at the gorilla walk, and I think he'd probably say he was proud of us all.

I couldn't bring myself to go to the inquest. But it was a misadventure verdict, I think that's what they called it when someone died through an overdose. It was ages after he died. I had just got life back on track and the death certificate came in the post. Then I got a letter from the police station to say, "If you want to come and collect his possessions." That was just awful. I got that, then I rang my friend Gerry, who I'm still friends with. I said, "Gerry, will you do something for me? Would you come with me to the police station in Norwich, so that I can collect Jason's possessions?" He said, "Yes, of course, I will."

So, we arrive at the police station, and I said, "I've had a letter from you to say that you've got my son's possessions from when he died." I can remember this vividly, this guy had his glasses on the end of his nose, and he looked at the bit of paper I gave and he went, "Right, then." He puts the bit of paper down, he trolleys off and then he sticks his head back round and he says, "Sit over there." I'm one of those people that giggles when I get anxious. I started giggling, and then Gerry is next to me and he starts giggling. We had fits of laughter. It was just so incongruent. Then he comes back and he goes, "Here you are, madam. Sorry for your loss." He puts his glasses back on properly, then he turns around and starts doing whatever he was doing.

I picked it all up and I was giggling and then Gerry said to me, "Are you all right?" I said, "No, I'm not," and I burst into tears. Because it just felt like such an insignificant amount of stuff to represent the end of somebody's life, and it was given to me in such a callous way. No respect or accounting for how that might be for that person. It was bloody shite, really. There was no privacy, no "come into this room and I'm really sorry for your loss. How awful. How are you?" I didn't know what to do with the money. They gave me some money that was in his pocket and a couple of other things. I asked Stacey, "What should we do with this money? It's your brother's money; it was in his pocket when he died." He said, "He was into War Hammer. I'll buy some paints with it and I'll paint something from War Hammer that will be a representation of him." That's what he did. He kept that in his room forever, I think. I don't know what happened to it now. So, something good came out of it.

I remember the local paper wanted to interview me, and I said, "If you interview me, I want you to write verbatim what I say," and they did. For months and months afterwards, I'd bump into people I hadn't seen for a long time, and they'd say, "I read what you put in the newspaper and I thought it was brilliant. I'm so sorry about what happened." The local college got involved too because a friend of mine was working with the Drugs and Alcohol Agency run by the NHS. He contacted me and he said, "I got a friend at college, and they've decided to make some posters for the drug campaign against drugs. They would like you to come along and choose a poster, and we will do it in honour of Jason." That was really lovely. I went along to look at their work. I was really touched. I found it really hard to choose something, though, because they were all brilliant. There was publicity, and there were his posters everywhere. Which was really nice.

I think I was angry with Jason for a while as well, for being such an idiot. Obviously, kids are kids, aren't they? They just do stuff. These kids do things like that, they either dabble in drugs or they do a bit of something against the law, a bit like they get measles but they get over it. I remember I was doing stuff when I was a kid that I shouldn't have done, it's all a part of growing up. I got my head round it in the end.

I've had some support from two of my brothers who came to visit me, but not from my mum, dad, or sisters. In the office the first day I went back to work, no one said anything, nothing at all, which was weird. My senior boss was very supportive, but my direct boss didn't say much at all. Just said, "You're all right? Glad to see you back." I had other friends who I work with who didn't work in the office; they were pretty good. The admin staff were brilliant. They all got out of their chairs, they all hugged me, and one of them burst into tears. I had a couple of friends who worked in the elderly team and another friend who worked elsewhere. They came around lunchtime and said, "Come on, let's go have lunch," and were really supportive for a long time, and let me talk. But the other women in the office were just completely hopeless. I don't think they knew what to say. I think it's partly because we hadn't been together very long.

That stuck in my mind, really; everywhere I went for the first time, I used to say to myself, "Last time I was here he was still alive." Everywhere I went,

I would do that and be reminded. So many places I've been with him, and it was only a small town as well, so many people knew him. It was only really difficult when I knew people didn't know what to say. I remember about three months after he died going to a local pub, something happened which was really funny, and I was absolutely falling about laughing with a friend of mine. Another person I had known came in and sat and looked at me. He looked like, "Why is she laughing? She shouldn't be laughing. She should be mourning."

I sometimes had a sense of having to manage other people's emotions and processes certainly with my family. Even when I went to see them and mentioned Jason, they would change the subject. I remember telling my mum about the posters, and whilst I was just talking to her, she just changed the subject by saying, "Did you know such and such body has died?"

I don't think I'm without Jason. I do miss him, but he's ever-present, really. You just manage the grief, I think. It doesn't go away. It just becomes that much easier to put it somewhere for a while, and then something will happen and then you'll remember and cry. I cry because I loved him, and I miss him. I think that it's really important to keep on acknowledging actually, because it helps in a way. It becomes a big build-up otherwise, if you can't talk about it. Like I will say, "Today is Jason's birthday," and I will light a candle to remember him. I remember him on the day he died too; his brother and I talk about him a lot. So, that's how I manage. I think if you push it down and bottle it up, you don't manage, because it becomes like a thorn in your side.

I think, the one thing that you need to do, and I feel very strongly about this, is if you lose somebody you love, they leave a hole in your life so you have to fill it, yes, but also you can't forget them. So, you have to keep on just reminding yourself that it's okay to think about them. It's okay to talk about them and it's okay to sometimes be sad, and most of the time you just think about them fondly, I think.

I have kept things of Jason's, but I'm less obsessional about them. I've kept his running shoes because he was a great runner. I don't get them out as much as I used to. I used to just sit and hold them. I still feel very connected to him. I guess the intensity of his loss is not quite as much as it was because it's a long time ago now, 18 years. Sometimes something will happen, and it will really propel me back to that feeling of loss, but not often. I think about him at Christmas and on birthdays, anniversaries of his death, and I feel sad. The other times I think about him, I'm not quite so intensely sad. Being able to talk about him and share my experience with people who have had similar experiences and seen me for therapy has helped. Not wanting his death to be in vain really has helped me get through, that sense of having a purpose and a value to his life by being the way I am.

I did get those letters of support; they were just amazing. I was able to get them out, I constantly needed them. Sometimes you forget people's words, but when they're written, there was a slightly different quality to them to the sympathy cards you get. They were all wanting to give me strength and courage to face this and to carry on, they said things that helped me do that. They are a lovely bunch of people.

My history, feeling terrible about how I was as a mother, blaming myself, feeling guilty, all hindered my grieving process. It took me a long time to come to terms with not feeling like it was my fault. Those things got in the way. I did a lot of therapy on that. Therapy helped; it was really good.

I found some people just said the wrong things all the time. Things like, "You mustn't blame yourself for your history," or "You were the cause of him dying." I spoke to a couple of people who were friends of mine, and they said, "Yes, it's a shame. A shame what happened to him really, but you did have a bad history, didn't you?" That was awful. Things people say sometimes can be very hurtful and cutting. They open their mouth and don't put their brain into gear; that can hinder your recovery. For example, I've had, "Oh, I thought you'd be over it by now." I remember when he first died, going shopping, I must have looked really terrible going into a café to get a cup of coffee and people deliberately avoiding sitting with me. They saw me and pretended they didn't see me. I guess because they didn't know what to say. I think people hinder your recovery just by how they are. Thankfully, I did have lots of other friends who were great, so that counterbalanced it, but it is more jarring when someone says something that's insensitive or crass.

I think I believe in a higher power. I do feel very strongly that there is an energy within us, and I feel it very strongly. It informs me in lots of many ways. It informs me in my work; sometimes I don't know why I'll know to say something, I don't how it's come or where it's come from, but I just know it's the right thing to say. It's always the right thing to say. Sometimes, you can react from a feeling level, or you can react from a thought level and you might get it wrong, but there's a spiritual level in you, I think, where it's just the right thing to do or say. I do feel very spiritual in lots of ways. I have Reiki healing every fortnight with somebody who has been doing this with me for eight years, and I find that really spiritually healing. I do think that I am meant to do what I do, and I feel that there is a spiritual process going on that's really supporting me in this. I think I had it before Jason died, but I didn't pay any attention to it. I remember going to see a spiritualist after he died. During the funeral, I was standing holding Rick's hand and both of us felt an immense surge of energy; it was weird. When I went to see this spiritualist, she said to me, "At the funeral, Jason sent you some love and some energy because he felt like, at that moment, you and Rick really needed it." I thought, "Oh, my God. That's weird, it's really weird."

I have always been very slightly aware of something about my energy. I pick things up so quickly. I just thought I was really empathic. Maybe that's what it is being an empath. Maybe that's what happens, that's why you are an empath. I can pick things up so quickly. I'm more open to that now. It's an odd experience, but it's in me. I think I do have a strong spiritual aspect to me. I have a belief, I believe in God, I am a Christian. Maybe that's part of it. I do have a sense that at some point, Jason and I will be reunited. I think he's already been reunited with my brother Matthew, my mum, and my dad.

I wish I'd known early on that we all have a purpose in life. Just because you die, doesn't mean you don't have any value or haven't had purpose because sometimes, the very fact that you die affects so many other things in the world. In some ways, I know it's going to sound weird, but Jason's death was a gift for me because it changed my life. It made me realize how valuable life is.

Something has to come out of it that's positive, otherwise it's just a waste of life. I think I've helped a lot of people with my experience, sharing my experience. I think my positivity, not just my experience, has helped a lot of people. You know, I don't always say what's happened to me, but my energy has impacted people. I'm not defined by my past. However, I can live a fulfilled and happy present and future.

It was the worst thing that could have ever happened to me, to lose Jason. The worst. But out of it, I really had the best of lives, strangely. My life's changed so much. I've become a psychotherapist. I have an amazing job. I love my life. I have a really good husband. I have a gorgeous son, two gorgeous grandchildren and a fabulous daughter, because I decided that that's what I was going to do. I was going to live my life fully and not live the crappy life I had before.

Matthew

Matthew was my mum's last child. My mum and dad split up when he was about three or four. She went off with a guy who at first said, "I don't want anything to do with your daughters." She blanked us for eight years. Also, he was not very happy about the idea of her having the boys, but she did have contact with him. My brothers were really impacted by my mum leaving, especially Matthew as he was the youngest. I'd left home by that time.

She'd left with the same guy before, for about 18 months, when I was still at home. I took over being the mum of the family. Then, she came back for a short while. Then, about two years later, she left again for the same guy and married him. My little brothers were really quite badly impacted. It didn't work out, so she came back and mum and dad remarried. Dad really adored her; she led him a merry dance, really.

Matthew was quite impacted by all of that and so, he had issues, alcohol issues. He came to live with me for a little while in King's Lynn with me and Stacey. My dad, who was a prison officer, chucked him out because he caught him smoking cannabis. I said to my dad, "Oh let him come and live with me and I'll see if we can sort him out." He was a bugger. He used to go out and get drunk and have fights, and in the end I chucked him out because it started to spill over into my life. He went out with my friend, and he threatened to beat her up. Even though he was quite out of control, I still got him an appointment with drugs and alcohol people, but he just didn't get his head together. It was really sad because I really loved my brother.

Eventually he met this girl, so he went to live with her; that was okay until they split up. He met somebody else, and he moved in with her while I was living in King's Lynn, and she had a baby by him, Dion, my nephew. That didn't work out so he went back to live with mum and dad. Then, he went off to live with my brother in London. He was always a bit of a troubled soul. One day I had a phone call to say he'd had an aneurysm on the brain, and he was in intensive care. I travelled down to London, met all my family. Everyone was really upset and devastated. He lived for five days before he died. That was really sad. My mum and dad were devastated. I don't think my dad really got over it.

It was really hard for me too. I remember me and Stacey had gone to the funeral, it was the same day as the 9/11 bombings. We left the funeral and I was going on holiday the next day to Cyprus with Bob, my husband, and Jess, my daughter. She was about three. I remember when I was on holiday, blocking out the fact that Matthew had died, because it was just too much for me. When I got back, my dad told me off for not being in contact with him. I thought, surely, he must have realized that this was like a repeat performance of losing Jason. But he didn't. They were just so absorbed in their own grief. I said to him, "Sorry, dad, but it was just too much for me." They didn't get it. It's interesting because he asked us all to help him with the funeral. He asked us all to send money. I sent some, but it made me think, "God, I never got any help." It made me realize just how selfish my family are, really.

It was always all about them. They never really talked about Matthew after that. Now and again, there'd be something. My mum said to me, "I never thought I would have him for very long. I always thought I'd lose him." Sometimes he crops up. His gorilla walk – like Jason, he used to have this gorilla walk. They both used to do it; you can imagine two really skinny, six-foot guys doing the gorilla walk. They were both really hilarious. His humour is talked about quite a lot because he was really funny.

I felt very sad and very guilty that I couldn't have helped Matthew more, but I don't feel responsible. I just wish I could have done more. I've just got a dysfunctional family. We have a history, my dad was in the army so he was away a lot and my mum wasn't a very together woman, really. I think she should have married somebody very rich and not had kids and be treated like a princess.

If I could have a conversation with him, I'd say I miss him. I would say, "You would absolutely love meeting your niece, Jess." I think he would have become really good friends with Stacey. They already had a budding friendship as Stacey looked after him a lot when Matthew was in King's Lynn because he was always getting drunk. He got him out of scrapes and brought him home, and looked after him, and watched over him.

I think he'd be sorry he can't be here. He would really want to be there with us. He was always in the thick of it, a bit like Jason really. They both were a pair together, always in the thick of things.

Friends were fabulous, because when it happened, I got this phone call, they could see that I'd gone white. I was at my friend's house. They said, "Are you all right?" I said, "No. My brother, he's had an aneurysm." Amanda said, "Get on the train and go down. You've got to go now. Get on the train and go down. Go now. Go home, get some stuff together. We'll have Jess and we'll – Do you want us to contact Bob?" I said, "I can't get a hold of him. I've left him a message but can't get a hold of him." She said, "I'll contact him and I'll tell him where Jess is, don't worry." I just got in the car and I went home, grabbed a few bits, got on the train and went to London straight away, to my aunt's house. My dad took me to the hospital. That was horrible, because everyone was there. All my brothers and sisters, everyone, all waiting in the waiting room and my mum in a complete state.

I have vague memories of my cousin's wife throwing her arms around me. People have this habit of doing that to me. I'm the one that people go to. I hadn't seen her for years. She went all histrionic and I had to calm her down. Then, I went in to see my brother. That was awful, because he was on a life support machine. They put this gel thing on his eyes to help keep his eyes closed. I remember holding his hands and telling him I was here, and he gripped me. They told me that he was unconscious, but he knew I was there. I think I went twice and then he died, so I never got to see him again.

What happened was, Matthew lived with my other brother Mick, who was in a relationship with a woman. She had come home from work and found Matthew on the floor of the flat unconscious, so she called the police, not an ambulance. When they arrived they said, "Why haven't you called an ambulance?" She said, "Well, I just told them I don't fucking know what's wrong with him. He could be off his head on drugs for all I know." Anyway, he ended up in the hospital, but he apparently had been unconscious on the floor for a long time. He worked on the railway, had finished his shift and got home about midnight. My brother who shared the flat with him hadn't been back for over a day. Matthew must have been on the floor for a good 12 to 14 hours when he was found. I don't really know much about aneurysms, but they're not a good thing to have. I kind of knew that this might be the finish of him, really. I did get to say goodbye to him, to say I was sorry that it was happening to him: thankfully, he wasn't in pain.

We had a big funeral. My husband couldn't be at the funeral, so I was pretty much on my own with the family, living with mum and dad and helping them arrange the funeral, and sort things out. It gave us all a purpose. Even making the sandwiches, because we had the wake afterwards at the house. Quite a few people came, quite a few family members came, which was good for my mum and dad to see.

I don't know as I had that much help afterwards. I had therapy but it was a really difficult time because it brought such a lot of stuff back up. I did things like I got a picture of Matthew on the wall and thought about him a lot and did the same things I do with Jason, light candles and stuff like that for him. I visited his grave every time I went to visit my mum and dad. I'd go and talk to him and say, "Hi, Matthew. How are you doing? Missing you, you mad bugger." Having a place to go to, it was helpful actually. Because my parents were in Leicester, I was here, I just did my own thing, really. Every time I went to see them, we did talk a little about him. Dad would say stuff like, "Poor old Matthew, what a terrible thing to have happened to him." My mum would direct all her grief through anger onto my brother's girlfriend, the one that called the police. She'd talk about her all the time. That was her way of coping, I guess.

Matthew's left a big hole because when we all got together, him and Mick used to get us absolutely in creases, laughing. He still does, but this hole is obvious. It's just obvious there's a bit missing. I'm conscious of it, because he has to be the one-person stand-up comedian now, not the duo that they were. I haven't really had very many conversations about the loss of Matthew because we don't see each other very often. Maybe once a year at funerals or weddings or special occasions. We do communicate constantly through social media, though, liking and sending hearts and asking "How are you?" They'd make a comment about something and we come back with, "Oh God, how did that happen? Hope you're all right," type thing. Good old social media, even if we don't have face-to-face contact, I always know what's happening. I will post, "We're remembering Matthew today on his birthday" and everybody else would join in or they'd post it. He gets remembered. They don't remember Jason. I'm the only one who does, that's typical. They don't even remember Stacey's birthday or anything like that. It's like, I'm just over there somewhere.

I do think it's really important for families to pull together and support each other, really. I'm sad that people don't always do that. I feel very blessed I've got the friends I've got because they help me pull through. I'm really, really happy. If you don't have those friends, and you've only got your family and if they are hopeless at supporting you, that's awful.

Notes

1 Bonce boppers are a headband with two springy extensions resembling the antennae of an insect, often with novelty items attached on the end. They are sometimes called head boppers.
2 *The Prophet* was first published in 1923; later editions are still readily available.

8 "They laughed at me and said, you've got to be joking"

Nancy's story remembering her daughter Angel

Angel was just the light of my life. She was born in August 1995. From that day she just spread happiness everywhere. She was a very sunny, bright child, lots of fun, lots of laughter, very creative, very empathetic even from an early age. She did lots of things and loved to dance. She did ballet, tap, modern, and gymnastics. She loved the water, loved swimming. She laughed a lot. She was very close to all her aunts and uncles, and especially her nana, my mother, and right up until the age of seven there were no problems at all. She just accepted everything and took everything in her stride. She had lots of ear operations and wore a hearing aid in her left ear, which she was fine with whilst she attended her first school, which was in a little town where I worked. Unfortunately, property was expensive and for her to attend the senior school we wanted her to go to, we needed to live in the area. So, I changed jobs, and it meant a change of school for Angel. That seems to be where all the problems started.

The school was in an area where my sister lived and, as her son went there, I thought it would be okay for Angel. My sister's son was quite quiet and seemed to be happy at the school. Angel was sadly bullied. The headmaster spoke about her being a sullen child, so I went in with lots of photographs and I said I think it's the school, I don't think it's my child. Nobody really took me seriously and the bullying continued, resulting in her becoming more and more withdrawn although there were still moments of the happy Angel. I just don't think she liked school from that point on, as while at home she was absolutely fine. When she was 10, we moved to a new house. Angel was dyslexic, and so I wanted her to attend a senior school that would be able to provide the additional support she required. Angel was initially very excited about changing school, ever hopeful.

Her first tutor said that she stood out because she was so empathetic and such a lovely child. By the time it came to her second year, that tutor left, and everything just went downhill. Again, she was bullied. She'd come home with maple syrup and other substances in her hair and ripped clothing. Although I attended the school on many occasions, the staff took very little notice of my concerns, and then in the end when Angel started hitting back, she was labelled the bully.

The summer she turned 14, she had a couple of friends stay over. She went to a park in the town with these friends, and whilst there they met a group that were known for grooming. I think from that point they started grooming her, which I didn't realize at the time because I'm pretty naive. She started seeing an older man, which I didn't know about, and I'd get phone calls where she would be drunk. She tried to take her own life on many occasions; the first time taking a massive amount of iron tablets but didn't say anything. I was due to go out but stayed in as I felt something was not right, and had I not, I think we would have lost her sooner.

I do not understand why she was bullied, although she would say it was because she did ballet and because she spent a lot of time with me, so that resulted in her withdrawing further away from me.

From 14, Angel was involved with Child and Adolescent Mental Health Services (CAMHS). Our relationship became fraught, and my beautiful, fun, lovely daughter became angry and challenging. Her school life continued to be difficult and stressful, where she would do things in class to be excluded because she couldn't cope being in the class, and although I asked if she could complete her last days in a room on her own to allow her to take her exams, my request was refused. Angel did not return, and we looked for another school. Again, we chose the school after being advised of the wonderful and amazing results accomplished with struggling pupils, and because she was an August child, it was agreed for her to retake a year and have two full years to support her to complete her exams.

Sadly, she did not last a year there. She was bullied, people waited at the gate for her, she was told, "You're not one of us, go home," and she would take the train back home. She started drinking and although the school obviously recognized this, they did not advise me. When I would meet her after school she would smell of alcohol but she would say that she drank at a friend's house after school. In hindsight, she probably didn't even go into the school. I would find alcohol hidden everywhere which she had mixed with Coke. Everything I found, I would throw away. I would come home from work and the house would be smashed up, there would be writing all over the wall, all over the ceiling. I tried to phone Crisis for support to help me with Angel, but nothing was available; they just advised me to call the police.

Things escalated, getting worse and worse. By the time she got to 15, nearly 16, I agreed for her to move out because she was running away so much, I was worried for her safety. I didn't want her to go but was advised that she would have 24-hour support. Had I known that the staff would not be trained and didn't know what they were doing, I definitely would not have agreed. She was moved from place to place, living in environments with other, much older vulnerable adults who encouraged her to take drugs.

She would return home on occasions, and although I tried to encourage her to stay, she would disappear again. Her transfer from children's mental health services to adult services was a really appalling experience. The psychiatrist from CAMHS said during the meeting that Angel was very fragile and had experienced lots of dreadful things, which I didn't know about at the time; she advised that she needed people to be gentle with her and give her time to build up trust. The new psychiatrist and the mental health social worker replied, "Right, Angel, you're with Adult Services now. If you don't engage, you won't get a service," and that was the transfer. Adult Services from then on were unhelpful, to say the least.

Angel got involved with a woman, who was extremely horrible and violent; she ended up in prison after using a hammer over a young man's head. I don't know for certain, but I think she encouraged Angel to do things on the wrong side of the law, as she appeared to have an unhealthy hold and control over her. The woman beat Angel up very badly a few times but even the safeguarding team where I worked wouldn't do anything. Although I sent photographs, they said that as Angel was 18 years old and would not give consent for further action to be taken, they were unable to do anything. Angel was petrified and under coercive control. The police were unhelpful; the one time that I asked them to come and help, they told me to go back in the house. I explained that Angel was very vulnerable and could not be left anywhere. They told me they were taking her to the police cells, but they dropped her off at the end of the road and told her not to come anywhere near me. Whilst they were with her, one of the officers had thrown her forcefully on the ground, resulting in her being badly bruised and grazed all up one side of her body. She came back and knocked on the door in tears, so I let her back in the house. I think she was let down by all services.

The drug-taking went on. Most of the time I found out or I would get a text. I'd take her to A&E and she'd be in hospital for a few days and come back out again. They wouldn't section her, it was all, "Well if you'll take her back home, we won't section her," and I kept trying to say that I didn't know how to look after her. She'd come back to my house with hidden tablets and try and take an overdose. Although I explained I needed help to look after her, they wouldn't disclose any information because they said Angel was an adult. There were quite a few ambulance calls where the ambulance crew said that they could see she was unwell, but they would not take her to hospital as she refused to go and she was capacitated. I was advised to call back when she became unconscious. It was absolutely horrendous. Because Angel would see different doctors, she would get different medication from different practitioners. She was prescribed Amitriptyline by one, which should not be prescribed to people under 25 anyway. Services were not joined up; no one knew of the other professionals' involvement.

One occasion when Angel was taken into hospital having overdosed on prescription medication, she needed to be intubated. The doctor who saw Angel at the time thought she was 12, as she was so tiny. Whilst Angel was in hospital, we spoke to a number of health practitioners. One in particular stands out as when Angel's dad and I advised we needed help and suggested Angel having residential care, "just to get through her demons knowing someone was there for her 24–7." They laughed at us and said, "You've got to be joking. They won't pay for that." We explained that we would be happy to pay for the service but needed support sourcing somewhere appropriate. We said that we were worried that she'd be dead by Christmas if she did not get this support, and we were told that we were being overdramatic. However, by the end of June that year, she was dead. I kept trying to say to mental health services, she hasn't taken the drugs and then become ill. She's taken the drugs because she's been ill and to quieten the voices she hears in her head, but they wouldn't listen; they knew best.

Before Angel died, she was admitted into a mental health unit for assessment and treatment. She was put on a female ward and although I was advised that all visitors would be searched and that no male visitors would be allowed in her room, she had a male friend visit who took in alcohol. Whilst there, Angel was not treated very nicely by some of the staff. As Angel was deemed underweight, she was prescribed build-up drinks. While visiting on one occasion I saw a male nurse put the build-up powder on top of the milk, give it a quick stir and forcefully hand it to Angel. She looked so sad and felt worried about what would happen if she refused to drink it.

I advised Angel that she did not need to drink it. I was shocked by the way she had been treated; the nurse had not even spoken to her or made any attempt to make the drink appetizing. Angel stayed in the hospital for about two weeks, there was no real evidence of any assessment or treatment and Angel appealed her section. I was surprised the day I received a phone call at midday. I was at work and was told that Angel was being discharged. I explained that Angel had just got a new flat and that there was no furniture or heating. I was surprised that they were discharging her at such short notice with no prearrangements of support. I was advised, "If you can get here, you can take her home; otherwise, she can get a bus home." I had to quickly make arrangements because I was on the duty desk that day. During the discharge meeting the psychiatrist said to me, "You don't agree with this, do you?" I said, "No. I don't think she's ready. You haven't done any work with her here. She's just been contained." He replied, "I hear what you're saying, but if she goes out and wants to come back in, even if it's the next day, then she can." So, even though he knew that I felt that Angel would be unsafe, she was discharged.

Angel received daily visits to start with, and although she very quickly requested to return to hospital, she was told, "You can't mess them around, what are you going to benefit from going back into hospital?" Angel was unable to reply although was clearly struggling and so traumatized, she needed to be prompted to undertake daily tasks including showering and eating. Angel withdrew from services as she felt she was not being listened to.

My relationship with Angel broke down further, and she only contacted me when she needed more money. Eventually, having tried many different approaches, I said, "I can't do this anymore Angel. I'm your mum, I know that when I give you money, you use it to buy drugs, and I can't do it anymore." I said, "I'm here to be your mum." Just before she took her own life, she asked if she could come back home. My partner refused; worried of the impact her return would have on my health due to her previous behaviours. She had her own flat by then, and both her dad and I said we would take it in turns to stay with her, making sure she had somebody there with her at all times. This action will continue to haunt me for the rest of my life.

Angel deleted both her dad's and my numbers from her phone, and having tried for nearly a week to make contact with her, phoning and visiting her flat, I eventually phoned mental health services, who initially advised that she had been seen that week, which I later found out was not the case. Although she had an appointment, she was not seen, and nobody made any effort to check she was alright. They were very condescending towards me, "Haven't you called the police?" At the time I didn't know I could, so I called the police straight away to request a welfare check. Angel was found dead; she died on 27 June and was found on 2 July. She was alone in her flat, another thing that will haunt me for the rest of my living days. She had taken a mixture of prescribed medications with the intention of taking her life. She was only 19.

At the inquest, I made 13 recommendations. I was asked to consider whether I believed my daughter's death was misadventure or suicide, not something you really want to ponder over, but I did as I was asked, although it was very traumatic analysing all the information. I believed she had meant to take her own life as, although she text friends to say what she'd done, she'd deleted her dad's and my phone numbers. Her friends did not act and were unlikely to have acted; one friend texted, "just sleep it off," another lied about sitting and drinking tea with her. They couldn't have done it; she was already dead. The coroner's verdict was a drug overdose, not suicide. Why did they ask for my rationale?

My experiences with the mental health services resulted in me taking another role at work where I no longer work on the front line. I control my feelings of anger daily. We experienced five years of trauma with no support. The health organization that prescribed Angel Amitriptyline refused to even come to the inquest, and that appeared to be okay. The psychiatrist that had worked with Angel also was not present. In a statement he said that he could not remember saying Angel could return to hospital if she felt she needed to, and as his record-keeping was poor, there was no evidence that this was said during her discharge meeting.

The mental health practitioners that were present blamed Angel. They said she was a drug addict, and although I kept reiterating that Angel took prescribed medications because she was ill, they insisted otherwise. They stated that as Angel had a borderline personality disorder, she was "bound to die young." Although mental health services agreed to continually provide updates on the progress of my recommendations, this has not been done. Angel has become just another number.

The local newspaper reported on Angel's experiences and death, and although I was concerned their report would be damning to Angel, it was sympathetic.

I pay tribute to my beautiful sister who, although gravely ill herself, supported me throughout. She was at Angel's birth and also supported me to lay her to rest, helping to wash, dress, and lay Angel in her coffin and to also accompany me out to sea to take her ashes to her final resting place.

I think it took me at least a year to emerge from my shock. I haven't had time to grieve for my mother, who died a few months before Angel; I was consumed with worry for Angel. I think I have disconnected myself as far as I am able from the world; I function, but I do not live. I am afraid to feel too much for fear of my actions.

If I could speak with Angel, I would ask, why? I absolutely adored my daughter from the day she was born; she was my reason for living. If she'd said she could no longer live in this county, I would have moved. I want to know why she cut me out and listened to her friends, isolating herself from those who really loved her. I want to know why she let others abuse her and beat her black and blue when she had a family that absolutely adored her and wanted to protect her. I really don't know why it all began, I don't know whether it was the bullying, which made her feel she wasn't good enough. I don't even know why she was bullied. Angel was quite an easy-going, beautiful, loving child. I don't know whether her lovely nature made her an easy target; I haven't got a clue. There are too many unanswered questions which haunt me daily.

Since Angel died, I tend to keep myself to myself, really. I go to work, I come home. I've stopped going to the gym; I exercise in my basement. I have a few close friends, and the people I work with are supportive. People that know me really well talk about their own children and Angel will be included in the conversation, while others avoid conversations and sometimes me. I can't bear to think that she's forgotten just because she's not around; she touched too many people's lives. I think I just get on and do. It just feels like I'm in limbo, really, just marking time until the end, really. I'm not quite sure when that's going to be. Some days it can't come quick enough.

Angel has a stone on my dad's grave; her middle name was a remembrance to him. I go up there regularly, clean the stone, and put fresh flowers. I do this because I need to continue to do something for her. Angel and I used to go to church regularly. I don't go any more, not since she died. She used to like sitting in the Lady's Chapel. A couple of times after she died, I'd just go and sit in there. Although there were people present who knew me, they avoided me. Nobody spoke to me. Nobody even said hello. So, I don't go in there anymore. I don't think I have any faith anymore.

I guess I just believe what I believe. I'm hoping there is a life after death and that I will actually meet with Angel and other family members again.

Angel had this thing about fairness, which I have as well. It wasn't that I would have sued the mental health services or anything. It's just that I wanted them to hold up their hands and say, "Yes, you're right. We did a really bad job and we've taken your recommendations, and this is what we're going to do." They said initially that they would let me know every stage, but I ring now, and they can't remember and don't even know what they are. Angel was let down by so many people along the way. I just don't think people think enough about the consequences of their actions.

If I were to say something to someone in the same position, I'd would tell them to "stay true to yourself, do what you need to do, and don't allow others to tell you how to grieve or how to live your life. You have to do what feels right for you in spite of what anybody else says, and however mad it might seem, just do it." Whenever I've had a trauma, I cut my hair really, really short. I have always done this. I think it is my attempt to cleanse and move forward.

I believe mental health services, especially here where I live, need to re-evaluate the way they support people with poor mental health, throw everything out, and start again. I think they work with the wrong people. They work with people that shout the loudest. The last time I visited the mental health hospital, there was one person who was being discharged, and she was laughing whilst saying "They're letting me out. I'll see you again in a few weeks." In my experience it is the quiet ones that need the support; they take their own lives because they feel no one is truly listening, and so eventually they give up and stop trying to be heard.

I admire Gloucestershire Sunflowers; it's a support service that started fairly recently, and they have done so much in such a short space of time. These people and services are needed as, sadly, I cannot see much has changed in the mental health service since Angel's death.

9 "I think I was in shock for a year"
Carol's story remembering her son David

Things that were important about David were that he was a very free-spirited person, did his own thing. Some people would have said, "Oh, crumbs, has he got some difficulties." I just thought he's a free-spirited individual, and I didn't want to dampen that, but "he is a little bit too spirited at times," is how I referred to him. I just thought some of his excess energy really needed to be channelled. That was done as he got older through sport. He was very sporty, played football and rugby to county level and held the record for 300 metres in our county. He could turn his hand to any sport, and he tried them all. He was just, "I think I'll have a go at that." Fishing was a passion; he lived for it. It was such a contrast because he was this ball of energy yet could sit at the side of the lake for eight hours. I used to say, how does he do that? How does he go from being so full of energy to suddenly just being completely calm, chilled?

Music – he was absolutely passionate about music. Even at a young age, he listened to things that were a little bit different for his age. He discovered the Beatles and various things when he was younger and listened to them. As he got older, he got into more dance, house, that kind of music, and had his own decks, wanted to DJ. Managed it at one point at 15. Him and his friend managed to set up an illegal rave. I have to laugh about it. I think, "good on you, you did something a bit different." They set up all their decks and everything with a generator on waste ground and the crowds came basically until they got raided. I look back on it now and I sort of think, wow! He crammed a hell of a lot into the time he had. He was incredibly sociable, made friends everywhere. God, it's weird talking about him.

He made friends all over the place with really diverse people, not just his own age group. When we went on holiday, he was always the one that came home with the names of three people who he'd met and was going to meet up with afterwards. If you met him, you'd think, "Oh, gosh, he's confident, he's sociable," but on many levels, he wasn't. He was actually quite a sensitive person.

I think that came through in how he enjoyed music; it really spoke to him. He didn't just listen to it, he really felt it. He didn't have the confidence to do some things. We were trying to persuade him to go to college and study, whether it's music production or something; but he was, I think, too frightened in a way of just stepping in there and thinking would he be good enough.

A lot of these insecurities, I think, are what took him down a path of getting into company where those people would cover up for his insecurities and lack of confidence. That he would almost get some kudos for being in a certain group. He desperately wanted to be popular. He really wanted that, and it took him into hanging around with people where exploring drugs became a natural path from quite a young age. Everything seemed to go wrong from that point of view from when David was 11. I'd split up with his dad in the summer and he'd transitioned from primary up to high school, but with a combination of all those things, he just seemed to change. He seemed to be wanting to prove himself somehow.

One day I got a call from his school to say, "Somebody has come to us to say that David's walking around the school bragging that he's got cannabis on him." Well, I laughed, if I'm honest with you. I just thought, that's ridiculous. I've never heard anything so ridiculous in my life. I went up to school thinking, something's gone badly wrong. What's all this about? I went into the headmaster's office, David's sitting there. The headmaster said, "Well, this is what the lad's saying." I waded into David's school bag saying, "That's absolutely ridiculous. Come on. Let's have a look." I'm pulling things out and throwing them around. Got to his wallet, and David went, "It's in there." I went, "What's in there?" He said, "It's in there." Back then I wouldn't even know cannabis if I happened upon it because I'm very naive, and it was just like a little block. I just pulled it out, and he said, "Yes, it's cannabis, whatever." You could have just blown me over. I didn't have a clue that he would even know what cannabis was or how to get it. He got suspended from school for six weeks. I thought, what on earth do I do with a 12-year-old who's put his foot into this territory? I tried to scare the life out of him, basically. I took as much time as I could off work, lectured him about what I could find out about drugs and basically put him to work painting a bedroom at home.

I was trying to think of what kinds of things, punishments, but education as well that I could do. I thought, "What on earth is going on here? Why would he even know about drugs?" At that point, I naively thought that this was an isolated incident, that he'd clearly just ventured into something that you could close the door on and walk away and everything will be fine. Unfortunately, it just became a persistent theme where I was just trying to stay ahead of the game with him, but I never did. His sister Charlotte would come to me and would say, "I found matches and I found this, and I found that." He would be saying, "She's a little snitch, she's a little rat," but she wasn't. She was just worried.

As time went on, it felt like everybody around him was smoking cannabis. The whole of his peer group, everybody around my area at that time, it seemed to just be absolutely rife. My lectures were falling on deaf ears. I say lectures, they were lectures really, I suppose, when I think back. I was trying to learn about drugs myself in order to educate him. He just kept falling into or finding company that I suppose gave him acceptance. I think he was a bit conflicted. I think he wanted to do the right thing. He'd say a lot during his teen years, that he wanted to make me proud. I'd think, "God, I must be making him feel pretty awful actually, for him to have to say that." I was proud of him. I just didn't want him to go down certain paths. I was educating myself much more about the long-term effect of drugs. I was getting really concerned. Your brain's still developing through the teenage years; it's still not reached its full potential. He was doing something to it that was going to hamper that. I was getting really frustrated and worried about what that would mean for him.

When he got to about 15, he was friends with one particular lad whose parents had separated. When his mum couldn't cope, he went to dad, and when dad couldn't cope, he went to mum. I was determined that wasn't going to happen with us, I was there for the long haul, "There's nothing that you can do that isn't going to make me dig in harder." That's kind of the attitude I had. In hindsight, I don't think it's the right attitude, but it's the one I took. So, him and this lad would be in each other's company a lot, just taking it up a notch, taking it up another level. I think that other lad was possibly dealing, and David was getting into the realms of dealing as well. I kept finding stuff around the house that gave me cause to think that was what was happening. I was getting more worried. Nothing prepares you as a parent to deal with that. I was completely out of my depth. How do you tell a 15-year-old, who seems hell-bent on doing what he's doing, the consequences?

When the consequences would just creep up on him, even that didn't seem to be the thing that would say to him, "I'm going down the wrong path here. I do need to start listening." Sometimes he'd have a little moment of clarity and say, "Yes, I'm stopping this and doing that," and then get back into whatever was going on. I'd have serious conversations with him.

I would go to bed at night, and always that thought was there of what's going to happen, what's going to be the end outcome? Always that worry, that fear, because we could see that his behaviour was risky, but he was absolutely blind to it. He would say to me, "You always think the worst, mum." I said, "Well, somebody has to. Somebody has to be the one worrying what the end outcome will be about the things that you're doing, because you don't seem to be doing it yourself."

Then when he got to 17, I discovered he was using cocaine. From that point on, the worry went up another level. I'd say things really escalated into just the most worrying period of time because it just seemed to be one thing after another. I think he knew that it was getting a hold of him, and he kept trying to do things to step away from it, like joining the army. The first time he did it, he came out because his girlfriend was missing him, they were missing each other. At a slightly later point, he said, "I'm ready. I'm more mature. I'm going to do it again." The minute he went, myself and my daughter realized why he had gone off in such a hurry, because people kept knocking on our door. He obviously owed people money. I think he'd gone in the army to flee that kind of pursuit but left us with the difficulty of people knocking on the door, and not nice people at all. I had my windows put in which was very scary at the time. My daughter moved out for a few weeks because she was too scared to live in the house, and I slept on the sofa because I didn't want to go to bed.

This impacted on my relationship with David. It meant that there were far too many conversations that were negative, that were about drugs. It got to a point, perhaps in the last year before he died, where he'd come in the house sometimes with the phone glued to his ear talking to somebody, every conversation would be about something drug related. Charlotte and I would be saying, "Please, we don't want these conversations within our orbit. We don't want to hear them. We don't want to know." He seemed to be just in his own bubble; what was going on beyond him was almost irrelevant.

He was anxious and worried; his life was out of control in terms of his own cocaine use, debt, and all the stuff that comes with it. Yet he was holding down a job working for a local housing association as a builder and plasterer. He was in a relationship and had a child. If you did not know David very well, you wouldn't have a clue what was going on behind all of that. He was a really nice person, sensitive, caring, but he was trying to run in a world that actually was so different to him. He completely wasn't meant for it.

If I think back to when he was 17, cocaine was there at some level influencing and impacting his life, creating consequences for him. It's the reason why he got discharged from the army the second time. He'd been doing exceptionally well. He'd been out for a weekend's leave; knew without fail he would be drug-tested, and he used drugs in that weekend's leave. How would he not think that that would be picked up? He went from doing really, really well, to ending up at Colchester before being discharged. I remember him saying to me when he came home that he'd spoken to a priest when he was at Colchester. The priest had said to him, "I think the trouble with you, David, is you just don't listen to the advice of well-meaning, well-intentioned people who could give you, tell you what's good for you and what isn't. You're just head down blinkered and just go about it your own way."

I think everything falls by the wayside next to drugs. That's not because he didn't value all those other things. He just needed that more. That's the tragedy of drugs, isn't it really? It's like everything else just completely falls to the wayside. The things, the people that you care about. It's all about your next fix. I knew things were bad with him, but in the last, say, 12 months or so, it just became this revolving door of him falling out with his partner because of his behaviour which was linked to drug use, and then coming back to stay at mine for three, four days, until things cooled. Then he'd go back, and things would go wrong again, and he'd say, "Mum, can I come up?" I'm like, "Yes."

I must be honest: I'm not a tough-love person. I just had two rules with him. I said, "You can't come through the door if you have drugs with you, and you can't come through the door if you are obviously on drugs, or if I look at you and think that you're under the influence of anything, you won't come through the door." That didn't work very well. I realize now, though actually his need must have been enough for him to even risk that. Since he died, I've gone down to our utility area when we would often go and found a lot of secreted packets, of empty packets pushed behind things. He had clearly, despite having given me assurances, known that "Mum's a soft touch. She says one thing, but she loves me enough to put up with it." I don't know.

I have been thinking about this the last few days where some people say 'tough love' don't they, and yet imagine if I'd kicked him out and said don't come back. My son could have died anyway, and I'd have had that hanging over me. As in not only did he die, but I wasn't actually in relationship with him for a period leading up to his death and I think that would've been worse. I think that because the outcome can be the same regardless of which choice you make, can't it? You know there are people who just completely wash their hands, I guess in the hope that it gives that person the wake-up call they need. They need to hit rock bottom and all that kind of stuff, but the outcome can be the same either way. You've got no guarantees when you make that decision that the outcome is going to be good. You don't know, do you?

I guess, because he'd been using cocaine for a long time, his tolerance had built up, so he was using more and more. I think he was in such a pit of despair; so, he was using more for that reason too. It was affecting his relationship, his work, his finances, and his friendships, everything. Because he was using more, the effect of coming down was having a really bad impact on his mental health. I mean horrendous. At times I didn't know whether it was the drugs or whether he was experiencing some kind of full-blown episode of some sort. He had gone to the doctors a few times and had been to substance misuse services, but he'd not really engaged in a meaningful way. I'd gone with him as well. I was trying to see if we could help him get motivated to do something. My daughter and I took him to a Narcotics Anonymous (NA) meeting, he didn't want to be there, and he never went back. I think he had an appointment or two with mental health services. We were at our wit's end.

What kept happening was David just kept falling between substance misuse service, mental health services, or the police. Nobody said, "Let's try and do an assessment with David that was actually holistic that actually considers the drug use and his mental health." This doesn't happen. In fact, they were most quick to criminalize him. I think that's the easiest route, from a young age he just became criminalized.

The final morning, I saw him, he'd come back up to my house, he was lying in bed using the iPad or the laptop or something, and I went out. Later, I was getting phone calls off him. He started fairly rational where he just wanted to talk to me. He said he wasn't in a good place, and I said, "Look, just come home and we'll sit down and talk, we'll do a pros and cons list, look at the options around things." He didn't want that. I think he phoned his sister that night, and his dad, and his girlfriend who he'd probably be rowing with because it was pretty clear he was becoming more and more under the influence, we could all tell that from how he was sounding on the phone.

He'd gone out driving with a friend and was heading back on his own. We were all getting quite concerned but also annoyed with him, because he was clearly under the influence and making phone calls that made no sense whatsoever, and you couldn't reason with him. Well, in the end, I regret it a lot. I turned off my phone and went to bed because everything I was saying was making no impact whatsoever. He was just doing his own sweet thing.

Next morning, his partner rang me saying, "I still haven't heard anything off David," and at this point, we were both starting to think this was really odd because actually, as much as David would do silly things, one thing he never did was be out of contact with us, I'm talking about a tiny amount of time; even if it was just to argue with his girlfriend by text message, he would be in some kind of contact. She started saying, "I've got a really bad feeling," so she'd contacted the police. I spoke to the police too and mentioned that when under the influence and certainly when coming down, David's behaviour could be so irrational. They took it quite seriously from that point and started looking for him; I think they had a helicopter and police dogs out. They discovered the car at a nearby garage, interviewed the person who'd been on duty through the night. She said he'd come in, wanted cigarettes, but then started behaving really irrationally, was shouting, "Don't make me go out there again, don't make me go out there again," and then ran out.

David's partner, Sadie, and I decided we'd go in the car and looked around certain areas. The next thing, we see a police car flying past us, and Sadie says, "Carol, that's travelling at speed, they must know something," so we followed it to an industrial estate, and there was a police officer standing on the corner, and I thought this looks a bit official. We pulled over, and we were just going to walk down this area but were stopped by a police officer. Then, I saw two police officers walking towards us, and one of them I recognized, he's a really nice police officer and Sadie had said to me he'd always been really nice to David. I looked at his face as he was walking up. I could tell that he looked devastated, as though he'd seen something that'd obviously really upset him. He came up and told us that David had been discovered.

It was a completely surreal moment; it was almost like I'd anticipated this moment. I mean it's like a cliché, isn't it? He'll be found dead in the ditch. It was a thought when I went to bed at night. Like, how the hell is this going to end?

I remember police officers taking me and Sadie back to her house, I don't know if it was just a case of phoning people who then came to her house. Charlotte had been ringing Sadie, but I guess there was too much going on and she just wasn't relaying to Charlotte what happened, because she was in a state of shock, so Charlotte rang me and I think because of the emotion, I didn't filter what I was saying whatsoever. In hindsight, I think, my God, to lay that on her, she was away, but I couldn't hide it. She and her boyfriend had to drive back knowing that this had happened. There was no way on God's earth I could actually hide it.

If I look back, I think I was in shock for a year, and I'm grateful to it, if I'm honest with you. I think it protected me, but when it lifted, which was probably sometime into the second year, the reality was horrendous. I think I almost wished I was still in a state of shock. It's hard to say if it was a sudden or gradual lift. It felt quite sudden. I kind of shut down even walking – I felt like I had lead boots on, everything was heavy, everything was an effort. And I could remember being in the car and I thought it was in slow motion, and at times, music would be playing; it sounded like it was underwater. That didn't last long, that effect, but the whole energy zapping, I felt exhausted, absolutely exhausted. I was in a fog, and I think the fog lasted longer than that. It started to scare me, actually, because I couldn't concentrate, I couldn't read a book. If I read a paragraph or something at work, I'd have to reread it, thoughts were flitting to other things. I did start worrying about that because I had to hold down my job.

It will be five years from next February since David died. I think my ability to concentrate has come back a lot better than it was; I can stay on track with something I'm doing longer. I still can't read a book very well for pleasure, but I can keep my concentration long enough to work and not feel anxious. If I try and read for pleasure, my thoughts suddenly drift off to the 'what if' scenarios. I think the first year, perhaps a year and a half, was plagued by that. In the end I just sat myself down and went, stop it, just to stop it, you can't change the outcomes, so stop torturing yourself. I think I really gave myself a stern lecture around, "This is getting you nowhere. You are actually going to drive yourself absolutely mad with this if you carry on; there's some things that you will never know." I think my faith belief tells me at some point I'll know. I think for me there are some unanswered questions about his death as well.

I'm somebody who needs to know detail, so when I got in touch with the coroner after David died, it was the assistant coroner at the time, and I said, "Look, am I allowed to see what you can see?" and she said, "Yes, you can see everything," so I asked for everything. I got all the statements, the post-mortem report, which I know this sounds grisly and horrible, but I just needed to know; I needed to put every single piece together. I didn't really want to read it, but I *had* to read it. I was ordered thinking like, okay so this was the lady in the garage, so then we moved to the guy who was with him and walking through all of the witness statements. Then I came across one that was from a motorist who had seen him at something like 4:20 in the morning, which was literally minutes before he died. The police hadn't mentioned a motorist had seen him that close to his death. So, I was like, why wasn't I told? Why would they not mention this? Why would they not think it's important? And then as I read through his statement, I'm having just this massive gut instinct that something was wrong. The statement itself had no meat in it. It was flimsy, as if it was just an add-on. There was no real evidence from somebody who'd seen him that close who had things to say about how he was and what he was doing.

It had one particular bit that said, "I was going around the roundabout, saw somebody running across it. I thought he might be running from somebody. He ran off the roundabout and he literally flipped and fell into the road." Then a new sentence, "I stopped my car." Why did you stop your car? Did you stop the car because you had to brake because he was literally in front of you? Did you inadvertently hit him? No one's going to blame you; he was running at speed. The thing I couldn't get my head around was, the edge of this roundabout has chest-high chevrons that you cannot run through, so where has he run off, and where has he stumbled? Because there were all these unanswered questions, I was driving myself insane, because it did not make sense. I became like a woman obsessed and possessed.

I got in touch with the police and raised it as an issue. I think they said they attempted to get a hold of this guy and get a more comprehensive statement, but they couldn't get hold of him or something. A police officer came to the house, and I can remember him sitting there, and I was saying, "I have no way of knowing if this man inadvertently hit him or not. You've not investigated that." He said, "We work on the basis of a hypothesis, so the hypothesis is David was using drugs and that was what led to his death." I said, "Well, yes, I agree, but there could be other nuances to this, and you're just not investigating them," so he got angsty with me, accused me of being judgemental. I didn't get very far with that, so I made a written complaint to the IPCC and they told the police to investigate it. There were about five or six points in the complaint; they upheld only one part, which was that the statement was not fit for purpose, the consequences of that being that the police officer will be schooled to make better statements in future. That's as far as I got; by this point, I was drained.

We had the first inquest, and the assistant coroner said to me, something like "We've not been able to get that statement from the motorist. Are you happy to proceed?" I said, "No." She said, "Okay, then so we're going to have to adjourn this inquest, go to a further inquest, once we've got it," I said, "I won't be happy until either I've got a statement that's fit for purpose, or you've called him to the inquest to give evidence. That's it for me because until I hear from his mouth, or by means of a statement, that's adequate, exactly what he saw, no, it's not happening," so I was quite stroppy.

The upshot of that was, I think my stroppiness led to it being passed to the senior coroner, who did actually get him to the inquest. He was in his

40s; he burst into the inquest. I got told by a paramedic who was there, a really nice guy who'd found David, he said he just came in and he just went, "I don't even know why I'm here," and the paramedic apparently turned round and said "Well, I think it might be because you're the last person to have seen him alive, mate." When he gave evidence, he said he'd had to take his car in to be examined. He said it was really inconvenient. The coroner actually told the guy to respect the fact that we had lost somebody very dear to us and actually to frame that a bit better. I try not to think too much about it, but I cannot get out of my head that the last bit of the story just does not make sense. It could be that there's a really innocent explanation, but I'm not being given it. I've even gone back in the dead of night and walked that roundabout because I wanted to know. If you walked as he's described it in that statement, you just walk straight into chevrons of chest height or dense bushes and trees that you cannot get through. Why would anybody not think that doesn't add up? It's almost like saying, "Well, it's kind of irrelevant, even if the poor guy had hit him well, what a shame because David was off his face anyway." It's that whole not knowing and not being able to get a straight answer to a very straight question. It changes nothing. It doesn't change the outcome, but it would help put that sort of that final piece of the jigsaw in. There is a bit missing. I know it's missing. There are bits of it that just don't make sense.

I'd say it's only in these last 12 months that I can feel myself moving incrementally forward in terms of not obsessively thinking about the whole situation. I started thinking, this isn't healthy for me, stop it. It wasn't healthy for my daughter and those around me to have me constantly doing this whole, "I need to know, I need to know." They got to a point where they were saying, "We're maybe never going to know, and you're going to have to live with it" and I came around to thinking, yes, that's true actually, I have to let it go for my own sanity.

I kept my daughter close, obviously, and my sister and my brother-in-law, nephews, and nieces became my go-to people. I became much closer to them. We've always been reasonably close, but they were and still are, not around at my house all the time or whatever, but just showing up in the evening, because they knew that probably I wasn't doing anything or going out. I had isolated myself a bit, but my niece would come around, we'd sit and watch telly together. My daughter and I talk about this now. We talk about that period and she says, "Oh, gosh, I did go to Dave's a lot." I said, "You know what, Charlotte, we actually did a really healthy thing because we realized that if we were in each other's company, totally we were no good to each other. We had to have freedom to grieve independently. I think it was a really, really good thing that we did." We came together at times, and then other times, I would drive her from my house to her fiancé, we'd chat on the way, I'd drop her off, and then I would drive crying all the way home. But it gave me a release because I could cry, because I didn't have to worry about how she was feeling. She could cry with him or not, but we had that time separate and then we had some time together. I think if we'd been in each other's company all the time, it just wouldn't have given us that permission to do what we needed to do for ourselves. You feel like you have to put on a bit of a face for other people.

I did go and see David in the morgue. I don't know where it came from, but I actually thanked him for teaching me about loving unconditionally, because he really did. We used to have this discussion quite a lot when he was growing up where I would say, you shouldn't hang around with that one, you're going down the wrong path, and if you hang out with him it's going to end badly, and he'd say, "Mum don't be so judgemental. Don't judge people." I'd bristled a bit at that because I don't want to be judgemental; we would have this discussion quite a lot, really. It's like a theme because my mum would say walk a mile in someone's shoes, and I'm all for that, completely; it's something I massively believe in. But when it came to my son and keeping him safe, I'm really sorry, but there were people that I would say, "Please don't seek out their company."

I felt very deflated after the inquest. It felt all very unsatisfactory. I thought I'd done so much communicating with the assistant coroner beforehand. She'd been so good. Thoroughly answered my emails, listened to me. Set a train of investigation in motion. That made me think, "My gosh, we are going to learn a lot. We are going to find out a lot of these answers." She'd requested stuff from BT with regards to his phone. She was keen for this whole statement thing, for this guy to give an account. I felt really pleased she was being thorough, and then it got taken over by the senior coroner. It's like he squashed it, he wanted it just to be done. Almost like I was being a nuisance, he called me into his room actually just before the inquest. He seemed to be saying, let's park this here now because we don't want too much discussion going on about your son's drug use. But actually, the friend, who'd been with my son, actually went to town in terms of how much they'd used together, so that became a big feature.

None of it made sense. I just came away thinking, I really don't get this. I feel like I'm being reigned in. It wasn't a good feeling. The previous coroner had asked me to email to her all of my questions that I wanted to ask the driver. I put a load of questions in. Then at the final inquest, I'm pretty much getting told to ask these questions myself. I was in no emotional state to do so, and the coroner wasn't taking that into account.

When David's body was found, our local newspaper messaged my daughter on Facebook and wanted some information about whether it was him. I came to the conclusion that if they were going to put something in the paper, then I'd rather it'd be something warm and loving from his family than something that they were going to say. Looking back on it now, I can't remember what I said, I think it was probably clichéd rubbish. If I was to be asked again, I'd probably say something completely different, but I think I'm still grateful that it was loving family stuff rather than just a cold piece that told you nothing about him. There was some more publicity after the inquest. Again, looking back. I can't decide whether I was too honest in terms of talking about David's drug use, but equally, I didn't want to have anything about that made shameful.

There is no shame, it is what it is. I wouldn't want anybody to think that that's what his life was all about. It wasn't. Equally the fact that he did use drugs, I don't want that shame thing attached to it because at the end of the day, how are we going to have conversations as a society about these things if we don't talk about them? What if there is some other parent out there who thinks their kid is innocently doing drugs at the age of 17. I'm really sorry, this is where it really can go. Be concerned, be worried. Get help for them.

My level of tolerance for people changed. They were probably trying their best, but my God, my level of tolerance had disappeared. I ended a romantic relationship that had been going on for about seven years. I think the people that I've actually been comfortable having around me are the people who have a level of emotional intelligence, who are able to tolerate me getting angry or being quiet, or can just be in my space and the ones who've actually even asked me, "What can I do?" "How should I be?" People who have been brave enough to say, "I don't know what helps, tell me." Those people are worth their weight in gold. One of my friends, she's a social worker, she's said to me, "I felt awful at the start. I just backed off. I just didn't know what to do." I said, "Well, can I just tell you that there is nothing that you can say that's going to help me. If you ever just wanted to sit here quietly, and just be in my company, bring a book with you because I might not want to talk, but I do probably want somebody to be in my space." She's been okay with kind of listening to all that. I think she'd probably say she's learned quite a lot too.

I withdrew into myself and the person I used to be, went. I think that's a big loss there, the loss of me. I think I'm just starting to regain that a little bit. I'm not very good at asking for help or telling people how I'm feeling, and I think perhaps if I'd opened my mouth and said what I needed, things could have been different. But there's a part of me also that thought, my ex-partner should have known. He's got two children. It doesn't take that much to know that it would be devastating for another person.

My relationship with David's father has changed. I'd say actually as a family, we're all a lot closer. Actually, I think we can all empathize with one another. I think that's something that's made us more compassionate, more understanding. There's a bigger picture, isn't there? Life's too short. I think we're all quite kind with each other.

I loved David to bits, but there was so much of all that other stuff that was almost like a full-time job, every day worrying. Every day him phoning me and there would be a concern or whatever. It just leaves a massive chasm. I feel like a lot of my life purpose is gone, because I think I identified myself as being primarily a mum. Yes, I am still a mum, but my little brood is dwindled. I still have contact with Sadie and with their daughter. She comes to stay with me every fortnight. I have a good relationship with both of them.

I always feel really responsible. I feel like somehow, I should have known. I actually think partly this is why I went into social work. When he was in his teen years and he was getting into trouble and what have you, in the early days he got referred to the youth offending team, and I can remember a student social worker coming out. I was sitting watching her doing some work with him at the dinner table, probably about consequential thinking or something like that. I'd always had an interest in social work, and I was watching, and I thought, "That looks quite interesting." Then, I started talking to her, and she loaned me a book or two. I started reading some stuff.

Then I got made redundant after being a civil servant for 21 years. I got a good package which gave me enough money to go off and study. I went for an interview for the social work course and got on it. The first job I took as a practising social worker post qualifying was in the youth offending team. I was feeling like I was trying to unravel what was going on with David. Then I applied to be a childcare social worker. I went off to childcare, child protection, care proceedings, adoptions, stuff like that. Again, there was an element there of interest in what's going on dynamics wise. I suppose to latterly since he died, my interests moved more into mental health. I feel like I'm always trying to unpick the puzzle. To get more and more pieces.

Having some people who are willing to be with me helped me through the grieving process – they're worth their weight in gold. I knew how angry I was, this real dangerous anger was there, and I recognized that I could actually explode over all the wrong people. I got counselling pretty much straight away to deal with the anger, because I knew that it was so powerful that I couldn't think of anybody, in my close circle, that should have to tolerate that level of anger. I didn't think it was appropriate. The counselling helped enormously. I would just go there, vent, and he would just listen and sympathize, very helpful. Some friends who were able to listen to the hard stuff helped, and one even volunteered to walk around the roundabout with me in the dead of night just because she knew how much it mattered.

Family who did the nurturing were amazing; they made sure I was eating and took me out for food or just spent time in my company doing that. We did a lot of getting together and eating as a family. My daughter's worth her weight in gold too. When she come back that awful day, she came up to me, she grabbed my hands, looked me straight in the face, then went, "We'll get through it, we'll get through this mum. We'll get through it." I believed her. I did. She's great. I'm a naturally introverted person, so I don't go seeking out people and I don't reach out a great deal. I've always enjoyed my own company, watching films, solitary walks. I know that about myself. So, that has probably complicated for me how I did my grieving. Maybe it's also been quite cathartic. I have done a lot of my own thinking, and reading at times, looking through articles, reading an awful lot about grief.

I read a book, *It's Okay Not To Be Okay* by Megan Devine.[1] I really liked and can relate to that a lot. I like her take on grief. She reckons as a society we've got it all wrong, which is absolutely right, we have. The minute you bring in the death of a child, it can stop a conversation in a moment. Let's be honest, it can literally end the conversation; but actually I'm at the point now where, for example, I was sitting next to a colleague today he started talking about music, I start telling him about David's interest in music and he just asked me, "Are you happy to talk about him? You're okay to talk about him." I said, "Yes, thank you for asking, yes, that's fine. I want his name to be mentioned, so yes, please." It's taken me a hell of a long time to get to this point because for first three and a half years I didn't mentioned his name, but now I think, no, I actually do want him to be talked about. I'm really happy when friends bring him into conversation, it's important.

I attended church for many years. I've always had my faith, but I haven't always been a churchgoer. I've done church in various forms. When I was younger, I went to a Methodist church. When my daughter was younger, we went to an Anglican church, then because she was getting older and we wanted something a bit livelier, a bit more upbeat, we went to the Evangelical church. When David died, I couldn't bear the idea of going into a church and feeling emotional because the minute you start worshipping, you're praying or you're singing, I would feel the emotions so intensely that I thought, I'm actually going to collapse in a heap here. I just wanted to go in be left alone and then go. I didn't want to have conversation. When I think back, I was having conversations with some people and I felt like my heart was caving in, like I literally cannot cope with having this conversation.

I seemed to know very early on that my energy became depleted by certain people and certain conversations. I would almost physically recoil. I knew that I had to place myself somewhere else because it was too draining. I could feel what little energy I had left just because I have no tolerance for the insignificance of their bloody banal conversation, my sense was, "Seriously, we're standing here talking about this. Oh my God, I've got to get out of here." I couldn't cope with the people. That's no reflection on them; it's just where I was at. I have my belief. I hold strong to that because what I can say to myself is, none of this makes sense right now, but it will make sense one day. David is just absent from my physical sight, but that doesn't mean he doesn't exist. It is a case of until we do meet again, really, and we will meet again. That's what keeps me going.

I don't think that grief conforms to anything prescriptive, it really doesn't. It takes you on the most horrendous ride, and you could go through any range of emotions in a day. I wish I'd known sooner that being foggy-headed and absent minded is actually normal. Don't think you're losing it; you're not. You're actually experiencing, whether it's shock or trauma. It's actually normal to have a foggy head, and it will come back because I really thought I was losing it in that respect.

If I were to say anything to someone else, I'd also say that it will massively alter your ability to tolerate certain people and situations; be prepared for that. Preserve your energy. You've got a really small amount; don't give it out in the way that you previously did. If you were somebody that runs at every situation thinking you can help out, don't; it's important to just sit in the grief. You'll grieve for as long as you love that person, and that will be a lifetime. It will change, that fragility that's there does develop into something a little bit stronger over time. It dips in and out, but it starts getting that little bit stronger. Self-care is important, I now demand my own time, my own space. I don't conform to what other people want me to do. If I don't want to go somewhere, I won't go, because I'm not going to put myself in precarious positions. I'd also say don't be hard on yourself. Just don't be hard on yourself. As much as you can, be compassionate with other people, be compassionate with yourself. I struggled with being kind to myself. I still struggle with it, but I know it's really important.

I've started prioritizing my physical health a bit more too. I realized just over a year ago, from when David died until that point, I'd been so inactive. Again, through lack of energy, lack of motivation. I was pretty much glued to my sofa, I can tell you everything that was on Netflix, I watched it all. I had a conversation with a friend, she's really into her fitness, and she said, "I can't help thinking that if you became physically fitter and stronger, it might have a payoff." Like feeling physically strong can make you feel mentally strong. I was thinking about that, and then there were a couple of other things. I'd been on a walk with my sister and brother-in-law and I was huffing and puffing up a hill. I thought, "This is awful, I don't like it." I started little baby steps going out for a walk, then afterwards thinking, "My head feels a lot better for having done that." I then started getting a little bit competitive with myself with the number of steps I was doing and sort of went from doing just tiny little things, with that friend really constantly touching base with me, to getting that little bit more active. I really did start to see the payoff. I would make a point of walking up the mountain as well because the view at the top was great and I could see the coast. Then it was like, well, why don't I walk down to the coast. Then I was pushing myself a bit more and a bit more. Going from doing tiny little walks, to now I could go out and walk 20–30 kilometres on the weekend.

I do feel so much fitter, I'm so much better for it. When I get out there and I'm in the mountain and my head's clearer, I've got my perspective back a little bit. As long as I'm moving and I'm moving forward, I'm not stagnant. There's something really powerful about moving in the right direction.

Note

1 M. Devine (2017). *It's Ok That You're Not Ok: Meeting Grief and Loss in a Culture That Doesn't Understand.* Boulder, CO: Sounds True.

10 "Tell mum not to worry. I'm going to the pure land"

Susan's story remembering her son Michael

Michael was born in 1971; he was the middle of my three children. I have two daughters as well. He was rather a troubled child because he was dyslexic and when he was young, it wasn't really recognized. We eventually taught him to read when he was eight, but he never could write properly. He couldn't do maths either, so he didn't do very well at school and had all sorts of problems, ended up as a teenager with psychiatric problems, left home quite early, and got into drugs.

He had lots of problems as a young man. When he was about late 20s to 30, he was able to overcome that. He was in a relationship which meant a lot to him and was also a practising Buddhist. Despite all his ups and downs, I never lost touch with him. When that relationship ended, he had gone on to heroin again and was in a very bad way. He returned to live near me when he was 35. Once he came back here, he went on to methadone prescriptions under the guidance of the drug team. Things started to settle, and he got his own housing association flat. He did rely on me a lot for support. Over the three years, before he died, I think he started to enjoy life again.

He certainly felt very close to his family, was making a lot of progress emotionally, and was looking to apply for a college course. He had always been a huge fan of motorbikes and fast cars and in fact was a brilliant driver. He was going to an art group for people with mental health problems, and he met someone called Peter who became a friend. Peter was an absolutely mad motorcyclist, we found out later.

On the day Michael died, he had planned to go to a local park where his father had a memorial bench. He was going with Peter, and we thought he was going by car, but in fact, he went as a pillion passenger on Peter's motorcycle. In the morning, he'd been to a support group and apparently had them all laughing.

He had a great sense of humour, very good telling an anecdote. He came to my house for lunch and it was a lovely sunny June day, and I waved him off. His sister Louise was with him as they walked towards his flat and she said goodbye to him. The next thing I knew was that at half past three in the afternoon, I had a phone call from Peter's mother to say that they'd had an accident and that they were taking them to the local hospital. I was dreading the worst; I don't know why. I got in the car and drove to the hospital, went into A&E and they showed me into a room at the back of the reception called the family room, which I hadn't known existed. I then knew that it was very, very serious.

They brought me a cup of coffee and said, "Is there anybody who could be with you?" I phoned either my sister or Louise, one or the other; they were actually together, and they both came to the hospital. I asked, "Can I see him?" They said, "Oh no, we're doing stuff." I said, "Tell him I'm here." Every few minutes they came in and the story got worse and worse. Then I think it was about five o'clock, they said that he had died, they couldn't save him. He had a serious chest injury and had bled out, I think. They said, "We'll just get him ready and then you can come in and see him." We went in to see him and he looked asleep, but very pale. I passed out. When I came to, I said, "I've got to get home." I rushed out, Louise came with me. I got in my car and drove home, which I shouldn't have done. My sister, Denise, stayed because they wanted somebody to see the police when they arrived and do an official identification and all of that stuff.

She told the staff that Michael was a Buddhist. I think they got some Buddhist person to come to the hospital to do something, I don't know what. Somebody rang Julie, my other daughter, who lives in Spain. That was Wednesday afternoon, and Julie arrived on Friday.

Then the following few days are all a bit of a blur. We had a police liaison person. The first person was okay, and then he appointed somebody else and then we never heard anything. We complained and we got the first guy back again; the information we got, very patchy. They did give me something that was incredibly useful. There was a book for bereaved relatives of somebody that has died on the road and it was from some charity, but I now can't remember what the charity was called. It explained quite a lot about how you feel, because initially, I felt physically ill, and I think that's quite common. I hadn't expected to feel physically ill, so that was one of the most useful things they did, was to give me this booklet.

My sister was very keen that Peter should be prosecuted. Looking at the evidence later, I think he was definitely at fault because the front wheel of the motorcycle was five foot off the road and then it fell onto its side and skidded, and Peter fractured both his wrists. Michael hit a stone wall belonging to a house next to the road, and that was what killed him. The accident happened on a very, very nasty bend on a main road. The police said, "Could you please tell people not to put flowers on the bend?" I said, "I wouldn't do that anyway. I think it's a horrendous thing to do because they just end up dead, don't they?" Somebody's got to clean up piles of dead flowers.

I didn't want Peter to be prosecuted. I just wanted him never to ride a motorbike again. He had mental health problems and tried to commit suicide twice. On one occasion Julie went to see him in the hospital, and I wrote a letter to him to say, "Michael wouldn't have wanted you to be like this. He would want you to get on with your life." I don't know what has happened to him, I've never heard anything since. My sister was very, very angry with him, and she never let go of it. A year previously, she'd had an operation for breast cancer. Two years after Michael died, she died from secondaries, and I just wondered whether all that not letting go had had an impact. It was very hard. There were four people I was very close to, my sister and my three children, and in the space of two years, two died.

The inquest was delayed by 14 months because of Peter's suicide attempts. When the inquest was finally held, he went as a witness and said he couldn't remember anything. He was very sedated apparently. I didn't go. I had no interest in going. I don't think those sorts of things give people justice, really, or answers. I didn't feel it would be helpful to me. Something Louise said to me later hit home. She said, "Michael was an idiot as well. If he'd been on the front it could have been just the same if he'd been driving." She was right.

After the inquest there was an article in the local newspaper because Michael's father, who had died in 1989, had been a prominent local councillor. This was mentioned at the inquest, there was a reporter who sat in on inquests every day, they picked up on this fact. I didn't want Michael's name in any kind of publicity, but I didn't have a choice. Thankfully, it didn't really have much of an impact on me.

Afterwards, people were incredibly supportive, and I couldn't have got through it without friends and family who were brilliant, absolutely brilliant. Louise organized the funeral. Her husband managed to crack Michael's email and sent a message to everybody on his email list. Those people sent it on to other people. It spread around his friends and the New Kadampa Tradition (NKT) Buddhist community. They said special prayers in a lot of the Buddhist centres all around the UK and abroad for him. Even the guru, Geshe-la who is a Tibetan monk, said special prayers. He knew him, you see. A real mix of people came to the funeral which was the day before his birthday. From the elderly couple who lived next door to him to others who'd known him from the Buddhist days. Some who'd flown in from Europe, others had hitched lifts and had rucksacks and sleeping bags, and it was huge. People really made the effort to come. We didn't want them to wear black.

The majority of the funeral was done by a Buddhist nun in robes. I read a poem which was quite hard, but I wanted to do something. It was one I'd found that was very touching, very appropriate. Louise managed to persuade a café in a country park, that he liked going to, to do the funeral tea, although they didn't normally do that. They closed this café and did this funeral tea. There were all these people there. It was quite a strain because I felt I had got to go around and talk to everybody.

I'd never been to a Buddhist funeral before or since. I didn't know what a Buddhist funeral was. I'd been with Michael to some Buddhist services and things, but I'm not religious myself at all. But I had a very strange experience the day after Julie arrived; she's a Buddhist as well. On the Saturday morning, I got up and I said to Julie, "What's the pure land?" She said, "Why are you asking?" I said, "Well, I've just had a message, 'Tell mum not to worry. I'm going to the pure land.'" That was the message that came to me, in my head. Apparently, it's Nirvana. It's where you go when you don't need a body anymore through these various lives. I still can't explain it.

It was about three years before I could have his picture up in the room, because it was too painful every single day. Which is the really difficult thing about losing your child. It's every day, and I think it must be every day forever, but it doesn't feel quite as painful as it did.

I happened to know somebody who had lost a son and ran a Compassionate Friends group. Somebody obviously had told them what had happened, and they wrote to me. They were lovely people, really lovely, but where they live is a really long way to go for a support group. I'd heard that there was one locally and I'd gone to one meeting of that, about a year after Michael died. There were probably seven or eight women. They obviously knew each other very well and they'd been going for a long time. Their most recent death was seven years before, and the longest one was I think something like 15 years before. I came away thinking that isn't how I want to be. The fact that they were almost, "I'm a mother whose child has died," as a kind of raison d'être. I can understand it in a way, if it was an only child. I think that must be so much more difficult, but also, I thought, well, I was never just a mother. That's not for me to sit talking about that and not moving on. They seemed very stuck, and they were keeping each other stuck. Now, that probably isn't how these groups are run in other places, because it depends on the personalities involved; that one later fizzled out. I had hoped it would be people learning from each other how to carry on living with their loss, really. How to find the resilience that they have within themselves somewhere.

When Michael died, I was about to start with a bereavement support group at a local hospice as a volunteer. I'd done the training, but then I couldn't do it because you have to wait two years since your last bereavement. Then by the end of the two years, Denise died as well in that same hospice. It wasn't until four years after Michael died, that I started doing that. I didn't actually work with anybody who had lost a child, but with other people had lost someone significant for them. But I did find that you could find ways of living around the loss.

There was one woman who had lost her mother. She had a husband, children, and a job too. Her mother had been her best friend and had been involved in all areas in her life. She said, "People keep saying, this will eventually get better, but it's this big hole." I said, "Well, let's look at what the hole consists of," and that's what we did. I said, "there's going to be a little bit in the middle that's never going to go away. Some of these other aspects, like the things you did with your mum, can perhaps be done in a different way. To sort of fill in some of that void." She was able to do that very successfully. I worked with her for about a year. It really worked for her. She didn't want to hear that there won't be a hole in the future, because that wasn't right. There was going to be a hole.

All my life I have suffered from depression, but I could live with it. I've managed to have a career, but after Michael died it got much worse. For the last eight years I've been seeing a psychiatrist. I never saw a psychiatrist before; I was just getting some tablets from the GP. I suppose when the depression gets worse or things go wrong, that it feels harder and my hole gets bigger. I have thought of ending my own life, but I don't because I've got two daughters and four grandchildren. Sometimes I don't for me too. I suppose having always suffered from depression, I do know that it will get better. But it never gets as better as it used to. I used to be kind of normal, at least part of the time. Now, that isn't the case. The new normal is a lot more difficult. I do try to keep busy. When I'm not feeling too depressed, I've got lots of plans and things I like doing. I don't think it helped that my marriage had ended, and I'd been forced to retire only a few months before Michael died; that didn't help at all.

I've got some friends called Jane and Terry, who I've known since before either of us had children. They arrived the following morning. My sister had rung them and said, "She doesn't want to see people." Jane walked in with a carrier bag with stuff to make sandwiches and milk. She said, "I've known her for 40 years, so I'm not staying away." With my two daughters, I think I couldn't have coped without them. They actually cleared Michael's flat. We were given a week to clear it by the housing association. That felt brutal.

Another friend called Jean was running backwards and forwards picking up Julie from the airport and things like that. I don't know what else people did because a lot of it was a blur. Louise was amazing. I mean obviously, she's got the loss just the same. I think the other thing was that they didn't let me be on my own for a while. I can't remember who was there. That was just right for me. I got a lot of letters, emails, and cards. The GP sent one which I thought was very nice. I felt able to put them up; in fact, I've still got them. I said to Louise the other week, "I don't think I need these cards anymore." She said she didn't want me to throw them away. She wanted me to keep them. For a long time, I kept the reports that had gone to the inquest, the police report on the accident, but I threw those away quite a while ago.

The other thing that's happened that's been very difficult is, following Michael's death, I put on three stone in six months by binge eating. I've not been able to overcome that. I think it's now actually become a sugar addiction. There's been some talk about that recently, about how addictive sugar is. I now see it as a sugar addiction. But no doubt, other people have turned to drugs and alcohol and all sorts of things.

The effect on my body has got worse and worse over the years. I now have diabetes, high blood pressure and all sorts of problems health wise. I did try quite hard to overcome it. Five years or so ago I went to a health retreat in Spain because I got some compensation after the accident. I used quite a lot of that money to try to solve the problem. I think it probably delayed me going on to medication, but I'm now on medication for the diabetes. I haven't given up yet, but I'm not finding it easy. Because my marriage had ended, I had a problem with loneliness, Michael used to come over every day, and we were very close. So, it was a double whammy, really, in that sense. Which is one of the reasons that Louise and I moved in together; she lives upstairs and I live downstairs. It's a bit of a solution to it, but of course, Louise's very busy. She's got her own life, and she can't be company for me.

When you're depressed, it's very difficult to motivate yourself to do things. Over the years, I've tried counselling. I've had various experiences of counselling. There was one counsellor I saw, after a nine-month NHS waiting list; during the first interview I was talking about things and she kept forgetting Michael's name, and I never went back. That's fundamental, isn't it, remembering someone's name? I don't know if she was just inattentive or whatever was going on for her. When I was working, I would put that to one side and concentrate on the person. So, that didn't work. The one I went to at the hospice was very young, had very young children, she didn't seem to get on to my wavelength. It's very tricky, isn't it? You've got to have the rapport. I think you need somebody who's been around the block a few times. I don't necessarily mean having had the same experience, but I do think they have to have had children to understand this. I remember after Michael died and I couldn't do the bereavement counselling, I went to work in the hospice charity shop instead. I told the manager what had happened, I said, "I don't want you to tell the other volunteers." She said, "Oh, I know just how you feel. I lost my dad from cancer." No, it's not the same. Cancer's not the same. You've got a little warning, haven't you?

My sister and I were very close. She died six years ago from cancer. I was with her when she died, and I don't think about her every day. She's what I call a normal bereavement. It's now and again and something will trigger it off. We used to go clothes shopping together. I go on my own now, and I might be reminded of something she did or said. It might be something she did that was funny, that Louise and I might be laughing about. I did the eulogy at her funeral, and I got three laughs at the end of the eulogy. It was hard to do, but it was the last thing I could do for her. But that's normal bereavement, isn't it? It isn't every day. Actually, my mother died when I was 18. She was only 47 when she died. I've had a lot of bereavement. My mum, Michael, my sister, and my ex-husband.

Going back to Michael, I'd love to ask him "Why did you get on the back of that bloody motorbike?" He'd probably say, "I thought it'd be fun." He was fun loving and mischievous. He was very kind too. He had a very warm personality and was very funny.

I mentioned earlier that he had problems at school, and he was dyslexic. He was one of those young people that was then stereotyped as being a bad boy. I think that contributed to his mental health problems later. His father died of cirrhosis of the liver, and his cousin has died of it too. I've often wondered whether there was some brain chemistry thing going on for Michael so that other things got triggered.

I don't have any religious beliefs, and I think the jury's out on any spiritual beliefs. Partly because of the message I got that I mentioned earlier, but I also had another interesting experience some years ago. I was with a party of people on a canal boat. I was sitting on the top with some people and there was a guy steering it from the back. It was a singles group; we'd all been drinking. Inside there was a guy serving drinks and another guy doing a pop music quiz. There was a woman sitting in the half-open doorway of it, looking at what's going on.

We started to go through a really narrow bit with rock on both sides. She must have been hit by a rock and fell into the boat. A friend of mine said, "Mary's hurt," and she was going to go downstairs. I said, "There's no point, she's dead." She said, "What do you mean?" I said, "Something's just left the boat." I didn't see anything or hear anything. I just had a sensation that something left, and she was dead. It had fractured her rib and it had pierced her lung.

I think with Michael I had that sense really driving to the hospital that he was about to go. I was really very upset driving to the hospital. Yet, what they said on the phone was that they were going to the hospital in the ambulance. It could have been a broken arm, couldn't it? I wasn't told anything serious. So, the jury's out on any spiritual beliefs, but the existence of a god just beggars belief. It's just a ludicrous idea to my mind. I mean, if Michael's somewhere nice, well, nice for him, but I've got the loss. It's a selfish thing, isn't it? I miss him, and I wish he was here. If somebody's suffering, like when my sister died of cancer, it's not quite the same. Because you don't want them to suffer, just to be here for you. Bereavement is a selfish thing, really.

I wish I'd known more about what to expect after Michael died, how to deal with it and what the future would hold. Some of the things about the physical impact that the booklet from the charity told me, were very helpful. I think one of the things I'd hoped to get from that group, was little tips on how to live, how to cope. What sort of things have helped other people. I think nature's very good. That certainly helps me. Gardening is good. For some people, music. There was a rather sentimental song by Josh Groban, that I think he wrote, or somebody wrote, and it was something to do with the 9/11 people. I think they must have had a ceremony where they built the memorial and he sang this. Something about, to be where you are. I found that quite helpful, although Louise said, "Michael would have hated that song, it's so treacly." But it helps me. You have to find a purpose, don't you, and that's quite difficult, because everything's changed. Even if you had a purpose beforehand, when you lose a child, it's a 90-degree turn. A completely different direction and you don't where it's going to go. I've got a new counsellor now, that I've been going to for about 18 months, who is very, very good. So, I'm making some progress.

11 "What more could we have done?"
Wilf and Kath's story remembering their son Michael

Throughout this chapter, Kath's words are in normal font, her husband Wilf's are in italics.

Michael was lovely. He was a much-wanted baby after we'd had Keely and Jay. Keely was eight and Jay was five when Michael was born. He was a really good baby and lovely little boy, and he was outgoing when he was younger.

He played with all the children in the street. He didn't have any shy, retiring qualities, I would have thought. He was normal.

He was a very sensitive little boy. Clever too, he passed the 11 plus and went to grammar school, but he was a bit out of his depth really at grammar school. He didn't like it there, there were probably other issues as well. He always did well at primary, but he fell out with all his classmates.

Well, something happened; we don't know what it was, really. We didn't actually know at the time. It wasn't until much later when he was adult, really, that we found out that all his friends had sent him to Coventry and didn't speak to him for quite a long time. It really hit him badly as a little boy of, I think he would be nine or ten. The teacher intervened in the end and she put a stop to it, but it was too late by then. The damage had been done to his confidence. Anyway, he did well, and he got to grammar school. He didn't want to stay on to do his A Levels. So, he started working at a nearby university in the biology department, and he was okay there. Then he went to day school and got some qualifications to go to University.

While he was at the biology department, he worked with two older men that had been there for years, and they were really kind to him; they got on well with him too. Unfortunately, one of them, cut a long story short, hung himself.

He was working with Michael in the morning and he more or less said to Michael, who at that time was only about 20, that he wasn't feeling good and he was going home. He went home at lunchtime and hung himself. That had quite a big impact on Michael because he felt really guilty that he hadn't supported him more. But as a young man I don't suppose he knew how to support somebody that was depressed. Nobody did.

Michael got married to Charlotte; they'd been together since they were 15. They got married but it didn't work out, and Michael went to Australia. He was using drugs, he started off using cannabis. It was his use of drugs that contributed to the end of his marriage. Marriage didn't fit in with his new lifestyle choice.

Charlotte, his wife, was absolutely lovely. She was like a daughter because her mum and dad had split up and she used to spend a lot of time at our house. But her dad was a drug user and he was also a teacher at the grammar school where Michael was. He allowed some of the boys to go back to his house and smoke. He was a drug dealer really, and he died of drug use.

We didn't know all this till much later. Charlotte wasn't happy with Michael's lifestyle. So, Michael decided that he would up sticks and go to Australia for a year. Charlotte went out to join him for three months. She went to try and patch things up, but it didn't work out.

So, she came back and Michael stayed in Australia for a short while and then he came home. I don't think he had a very happy time out there; he was homesick. He came back and then he went to Leeds Uni and started a degree in dietetics. He was very interested in nutrition and keeping fit. When he was well, he really was into it. He was a really good-looking lad; he had a good physique, and he was proud of that. It was one of the things I suppose that helped him, because by this time looking back, he was starting to fade away, shall we say, losing grip on being able to maintain a healthy lifestyle. His mental health problems had kicked in by then. We don't know which came first, the mental health problems or whether the mental health problems were caused by drug use. He was using cannabis at 15 and ecstasy; he used to go to raves in Leeds and Manchester.

Jay, our elder son who is now 52, is a heroin addict, but he functions well, he's got a job, and he's got two children. He has really good periods working his butt off to be okay, and succeeded to a certain degree, but he was a big influence on his younger brother. Michael looked up to Jay, and he wanted to please him. We don't know whether Jay had any influence on Michael's early drug use. I think it did. That is a big issue for me and my relationship with Jay.

Michael came back and started his degree. He had to defer for a year, in his third year, because he had a breakdown. He was in a very toxic relationship with a woman that was about eight years older than him. She was married with two children. She was very, very controlling.

She didn't like me, and she didn't like mine and Michael's relationship. She did try to help him, but she wanted to control him. She wanted him to herself and it didn't matter what he did as long as she could have him to herself. Well, Michael just could not cope with that. It was a really bad time. We were back and forth trying to help him.

This was after he got a 2:1 at Uni. He got this job with NHS and was setting up cooperatives with single mums, showing them how to live healthily on a low income. He was trying to help them to cope, but it turned out he couldn't cope with himself. I don't think he was using then, but he was drinking a lot.

He went into rehab for a year. He had a lovely, lovely girlfriend then. She absolutely loved him. We thought he'd cracked it. He was living with his girlfriend at her grandma's, his girlfriend had got him a job with her uncle. He was really keen on swimming in those days, and he had this Land Rover that was full of equipment to do his job. He went to clean a pool and when he came out, the Land Rover had gone. It had been stolen. You can imagine the guy who was his boss wasn't happy about that. I think that culminated in him leaving or getting sacked.

After he split up with his girlfriend, Jay said to him, "If you can't function using alcohol, have some of this." That's when he got on heroin. That was the beginning of the end, really. All the time it was the drugs drawing him back. Getting in the way of everything.

Then it got really bad and he was sectioned into a psychiatric hospital twice. It was an absolute mess, that place. Absolutely terrible. He was sectioned and shared a little tiny room with a curtain in between him and another lad. He tried to kill himself.

We had to bring him home. The psychiatrist said, "You take him home. You can look after him better than we can." So, then we had the Crisis Team coming in here every day to see Michael. We couldn't leave him. We were on 24/7 watch with him. We never knew on a morning whether he was alive or dead. Whether he'd tried to kill himself during the night, or anything.

Then Michael moved to a flat which Jay had. Jay moved out because he got a girlfriend. It was a terrible place. It was right draughty and all the rest of it. Anyway, Jay moved out to live with this woman and Michael moved into this flat. We were backwards and forwards. I mean at one point, we were walking through the local town doing something, and we saw this big piece of wood. It was a skirting board about eight inches deep. I said, "Oh, that look –" because Michael wanted some shelves. These are just the side issues. But we carried this piece of wood back to his flat and put it up. All this was about trying to help Michael, which when we look back, we think, how feeble was that really, but you grasp at anything, don't you? We were grasping at anything to try to make him feel good and help him and all the rest of it. Then he left there because I think he'd fallen out with some bad people there, and he couldn't wait to get away. I went over there. At that point, we had a little camping trailer and I went over there. We filled the trailer up with everything he had and brought it back here.

So again, he was living here, but it was awful. I mean one day I was here, and Michael was still in bed. It got to 11 o'clock, got to 12 o'clock, got to one o'clock. In the end, I went upstairs, and I had a word with him and he got real stroppy, and "I'll go I'll f-off then" and all this. I think he was on the point of hitting me, but he, even in his bad state, he just had too much respect for his parents.

The thing was, when he was here, it was really hard to cope with him. It was awful. Every time he came in, I knew, I could tell as soon as he came in if he'd used, or he'd been drinking or whatever, and then that would cause problems. I could tell if he'd been on amphetamines, he would be as high as a kite and he would just deny anything you said to him.

I couldn't see what Kath could see, I wanted to believe that everything was okay, I suppose I always believed that things would be alright.

But I knew they wouldn't because I knew there was no going back for Michael.

Then, the year before he died, he got a spiral fracture in his leg. The thing was, he had his leg in plaster from thigh to ankle and he lived in a first-floor flat, so he couldn't go upstairs, so he had to come here. Of course, he couldn't get access to any drugs. He was on a script for methadone. That was another thing we had to sort out because he was on a daily pick-up because of his chaotic lifestyle. He'd got off his daily pick-up prior to his leg being broken and then, he was back on. So, when he first came here, we were having to pick up daily for him.

He was with us for nearly five months. We thought, he's doing right well with the help of the fact that he was incapacitated with his broken leg, we thought he'd done right well. Anyway, after five months, he went back to his flat and that's when things really hit rock-bottom.

He was using more than heroin. At one point, it was Jay, Michael, and his girlfriend all living in this one-roomed flat. There was no chance of anything good coming out of it. I went around there, and we bought a television to go up on wall. It seems pretty stupid but, I thought, "If we can make it somewhat, I don't know, comfortable, or what have you. With them all living there, they might work it out." How stupid. Jay had to sleep on the floor. It was complete chaos. I was unable to do anything other than practical things to try to find some good in all that.

That caused some conflict between us too. We both wanted to be there to support Michael and Jay, but I could see that there was no coming out of it. Wilf always had this hope. He was giving them money and I kept saying, "No, don't give them money."

I was convinced that, I suppose, where there's life, there's hope, but I've realized that, with drugs, it's not the case.

Thing is, it's up to them. It's up to the person to help themselves.

But you do hear about people coming out of drug addiction. So, I suppose I thought, "That could be our lads, you know." In the end it dawned on me that it never was going to happen, that Michael would get better. To be quite honest I felt that death would be a release. It would be a release for all of us.

We wanted him to die. That is a horrible thing to have to say about your son, but when it happened, we wanted him back.

We did, but Kath, it did take a massive weight off us, love. It's devastating, of course. It was devastating.

We were getting to a point where we were thinking about turning our back on him. We'd had it for 30-odd years. We're both in our 70s. It was just hopeless, and we just felt helpless.

But then when we knew there was no chance. I did say more than once, after I'd come to the realization that there was nothing to be done, that I knew he was going to die. I just thought that will be a blessing. It would certainly be a blessing to me.

It was a relief. It was in the end. Living with his loss now, it's awful. Living with it. We talk about him all the time. We say, "What more could we have done?" Should we have kept him prisoner here?

No. What bugs me is I wish that I could have seen all this coming years and years and years ago, long before things started to go wrong, because I believe that parents are the most important thing in a kid's life. I can't help feeling that I could have probably rescued Michael years ago. And Jay, but I was always at work, working overtime. When I came home, I was tired and short and impatient. I do believe that it's the parents' fault, really, these things.

We definitely feel to blame, anyway. That's hard to live with. Well, like Wilf said, he worked 12-hour days and we had a good standard of living, the children never wanted for anything. I was there, but you see, I don't know whether there was a bit of a divide between us, in our parenting, how we parented. Wilf was quite strict; I was the softer one. When they were with me, they got away with things, and then obviously when Wilf was there, it all had to be done properly, which caused conflict between us – I felt, anyway. Children pick up on that, don't they?

I had Keely when I was 19, and I didn't know a thing about babies. All I knew was what the midwife told me, which was keep them to a routine, don't feed before the four hours is up, swaddle them and put them down to sleep after the feed. I was watching a programme on the TV the other day and mothers were talking to their unborn babies in their tummy. It broke my heart to think that if I'd have known all that when I was 19, I don't know how things might have been different.

Jay told me this later, that when Michael was born, he thought we didn't love him anymore because we'd had another baby. Obviously, because Michael was so wanted, I lavished a lot of love and attention on him, that I do feel I maybe didn't give as much to Keely and Jay. He was just such a lovely little boy.

It's one of those things, we can always look back and think, oh, I wish I had done this differently, or maybe I shouldn't have done that. Unfortunately, it doesn't bring them back, it doesn't change what happened. If anything, it's more painful, you're torturing yourself all the time. The pain is a double-edged sword, really, because on the one hand, we've no stress now. We haven't got to see Michael in states which were horrible, but we haven't got him either. So, there's the guilt of feeling relief that he's not here, but the heartache that he's not here to see all these lovely family events that are happening now, marriages, grandchildren getting married. I don't know if we'll ever see an end to the guilt.

I don't think you can assuage that guilt. I don't think it's possible. Why should it be possible? You've got to live with these things. Some people lose their limbs and have to live with it. Get through it as best they can, and that applies to me. I've got a lovely family. I can have plenty of moments that don't include feeling bad or anything. It's just part and parcel of someone's life. It's as simple as that. Some say time heals all wounds. I would have said, "Yes" at one time to that, but – not anymore.

Not when you lose a child.

So, I think I was very immature when I look back, very immature. It's a terrible thing to say, but I was more often than not focussed on myself, you know. It wasn't really until I got into my late 40s that the scales began to fall from my eyes, and I began to see what an awful – I'll admit, I'm a good grandfather, but I was a pretty poor bloody father. But, at the time, I never realized, you know.

I know I was busy bringing in the money and working hard, but there was still time to be a decent father, to have understanding. I had no understanding of my kids' needs, really, or anything. Their emotional needs and stuff like that. When you think, it's so simple, really. But I just didn't have that capacity, that ability. Being able to see it now, that's terrible. Too late, of course. I can try to make up for it being a decent family man now, which I am aware of doing or trying to do. I can't see me being able to forgive myself, and I can't see what good it would do. In spite of what I've said, I still have a good life that doesn't involve self-pity and torture. We go dancing, and I can enjoy that. I paint and enjoy that. As I said, it's all part of the jigsaw of life, isn't it? I think I make up for it, or try to make up for it, by being a good grandfather. I don't think I lay it on anybody else. Sometimes Kath gets a bit fed up with me, but I try not to be that person who wallows in my grief. I simply think that you've just got to get on with it – it's as simple as that, really.

We've had some really good support, from family and from friends as well. We have some friends that go dancing, and their son took his own life, so they've been really supportive. Then we have other friends that know. We have had other people that avoided us. They don't know what to say, which can be hurtful, but that is their problem. We talk about Michael all the time. My biggest thing is the guilt that I feel relief. I do. I just wish it could have been right. He did have a nice life in short bursts.

We decided not to go to the inquest. I said right from the word go I wasn't going. I felt that Michael had that life, different to his life with us. To be quite honest, I did not want to know about that life. Anyway, the outcome of the inquest was that Michael died from an overdose, it was an open verdict.

But what we were concerned about was that it would get in the paper.

We asked for no publicity, and the coroner said, "Well, we cannot guarantee that." She then said because it was the first one of the morning, and they were so short-staffed at the local press office, that they probably wouldn't send anybody at that time on a morning.

Jay saw Michael a day before he died. He said, "Dad, mum, I've never seen anyone look so awful." He said Michael could hardly walk because he had an abscess in his groin. He'd locked himself out of his flat. Jay met him at his flat and they tried to get in, but they couldn't. It was a bank holiday weekend and flat owner's offices were closed. Jay said he just had to walk away from him. He said, "I can't be with you Michael, it's too dangerous for me to be with you. So, Michael went to his girlfriends. That was two miles away. He walked over there in the state he was in. He just said to her, "I'm really cold, I need to get in bed and have a sleep."

He went to bed, and that was about teatime. Then she went to bed later on. She said he was still awake then. Then she woke up the following day to go to the toilet, then she got back into bed again because she'd been using. She said to us that there was a funny smell, but she thought it was just the state of the flat or whatever. She got back into bed and she didn't wake up again until the following day. That was when she realized he was dead and called the ambulance and the police.

The policeman asked Michael's girlfriend, "Why did you have the electric blanket on?" She said, "Michael was cold, and he wanted to get into a warm bed." He could have died in a back alley; he could have died anywhere. He could have been beaten up in the street. That is one thing that we're thankful for is that he was with his girlfriend in a warm place, and she said that he said to her, "I love you, come and lay with me." She just laid on top of the bed with him and he went to sleep, and he didn't wake up.

The police told us a lot, really it was too much information. I said I wanted to see Michael, but he said, "No you don't, he's started to decompose."

So, we didn't see him anymore. We saw his coffin at the funeral place. Really, talk about mixed emotions, you've no idea.

The funeral director said, "We'll make him look nice." We gave some of his really nice clothes to put on. We put some things in the coffin. I got a lock of his hair and his fingerprint. I asked the doctor, "Would he have been in any pain?" The doctor said, "No, it's actually quite a nice way to go."

Which was a consolation of sorts, of course.

That's the only consolation, really, I've got anyway.

Since Michael died, life is still a bit up and down for us. I was quite bad last week. I cleared out the stuff in the garage. We got rid of lots of it, but occasionally sometimes I will come across something that will just poke your emotions. It's awful for us when we see a young couple walking along, a nice young girl and a nice young bloke. That can really stab you.

Michael built a couple of bikes, and Wilf helped him. Then they'd go cycling together. This is all the things that he feels that he's missed out on, or we've missed out on.

I'm getting worse and worse with the loss. I have difficulty watching men, fathers with their kids, or mothers with their kids. I find that really terrible to watch.

We do have some really happy memories with him. One year he did the Great North Swim at Lake Windermere. He did that and when he came out the look on his face, he was absolutely elated.

He looked lovely. He had a wetsuit on, and he had a magnificent physique. But he couldn't build on that.

We told him time and time again how wonderful he was, and what a lot he had to offer. We always said, "You have so much to offer, Michael."

Something that I could never understand was how anybody could let drugs into their life to that extent.

Well, I think it was simply that he had so much pain and mental ill-health. He was diagnosed with bipolar and with borderline personality disorders. So, there is all that conflict, that pulling apart and self-medicating to get out of that pain in his head. He said to me, "That is the only time I get any peace, when I'm asleep or high." That is heart-breaking.

I used to run a support group for parents and partners of drug and alcohol abusers, and the number of couples that came that had split up because one wanted to support and the other one didn't. That's the thing with Wilf and I, we've always been of the same mind, of wanting to support.

That's one thing that has certainly supported us or given us comfort is that we never turned our back on him. As a couple, we never turned our back on him.

We've had some good support from friends. Not all of them know the whole story. We haven't told everybody about Michael's drug problem because, I think with people being people, they will say, "Well, it was his own fault." What we have said is that he had mental health problems, which he did have, that's not a lie, and I would say 95% of that was part of it.

I'm afraid Michael did have a lot of these massive mental health problems. A lot of people will see Michael as just a drug addict. I know there are some terrible, bad, awful people. Michael was never one of them. He never robbed anybody or did any bad things towards anybody or anything.

He never robbed us or abused us. There were a couple of times when he was really bad that he was aggressive towards Wilf. He never asked for money, really. These homeless people we see, it is heart-breaking to see them because Michael could have ended up like that if we hadn't been here.

That's one good thing it has done for us, I suppose. A friend of ours whose son hung himself, they'd thrown him out, turned their back on him. So, that's something else they've got to live with. We feel bad enough and I'm grateful we don't have that added pain to deal with.

Having each other and the family support has really helped.

Without a doubt, Keely has been a massive support, she's kept things together a lot of the time in a way. She really has. She's so brilliant and she's got a lovely family and we are part of that lovely family, of course. We wouldn't want to destroy or make anybody unhappy. Having a family around you like we have is all I need. I've never gone to any of these support groups, and I wouldn't start going now. Certainly because, as I said, there's no need for me to go. We've got a lovely family around us.

I did get in touch with a local charity that's for parents whose children have overdosed. I was invited to go to one of the support groups. I was going to go. Then I thought about it and thought, "Do I want to sit in a group and listen to everybody else's sad stories? I've got enough sad story of my own." Because it was a support group, it wasn't a one to one, and so I didn't go. I did think in the early days that I might have some bereavement counselling. But I think having each other as much as anything has been helpful, because we cry together, we remember together.

Our family are great, they understand. They're not critical, they don't condemn anybody, they come around, the grandchildren come around. They're all grown up, all the grandchildren.

We don't talk about Michael. He might come into the conversation very, very occasionally. The very fact that they're just such nice people is what helps me, they accept us as we are. I'm just grateful that that's how it is, that they are such nice people.

When it first happened, I was a member of quite a few different classes. I couldn't go back to any of them at all. I didn't want to see anybody that knew my situation, that we'd lost our son. They didn't know the circumstances, people in my classes. I would tell the person that ran the class, "I won't be coming back, our son has died." I didn't want to go anywhere where people would come up to me and say, "I'm sorry" or whatever. We never went dancing, for about three, or four months.

But then I joined a class where I didn't know anybody at all, and I went there about three or four times a week. I had to be out of the house all the time; being at home I could just 'see' Michael sat in that chair all the time. That's where he was for five months when he broke his leg. So, I had to stay out and keep busy. That helped me through about the first six or eight months.

We go walking, and last week we went to one of our favourite places where we used to go with Michael. We'd have a coffee and then walk around the lovely gardens. Michael loved gardens. He was into bonsai and loved all that sort of stuff. He had so much talent.

We went there and had a walk; it was quite sad because we have a photograph of him on a little bridge, and we remembered that. There's another place where we used to take him. We used to go there and have a coffee and a picnic. We haven't been there since, yet though. It was sad, but we did it.

You cannot just blank someone out of your life, can you? Certainly not your son. It's not possible, and you wouldn't want to.

Another thing which some might think strange is we've still got his ashes here. Well, I can't let them go at the moment.

No, that's right. We can't bear to think of him in some lonely wind-swept place, really.

But when it was his birthday, we went to a picnic area that we used to go to when they were little, where Wilf was brought up in a little village, and we planted a wild primrose. We have wild primroses in the garden, and we took one out and planted it.

We're going to have that as somewhere to go on his birthday. We're not going to go on the anniversary of his death, just on his birthday.

I was forgetting about that.

Everything seems such a long time ago to me. In some ways, such a long time ago, and yet in other ways it feels like he's still here. I was thinking about something when we went for a week for Wilf's birthday in September, and I can remember thinking, "Will Michael be all right for a week while we're away."

Although I didn't really want to talk with others, what I would have found helpful would have been reading other people's stories and how they coped with it. How their experience affected them, and how they managed to move on. What I would say, about moving on, is just do it a day at a time. That's what we've done. The day we went on that walk was another milestone for us because we visited where we used to take Michael. It was painful, but we did it. Next time, we'll go to somewhere else where we went a lot and picnicked. It's just those little milestones that you're moving on. Another Christmas without him. When our grandson got married, that was quite sad when he said his speech and raised a glass to absent family.

A book like this needs to be read, really, by young people, I think. It's too late when it's – too late. I'd want them to understand the potential impact of the decisions they may make, especially about taking drugs.

12 "Her horror penetrated me"
John's story remembering his brother Jamie

Jamie was my younger brother. When he died, I was eight and a half years old and Jamie was ten months old. I had an older sister Theresa, 14, and a younger brother, Richard, 5. I'm 57 now, so I don't particularly have a lot of memories of Jamie – I suppose because his life was so short. This isn't something I particularly have ever thought about in adulthood, about other memories of him. I'm not really sure that I've actually got any memories of him in terms of playing with him, him being in the house or part of the family, and yet I suppose he is still part of the family. Sometimes he will crop up in conversation, particularly between my sister and I. He hasn't physically been with us for a long time, but I'm aware that in some ways he has been. I've never thought about him in that way.

He's not a topic of conversation all the time. Equally, it's not a taboo subject. My sister and I will talk quite openly about him. I think typically we talk about what happened, our experience of it, almost the craziness of it, and what it was like for us and how we experienced our parents. I think that's probably more about what we would talk about. Rather than talk about him and things he might have done. Though I'm sure if I were to ask my sister, I'm quite certain that she would have more memories of him as a baby than I did. Interestingly, I'm also aware how memory is fallible and incorrect sometimes, because when I asked her something, checking about ages, and said, "I want to ask you about Jamie's death," and she said, "Oh it was Rick that found him" I said it – "No, no, no, no, it wasn't, it was me." She said "No, it was Rick," I said "No, I'm absolutely, absolutely certain. I can remember it because I could remember his colour." She wasn't aware of that, and she said, "What do you mean about his colour?" I said, "What I've subsequently learned through all of the bodies I dealt with, as a police officer, that depending on various things it's like blood, everything settles in the body, so you get a reddening." That's one of the things I noticed. That memory stayed with me for a long time about the colour of him.

My mother and father always had a chaotic relationship that I really became much more aware of later in life. We're talking of 1970 – my father would have been reasonably successful in his work in commercial construction, my mum being busy as a housewife as well as her somewhat dysfunctional relationship with my father. At eight and a half, my memories of that is always fighting and squabbling with Richard. Always, always fighting and squabbling, and we were just like that. I suppose it would have been a little later, about the time of me wanting to tag along with my sister and her boyfriend or being sent along by my mum. I guess that was to make sure that nothing untoward was going on. I think sometimes like many people, if you ask about childhood, they say, "Oh, my family life was quite okay and quite happy then." I know through a lot of the personal work I've done, there's also another aspect to that. That's my recollection of how it was in the family.

I'm fairly certain it was the weekend when Jamie died. In our house – it was a detached chalet-style house – downstairs there was a lounge next to the reception room. With the birth of Jamie, I think that became my sister's bedroom. There were three bedrooms upstairs – two bigger ones and a small bedroom. The small bedroom was Jamie's bedroom. I remember there was a cot in there. It must have been a Sunday, because my father went to work the next day. Mum would have said to me something like, "Wake your brother up," so I had gone in to wake him up.

My memory as I pay attention to it, I noticed there was something about his colour and I couldn't wake him up. I shouted out and said something to my mum about I can't wake Jamie up, and my sister vividly remembers it, just the chilling scream from my mother. That's what's really lodged with me. In that moment, there was something about the horror of it. My mother just knew. There was something about her, the only way I can make sense of is that her horror penetrated me and lodged. Yes, there was something about Jamie's colour, but that's a hazy memory.

What really has absolutely stuck with me is the horror of it. There was a lot of what happened, and there was a lot of screaming and chaos, really, and my mother being hysterical. I think my mother was also prone to being histrionic anyway, but that's a side issue; she was being hysterical. I remember sometime later, lots of people in the house. There would have been ambulances, priests, police. You can imagine all of this turning up. My sister, as I was discussing with her just the other day, remembers our next-door neighbour. The woman's name was Joyce. It was a time when, and a generation when, we referred to her as Auntie Joyce, but she wasn't a biological auntie. My sister recalls this neighbour coming in and shaking her and saying, "Get it together, be strong. You've got to be strong for your mother here." She was saying to my sister, "Pull yourself together. Your mother's going to need you. Be strong here." I remember the chaos of that morning. I've got no particular memory of my dad being there. Just this horror of my mother. My father went to work the next day, quite a big 'Be Strong' there and 'Don't feel.'

I think at some level I must have known that he had died, but I don't have any memory of it or any understanding around it, and I don't recall anybody saying, "This is what's happened, and Jamie died," or anything.

I just knew we were just left with it. There wasn't any discussion or explanation around it. I've got a really hazy memory of being with a lot of people in the house, and now I can understand why there would be, but after that my main memory is of my mum's ongoing grief. I remember her crying. I have a hunch, but I can't be certain that perhaps her wanting to be closer to me, as in "gives us a hug" or "your mum needs a cuddle" or something like that, but that being – I'm not sure what the word is I'm looking for, not unrequited, but not welcome by me, I experienced it as an intrusion. I think that's about my mother, she did not understand, not calibrating enough, not being attuned enough to me. I think it was just the pain that stayed with her for the rest of her life. She would often be physically there and emotionally absent. I mean, if she was particularly in her grief, she wasn't present. I think in some ways that also my parents in some ways weren't available before Jamie died. This maybe just fed into that part of me, the sense of, "Hey, I am really on my own. I need to look out for myself."

I remember the day of Jamie's funeral, we were not allowed to go, and I know that my sister's really quite upset about that. I think that was also something of the time as well, children are better off not being at these things. It's how I understand that, but we were not allowed to go to the funeral, and I remember each of us being given a toy or something, and I remember at the time, even at eight and a half, this kind of feeling of incongruence. It was something about "I don't want a toy. You're giving me a toy to distract me or something. Oh my God, all this horrible stuff has happened and you're buying me a toy to keep me happy or something like that." I realized that this wasn't a normal way to get a toy. This wasn't my birthday or Christmas. There was some other intention behind getting this toy.

My other recollections of it were that Jamie was never particularly spoken about, although I don't think he was intentionally not spoken about. Sometime later, I moved into his bedroom, and that really troubled me. I think now I understand it because that was unprocessed stuff for me. I think there were childhood fears that something might happen to me, or the room was haunted, or there was something bad about it. My sister shared with me recently, she didn't even like going upstairs on her own, going past the bedroom where Jamie died. There was something when Jamie died, I just couldn't make sense of because it was scary. It was very much a felt experience for me and for my sister too.

Every Christmas, and I think my mum may have gone on his birthdays, first thing in the morning, my mum and dad would go to the neighbouring village to Jamie's grave and put some flowers on his grave. I've often wondered about that, and I've been back to that part of the world since and thought, "Do I need to go and have a look," I don't know. I've never done so. I'm not sure what that's about. I think maybe a part of it is because in some ways I know that's not him there. Even though I know his remains are there, but for some reason, it's not him, it's just something representative of him or it's some kind of block, like walking past his bedroom. I don't know. As of now I've never been to his grave.

I don't think Jamie's death particularly impacted on my relationships with Theresa and Richard. I think that in some ways, yes, he was spoken about but, we didn't speak about what happened, not in a helpful way, to bring understanding or to help me as a child understand feelings or emotions. So yes, memories of Jamie would be spoken about, but for me, it's really different from speaking about what I might have be experiencing as a child. It was just something that was held in the family. I'm not sure, but I do wonder if there might also be something about shame in there, because I'm reasonably certain that on the Sunday that he died, there were all these people coming into the house. I do think there was something going on in me about what's everybody going to be making of this. What are all the neighbours going to be thinking? Something that I'd been concerned about and not in a positive way about what people would be making of it. We were now the centre of attention.

At some point that day we were all taken next door to this woman Joyce and Eric, they had a couple of kids at similar ages. My guess is we would have been looked after there, whatever else was going on within our family home. We were just left in there. No discussion, nothing at all about it. I think that was familiar, just because that's how it was. I certainly remember being left with this notion of having been penetrated and taken on some of my mother's horror, possibly, a bit of both. I do remember being scared around that time and of just being left with it. I think there was something about the immediate trauma. It's slowly coming back a little bit. I think I had some real, like a PTSD type of thing of actually seeing my brother. I mentioned the colour of him, so the shock of that. I don't know how much later it would have been, but at some subsequent point when I moved into his bedroom, I could well have been in my early teens by then. It still felt scary and uncomfortable, and that there's this unknown that had been left unprocessed.

I'm going to take a tangent here. It was only much nearer the end of my own personal therapy when I made a link to this feeling, so I don't know how many dead bodies I dealt with as a cop, loads. I always felt really uncomfortable about it. Got on and did my job, but I was never one that would volunteer for it. I'm aware the majority of police officers, there were the weirdos that really relish it and enjoy it, and I wonder what that's about; but for the majority, it's not on their radar. It doesn't bother them one way or the other, I think. They just get on with it. But for me, I always had a really uncomfortable feeling. There was something I disliked about seeing dead bodies, and I had to really force myself to do this, and to engage with what was happening. I did repeatedly, but when I made this link, "Ah! You know what, I think that fear was the fear or the horror from way back then with my mother." I think that was getting re-enacted at a felt level. I felt that every time, even before I got to a sudden death, it was the prospect of going.

I think this was active because it had never been processed. I think when I made the connection, "Okay, I've always known, and I really experienced at a felt level some real discomfort around dead bodies," and that made a lot of sense to me.

Sometimes if the three of us siblings are together, there may be a discussion about, "Oh, Jamie would be coming up to 49, that would be right?" "Yes." I remember that throughout the years the conversations would have been "Jamie would have been this" and "Jamie would have been that age."

We didn't ever do anything around his birthday or the anniversary of the day he died, nothing at all. I find it really weird now. I don't even know when his birthday was. That's some information there that I didn't even know that. I think I have some memory of being treated or feeling that I was being treated differently. It was something about at school, people would know that I was this boy whose brother died. I'm not sure I liked that either. I don't remember any teachers or anybody particularly going, "John, poor you, how are you doing?" I've always been pretty good at calibrating others, and I'm pretty certain even at that age, I was picking up on something that the teachers knew about me. There was something I can't quantify, different in how they were relating to me. I could think of this probably coming from a caring place, but it was that sense of something different is going on here. What I now know is nobody was speaking to me about it.

If a teacher could have just said, "John, I've heard this horrible news about your brother. How are you doing?" or something like – a human response like that would have helped me then. I think that would've probably helped me contextualize all that was going on. But no one talked with me. Auntie Joyce just spoke to my sister and told her to pull herself together. I was only close to one set of grandparents. The other grandmother wouldn't even have me in the house until I was over two years old because my parents weren't married when I was born. There were some really strong values around. I used to spend quite a lot of time with my father's parents and was close to them, but none of this was spoken about with them either. In fact, I'm not even aware of them being in any grieving process.

I think it would have been really helpful for me back then if I've been consoled and been given some way of talking about or exploring something about the horror of finding my brother, the colour of him and the shock that went with that. I think the only time I've mentioned it was probably a few days ago to my sister. When she said, "Colour, what do you mean?" that's just been there all of those years. It was horrible. I want to make that really clear. Eight and a half years old and the horror of that. Even though I probably didn't know he was dead, there was something about the colour and the red and blue of his face that was quite unrecognizable that I've never spoken about.

The horror of that day has impacted on me with my own children. My son's 29, my daughter's 27. I remember that fear was there in the background. I suppose for a while, I did a lot of checking on him in his cot and making sure he was okay. It wasn't in any way paralyzing or obtrusive, just that kind of background niggling away. It was definitely a residual effect from what I went through with my brother for sure.

What's just come to mind is I don't think I've ever grieved for him. I can understand why. If I could talk with Jamie, I think I'd say, "I miss you." I don't know what he'd say in response, probably, "What have you been up to?"

My father took himself off to work and just left my mother to it the next day. I can't even begin – well, I know what he was like as a person. I can make a sense of it, but on another level, I can't make any sense of that at all. I don't have any strong memories of being kept at home for a period of time. I think we were packed off to school; that would fit with everything.

I did have an older sister who died. Mum didn't particularly ever talk about her. Again, it wasn't a secret. She was in the family narrative, but that's all. She wasn't spoken about in the same way that Jamie was. It wasn't a total secret, but she was never mentioned. We all knew that this had happened to my mum because she told us. She'd shared it, but her loss wasn't talked about either. I didn't have any context. It's just the way it was.

My mum died about 18 years ago now, relatively young at 66. She had a secondary from breast cancer. She had a tough life; her childhood was pretty brutal. I'm pretty certain my mum had some aspects of bipolar process, because she could certainly be manic and then be laid out with a migraine for a couple of days. I'm pretty certain that she had a big dollop of a borderline process as well. So, with losing two children and having cervical cancer as a young woman, surviving that and then breast cancer, and statistically surviving it, but she got a secondary from the breast cancer, her life was hard. What a bloody hard life that is, having cancer three times and losing two children. It's brutal. So, whilst my mum would speak of Jamie, "Oh, your brother would be such-and-such an age now," there was never any reflection or discussion about what happened, which I now know is so important, to talk about the actual event. "What do you remember?" "What was it like for you?" "What happened at this bit and that bit," actually talking through the chronology of what happened; there was none of that.

I realize that I haven't spoken much about this with Richard. But as an adult man I think it's prompted me next time I speak with him, to check out some of what he remembers about it. I suspect it may not be much given that he was five. There will clearly be some trace and element that for me will be helpful just to hear his recollection.

I've just realized something. My father up until his death about four years ago never ever mentioned anything about him. My parents split up when I was about 20, I think; that was only 12 years after Jamie died. I'm just putting this in context. I was a young cop when my parents split up, and that was only about 10 or 12 years after Jamie's death. He never spoke about him. My father was an out-and-out narcissist who would humiliate and put people down for his own gratification. When he died, I went out to Spain for his funeral; other than my daughter who came with me, I was the only family member that went. My brother, Richard, said, "No, I'm working." He wasn't my sister's natural father, so there was no way she was going. She hadn't spoken to him in years.

I look back at my family life and think how mad, unhelpful, sometimes dangerous, toxic, and unsafe it was. Certainly not emotionally supportive and encouraging and empowering. It was a pretty hostile environment to grow up in. My mum was also pretty handy at lashing out with a belt or a wooden spoon or a hand or that kind of stuff as well.

I don't think there was anything in the external world that helped me back then when Jamie died. My hunch is that it reaffirmed and strengthened the part of me that said, "I need to manage myself here because nobody else is helping me with this." Something about "toughen up and don't feel and all of that." I'm pretty certain that's how I would have managed "It's just me in this world. I need to get on and manage this." I was just lost. I have an archaic sense of loneliness, of being alone that goes very, very deep and brings up huge emotion if I sit with it. I think it would have resonated very much with that part of me.

I'm really not sure if it was the same for Rick. I've got a blank space there. I think Theresa coped with it by supporting our mum; she had a good and close relationship with her.

I'm beginning to see how unhelpful it is for anybody, but particularly to children, to be left alone with something as big as this. Of course, children should go to funerals if they wish to and be included in the process and be accounted for and helped and spoken with. I really would have liked somebody to know how scared I was, having that fear of being in or going past that room or the scare from the visual image that I carried for so many years. It's not as strong as it was; I have a different sense of it now. It's faded over the years, but for a long time that was a really powerful image, and it was scary because it was traumatic. It would have been great for somebody who was attuned enough to me who might have picked up on something and then talked to me.

My mum was Roman Catholic, but my father wasn't at all religious. I know my mum on some level would have made it about her, that she'd been bad or something. I don't think I went to the spiritual level even in terms of trying to understand what happened, but I think there was something in there about feeling scared. Could this happen to me? This unexplained event. Fuck, this could happen to me.

If this book had been written back then, I would like to have read about feelings and thoughts, that it was normal to feel scared. I'd have wanted to read something about, it's okay to ask for help, and something about sharing it, who I could share it with. As I'm talking about this, I am really shocked how much of this I had held for so long without realizing it was holding me.

There have been aspects of this that I've spoken about in therapy, but not the horror to me in terms of the trauma. I may have spoken about me experiencing my mother's horror. But the horror to me, the scare around Jamie's bedroom, being in it afterwards, of not wanting to pass the door, of not liking being upstairs. The horror of what he looked like, none of that's ever been spoken about, and that really surprises me.

I want to thank you because this will prompt me to talk some more to my sister about this, and also to talk to my brother and find out their experiences. This process has allowed me to reconnect with something that is still there in me and has been shut off. That feels really important to bring some more understanding and some more attention to that part of me.

13 "They're just living in their lovely little bubble and my bubble burst"

Rose's story remembering her older sister Lizzie

Lizzie is my older sister. We weren't close, but I wanted it to be different. I didn't really see her that much. Not as much as I would have liked. It would have been different if it were up to me, but she was always out. If we'd been closer in age, then it would have been different, but when she was 18, I was only 14. We couldn't go to the pub together or anything. That was the only thing to do where we lived, really. She did have a part-time job, but when she wasn't working, she was with her friends or in the pub or both. Although I love my sister, she was selfish and didn't really take much notice of me or what else was going on outside her bubble.

She got pregnant, but then after a couple of months she had a miscarriage. I remember it happened a couple of days before we were all due to go on holiday. I remember mum, Lizzie, and I all going shopping to get the clothes for the holiday, and she was crying. I didn't really understand the emotional impact of it because I've never had one. She still wanted to go on holiday, so we all went. I can't really remember a lot of that. I remember we just had a few laughs. She spent every evening drinking and came back to our room drunk. She'd crash about and then fall asleep. She used to snore really badly, so I kept hitting her to wake her up.

After the holiday, we got back home. A few days later I remember I was out shopping in the supermarket, and my boyfriend was there, and she snapped at him about something. That really annoyed me. I can't remember exactly what she said, it was something little like, "Move the trolley out of the way, you idiot." We fell out in the car on the way back home. That was the last time I actually spoke to her. I only saw her in passing once going down the stairs while I was going upstairs, but we didn't talk or anything and she didn't look at me. That hurts even now as it was the last time I saw her alive.

A couple of days later I spent the day with my friend and my boyfriend. We got Chinese, and we had that at our house. My friend went home, and me and my boyfriend were there in the bedroom, then my mum called me. I was like, "Are you all right?" She was like, "Not really." I remember thinking, "Oh, shit," because that was the "You've done something wrong" mum voice. I was like, "Oh, God. What have I done?" Then she came in my room and she said, "It would appear as though your sister has died." Then, me and my boyfriend both got up and gave her a hug, but then in my head, I was like, "No, she ain't. She's just fast asleep again." Then, we went down the stairs and outside to the annexe where my sister lived. There were people there. My boyfriend felt awkward, so he sat on the opposite side to the driveway, not far away. I looked in, and then I could see her on the bed and there was someone doing something, checking her or something. Then, I was like, "Oh, she's dead."

I think it was more unnerving than anything. I think I just cried. You just cry, don't you? The most unnerving part was seeing my dad cry, because I've never seen him cry before. I remember sitting on the outside wall opposite the annexe, then he just broke down. I just sat there like, "Oh my God. What do I do now?" I was pretty fucked up. I remember sitting in the annexe, and then I was stroking her hair and she was pretty blue by this point. It was really cold because the doors were open and it was dark outside. The bloke with the camera – I think he was a police officer – said, "Sorry, I need to take some photos," so then I had to leave. The next thing I remember is everyone sat in the kitchen in our house doing paperwork and stuff. My brother made everybody a cup of tea. He was keeping it together most out of everyone, I think that's because he's not one to show much emotion outwardly. When all that was over, I went to have a shower before I went to bed. That's the bit that creeped me out the most because when I was having the shower, the door was right opposite. I kept my eyes on the door because I thought she was going to burst through, like in a paranormal horror film. Looking back, I think that was the PTSD kicking in. That and her being blue.

I remember that I didn't eat for three days. I remember being at my boyfriend's house, but I can't remember if I stayed there or if my parents didn't want me to stay there overnight. I can't remember. I remember walking through town and then I had a little cry on the way down. That's the little bit I can remember from that point. I remember the numb bit because I didn't eat for three days.

The boyfriend I had was good for a couple of months, give or take. He was there. We spent all the time together anyway. He was there in that sense. I know everyone was all lovely to me because people were messaging on Facebook, things like that. In the beginning, that's all I can remember. People were nice to me generally. Everyone was suddenly my best mate. People I didn't know were my best friends, everything like that. There were numerous stories on Facebook about how she'd died, that was horrible. People just staying stuff about her that wasn't true just because they wanted their 'five minutes of fame.' These stories ranged from alcohol poisoning to a heroin overdose.

I wanted support. I just wanted my hand to be held, so it was sort of nice having all these new friends. It was nice at the time, but at the same time, it was usually shit. I'd rather be okay on my own rather than feeling like shit with a million people or what felt like a million people. People offered to be there for me, that I could talk to them any time or hang out any time, get tattoos together and all random things like that, going for a drink and things. But they aren't really your friend if they just pass you another drink or offer you other substances which drag you down further.

I can't remember the days after at all. How funny is that? I do remember being at home because I remember sitting around the kitchen table trying to choose the songs to play at the funeral. That was really shit because I grew up listening to her music, we liked a lot of the same music, so quite a bit of it is ruined for me now. It was hard. I felt like in the charts at the time, there were some really depressing songs. It was really, really weird. There's a song called "Say Something." I can't listen to that because it's like, it's too morbid. Even Olly Murs had come out with "Dear Darlin' " – it all seemed to come out at the same time, all these depressing songs, so it was really hard to avoid.

I was glad to be part of that process, though, choosing the music. Oh my God, yes, because we played Evanescence's "My Immortal." That song sung by Amy Lee is actually about her real-life sister who killed herself. I can relate to that. I was glad to be part of that process even though it was horrible. Because I feel if my family had just picked it, they would have got it wrong. If I didn't have a say, it wouldn't have been right. I felt included in that part of the process.

Since Lizzie died, life has been a bit of a roller coaster. A bit hard. Lots and lots of highs and lows. When it's been low, it's been low. When it's been high, it's been high. I'm trying to think, in the first two years afterwards, it was really, really bad. Then, it went really, really good. But that's just life, isn't it? I've been distracted by other events in life.

Alcohol and substance abuse helped me get through the worst bits and having a dog to talk to. The dog was the best bit. But then the alcohol and substance abuse got in the way and caused me more problems. I lived in this small town where there's just pubs and things. What I felt like is that I just wanted to be out and about. I was still quite young, so you do want to go out every night with your friends and things like that. If you hang out with people, you go to the pub. If your sister just killed herself, you can get away with pubbing underage apparently too. That's all very well in the night when you're distracted and drunk and things. The next morning, when you wake up, you feel like shit, and your brain is just tick, tick, tick, tick, tick. It's hard to put it into words actually because it helped me to grieve by lashing out, bouncing off the walls and things; but it hindered me because then, it was messing with my brain as substances do, and I really, really struggled with those thoughts.

I wasn't really at home very much. No, I wasn't. I'd go home when I was hung-over, so I could get some nice food or something like that. I actually can't really remember much. It wasn't that I didn't want to be with my parents, but I was only 16, and from the age of 14 onwards I'd get home from school and then I'd be going out with my friends every evening. I was still in that stage but was just doing it differently.

If I could see Lizzie now, I think I'd just hit her. I would. I'd absolutely smash her head in, get all that out. Then, I'd just see how I felt afterwards. I'd hit her a lot. If I was going to say something to her, I'd tell her how she ruined my childhood and I fucking hate her for it. After I get all that out of the way, I don't know. I might be sad. I don't know. The anger will never go away, and I'm not sure I want it to.

There was an inquest. It would have been all absolutely fine, to be fair. I don't think I would have felt negatively about it if it wasn't for the journalist that was there. He was an absolute wanker. He was sat there scribbling away. He was sat right behind me over my right shoulder. I was getting wound up the entire time because I was thinking, "I don't want to see this in the paper," because I remember, before we even got there, I was hoping it wouldn't go to the newspaper because publicity is embarrassing. Suicide is embarrassing. We're not celebrities. We're not famous. Why would anyone give a shit? Because I don't give a shit about other people in that way. Anyway, he was scribbling away, and I was getting more and more wound up, so I can't remember the majority of what was said at the inquest because all I could see was him behind me. We had a break for some reason. We were still out in the open area and I asked him, "Can I read what you wrote?" He said, "You can read it tomorrow in the paper." That really pissed me off.

I sat in this chair, and he stood in front of me with his hands behind his back holding his notebook. His notebook was right there. I just wanted to grab it and run off with it. I didn't, but I wish I did. I wish I bloody did it. Part of me was still hoping he wouldn't go into full details, but he fucking did. I was reading about the miscarriage and all sorts of things, things that weren't needed. Talking about her boyfriend. No one needs it. He wouldn't like it if someone wrote stuff about him. Journalists are inhumane about this sort of thing. Lots of things.

I had a friend at the time, and she put up some comment on Facebook. Nothing to do with me, nothing to do with anything or anyone, just some joke about dying. It was just a joke and I went mad, went completely over the top about it. I was annoyed at her, but I know we've hung out since then. It was awkward because of my age, no one I knew of my age knew what was going on, but at the same time, it was nice because then, I could hang out with people and it was all normal. But then inside, my brain was doing different things to what my mouth was doing. I could act normal and have a laugh with my friends, but it was in the forefront of my mind still, this like horrible nightmare going on that wouldn't go away out of my brain.

Then, my boyfriend couldn't hack it. I remember I was reading an old diary that said something about my sister and I threw it. I wasn't aiming it, but I just threw it and it just missed his head by a tiny amount. We just started arguing, just kept arguing because he didn't understand what was going on, but then I didn't realize at that time how much of a spoiled brat he was. He was getting all the attention he wanted and things like that. That went to shit. I had a best friend – we'd drifted apart a little bit right before

Lizzie died, but then he started being my best mate again, so that was nice. I'd asked him to come with me in the funeral car. Then, the day before, he texts me saying he won't go. He had to go shopping with his family or something. I haven't spoken to him since then.

The funeral was all right, really. It was more annoying because it was just supposed to be for close friends and family, and then there was fucking random people coming, people that I didn't particularly like sitting in the front row when her boyfriend and things couldn't even get inside the building. It was packed and they had to stand outside. No one could get in and he was in the back somewhere. I'm really annoyed about that still. It was a bit of a cock-up in that sense as I didn't really know him then and didn't pay attention, but no, it was quite nice. It was fucked up as it is, but it went as well as it could have.

I'd say Lizzie's death affects me every day in some way or another because I'm very cynical now and I'm very impatient; I'm quite short and blunt. It takes me about two seconds from going from liking someone to just wanting to say fuck off because I'm more judgemental. If someone's whining about something, I'll just shut up. Because they haven't had the things happened to them that have happened to me. I don't know that, actually. You don't know what people are going through, but it's like my brain automatically assumes they've never been through anything ever. They can do one kind of thing. To be honest, I don't really care, especially if their siblings are all alive.

I'm so intolerant. I know I can be quite cold. I think I was at a funny age when it happened because I was borderline adult anyway. I wasn't quite a child, but not quite an adult. It definitely stopped me from being a child. I went straight into the miserable existence of adulthood which I'm quite bitter about. Cutting my brain out would have been brilliant, but you can't just stop what goes on inside your head. You can't control your thoughts, can you? You can't control reality. It happened. Whatever, it happened. There's no point wondering about that because it happened. You can't change it.

I really think about things a lot. I'm glad I am how I am because at the time, I thought, "How am I going to cope without bossy, big sister?" But then I feel proud of myself when I think how much I've actually done and accomplished since. Obviously, I've cocked up a lot of things, but I've come a bloody long way. It stopped me from doing anything at first, but then that was during the really bad grieving period. It was like the first three years were the worst. I didn't want to do anything, but it was my parents that spurred me on.

First me and my mum went house hunting, and that was like one of my favourite parts of my life because that was brilliant. Staying in nice hotels, having a nice breakfast and things. It's basically just shopping for houses. That was nice because that's a little light of hope. Then, just before we moved, I didn't know what to do. I didn't really want to do anything. I didn't have the energy.

It just had been like two, three years just getting off my head and gallivanting with other people that didn't have jobs or anything. I didn't see the point in working if you could get money for free. Then, my mum made me inquire at the college and things like that, and then I just got the ball rolling and I went on from there to university and things. I'm glad about that as if I stayed put, I would have remained in the same shitty social circles, forever 'Lizzie's little sister'. God, I hated that. I lost my name.

Another thing I can think of that helped me is tidying and decorating. I'd feel really shit. I'd be having a bad week or something. Then, my room would be really messy, and I'd hate it and I'll be in that little squalor for a bit, but then I do my spring cleaning. It makes me feel so much more in control of my life. When I was in the annexe, I made it all nice and pretty and things like that. Things like that help. That only helps for a day or so. I don't think there's anything else really. I'd say food. Food always helps, but then I wasn't eating food. When you're off your head or drunk, you're not hungry. I think my appetite did come back eventually, but not for a long while because things kept going wrong after that. Bad luck comes in threes.

Lizzie died in August, and then in November, I found out I was pregnant, which was very awkward because my head was already like mashed potato. I couldn't think clearly enough to make a proper decision, and everyone was saying, "It's your decision," but I knew it wasn't the right time and you don't want a baby around. It was a huge fuck-up. Then, I had an abortion. I had mixed feelings about that anyway because then, I felt like a murderer. In hindsight, it was the right choice, but it'll always make me feel a bit . . . because I'd have a five-year-old now, but then it wouldn't have gone well because I obviously needed to have that big blowout for two years to keep going. But then during the big blowout obviously, other things happened.

If this book was available to me, then I would have wanted to read about other siblings who shared the same thoughts and feelings as me, who would have gone out partying to distract themselves, who suffered a pregnancy or something, got raped or something as a result, things like that, anyone you could relate to, anything would have been grand. To read other people's similar stories.

I didn't have anything like that. I was just around people who say the same things like robots over and over again, like, "I'm so sorry. Here's another drink," things like that. I couldn't find the support, but then I felt like if I go on about it, I was so sick of saying, "My sister, my sister, my sister," because I got bored hearing myself saying it, so what's everyone else going to think? Even now I do my own head in saying "my sister" just once. I'd love to forget her totally in some ways.

It would've been handy to read how others overcame it. That would've been handy as well because there were many points where I thought I was going to end up killing myself as well. But then I was quite lucky, actually, because my mum would come and give me a cuddle when I was in bed feeling like shit because I'd done drugs the night before and things like that, and she'd asked me if I felt that way, and I said, "Yes," and I was crying and everything. If it weren't for my mum, I think . . . I don't know. Don't want to jinx it. I've learned since then that that's just what happens. I saw a quote and it's like, "It doesn't end the pain, it passes on to someone else," and it's true. When she killed herself, there were four people in this house who were probably all fucking suicidal as well.

A little self-help section which doesn't involve going to a counsellor or ringing up a hotline, because no one would do any of that, would be good too, some practical tips. Things like "These are the kind of feelings that you might get after your sibling dies. You feel like you're going out of your head. You'll feel suicidal. You'll feel angry, you'll feel very angry, you'll lash out at other people. You'll go through a self-destructive stage. You might feel yourself drawn towards a drug dealer. Don't do it. If you do do it, then make sure you give yourself a set date when to stop that, though that of course is easier said than done. Sometimes, your mind goes blank and you're just existing, thinking you're done for." My memory is shocking because of all of it, actually I think it's getting worse. I don't know because everyone is different.

My life now is pretty good because I'm more in control. However, it's really, really hard because of other people that I just don't have time for. I feel like it's all well and good being around new people, but it's hard to meet new people. I'll chat with someone, say if I'm in a lecture or seminar, I'd meet someone, I'm trying my best, and at the end I'm like, "Yes, nice to meet you," and everything, but then I'm so ready to just leave and never see them again right after that. I don't like making close connections with people because when you do that, you have to tell them. I know you don't have to tell them, but it's like you've got that big cloud hanging over your head.

There are just constant reminders of it, like when that question comes up, "Do you have any brothers and sisters?" What the fuck are you meant to say to that, then? It's all sorts of things like that. I really wind myself up about it. Then, when I do talk about it, they use it against you eventually, in my experience anyway. They'll bring it up. Boyfriends specifically, because I've had two. One of them told me to take pills and join her and is even recently still bringing up shit even though we live halfway across the country to each other now. Then, the other one, I didn't want to talk about my dad or anything and he'd keep pressing and pressing and pressing. This is just a reflection on his personality but not the event.

When I'd actually open up to him, he'd then use it against me from having a grump on, or we have an argument, and he'd say, "You're crazy. No wonder your sister did that. It must run in the family," and things like that. Since I left him, he sent my mum an email saying I tried to kill myself, which isn't true. He contacted my sister's old boyfriend saying that me and my mum blamed him for Lizzie's death and things like that. So, making new friends is difficult. As I'm talking, I realize that I find myself drawn back to old friends because they know. I never thought about that before. That makes so much sense because they do understand, because they were there during that time. In a way, that's positive because I haven't got to explain anything. I can be myself, and they're probably not going to throw it back in my face because they knew me. They've known me for a long time. But does it have a knock-on effect which means that I'm maybe more reluctant to make new friends.

I have a couple of good friends. My best friend at uni, he knows because we do talk a lot. We get on so well because I have quite a messed-up sense of humour because of it, I laugh about it, joke about it, but then he's like that about things that have happened to him because his family has suffered from racism and things like that. We both have dark humour. That's really nice. No one else understands it, but that gets me through. It was quite funny, actually, because we were friends in first year, but not as close as we became right at the beginning of second year. What really helped was because we both lived with someone who was an utter nightmare. We'd end up hiding in one of our bedrooms having a good old rant about her radiating ignorance about life.

If I see someone being really pedantic about something really minor and just being a general idiot, and I'm thinking, "What's wrong with you? Go out and live in the real world and get your head out your ass," he sees that too. It feels like it's me and him against the world or against the middle-class wet flannels that we've got to associate with at uni because it's true. It's good. It doesn't make me feel as crazy as it did during first year when I mentally felt about 40 compared to a lot of them. I just wish they'd hurry up and join the real world. I know this sounds messed up, but sometimes I really wish something horrible upon them just so that they get their head out their ass and notice that there's more important things to life than a club or whether somebody did or didn't send an email or a message.

I can clock people really quickly sometimes. I remember in first year I was friends with this girl we met. We found out we were in the same accommodation, same course, and everything, so we agreed to meet up, and then I visited her flat and her flatmates. There was this one girl and I clocked on to her right away, and I said to Chloe and I was like, "She's a compulsive liar." Chloe was like, "Oh, no. Do you really think so?" and I was like, "Yes." Anyway, about a week later the entire flat fell out with this girl because of her compulsive lying because she said she got with one of the boys. With some people I do clock on to that quickly, especially girls.

I think that's probably why people might think I'm a bit crazy or I overreact about certain things, because I feel like other people are just too forgiving. If someone does something I don't like, or they say something I don't like or that I just don't think is right. I'm just like, "No, I don't like you." But other people just glaze over it, and I'm like, "Why bother?"

I think it's made me more sensitive in other areas too. I really wanted to be a primary school teacher, but when I'm actually around children, it's horrible. Like sometimes I look at a kid and I think, what's the point, you're going to turn out to be a little prick anyway. Sometimes you can tell that they are just going to be a little shit when they're older. What's the point, anyway? Because children are so sweet and beautiful, but by the time they turn to adults, humans are horrible people. We don't deserve to be here. I tend to see the bad in others, and sometimes it's so big I don't see any good.

Since Lizzie died, I've got really, really anxious, and I get really, really angry. I saw a counsellor for a bit, and she said that anger is an umbrella emotion for these other emotions. Sometimes I don't know what I'm feeling, but I do get frustrated a lot. Loads of stuff frustrates me. People being inconsiderate and rude. It is just a rough example, but it's what I come into contact with all the time. If you're going down a pavement and the pavement is wide enough for, say, three people, and there's three people walking in a row like a human barrier. You're walking the other way and they don't move. Things like that really piss me off because it's like, "Where are you even looking?" I hate feeling like I'm always the one weaving all the time. Things like that really do my head in because I'm always looking where I'm going, and I move out the way. You don't have to shoulder barge everyone you come across or expect them to manoeuvre around you. You can afford to stand behind your friend for a minute. You're not going to miss out on anything in the two, three seconds you are not stood side by side. Certain things like that – not holding doors open for someone and leaving a horrible mess, using other people's property and leaving it in a state – just really rude things. Basically, people being inconsiderate. Because I feel like, even if I'm having a really bad day and I'm human and I hate everyone, I still hold the door open for somebody. Other people who aren't like that I'm just like, "Fuck off. Go away."

I think I act more reserved, different in front of people I don't know. If I'm pissed off, I'll let people know more if I know them. I struggle with it. I feel like I'm either nothing or everything. The worst scenario is if I'm living with them. I was living with someone who lives like an absolute pig and was so unhygienic. I'd just want to make a cup of tea and I couldn't go and make a cup of tea without shaking with anger because it's so fucking disgusting. Then they just expect me to tidy up, and I'm not doing it because I'm not your mother. I feel like I'm so angry already, I don't want to have to put up with other people's disgusting habits. I don't want to unleash what I really think, because then I feel like it'd be too much, but then my problem is, I hold it in and then I end up exploding, and I've attacked someone before over it.

Lizzie's death has ruined my birthday. That was a big one. I realized the other day that when things like this happen to families, it's Christmas that's ruined for them. I remember our first Christmas after she died, we didn't put decorations up or anything, but we just did as we normally do. I love Christmas and I don't think anything can ruin Christmas for me, but it's my birthday that's been ruined. Because she was 20 when she died, and I was 16. Now I'm 23, I'm three years her senior. I find that really fucked up, and that's what I struggle with. I remember on my 20th birthday it was a of bit sibling rivalry, like, "Ha, ha, you're not the big sister anymore." As every year goes past, it's just sucked the fun out of it. It's just a miserable thing. It's just like another year she didn't get a chance to sort her shit out or be a mother or a proper sister. I don't know. It's just sucked the fun out of it, really. I didn't know if that's just because I'm an adult. I'm a boring adult now. Adults don't find birthdays fun. It could just be that, but the last couple birthdays I've had, I've just been crying my eyes out. But then I don't know if that's because I was with a horrible bloke two years ago or because for the last one, I was really drunk for breakfast. I don't know. I'll have to wait and see how the next one goes. But I love Christmas. No one is ruining Christmas for me. Christmas is the most magical time of the year.

I've always had a really good relationship with my parents. There's the occasional bicker, but that's normal. It's a bit fucked up, actually, because I know I'm more afraid of them growing old, because they're old already. Then it's just going to be only me and my brother, but he's . . . well, it feels like it'll just be me. It's a little bit annoying. There was a period like where I thought it would just be better not to bother having a relationship with anyone because they're just going to die anyway. That's how I felt all the time with my family. That was also partly because of the boyfriend I had. He would say things like, "I'm the only one that's here for you," "I'm the one that cares about you," things like that. It made it more real somehow. It messed with my head, but it's all right now. I came back to my senses. It was such a stupid fucking way of thinking. If you think about everyone you love and you think about them dying, of course you get upset about it. I can think logically in that way. I mean, as long as you're old, it's all right, isn't it? I suppose with Lizzie dying, my own mortality as well as that of my parents has come even more to the forefront of my mind.

There's something about my whole experience that has been a real "welcome to reality, welcome to the grown-up world," I guess you could call it. I think I'll always be bitter. That's probably why I don't like people as much because they're just living in their lovely little bubble and my bubble burst.

14 "Everything was coming together for him"

Shireen's story remembering her brother Tariq

My brother Tariq was one of twins. He was born when I was 13 years old. Born at a very particular time, I guess, because it was the first time my father had taken myself and my other brother and sister to Pakistan to meet our extended family. It was the summer that we met all our cousins, aunties, and uncles that we've never known before, so it was a very memorable time for me. The three of us visiting Pakistan were the children of his first marriage, and Tariq was born from my father's second marriage to a German woman, Inga. We knew that Inga was heavily pregnant with twins, which was a shock for my father because he had not anticipated a second family – let alone twins. He was completing professional obligations in Africa, so between continents and transitioning into a new life. This was the hot summer of 1976 in Europe.

Tariq was gorgeous. Both the twins were adorable babies to me. They really were. Tariq was more delicate and pretty, and the one that everyone wanted to pick up. His twin brother was calm, relaxed, solid and Buddha-like, whereas Tariq was a more highly strung child, more excitable.

I saw them about twice a year, usually Easter and summer. We saw them as newborns and then saw them again when they were about six months old. Because my brother, sister, and I were all older and bigger, we'd be quite possessive about these little babies. It would be a competition as to who could get one on their lap. Those are some of the earliest memories I have of him, of being a teenager and feeling very maternal towards these two boys.

It followed that same pattern throughout the rest of my teenage years, seeing them a couple of times a year. I suppose I was always the protective older sister. I felt quite strongly for these two boys, but of course the contact wasn't consistent, so they weren't a part of my day-to-day life. They were a part of me and my brother and sister visiting Germany and becoming acquainted with this new family. There is a sense of feeling cut off a little bit, like I feel quite cut off from my cousins because I haven't had consistent contact with them through my childhood.

The contact developed along those lines. We saw them when they were six months, then again when they were nine months. My strongest memories are of them up to the age of two and then as small children. I'd also continue to see my father. Once they were about five or six, I was 18, 19, and off at university then and probably only seeing them once a year.

Tariq continued to grow into a handsome boy. Which is very bittersweet because that also led to him being sexually abused when he was, about seven or eight. I learnt that this had happened to him when my father separated from his second wife, and I asked my father why. He said that the relationship had broken down when the sexual abuse had been discovered. It was a friend of the family that would occasionally babysit with the twins. I think it was only Tariq who was abused. The story I've told myself from the little bits of information I have, is that it was just him. He grew up – you know, it's complex, isn't it? – he had a Pakistani father, a white German mother all living in Berlin before the wall came down. It was such a different time.

In his teenage years, he and his brother got into smoking a bit of pot. His brother stopped at that. But Tariq went on to harder drugs – my sense is that part of that was because the unresolved trauma hadn't been worked through, and with the separation of their parents, I guess that was further distress. Part of the difficulty was that their primary attachment was with my father, because when my father reached 50, he retired from his job in Africa and went to live in Germany with the twins. He raised them, and their mother went out to work. So, he was their primary carer and they were closely aligned with him also in terms of their identity. Having and using their Pakistani names meant wearing it and owning it, with dad as their main carer. So, I think the separation of their parents must have hit them very hard on top of everything else.

I don't fully comprehend exactly what happened between my father and his wife. They continued to have a practical arrangement and relationship as parents, but the relationship between them broke down completely. I imagine it was complicated, because this was a complex blended family; the woman he married had got two children from a previous marriage. She had separated and divorced in order to marry my father. I think that was difficult. That marriage had also included separation of her children, because in Germany, divorce laws worked differently from the UK at the time. The little boy that she had went to live with her ex-husband, and the little girl that she had stayed with her. So, I had a white German stepsister who was raised with these two boys. She was younger than me; she would have been about six or seven when they were born.

Therefore, there was a lot to contend with. I think the breakdown wasn't just about what happened to Tariq, although I am guessing that was a big contribution. I think what may have happened, thinking about it a little bit more now, is that my father had been somebody in Nigeria. He was an academic, and he'd sometimes broadcast on radio and TV. He was somebody to be respected and admired in that context, and in many ways, he didn't have a problem living in Germany and raising the boys. I think he felt that he was getting a second chance because of his separation from us. But for his German wife, I think, that must have been difficult. He wasn't now the man that she had talked to and admired in Africa. He was a househusband, happily looking after the children, happily cooking the dinner, but I think she started to resent him for that.

I continued to have contact with Tariq throughout his childhood. I wasn't really in contact with him when he was a teenager. By the time he got to about 15 and he was starting to use drugs, I was 27, 28. I was much more embroiled in my own life, although I still made contact with my dad, the contact with my brothers was less. It would be like meeting up, going for a meal together. It wasn't like living or staying over in the same place as them.

Tariq had been on heroin and was really bad; he went into rehab in his 20s and got clean. He got a job and was really beginning to get his life together. He was working in some form of social work and was enjoying it. He had a really good manager. Everything was coming together for him.

Then, he got some sort of infection – I'm not quite sure what, like a chest infection – and went to the doctors about it and was given some medication. I'm not 100% sure about this, but I think the inquest said that he couldn't tolerate the medication because his system was so vulnerable. He was just 36 when he died – this is about seven, eight years ago now. It was a terrible shock. Because we were feeling optimistic for him; his life was being turned around.

The other distressing thing is that he died alone and wasn't found for two or three days, not a huge amount of time, but nonetheless. It was his manager at work that found him; she wondered where he was because he didn't turn up for work, and she knew that that wasn't like him. She went around to where he lived, and that's how he was discovered. I think that haunts my father.

I immediately planned to go over to see my dad and to be there for the funeral. Tariq reminds me of my younger sister – a little frail, a little bit excitable in temperament and in body and in looks. My sister had estranged herself from our father. She wasn't involved in the funeral. It was sad, really, not to have her there. She's just never said anything. I think she's just banged the door firmly shut on my father and anything to do with him in a way that I find difficult. As much as I am very invested in continuing to have a relationship with her, I don't like how she treats my father. And, I also feel very sorry for her. I'm still connected with her, but I'm not close to her as I am with my brother. I always felt she seemed much more ashamed of her heritage than my brother, John, and me. She's fairer of skin than us – actually passes as white. No one would necessarily know, but she's the one that's needed to kind of put some distance there. Also, I think she genuinely didn't quite bond with my dad because when she was born, his career was at its height.

John and I always had a closer connection with our father. So, we had to go to the funeral, we had to be there. My brother has been someone I could talk to. I'm so glad we went together, and I wouldn't have wanted to go alone. That would have been really, really hard, and so he and I could talk together about what happened at the funeral. We did our grieving together.

When I got to Germany, I found my father looking traumatized, frail, and very vulnerable, which was really difficult to see. Particularly, I found it difficult to see him age. But his new partner is really warm, kind, and loving. That was encouraging that he has her in his life. She's also incredibly loving and warm towards my brother and myself. She's only known us as adults, but she treats us like we're part of her family. It's very touching.

I'll never forget going to the funeral. It was extraordinary because I saw my stepmother again, Tariq's mother. I hadn't seen her for about 30 years or more when she was still quite in her prime. To see her as an old woman and to see the trauma of a mother who's lost her child, she looked broken. I really felt for her. She was completely all right with my father, but he suffered an attack at the funeral from her daughter, our old stepsister, who went for him. She spoke German and so I couldn't understand everything, but I got the gist of what she was saying. She was attacking him for his lack of protection and some other things. She was partly blaming him for the demise of her brother, and everyone else stood around in a stunned silence apart from me. I stepped in and I stopped her. She speaks fluent English, and so I said, "Not now. This is, not for now."

I saw other people that were gathered there. The other twin brother was there with someone who was supporting him. My brother and I weren't sure if it was a social worker or a possible partner. He obviously had someone there that he really trusted that was a really nice support for him. There were other people there that I didn't know at all well, as well as people that I hadn't seen for 30-odd years. It was difficult having this sort of public attack on my dad. So, it was good that everyone came but terrible for my father that he got humiliated like that.

The truth is, he wasn't a great father. He wasn't great on structure. Folks think sometimes of Pakistani and Indian fathers as being very strict, very this, very that. He was none of the above. I think he almost went to the other polarity, "Children need to be free." Which was a nice antidote to my mother's strictness for us, but perhaps did not always feel safe.

Much as I do love him, and I think he's a very interesting man – now as a grown woman, he was not a good father. However, he did offer consistent love. He's always been a very loving man, a warm man. But, my God, he left a trail of destruction behind him: broken marriages, broken children, separations. I think holding all that complexity is quite hard.

The German woman he'd married was similar to him as well. I think that that was part of the fury in my stepsister, that someone needed to be blamed for the lax boundaries in the family and for not being on the alert, for not being vigilant. And for me, it also felt reminiscent of racist attacks. Because there was a strength of hatred in her, and I'm not saying that that was part of it, but that's what it felt like. It felt like everything he stood for had to be condemned somehow. We were a broken family, and a broken family that was trying to come together over the death of a broken child. My brother said to me, "She's very aggrieved." Him just even saying that, kind of helped me to think about what might be going on for her.

I was very touched that Tariq's mother came to my brother and myself and was appreciative that we'd come to the funeral. There was a moment of genuine soulful connection between us. I hadn't particularly liked her as a child. I'd always been a bit wary of her, but she had always been very kind to me. It was a moment of genuine compassion, connection between us as two women. I could see and feel her terrible, terrible, terrible grief. It was even sadder because she died shortly afterwards. She'd had cancer and she had recovered, but I think her body probably couldn't hold and survive the grief.

As for Abbar, Tariq's twin, I think he dissociated. He was clearly deeply disturbed, and he stayed with us after the funeral. He looked traumatized. When his brother got addicted to harder drugs, Abbar did all he could to try and get him off them, but it didn't work, and he couldn't bear it, so he separated from his twin and had less and less to do with him. I just think this continues to be a grief that he holds. What I notice about him when I meet up with him is his tenderness towards my father. He's very caring as a son because my dad was an older father to them and now, he's 88 and frail. I'm really touched by how kind Abbar is to him. You know, watchful in that sort of caring way. He's in his early 40s now, and I feel when I talk to him about his life in Germany, he's very attached to his German identity.

Abbar had visited Pakistan alone, to have the experience that I had, when he was 12, 13. He had this one meeting where he met all of his cousins and his uncle, and I think it had a profound impact on him. So, it's not that he feels he has to distance himself from that, but when I see him now, I feel like he's trying to cling onto his motherland. He's lost his mum. He's lost his twin. He's got an aging father. He's got my brother and myself, but he doesn't feel close to us, really. I feel his tragedy and his loss more than he probably realizes I do.

I carry a deep level of guilt around for not nurturing a closer relationship to the boys when they got older. Added to that, there is even more guilt on my part, because when Tariq was coming off his medication, when he was in rehab, he met a woman who was also in rehab, and she was HIV positive with a terminal diagnosis. They had a child together. The baby was going to be HIV positive, and because she had a terminal diagnosis, they put the child up for adoption. My husband and I came close to adopting the baby, but we didn't partly because of German bureaucracy, and partly the influence of my mother telling me not to. I don't quite forgive myself for that because, I wish I had adopted the child anyway. It's the feeling of there being a relative out there, I don't know. Perhaps there's also a sense of, maybe that child represents all the lost connections in some way. It's another can of worms potentially.

My twin brothers never came to my home in England. I went to Germany and visited them in theirs, but they never came to mine. I would have liked to have had that sort of relationship with them where they came to stay. It didn't happen partly because of the arrangement of us as divorced children going over to spend time with my dad. I've consistently invited my brother, Abbar, to come over and stay and visit England. He always says thank you, but he's never done it. I think he's never done it because, I think, his life is in Germany, and I don't think he feels the same. Maybe – I don't know, actually, because there is something intimate about the way he greets me and the way he says goodbye. There is that longing in him I perceive for family.

Abbar seems to have a strong, close network of friends. Being a twin, you have such an urge to have that, I think. I notice that about him. He does have very strong connections with friends, and he has quite an active social life. He goes on holiday with friends and that sort of thing with the group. I think that he's very invested in that. My dad's partner said once over dinner, "Abbar would never leave Germany. He would never leave Berlin." And that's where I learned about the strength of this feeling in him. So, I wonder if there's just been so much loss in his life that he clings on very securely to what he knows and what's familiar.

I sense that in some ways my relationship with them feels not like a sibling. It's more like an auntie, because I was older than them. It feels like there's that strange feeling of being another generation of looking down where I see them as younger people that need protection and connection, and sometimes like a parent looks at a child and thinks about a child in a different way from how a child thinks about their parents. Maybe it would have pleased me more than it would have pleased them if they'd come to stay. Maybe it would have satisfied some need in me to be maternal and to have that role in a family.

I have some regret that I can't pull Abbar closer. He's very happy to see me, and when I do see him, there's a real connection it feels, even if we do have very different political views. There's a real connection in the way he hugs me and the way he looks like there's this longing for connection. Also, for him to see my brother and I as children of dual heritage, I feel that there's something quite primitive that goes on for him there. That he doesn't really get that anywhere else. He probably gets mistaken for being Turkish in Berlin a lot. There is something I think about his racial identity, the union of us being our father's children and reflecting something of my father's life, his sort of global identity. I think Abbar's obviously very involved in his own life out there. Every now and again, I drop him an email, he does respond but not elaboratively. I'd really be up for a close relationship.

I think being able to talk to my brother, John, has been very helpful, having someone that could identify with me but also had a different perspective because he hasn't got that older sister thing going on for him. He's not coming at it from a maternal viewpoint, maybe a slightly paternal viewpoint. Definitely having him and personal therapy has helped. Thank God I did have my brother and my husband. My husband has his own versions of trauma and disturbance in family. He wouldn't use that language, though he is emotionally literate enough to understand the complexity of the situation.

My mother has got so much unprocessed loss in her, there's never been any way that she could respond to this. She isn't somebody I can reflect with, think about things with, get help or wisdom from. It's probably partly why I get quite a strong maternal urge with my younger brothers and sisters. My mother was a very capable woman in her day, not now but in her day, she doesn't really get that feelings need to be processed. I guess that's one of the things that makes grieving more difficult.

I don't follow any religion or any organized religion. None have really spoken to me. I've tried occasionally with Christianity, then I wondered if I could get into Sufism, though in the end I've not really pursued organized religion. I believe that we have soul and in the spiritual connectedness of everyone. I feel quite resistant about getting into a more new-age kind of thing about that. I believe in that because that's what I experience.

There is something about the connection I feel with my siblings that is more than just, they're my brothers and sisters. I sense a deeper connection that maybe hasn't even got words. The same to some degree with my parents. My relationship with my mother is complex. I'm probably the child she feels closest to, but I'm also a recipient of a lot of her hostility. I suppose I feel that kind of ancestral connection even with people that I've never known. I've never known my grandmother. I find myself just wondering in my imagination and my fantasies about my grandparents and my lineage.

My mother's mother, my grandmother died when my mother was pregnant with me. For some reason, I've always felt maybe that's just a story, and what do I do with it? I feel like all of these things might mean something. I suppose I feel a sense of spirituality from all the experiences we have which take us beyond ourselves, which feel bigger than who we are as individuals.

Perhaps I have been partly changed by Tariq's death in the family, not that it's a source of comfort except from a sense of what it represented for the whole systematic organization of our family. Like it belongs to all of us, not just Tariq who died. I feel that. I'm not sure how much that has changed, but I think it has a bit. I also think just getting older has made me think more about that, and maybe a sense of him also dying and me getting older. Of course, this came at the time when I was coming to a change in my fertility as a woman, so I was also going through a life stage. I think that change has got me really reflecting on how short our lives are.

I feel a sense of urgency to contribute meaningful things in the short space of time, as well as the self-interest of, I want to enjoy being alive for a bit longer. I do want to look at the seasons changing. I do want to be connected with nature. I do want to get out in the spring with gardening, and then that helps me to appreciate my time on this planet.

I feel more accepting about my death generally, a bit more like I'd want to do my best to live. It's so tragic, Tariq's death. It's so tragic. It's such a young life that could have been so much more, so much more. It's so sad that in some ways I want to honour such tragedy, I want to appreciate life while I have it, as best I can. I feel just that little bit more resigned to the inevitability of death.

The other thing I'm searching for and wanting to understand and connect with is the difference between parents and siblings in how the grief affects them. I want to understand that a little bit more. I think if my close brother or sister died, I would feel like a part of me died too. From a position of an "auntie," I can step into maybe thinking like a mother or imagining what it would be like if my brother or sister died. I guess I'd be really interested in the different family positions and relationships.

15 "Don't judge my life on the chapter that you came in on"

Beth's story remembering her brother Jim

Jim is my brother, and he was nine years younger than me. When he was born, I was in the first year of Juniors. I remember he was just a lovely baby, a really big, fat baby. I was at an age where I could help mum and things like that with him. I've got another brother, Baz, who is three years younger than me. We all just got on really well. We really loved each other; we used to play out in the street.

When he was a little boy, Jim was really interested in nature, and he was a member of the RSPB. I always remember that his letters came from Sandy in Bedfordshire. It was really cute because from being little he used to get mail. Baz and I, we used to call him the golden child. He was golden in colour; he was the one of us that would tan. He was the youngest, had blond hair, and he was really the apple of my mum's eye. I just accepted him; we all loved him.

When I met my husband, Brock, I was 18, so Jim was 9. We used to babysit for him, and Brock used to carry him up to bed. He was just getting gangly and long-legged at that time. He was . . . What can I say to you about Jim? He was someone that everybody liked – everybody loved him, really. He was a very beautiful looking person, actually, and inside he was as well.

As he got older, it became obvious that he was really troubled, and he was diagnosed with bipolar disorder and with a borderline personality disorder. The two are kind of similar, but he was diagnosed with both. He struggled with that, and it increasingly affected him as he grew older.

He was really bothered about what other people thought of him, really bothered. We were very close as friends and as siblings, and we talked a lot. Well, I think one of the things with Jim was because he was so stunning looking, people were attracted to him, they just were. He didn't really have to do anything to be popular or to stand out in the crowd. I don't think he could really marry up how he felt about himself with the way that people responded to him, so he ended up sort of always trying to be someone he thought people wanted him to be and forgot to be himself.

He was someone who really liked nature and birds and bonsai trees, and that didn't fit with how glamorous he looked, and was. He became a personal trainer, and so he had a really good body as well. He felt boring; he didn't look boring, but he felt boring inside. Obviously, we didn't really know then that he had these mental disorders.

You can imagine from 18 onwards, I'm just living my life. I'd left home, so I wasn't in a great deal of touch with him at that point; he was a young lad. For me, in terms of what happened to him in the end, there are questions about this time when I wasn't so in touch with him when he was living at home with my parents growing up, being a teenager. As a young woman, nine years older, I was doing my own thing. So, I don't know really what happened then, but then when our first child was born, when I was 26 and Jim would have been like 17 or 18. He had a girlfriend and they were really close. We chose Jim to be our son's godfather. The friends that he was with were really lovely. They were from an area that was quite Bohemian, they were really lovely, politically minded and bothered about the environment, and those sort of things at quite a young age.

He went to university, and one of the things that he had to do was a placement, and this placement abroad. He went away and set up a diabetic clinic in the jungle, and he was teaching people there about how to avoid diabetes and all of that sort of thing, and we got all these photos of him. While he was there, I think he started to feel frightened and isolated and really cut off from his family. He started drinking to cope, and in these rural communities they made alcohol out of cane sugar and it was really, really potent.

He used to ring me, he'd be crying and saying he was homesick, and it was a horrendous feeling of powerlessness because I couldn't really do anything. Then he came back and he was in placement at a hospital in the far south of the country, and again, I think he felt isolated. He used to ring up and be really upset and not in a good way at all. I had three little ones at the time.

Then he really started to display bizarre and harmful behaviours towards himself, starting with addiction. It's this weird thing: he was my brother, I loved him so much, but then this other side to him would be there, and it was a bit like, I don't know what that is, that feels not really like you, but it must be you. It was really, really strange and sort of horrible.

I mean, we were really close and continued to be close, but there was this whole drug thing happening. Then there was a period of time he would do things like ring me, Brock worked away for three or four years, and so I was at home with the kids. On a night I'd be on my own and Jim used to ring and there'd be this noise, this rattling noise, and he'd say, "I've got loads of pills here and I'm going to take them." I couldn't do anything because I was with the kids, and it was really horrible, and it felt punishing on me.

But I didn't know why – and it was just crazy at times – he was diagnosed with these illnesses, and yet he could not bear the mental health label. He didn't want that, and he wouldn't engage with any drug regime for bipolar disorder, which we know takes ages to get right. He wouldn't, he just would not go there. He said, "I can't bother with that, it'll make me put weight on," and all of this sort of thing. He decided to self-medicate, so he just took loads of different drugs – heroin, he had alcohol, just all sorts of things.

I had a lot of guilt myself about not really protecting my children from my brother, but I just loved him so much. I couldn't bear to abandon him. But eventually, after many horrible incidents, I just had to put a barrier there and say, "You I love, your behaviour I don't, and I can't really." Then it was a bit like a Russian doll, I would support my parents with supporting him, but there was probably about maybe three or four years where I didn't have a lot to do with him.

I was aware that really, really hurt and wounded him, and it was awful, just awful. He wouldn't and couldn't contain some of his behaviours, that were so harmful, and he'd done some awful things. I couldn't really bear to see him like he just was on this self-destruct, but nothing we did could really help him or be enough for him.

When he died, I just thought that he must have felt abandoned by me, and so he didn't feel like he had anything to live for. Not that he was only living for me. I mean that I feel like I could have talked to him. I could've helped him to maybe see things differently or just get a different perspective. He had for probably about a good ten years been making regular, quite serious attempts on his own life, had twice been found in the nick of time and revived after an overdose.

He'd written a note before one attempt 15 years ago, that we found after he died; he didn't leave a note when he did die. When he was found, 15 years ago, he was really angry with us and I remember him saying to me, "You're really selfish because you're making me stay alive and I don't want to be."

For a couple of years before he died, we'd really been rebuilding our relationship, and he had been to us for Christmas, the Christmas before he died, and the one before that. We'd seen each other and been in touch and talked, and it felt like we were getting back to somewhere. There's just so many questions for me that I can't ask. I just miss him, just really miss him, and he was someone who loved me. I know that he loved me. I hope – I think he knew that I love him.

He was part of a big online community. After he died, we found out that he had loads and loads of messages from his online community. They were people who were drug users and who just shared and supported each other and helped each other. He was really community spirited, so he'd have good times if you like, where he was part of a community allotment project. He did a lot of teaching around diet and healthy eating and exercise and things like that.

These were the poles of him, so it would either be "My body's a temple and I'll only eat organic food," or "My body is a cesspit." He just swung between them, really, and it was quite hard to be with. As I developed and trained as a psychotherapist and really gained an understanding of psychiatric disorders, I could see he was experiencing borderline PD. He couldn't be in this middle place, and the middle place was where he needed to be.

He could sometimes be there, but there were always these extremes and these swinging things, and he couldn't really bear it, either, so he medicated himself.

It was an exhausting process, really exhausting. He would talk about it, and we would talk about it to exhaustion, a lot. I think the thing is, it was so disempowering as a sister, but I accepted him as he was, I never denounced him. I just didn't want him to come to the house when he was like that and be around the kids because he wasn't necessarily the same. In all the time when I wasn't really having a lot to do with him, we still were in contact and sometimes I would see him. That was heart-breaking, because sometimes he looked awful, and he looked like a really vulnerable, doddery, mind-fucked person.

Then, maybe something like a year before he died, he seemed to recover: he put weight on, he was available. I thought he'd mashed his brain so much with drugs that he'd never be able to find himself again, but he was there. Then, we all thought, this is how he'll really come back to health in a way, but he just didn't. He just went back to bingeing on drugs every so often. When he died and his flat was cleared out, a lot of diaries were found, and I felt that they were his diaries and that's not something that he imagined that someone else would read. But mum had a different opinion to that, and their relationship was obviously part of the whole thing. She felt that if it was his, it was hers, so therefore she could read anything and everything that he'd written. That was not really okay for me that she did that, and then she told us things.

So, I can't un-know those things, but in that time, immediately after his death, when we were all so vulnerable and so sort of broken, really, I felt I just had to let mum do what she needed to do. If mum needed to talk about those diaries and say what she'd read, so that she wasn't the only one with it, I just had to hear it. I don't feel the same now about that, but then it's what I did.

When he was not good was when he was doing not good things, and he didn't get in contact with us and didn't answer his door or his phone. To me, that was not for us. If you talked to him about it, he would just be cagy or just deny it. There'd be things that he was doing. He'd do things in front of your face and lie about it. That is the nature of addiction, or that was a part of it. I got to learn more about his inner world; it was more than he would have liked for us to know, and I really respected him. I respect that, really do. I feel like this is all coming out in a jumble.

We're not quite sure when he died. That weekend we'd all gone away as a family – my parents and our kids. One morning, all of a sudden, my dad just came out of the living room walking like – you know how people's body movements captures your eye if it's a bit strange? He was walking really stiffly, as if his legs were wooden.

He came in, and he was just as if he'd been hit by a car or something. He just said, "Jim is dead." Just like that. I was sitting on this sofa. I looked at him, and I knew it was true. Then I just heard this noise, like this wailing noise, and that was my mum, and that's how we found out. Basically, my brother Baz had been contacted by the police who had been trying to get hold of us all to say this body had been found in a flat, and he'd realized who it was, and he wanted to get a hold of us. I think it was about a day where they couldn't get a hold of him, then they did, and he got a hold of us.

It was just horrendous, as you can imagine. Then we realized that we needed to go back to mum's house to talk to the police. We met them there, and that was just awful, because they told us all these details that were just not okay for us to know, at all. This guy came in, he was the policeman that had been to the scene of the body. This story emerged that Jim had gone to bed, he must have taken a massive overdose before he actually went to bed and just died probably quite soon after.

These are the things that the police are telling us, plus many other horrible details. I still feel like I want to go back to the police and say, "We didn't need to know that at that time," but I haven't done so.

Then we could never see him, we could never see the body, but we just kept getting these phone calls. Brock was great; he was taking those calls – this was within a few days after he died, the pathology lab phoned. They said, "We need to take some tissue samples. What do you want us to do with the tissue samples afterwards? We can destroy them, or they can be used for medical science." I said, "Jim was a scientist. They can be used for medical science, I guess that would be okay." I don't know, it's like my brother had gone from a brother and a person to a body that was having these tissue samples taken.

I felt really fragmented, because there were all these pieces that didn't seem to fit together, really. Then, I couldn't really believe that, and I remember thinking, "Oh, he's not in the world anymore" and that was just awful.

Then, because we didn't see the body, about three weeks after he died, mum rang me one morning and said, "Oh, I've just thought of something, maybe it wasn't him." I said, "Oh, mum, it was." "But we never saw him, didn't we?" Oh God, that was just awful. That was just awful. It was so hard; any sadness was mum's sadness really. Dad was obviously sad, but we all knew that mum had this thing about Jim. It was like there was a Jim-size cookie-cutter hole in her. I don't think she still accepts it, really. But it feels weird to have one brother.

There are other things that are just coming up for me, like thinking about my brother's departure and what that was like in this case. Well, we had all these choices to make about what sort of coffin we wanted for him and all of that. I'd never done this, so we decided to have this cardboard one or eco-coffin, and it was all covered in what looked like leaves. There were photographs of leaves on it. It was really, really beautiful. He would have really liked that because he just was really bothered about that sort of thing.

They said we couldn't see him, but we could go and see him in the coffin when he got in the chapel of rest if we wanted to. We decided that we would, and this was another time it was all about mum. It was all about supporting mum, and mum was in this terrible place. I said, "Mum, I'll do this thing with them that they need." They helped to make this list of what she would like, because they couldn't even put any clothes on him, but they could lay clothes on him. What did she want to be put in the coffin with him? So we'd all written poems and things that we wanted to put in with him.

That was really heart-breaking, but mum was like, "Well, I can't really do that." She went off into the room to be with him, and again there was just all this noise coming out of the room because mum was just in this horrendous state. Then she came out and we could then go in. I think it was me, Brock, and my daughter, and so we went in. It was just a little room and there's this thing the coffin was resting on. The first thing that hit me was the smell, it was just horrendous. Well, obviously, something had been treated on the body, but still it was dreadful.

We'd asked for his photo to be put on top of the coffin, so it was and that was really great, actually. That really helped because it was like, this was him. I'm looking at him there, not this other thing in the coffin. Then again, when it was his funeral, we kept it to the family, because he did have quite a lot of friends who were quite unstable people, really. I was really mixed about that, but it could have been really upsetting if people were coming and being drunk or on drugs or whatever. It was quite small; we were in quite a small chapel. The smell again was just horrendous. It was really weird.

Then, I remember that as we were going out, mum and dad and I were standing by the coffin, and Baz was still sitting down. He had distanced himself for years and years, but anyway I just put my hand out to him, and he came and stood with us, and we stood together with hands around each other. I had this most bizarre experience or memory of it being the four of us again. At that moment I thought, since Jim arrived, Baz went out on the outside, and since he's died, he's come back in.

Now I feel sad. I feel like I, it's a strange thing because it's almost like, once he died, I could really grieve for the brother that I'd lost, and for the brother that I loved. There was a long time while he was still alive that he wasn't really available or present, or allowing himself to behave better. There was that sort of thing of, it's almost like while he was alive, I'd shut this door on my heart, on my feelings about him, and sort of said to myself, "He is what he is now, this is who he is. This is what he is right now, this is where we are with that." I think all of a sudden it sounds like I said, "Let's not be comparing him to now. This is how he is."

When he died, all of that grief came out. It was like this other layer of grief somehow was then allowed to be there, and the sadness of a life lived in torment really for him, and just all sorts of questions, and it has to be said, now we know where he is. We never knew where he was, if he was okay and what he was doing. We all said, "We know where he is now and that he's in peace. He can't hurt himself anymore."

Now, when I think of him, because I'm very visual, so I'll see things. So, it's not a problem to me to see him. I can still see him, and he's always looked the same since he died. He's been in a pair of really soft pale worn-out jeans and a white long-sleeved T-shirt looking okay and with bare feet. I can just imagine if he was here now with us, he would just be sitting like this looking at me and nodding and listening. He was a really great listener; he wasn't someone that would really interrupt.

When he died, one of his friends sent a card with a quote from Helen Keller. It said, "Those who we love the deepest become a part of us." I really feel that. I do think he became part of me, because he is part of me in a way. But I also feel that his energy is with me. I do believe in that sort of thing. I do believe that when something comes into existence, even when it goes and is dead, his body is gone, the energy from that thing or that being, that spirit is still there, and I don't feel uncomfortable about that. It's just what I believe. I wish he was here and okay and well.

I'd say I have a spiritual belief. I don't really like or subscribe to organized religion, but I would describe myself as a spiritual, a pantheist. I think, for me, I found my spirituality in probably nature and in relationship, really, in the space between. Since Jim died, I would say it's sort of crystallized that for me. Like I would feel it's there. It's been tested in some way. It's certainly tested my religious beliefs, because at no point did I ever want to pray or do anything like that. I never did at the time; I just wouldn't. There's the feeling of, there's some kind of imprint left or something. He's just there. That feeling didn't die with him. Things come to me that I feel, it's not just my memory of him, it's something else. I can't really say what that is. There, again, I used to be part of a Shamanic journeying group and things like that, so that really speaks to me, other planes of consciousness and that sort of thing. So, it doesn't scare me or anything like that. It has made me obviously think about my own death.

This is the really weird thing, the thing that keeps recurring for me, and I don't think I'm being a bit weird here, but it's the idea of a body breaking down and not being there anymore. I think because we had that horrible information to begin with, and then this irrefutable evidence that that was happening. That's been sort of helpful as well, because it's like it's altered now; there's leaves everywhere that are just going back into the soil. That's what's going to happen because there is a disbelief: how can someone not be there suddenly, that solidity of the person? The breath is gone, and then life's gone out of that body, but still, this energy is there. It's probably still a work in progress, but I think there is something still familiar about, how can he not be there? I know he isn't, but how could he not be?

In the order of service that we had for him, the poem that I chose was one that everybody knows, and people think it's cheesy, but to me it is that one where it says something like, "It's about going through a door and I know that you're just in the next room." It feels like that all the time. It feels like there's another dimension or something that we can't see, we don't know, but there is. I don't know whether that's just because that is nice for me to think that. I don't think I'll be reunited with him in that way because I feel like in the way we're united now is how it will always be. It's not as if I'll go down a tunnel of light and he'll be at the end in his jeans and white T-shirt; I don't think that. I think wherever he is, he will be feeling this, and the same will be for me.

If I could say something to him now, I'd want to ask, "Why didn't you tell me how you were feeling?" I think he would say, "There was no point." I'd also want to ask, "Are you all right? Are you okay? Do you know that we're with you? Do you come and be with us?" I feel like he does. I think he does. I think there's all sorts of questions I have, like, "Was there anything I could have done? Was there anything I didn't do? Could I have made a difference?" He would say – well, this is just what comes to mind – he would say "You did make a difference. I just couldn't do it anymore."

There was an inquest; that was another horrendous thing. I had, really, a bit of a battle with my parents because my dad wanted to go. I said to him, "Let's just imagine that Jim was sitting with us now, what do you think he'd say if we said, 'Do you want us at your inquest?' " He said no, he thought Jim wouldn't want us to go. I guess there would be details of his life revealed that he didn't intend us to know about, and I wanted to respect that, I really did. And I said, "He's not here to really make sure that that's the case, but I want to do that." My dad was really not happy about it, but he didn't go. I don't think mum wanted to go.

You could imagine that there would have been a lot of stuff at the inquest which he didn't want to be really talked about or heard by us. I did what I could to really to make sure that his privacy was protected, and it wasn't always, really. My mum just needed to know things which I don't think helped her in the end, really; it certainly didn't help me.

So, we stayed away from the inquest and heard about it later. They recorded a death by misadventure, but we all feel that he took an overdose. They called it like an accidental overdose. Because of all this history of attempts and the notes, I do find that a comfort that it was a choice, not an accident. I'd find that really hard.

We have received a whole report thing from the inquest, and I don't want to read it. I won't read it. I think everything that was said was typed. I don't really need to know that; I don't want to hear about the state of his body and all of that. I don't.

Having an experience with undertakers was a whole new thing for me too. They were really great. I learned all sorts of things. For example, there were quite a lot of women involved; somehow you always think it is men, but ours were women, which really helped me. My boys and Brock and my dad carried the coffin, so that was okay. Then how the undertakers talked about Jim was really respectful. There was a photo of him, and they'd put a little message next to the photo saying, "Jim's family wanted you all to know what Jim looked like. This is Jim." They really wanted to know about him. She said to us, "That's really nice for us. We know who he was really; we have an idea of him, and we can say hello to him."

It felt so comforting and kind at that sort of time. I felt that he wasn't judged or anything like that because it would have been obvious probably what sort of lifestyle he'd had. Then just the things that they offer you, I didn't know. She said, "Do you want some of his hair?" I was like, "Oh, God," I would start thinking that there was something like that the Victorians used to do, rings with plaits in. I was a bit like, "Oh," but mum did want some.

As it happened, Niamh, who was our funeral director, on the day that they came with him in the coffin to go to the crematorium, she just handed me this little velvet purse. I opened it, and it was Jim's hair. Everyone I've told about it has gone, "Oh, God, that's a bit grim." Actually, it was quite nice; at that moment, it was okay.

My daughter, my niece, and I made the wreath that went on top of Jim's coffin. It was all wildflowers and flowers out of my mum and dad's hedgerow; it was really, really lovely. Also, on top of his coffin, we'd put a pair of his trainers because he loved his trainers. Then Niamh said, "It's the first time I've had a pair of trainers on top of a coffin." But you could have what you wanted, so that was really nice. It was really personal. The order of service was really personal too. The poem on the front page we had to fight all the way, because they kept saying to us it needs to say something in remembrance of him, and we said, "No, we don't want to say it like that." There's another bit to it which was the inside bit: we had all these little trainers and things, and the family had written tributes and things, so that was part of it, it was farewell messages.

Then we had this song, "I Can See Clearly Now, the Rain Has Gone," that he had said to us all, "I want this playing at my funeral." We also chose "Somewhere over the Rainbow" – I think that was when he came in – sung by the Hawaiian guy, and then "Tiny Dancer" was his girlfriend's choice, that was their song, so we had that. Now, obviously, when these songs come up, it's quite tricky.

He was very loved. One of the things that we really did share between us was humour. We really had the same sense of humour, and that was absolutely ace, it really was.

I've got quite a lot of what I would call close friends, and they were just great. They were really supportive on the day of the funeral. I've got friends that live down in London; they both came up and made a meal for us to be ready for when we got back from the funeral. That was really nice.

Other friends just sent cards and would be in touch with me. For ten years, I ran a counselling/psychotherapy service and I was a service lead. I left in 2015, but they sent me a big bouquet of flowers. That was really nice. People were really great, I think.

I went to see my private practice supervisor to see if I was ready to start working again. She was just great. It was such an important learning for me, about being a psychotherapist, working with grief, and then being in grief. She was talking to me about it. She said, "Tell me how you feel and tell me what's happened." I did – I was upset at times, but okay. She said to me, "Beth, I really think that you're okay to work because you are in touch with yourself. You're not defending and sort of going, 'I'm fine.'" It's important to know. I had a time with that, probably immediately after he died. That felt really important to me that I could be in touch with the sadness and I can hold myself too.

It was something as a family that we grieved, we did a lot of grieving together, a lot of talking. It was like a co-created grieving process; it was really important, and it meant that I could keep walking in this horrible landscape and eventually become okay on it. I did do that purposely because I did want to get back to work. I took three weeks off, I think. So, that for me, in terms of part of checking in with myself, "How am I?" I think having a supervisor was really helpful and other peers and things like that was really helpful.

Mum did not have a good experience with her yoga group where someone had said something really insensitive like, "Oh, she is not here today because her son killed himself" or something. Someone else in the group came to see her and said, "Oh, I hear you son's killed himself." And this was just horrendous, and it was not really someone that mum knew all that well.

I think when it's a suicide, people are a little bit like, "Oh." I do not shy away from that, I don't. I do say to people, "He took his own life." I don't say, "Commit suicide." I don't really like that way of saying it, but I do say that he took his own life because I just think we need to get more okay with just sort of saying the truth. "It's awful, I can't protect you from it, I'm sorry that's what happened, but you don't need to look after me because I'm okay." So, when people say, "What happened to him?" I would say, tell them what happened. Also, there was another thing where you get these little verses or things that are quite meaningful. There was one which was, "Don't judge my life on the chapter that you came in on." I really liked it.

I was talking to mum about this because she got really horrified about the yoga group, "Oh my God, they're going to know all this about me now." I said to her, "You know what mum? I'll come with you to the yoga group and we'll say, 'We've heard that you know about Jim, we just wanted to tell you a little bit more about it so you don't judge his life on the chapter that you came in on because that's really not all that there was to him.'" Mum thought about it, but she said, "No, I don't think I can bear to do that." I would have done it with her because it felt really important that this was a life. Jim had actually done loads of things, he had so much potential, and if you come in on that end chapter, it doesn't look that brilliant, but that's really not all that he was.

I know I'll always have two brothers, it's a bit weird now. One is not there but it's how it is. I remember being at a conference or something and being asked if I had any siblings. I just said, "I've got two brothers." I wouldn't go into it any more with that, I haven't talked about it a lot. I'll do tell people that I'm close to, but I'm quite private as a person. Last year at a conference, we were there on the anniversary of his death. I did feel horrible and I did tell my colleagues. I said, "My brother died a year ago today. That's happened. I'm okay, but I might be a bit wobbly." Probably I put a bit of a thing of, "Don't ask me about it too much or something."

I remember that really keenly because I was in this role and I take my profession really seriously. There was this leakage from my private life, and I had to really acknowledge to myself that I needed some help with it, but I couldn't pretend it was okay because it wasn't. But as soon as I'd told people and given myself permission to be a bit quiet, however, it was fine. They were really okay. I think it's quite important, actually, that with grief we have time to do what we need to do with it. Where I live, we have this "don't make a song-and-dance about it" attitude, but at the same time, I needed to say what was going on for me on that particular day.

Actually, the first anniversary of his death was worse in some ways than his death, which I had not expected at all. Because when someone kills themselves, you've got no idea, and then just on the day you know that they had died. When it came to the anniversary, in the three or four weeks up to his death it was just horrendous because I was thinking about what was happening for him at that time last year when he was going towards this final decision. I hadn't at all accounted for that, I hadn't even thought about that. I really broke down, actually, I was not at a good place in April at all. It was awful, really awful. I was talking with my brother because we were always close, but now we're closer. He's got loads of guilt. It can be hard, I think, to stay in relationship in grieving.

We did some lovely things like making a bonfire, I did force my mum, in the end, to burn those diaries, although the other day, she told me that she had kept some. I was like, "Oh God." We made this bonfire and all Jim's personal things went on the bonfire. We talked about him, that was one thing we did. We went and planted some snowdrops. We did all sorts of things that he'd have liked. Went to see things and to go to places; now when I go anywhere, I take a photo of him. He didn't do loads of travelling, but I know he wanted to, and I just imagine that he's with me. I think in this grieving, there's a part of me that wants to just go like a little rabbit in the snow, just be hidden, and not have to talk about it, or feel it, or think it, I imagine that's a fairly common thing, because it's just so horrible.

My mum is really great, and I love her to bits, but – say, if I rang mum and said, "Mum I've had an awful headache all day," and then she'd go, "Wait till I tell you, I'm having a headache, and I'm having a backache, and both my bunions." I'd be like, "Okay, okay, let's talk about you, then." It's the same with Jim. I've said to her, "I just can't get my head around losing my brother." She said, "But Beth, I've lost a child." God almighty, I am a mother, so I can absolutely imagine the horror of that. I can because I've been alongside her. I've got another friend that lost her little baby brother when he was two, and another when the baby was a year old. You can just imagine it, but it's different.

That made me shut up about Jim around her and not show her what I was feeling. It would be really helpful for me to show her my grief. I have done sometimes, but not much really. She would do it with me but I wouldn't do it with her, and so that's hindered me in my grieving process a bit. Some of my anger with him has hindered me too. I hinder myself too sometimes. Something of me being me and thinking, "That's awful and I don't want to really go into that," and just doing other things almost till Brock held my hands down to stop me and said, "Are you sad?" Then for me to say, "Yes, but I don't want you to be. I don't want to be." I do remember thinking, "I haven't got time for this," and "I don't want this. Why am I still fucking sad?" That was horrendous, and I'd still have that sometimes.

Baz and I made up this word called 'emocean', so it's E, M, and then ocean, because we said grief was like the tide. Sometimes we'd text each other and use this language. Sometimes I'd be like, "I'm fine today. I'm on dry land. There's loads of beach. It's fine." Then suddenly the sea would come in and I'd be at the till in Tesco thinking, "Not now." The grief would just come in, I'd be like, "Oh, no," I would go and put my shopping back, leave the shop and have a cry, and then go back.

Eventually, just using this metaphor between us as siblings, we really found a way to talk quite deeply about our feelings. I'd say, "I've made myself a raft, and I've got a pair of old knickers as a flag," and he said, "Was that you? Did you see me, I went past on a whale a minute ago?" It was really, really nice. Or sometimes he'd say, "I'm just on the bottom today, it's really dark" and I'd say, "I'm weighing anchor. Have a look out for it." Sometimes we would really be able to find a way to connect with that, to make meaning and find a way to place this experience.

I would like to have been able to read about other people who had lost a sibling. I don't know if I know anybody that has. I remember when I was at school there was a girl that died. Then when my kids were at school, a girl died, and she was one of three sisters. I always remember thinking, "I wonder what it was like for them. Suddenly, there weren't three, there were two." I think it would've just been really comforting to hear about other people's experience because it is horrendous and at times so horrible that I thought, "I just don't want to be here." I wasn't suicidal, but it was, "This is too awful, and I don't want to exist, for a minute or a day." I think there would've been something for me about knowing where they'd got to in their grief, about how they managed their parents' needs.

I suppose there might be something about this experience that is only occurring to me now that I might've done some more detaching from my parents because they couldn't be there for me. They are parents that are usually quite there for us. So, there is that kind of somewhat childlike tendency to turn towards them in adversity, shall we say, but that just wasn't possible. It was the other way around, a role reversal.

I'd want to say to other siblings, "Don't expect your parents to prop you up because they can't. Because they're in their own grief and you might get a feeling that your grief is somewhat diminished next to theirs. That's not very nice, but it just is what it is." I have worked with people who've lost siblings when they were young, and they felt that as the surviving child they were quite invisible really in this time of their parents' grief. There might be a message then to parents about, "Don't forget about your living children. They still need you." But then it feels wrong of me to say that.

I count this telling my story now as part of my experience, so that I'm really glad I did it. I feel like when you sit with someone who has had, what I would call, a catastrophic loss, it's a bit of a relief too because somehow you know that they know something about what it was like.

16 "Jacky was my most significant security base"

Edward's story remembering his brother Jacky

Jacky is my younger brother, four years younger than me. We have an older sister. He was very different looking, physically, to me and my sister. My sister was like me, so pale-skinned and fair-haired. He was a different shape. I'm quite chunky, he was quite slim, he had dark hair, I've got ginger hair or light hair.

Of course, as we were growing up, he was the baby of the family, the youngest one, and he was the favourite. It may well be heavily coloured by my perspective, of course, but yes, he was the favourite of both my parents. I think it's because he was the youngest, the littlest one, the cutest one, just because he was four years younger than me. He was the one that got all the attention. I've got photographs that prove it. I became a sour-faced, resentful, jealous, hateful person in relation to him, and I used to do horrible things to him.

I remember once being away in Ireland; my mum is Irish. I remember taking him out one day for a walk, taking him a long way away from the house, then running away from him and 'losing' him. When I got back and they said, "Where's Jacky?" and I said, "I don't know, he wandered off." Took them hours to find him, and so he was massively distressed, "He left me, he left me." I was found out on what were those bullying, resentful, retaliation things. It must have been horrible to be told off, but I don't remember that. It became the norm. I do remember getting to the point where in some ways I got some masochistic pleasure from being told off. It's a bit like I'd succeeded if I got told off. I succeeded in doing something to him. Those are my deeply affecting earliest memories, and so different from later. I mean later in our lives, our relationship, I mean were polar opposites.

My sense was that he went through that early part of his life just being the adored one. If someone had asked him during that period, "What about your brother?" He wouldn't have much to say. I think later on, because I wasn't bullying him when he was two or three, but later on if he was asked that, he probably say, "He's horrible to me. Why is he horrible to me?" That would be like when he was six to ten, or something like that.

But in the early days, I wouldn't be on his radar much. Maybe he started to think about me in some more significant way when I started to bully him.

When I say, bully him, I never beat him up or anything like that, but I'd just do horrible things to him like take him away and lose him in the Irish bog.

When I was 18, just before I went to Oxford, my father retired. He was a bigwig in British European Airways, as it then was. He was married before, and his son from his first marriage, Julian, lived in New Zealand, and cut a long story short, my dad decided, and persuaded my mum, to emigrate to New Zealand. But it was the time I was going up to university. So, my mum and dad, Jacky, and my sister Joanna went off to emigrate to New Zealand. I stayed in England to go off to university. By that stage, Jacky was 13, 14. It's one of the most significant parts of my childhood. It was massive, absolutely massive. I was a very rebellious teenager. Not surprising given what I've already said. I'd do all sorts of things to piss my dad off, basically because he loved Jacky rather than me, that was at the bottom on it. Yes, so I was convinced at the time that dad was glad to get rid of me. I was about to go off to university anyway, I have no recollection at all, of there being a discussion about whether I could have gone to university in Auckland. I'm glad I didn't, but I could have done, but there was no discussion about that.

I think I got into Oxford to please my mum. She'd grown up in Ireland in a poorish family with lots of kids. They didn't have the money to send her to the high school. Until I was about 13, I didn't apply myself in school, my school reports said things like, "Edward doesn't concentrate in class. Edward is a troublemaker. Edward distracts himself; Edward distracts others." Then it all changed. I twigged that my mum really liked it that I was clever, fulfilling her dream maybe. I worked hard and got into Oxford, and she told everybody, it was a big deal. I did that to get my mum's admiration or to please her and make her proud of me, and then they buggered off. They went to live there forever. It wasn't a visit. They went to emigrate.

There wasn't any internet back then. I remember they went off in September, and I went up to Oxford in October. At Christmas, I went to stay with Auntie Win. She wasn't our biological auntie, but she was a lovely woman who lived nearby. I went and I stayed with her and her husband. She was lovely, but it was horrible. Then a year later they came back, my mum, dad, and my brother, but not my sister.

They bought a house, not that far from where we used to live. It was weird. In some ways it was almost like they hadn't gone. Superficially it was like, "Oh well, they're back." At some point I stayed there a few years. Then my mum wanted to move near the seaside and my dad wanted to move north, so they moved to Morecambe where they lived for the last ten years of my father's life.

When I finished Oxford, I went out to America. I came back and I got a job. Then I went to live in India. Between them coming back and me going off to India, I don't really remember much in terms of me and Jacky. I saw him and he wasn't that much different than before. I was in India for a year and a half. During that time, Jacky got into acting and he was very successful. He blossomed in a way. He left home, got his own identity. He got the star role at some rep company in North London, so he was doing really well. The other thing about my brother, of course, which I haven't already said, but I think was true when he was little as well as later, he was very handsome.

He was very good looking, much more good looking than me. I remember it was the '70s, he'd let his hair grow; he'd got rich, curly black hair, and he's really handsome. He had this beautiful girlfriend, and he was this rising star in the theatre world. It was like my worst nightmares come true. It was like my childhood is just going to be continued throughout my life. He's going to be the one who's in the limelight. Okay, I went to Oxford, but that's small beer, academic success compared with, you know he's good looking, a star. During those years, we weren't close, he was very separate. He'd come up, we'd see each other occasionally and it just reinforced my fatalistic sense of doom. I was doomed to be the second best for the rest of my life.

When I was in London doing my master's degree, he came to live with me in the flat I had. It was out of the blue, and all that theatre thing had suddenly just ended. Just like a light switch going off. He was a bit lost. He didn't want to go home to live with mum and dad. He lived with me for, must have been the best part of a couple of years in London, and then I got a job in Manchester. He didn't come with me, but he followed me up later. That was where our relationship changed, because I saw a lot of him in London, I took him in, and we spent a lot of time together.

I found out later from him, years later, that he'd grown up seeing me as the successful one. There was truth to it. I was the one who was clever at school. I was the one who got to Oxford. I was the one that got good jobs. He was at the theatre, was a shooting star, then suddenly that all went, and he was a falling star and he needed my help and I gave it to him, I did. I am aware that it put me in the one-up position. He seemed to change. He had this gorgeous girlfriend and was in the theatre. You can't get more sociable in the theatre, lots of people around. He lived with me in London, then I moved to Manchester with some friends, and he followed up, lived in the house with us. Just following on my coattails really. He wasn't on a career path, and he was struggling, I suppose, struggling in being out in the world. He wasn't an emotionally expressive person, my brother. Despite all the stuff about being in the theatre, he was shy, not sociable, and quite isolated.

Soon after I came in Manchester, I met my first long-term relationship partner, Christine, and we began living together. I loved her. She was very beautiful actually. We had a very good and loving relationship. I was the one who had everything. I had money, I had a job, I had a career, I had a beautiful girlfriend, I had a partner, a house I rented.

Then I bought a house with Christine, and he rented a flat about 10–15 minutes' walk away. During that period in Manchester, probably the best part of a decade, we saw loads of each other. We'd run together, we'd go out playing backgammon in clubs together. We'd go walking, we spent a lot of time together. We really saw a lot of each other, and our relationship completely changed, and we became very close.

Then, in 1984, our father died, and Jacky went back home to Morecambe. When he'd been there a few weeks, I remember saying to him, "Look Jacky, you've got to be careful here because mum is going to get used to you living here." Basically, I was saying to him, "Be careful for your own sake. Do you want to be living here for the foreseeable, for the long term? Do you really want to be living in Morecambe with mum? If not, then maybe you shouldn't just keep living here because mum will get used to it." I remember vividly talking to him about that, but it didn't seem to register and, to cut a long story short, he stayed living with my mum until she died in 2004. So, he spent 20 years, living at home with our mum in Morecambe and without a partner. During that time, he used to come down to Manchester and I went to Morecambe a lot. A few times a year, we'd go off on walking holidays. Although I didn't see him as much as when he was in Manchester, we were very close, very, very close. So close, I can never really find the words to express how awful that two or three years of him having motor neurone disease (MND) was. When he died, the biggest thing about that, by far, was the realization that Jacky was my most significant security base. It wasn't my mum or my dad, it was Jacky.

Without ever thinking it, I had always lived as if he'll always be there, whatever happened in my life, and there were lots of things that happened. Christine and I ended our relationship – that was a terrible period of my life – and lots of other things, and yet Jacky was always there. In that 30 years, Jacky was always there, and I had that sense that he would always be there and he was such a soothing presence for me, because he was just always there.

After my relationship with Christine ended, there were a few years when I wasn't with anybody and then my relationship with Hazel started. Jacky and Hazel were very close as well. But, it's like, whatever point in my relationship with Hazel, I could not say as certainly as I could say with Jacky that she would always be there, because she might not. I'd had a relationship with Christine, I thought we'd be together forever, but we weren't. So, that could happen with Hazel, but it would never happen with Jacky. Deep inside, I knew he would always be there whatever happened. It's a wonderful thing to have, a sense of something solid, of refuge really. He was that, and when he died and that went, that was profoundly disturbing for me.

That's how important he was, and he was there for 30 years. I'll never forget reading Juliet Mitchell's book on siblings.[1] She wrote this book, basically was saying, Freud got it wrong. He was right that parents are crucially important, but that siblings can be just as important, if not more so for some people. In some ways, that's certainly true with me, not in my first 20 years, but in my lifetime, it's definitely the case in some significant ways.

Then that last phase which was about two and a half to three years, from the first limping, which was the first symptom, to his death. That was in the last phase which was absolutely awful. Hazel noticed it before I did, she said, "Is Jacky limping?" We were behind him and I was, "Oh, yes." I could see he was limping slightly. I didn't think anything of it, for all sorts of reasons. I said to him, "You got something wrong with your leg? Looks like you're limping a bit." He said "Oh, it's probably the ligament or something." We didn't think anything of it, really, and then it got worse. To helplessly, powerlessly, witness him week after week, and then finding out that he had MND, and knowing it was going to continue, you know, he wasn't going to get better.

Seeing him on a daily, weekly basis getting worse and worse, and getting to a point where he couldn't even hold a spoon, and spoon up some food, and put it in his mouth. He had to be winched out of bed to be put on a commode, and have someone else wipe his arse, and winch him back through the air back on to the bed. The extent to which I just hated, more than I've hated anything else in my life watching him suffering, everything about him sort of dying very slowly and watching him suffer. There's something about that, in a funny, perverse sort of way, that really bonds you to somebody. It's just unimaginable. If somebody had described it to me before I experienced it, I wouldn't have believed it. I would have been able to imagine it, but it's awful, in so many different ways.

I used to go and stay with him; I'd go up there on a Wednesday and come back on a Thursday and then go up on a Saturday and come back on a Sunday. He'd be in his room in his bed at night and I'd be in my father's bed in my parents' bedroom. I'd lie there and in the middle of the night, 2 o'clock-ish usually, two district nurses would come into the house because they had a key and they'd turn him over in the bed. They'd turn him over because he couldn't turn over.

He was just lying on his back like some fucking beached whale, he couldn't turn over. They'd turn him over. I used to lie there often awake when they came, or awoken by them or whatever, and I'd imagine it. I tried to imagine what it would be like to be Jacky lying in that bed unable to move, waiting to be turned over. My last years with Jacky were awful. Awful, but you know, as it went on such a long time, it became part of my life going up there and you get used to it in a way. You get used to the torture of it. It's weird, and it would be routine.

I'd go shopping and then come back and I'd cook his food, what he liked, and I'd sit with him in his room and we'd talk every week for over two years. We'd put things on the telly and watch it. Or when he was in the early part of that period, we'd go sit by the table with the computer and play backgammon. You get used to it, you know, I'd look forward to going and seeing him. It became a new normal, something I looked forward to, something nice. Something I looked forward to, something pleasurable. All mixed in with all of that awfulness. I hadn't had any previous experience of somebody close to me being ill for a period of time and getting worse.

What is it that bonds people together? It's the sort of thing that often comes to mind to me when I try and make sense of it or try to talk about it is a bit like soldiers who have been in war and there's Wilfred Owen's poetry and all everyone has written about war and that well-known phenomenon where people that have been in the war together have a bond because through that awfulness, through being together in something that's so awful, that is almost incommunicable or something, but they bond through it. Having been through something terrible together. I always think Jacky and I have been through it together. Well he was the one that actually had MND and I didn't, and I was eternally grateful that I didn't. But nevertheless, it was absolutely awful for me, absolutely awful, but in a funny sort of way bonded us. It's like we had that early phase of our lives when I hated him. He was a loved one, he became so beautiful and he was always so beautiful. He got the girlfriends and was going to be a star. I was just plodding along. Then somehow, what turned out to be 30 years, being really, really close and then for that MND to happen and for us to bond further through that.

He didn't want to die. He knew it was not going to be long, he knew it was going to be months at most and I'll never forget, maybe a couple of months before he did die, he said to me, "I wish I had longer." I remember being shocked by it because there he was lying in bed and couldn't move a fucking muscle, but he had two really, really good carers. Vicky was one of them, she was wonderful, and George. I remember their names, Vicky and George.

Vicky was a middle-aged working-class woman, a carer who tended Jacky for a long, long time and, when he was dying, she held him. George was a lovely man, and Jacky got really close with them. It was so good to know they were there, Vicky and George. He saw them every day and he saw me twice a week, and he didn't want to die. He wanted to be alive longer because he was enjoying some things, he still had a quality of life.

I'll never forget not long before that, he said he dreamt every now and then about, as he called it, striding out, with me and how he missed it, and that led me to imagine – I used to walk a lot and if somebody said to me, "You can't go walking anymore Edward," or if something happened to me and I couldn't go walking anymore, I can't even imagine how it would be. I can imagine it would be fucking horrible. I can't tell you the number of times I kept coming back to his statement, to that picture, back to that reality, to that unpalatable fact that he couldn't, he would never ever walk down the road again, never mind up Scafell or something again, and so that bonding in that last bit in some ways was the closest I've ever been to anybody ever.

You know when people say, "Oh they've not gone, they're up in heaven waiting," Or "They're there," pointing to their chest, I used to scoff at it, but since Jacky died, I know, he's inside me, I can access him any time I want, and I do. One of the main ways I access him is missing him and people say, "Does it get easier?" It does get easier. It gets easier in the sense that I think about him less often, that's certainly true. But does the missing of him being in my life get any easier? No, it doesn't, it doesn't get easier. I go to it less often, but it doesn't get easier. Even as I think about him not being here, it's like I ache. When he died, one of the things I was influenced by was William Worden's model of grieving: the last stage is finding some people in your life to replace what you had with the person you lost, and I thought I need to deepen my relationships with my male friends. I know I've done that, and it's good, but it doesn't detract, actually; it compensates, maybe, but it doesn't detract from missing Jacky. Wishing on a beautiful day I could just go off to the lakes, walk up Striding Edge with him and I can't do that, and I'll never be able to do that again.

Most times I go walking, I think of him and for a long time after he died, years, every time I went north, wherever it was I'd almost always come back via Morecambe and I'd drive down the road that he lived on and go past the house and stop, park, and look at it. In the early days, I'd go in next door and talk to the lovely woman who lived there. Once I called in about a year or two after Jacky died, and of course we talked about Jacky and she said, "Oh it's always the best ones that go first," and I thought, "Yes." You know, it takes me right back, it was such an echo of the first phase of my life.

I was with Jacky when he died, as was Hazel, as was Vicky. It was strange because I wasn't there when either of my parents died. I think it's the first time I had been with somebody when they died. The main thing was that when he died, I knew he was dead, but he'd just been alive, he'd just been alive and then he was dead, but he was still there, his body was lying on the bed. I couldn't make sense of that. It was profoundly disorientating for me, weird, strange, peculiar. It was like I knew he was dead. I knew he was dead but his body was there, and he'd just been there alive, making some noise or moving or something. It was just very strange and then I remember staying there for a bit, and then I left the room and we were waiting for the undertakers or the GP to come. He was lying in the bedroom on the bed for a while, and I'd go in a few times just because I didn't know quite how to be. I didn't know what was best to do. I didn't want to just shut off from it, that's why I kept coming back. I wanted to be there.

It was very disorientating, not sure how to be, what to do for the best for me. I was also surprised because I shut off at some point in the few hours after he'd died. I remember I didn't burst out in tears; I wasn't emotional. I know I felt like I'd switched off my feelings, a state of shock, a state of numbness. I sort of didn't like that, I wanted to be feeling, I tried to feel, but I couldn't.

And then they came, these strangers, and took him away. It didn't seem right somehow, but I knew it had to be done, but it didn't seem right. Then his body was gone. I remember vividly being in the bedroom that he'd been in for years, for two years, and then for the best part of his last year more or less all the time in his bed. Going into his room and there was the bed, and there was everything around it, it was familiar, but he wasn't in it. He'd been in it for such a long time. That was like I couldn't put the pieces together, the bedroom with him in it alive and the bedroom with him not in it, and his dead body going along the road somewhere.

I couldn't piece it together. Everything felt very empty, like there was nothing more to do. There was plenty to do when I was there with him in the house, and none of that needed to be done. All these objects around there were pointless, everything in there, pillows and cups, they were irrelevant. There were a lot of gadgets and accoutrements or whatever, more than in a normal house, and they all died; they had no purpose. They were all pointless, purposeless. Suddenly, there was just emptiness, metaphorically an emptiness. I wasn't wailing and tearing my hair out; there was emptiness.

There are just so many echoes in my life, so many things that can trigger stuff around Jacky. Over time, it's been much less often that I'm triggered, but I'm still surprised how powerfully and strongly I feel stuff around Jacky, and what happened to him about him not being here. He's still with me. The intensity is just as much now as it was back then, but the frequency is less often. There are lots of triggers around that put me back in touch. So many things – it could be something like a walk or more incidental like the way somebody looks at me, or the smell of something or a phrase. In some ways, it's like, I don't mind. I like it. I wouldn't like it to be otherwise. It is difficult in a way, but I don't want it to stop. It's like it brings him back.

Jacky was somebody who didn't have lots of friends, but if he liked somebody, you knew it. He liked Hazel and she knew it, because he wasn't close to many people, I think she felt quite privileged in some ways. One of my regrets is that I didn't get to tell him, even though I had a fucking long period of time while he was still alive on his way to death, how I felt about him. I did a bit, but not to the depth that I really felt. In some ways he wouldn't have wanted to deal with it, and it would have been an imposition. A lot of my relationship with Jacky was conducted very much with that sensitivity on my part. I think for a lot of it I was accurate, but I'm still left wondering whether I could have said more that although he would have found uncomfortable, he would have liked. I can't know that. I'm always in doubt about that. The fact remains that I didn't. If I had, I would have wanted him to know how in some ways he was the most important person in my life, and I would want him to know how much he meant to me. How much I depended upon him. How important he was to me. How he was my basic security. How much I loved him. How much it pained me to see him deteriorate. How much after all these years I still miss him. He's regularly missing. I would want him to know about his importance to me.

I wish he could say something like, I'm so glad, I'm so glad from the bottom of my heart that I've had you in my life. You've made such a difference to me for such a long time and I'm so glad that we found the way to find each other back there in London and carried on and deepened our relationship. It could easily not have happened, but for whatever reason it did. I'm so glad.

Jacky took a shine to Hazel, he let her in a lot more than anybody, and it was mutual. Hazel didn't go up every time I went up, but she went up a lot. She's a trained masseur and she used to do all sorts of things for him. She used to massage him, he loved it. Because his body, he had no life to it. It's quite an intimate thing really. Hazel really loved him, and Jacky loved her although, he didn't really express it. Hazel had a total awareness of what Jacky meant to me and how it was affecting me. Because she saw it every day. She also loved him and was loved by him. So, it was fantastic to have Hazel there. We both had that relationship with Jacky. That was the biggest thing by far that really helped me.

Another person who helped was Henry, who was a friend of Jacky's and a friend of mine. He lives in Nottingham, so I don't see him that often. He didn't have such an emotionally close relationship with Jacky as Hazel did. But he did to some extent. There's a bit of Henry knowing as well that made it felt really good when I was with him. Apart from those two, there's nobody else who really knew Jacky that I was close to. Because Jacky was like he was; he did not have people close around him. If he had more who I also knew like Hazel or like Henry, that would've been so much better for me.

I'm so glad I had Hazel in that place as well because I saw her every day. There were many, many times especially in that first year, maybe longer probably, where I'd be in social situations and someone would come up and I would get emotional and I'd start crying. People are nice. They didn't ignore it. They'd say things like "Are you okay, Edward? Must be difficult for you." It didn't do that much for me really. I don't think people are very good at knowing what to say. I mean it's conventional wisdom, isn't it, that we're not very good in this culture of facilitating grief, mourning, how to be with death. It's a subtle skill, a subtle quality. What I experienced with other people I think is quite normal in that sense. I'm not saying it wasn't helpful to some extent. But it wasn't helpful in a way that matched the depth of the experiences that I was having, and I had been having with Jacky. Not just his death, but his illness and his death. What I would have really appreciated would have been more space, more time and people to be able to share more of my experience, as much as I wanted to at that time. I guess it's partly down to me. I've never felt that I'm reluctant to talk about it or to get emotional about it, I haven't. I think part of my experience handling this has been consistent with the conventional wisdom that we live in a culture where people maybe are not very good at how to be with somebody who is grieving.

I think looking back on it, Henry and Hazel provided me with what I would call a rich experience of mourning Jacky, and I was in therapy too. I think I could have done more. For example, I could have gone to some workshop or other or one of these many events around out there like a death café. I could have sought out more, maybe. I've got a number of friends who I was close to, who I would open up to and are okay with me talking about Jacky and okay with me getting upset and finding it difficult and so on. But I think I could have been more active in that. It's a bit like I might happen to be with them, and something might happen to stimulate me and then I would talk about it or get upset or whatever, but I could have been more active in that. Effectively, I could have said or acted in a way that was saying I want some more of this rather than leave it to happenstance. Leave it to chance that something gets stimulated. I didn't because it was so painful. I'm more able to tolerate it now. To let it come, let it go, not move away from it.

It was towards the end of the first year after he died, I had the realization that Jacky was my number one security person and the significance of that. When that hit me, that was the biggest thing, really. It was more than losing him, it was very scary to realize that he was my number one security object, and he'd gone, so that was new. Before, it was just grief in terms of sadness and missing, but then it was scary and "I'm all alone" sort of type scary.

I've often wondered, how do we manage to live given all the challenges of living? Well, my version of the story is based on Nietzsche's idea of surrender. When I was a kid, we used to go to Jaywick. I remember vividly building sandcastles on the beach. They were great sandcastles with moats and turrets and things on sticks and things on top of the turrets, really good sandcastles. We'd use our buckets to get the seawater and bring it up and fill the moats up and so on and so forth, and it would take hours of work. We'd do it together. A communal activity, three of us or whatever or maybe some other kids, and then we'd come back the following day and the bloody thing was gone. The tide had washed it away and it was like, "Oh no, no." Then, we'd build some more sandcastles. Nietzsche says that it's like we build sandcastles and they're washed away, and we have to find in life, we have to be able to overcome that and build again.[2] It's a bit like the incoming tide of life will wash away everything potentially and everyone will live as well as possible, as best as possible, as happy as possible. We have to find a way to overcome that and still retain the capacity to build, using build as a metaphor. For me, it's been the experience of dealing with those two or three years Jacky was ill and losing him, especially given the realization that he was my deepest security, whilst managing the challenge of being alive.

I wish I could have read something that conveyed something about pain, about accepting pain, tolerating pain, and the value of that. For me it was all about bonding with Jacky. The early years of hating and all of that and the years of no relationship and then building a bond and then the bonding that came through me facing what ultimately ended with two and a half years of all that horror. In some ways it was, in those two and a half years, that we were most bonded. Not through the conflict, not through the absence, not through even the shared pleasure, although we did bond through the shared pleasure. But in some ways the bond was deepened in those two and a half years.

In a similar way I've realized a number of times how in some ways I've avoided my neighbour whose wife died a couple of years ago. To some extent, I have avoided him, and I've done that spontaneously. It's in a sense similar in that I didn't face the pain, it would be a different sort of pain, but I avoided it. I avoided something and in some ways that makes my life and probably his smaller. Smaller and less rich in a small way, but to have done otherwise, would have been to do some more facing of pain which I didn't do. Even if I didn't do it without thinking, but then, when I thought about it, to some extent I still didn't do it. I did to some degree, but not anywhere near as much as I could have done, and I think that's to my loss as well as his.

There's something about facing pain, and it's a funny sort of thing, isn't it? What's the best way to have a happy life? Oh, learn to tolerate pain. That's a testament to how hard it is, and that's why we take painkillers or we drink alcohol or we do all of those avoidant techniques or whatever it is to numb the pain, to avoid it, to avoid that task. But all those avoidances, that's a point of paradox that in some way, to avoid them is less painful but less life enhancing. It sounds like a really masochistic philosophy.

If Jacky hadn't got MND and if that hadn't happened and we'd have just carried on during that two and a half years just like we had been doing before and then he died of a heart attack, then I would have missed something. I mean, he would have avoided a lot of pain, but, because of what I'm saying about the bonding and through that, I would have actually missed out on something because I knew there was a limited amount of time, so it was like I seized the moment in a way.

To some extent, I seized the moment of going to see him. I saw him much more than if he hadn't been ill and in more emotional circumstances. Because I had a sense of time running out, I seized the moment in a way which, if that hadn't happened, I wouldn't. In some ways, and I remember somebody once, a really good friend of mine who also knew Jacky, actually said, "Look what you got from that. Look what you got through being with him during that period." How often I saw him, how deeply aware I was of what I had, what I was losing, how bonded we got even through that. In some ways I was better off with what happened in a funny sort of way. So, something about seizing the moment, maybe it's partly because I'm getting older as well. Because I knew we had such little time, I made more of it. Why can't I do that in my life anyway? Especially given I'm older and I've got less years to look forward to anyway. That's another reason for the same thing in a way. So, something about seize the moment. It's my parting shot.

I sensed in some way that sitting down and talking about me and Jacky for such a long time would be significant. I knew it would be and it has been. It's been important and valuable to me to have had the spaciousness that's been created to be able to tell my story. To have the space and engaged attention. That's been good for me. That's really helped me to get in touch with and articulate what I wanted to say.

Notes

1 J. Mitchell (2003). *Siblings*. Cambridge: Polity Press.
2 F. Nietzsche (1962). *Philosophy in the Tragic Age of the Greeks*. Washington, DC: Regnery Publishing.

17 "I think you have a sister"

Sally's story remembering her sister Rose

I think the overarching thing I want to say is that I feel so validated by you asking me to be part of your book. I understand that my situation is probably different for many people you've interviewed because I never met my sister. I really appreciate you including something in your book.

I've always known on some level about my sister, who I call Rose, although she was never mentioned, never spoken about, and she died ten years before I was born. I have two younger brothers, and I had an awareness of how fragmented the family was. I'm the one who's constantly been looking into the family history and contacting previously unknown uncles, aunts, cousins; some of them didn't even know I existed. That went on for years and years. I now think that was the manifestation of this unconscious knowing about Rose. Within the last 20 years, I started to think about various phenomena I was experiencing and I kept saying to my therapist, "I'm sure I had a sister." I had already been interested in Family Constellation work and in one particular constellation, the presence of a representative for my sister made a significant difference. My representative said to my sister's representative, "I always knew you were there." Julian, the facilitator, turned to me and said, "I think you have a sister." That was the moment when Julian and I jointly accepted that she had existed. This was about 20 years or so ago, I was in my 50s then.

After that it took me four years to find my mother's half-brother, Harry. Mum and Harry had the same father. What I realized when I did find him was that if I'd known exactly how to do it, I could have found him a lot more quickly, but I found him. He said, "I'm coming up to the Midlands to tend my father's grave. We can meet up, the least I can do is buy you a meal." It was lovely; it was like watching *Long Lost Family*. I remember clearly meeting him, he was a total stranger. It really was, "I'll be wearing a red rose." He walks into the restaurant, he's a total stranger, and there was an immediate knowing between us. We each felt that we knew one another. It was extraordinary. He put me in touch with his sister, my mother's half-sister, and told me about a third half-sister who died. He was also able to confirm dates I'd been unsure of. He confirmed the incest I'd always suspected in my mother's family and added that his father (my grandfather) had shared a bedroom with my mother and aunt for as long as Harry could remember.

Harry told me when he was 12, he was put to bed with another cousin. It was expected that they would have sex. He said he was too young and couldn't do it. In the context of this family, it makes the probability of incest more and more normal. "This is how we show our love." That was the family belief. If you think you're special, this is how you show your love, there's no shame attached to it. This is what you do. They were devoted chapel goers too.

More has come out since I met more of my relations. One of my second cousins said to me, "You know there's a family history of incest, don't you?" I thought, 'He's going to be telling me about my sister,' but he didn't. It was somebody else. I said, "Yes, three people told me."

I've got a file full of birth certificates from when I was looking for my sister. I found no trace of her whatsoever. I think I bought at least 20 birth certificates just to check, but there was nothing. I've been to adoption societies, and they could find no trace of my sister either.

My mother only mentioned my sister obliquely. A lot of my conscious awareness was gathering anomalies. For example, she told me two different birth stories. You do not normally confuse birth stories, do you? In one, she had told me I was a forceps delivery. Then when I was about 13 or 14, she said something and I said, "You said I was a forceps delivery?" she said, "No, you weren't." It wasn't just that contradiction, but the way she looked at me when she corrected me, there was an intensity in her eyes. Even at 13, it rocked me. There was something on her face that really, I didn't put any significance to it at the time, except that I remembered it. I thought, that's odd, two birth stories. I've got at least half a dozen anomalies like that. When I put them together, the only thing that makes sense of this was that she had another baby. This was before I realized that it was a baby to her father.

Another anomaly was, as I was growing up in the 1950s she would say out of the blue, "If I had a disabled child, I would have rolled over in bed and smothered it." It was like a mantra, she'd say it sometimes twice a day, sometimes twice a month. She even said it to my husband in the 1970s. She kept on saying it on an almost weekly basis to my knowledge for 20 years.

About four years ago, Richard, our son, phoned me and said, "Mum, I've just done a constellation. It was quite horrible. What emerged was that either your mother smothered her baby, or she was told to say that, or she believed that she had because they told her that she had. I don't know which is the truth, but it's something about rolling on a baby and smothering it." He hadn't heard my mother's mantra, but he was astonished when I told him.

All my adult life I was haunted by recurring dreams/nightmares. After I started doing constellations, they gradually increased. One was coming out of sleep screaming to see a man with no face at the bedside. Sometimes the man was walking across the end of the bed. Once an arm was snaking towards me on the pillow. The image always faded as I woke up. Not until I did a constellation did I know consciously that the man was my grandfather and that I was reliving my mother's experience.

After a constellation that included Harry's mother, Marie (the family housekeeper after my grandmother was certified insane), I had two further dreams the next night. I did a constellation, and it showed how powerless Marie had been in the family, as I had been told. My aunt told me how Marie had sent my grandfather to dry her off after a bath when she was 11. He said, 'Oh, you're not ready yet.' My aunt wept as she told me this.

I have not had any of these dreams again since the trauma was acknowledged in constellations.

Another odd happening was that when dad died in 2015, we cleared out his papers. My mother had died in 2001, but in her bureau was a diary for 1996. First anomaly, why keep one diary? Each page was quite large. I was looking at this diary, and it's completely banal but on April the 17th – I strongly believed my sister was born sometime late spring, early summer of 1937 – there's a poem. It starts "Tragedy, tragedy, tragedy," and it fills the whole day, about 10 or a dozen lines about lost babies, but she writes "lost babes." "Tragedy, tragedy, tragedy." Then the next day, the diary entries go back to "buy potatoes."

What I know now is the grief that I carried for Rose was very real. What I didn't realize until a constellation I did in January just gone was that I've also been carrying her terror. I've always been anxious. I can feel very sad at times without really knowing why. I suppose I attributed it to a dysfunctional childhood. I've had two panic attacks, both involving water, and now through the constellation I believe this was to do with Rose and how she died, so I suspect she was drowned rather than suffocated.

Since that constellation I feel that I've separated from Rose and it's now okay for me to stay living. I've often said I feel like I'm nearly dead. I can just feel like I'm hours from death and I don't feel like that anymore. I feel like I have permission to live. That I can be separate from Rose. It's almost like I was clinging to her.

I only met my grandfather once. I realized later he'd come to say goodbye because he was dying of cancer. I didn't know who he was. I just knew it was a very important occasion. I was 12 years old. To me, he was a stranger.

Mum was very bright. Just before she started her School Certificate, she and her sister were whipped away from home, whipped out to school, circulated in the family, and eventually returned to their mother who they had barely seen for a decade. She missed her school cert. I always knew something major happened in the late spring/early summer of 1937, but it took a long time to work out what it was.

I learned that mum and her sister went to court in 1937 – that was when my grandmother, who had barely seen her daughters for decades because she'd been labelled as insane – applied for custody of the girls and got it. After mum died, I learned mum had to stand up in court and testify to her own father's sexual behaviour, which is another anomaly. Why would that be asked about unless there was evidence for it – like a baby?

I think it's virtually certain that grandfather was told in court to keep away from mum and it was years before they saw one another again.

There's no record of a child being born, so they must have got rid of the evidence. That's what people did in those days. I told Julian about this and I said that I thought she had been buried in the garden. We had a mini constellation on the spot, and I said, "I want to go back to that house and dig her up." Julian said, "No, I feel like I'm representing your sister now. What she's saying is, leave me in peace, leave me in peace." Reluctantly, I agreed.

In other constellations I've had images of missing aunts and uncles. I would imagine the family had a habit of disposing of the babies born of incest. I suppose they were an inconvenient truth. My deduction is that our family saw themselves as special; that was how they showed their love, but they know other people didn't see it that way, so they kept it quiet.

My grandfather, mother's father, had an older brother Joshua, born of brother-sister incest, who was allowed to live, but he was always shunned by the family. I've got loads of photographs at weddings, christenings, the first grandchild, all set about 100 years ago, and Joshua and his family are missing on every single one. I've come to think he was shameful or inconvenient evidence of incest – the family kept him but shunned him.

Having done all the constellations work, I feel validated. It's easy to think, "Am I making this up? Am I crazy?" I now have validation of my thinking and my intuition. I've got more pieces of the family jigsaw, and what I've learned now makes sense.

It's been a progression, really, of realization and understanding, making sense of and then a desire to claim normality. It's been really tough, but what's inspired me to keep going is thinking of future generations, thinking of our children and grandchildren. If it's this bad, I've got to keep going for all our sakes, yes.

I think knowing about what happened was like another trauma. I think the constellations and the resolution has allowed the healing, but just telling people was really traumatic for them to hear. I felt I was fighting mum's corner really to help people to find some tolerance for her. I know she was dead by this time, but that's not the point. I did feel I was fighting her corner. Just finding out was only the first stage; it's the ongoing resolution and the healing that's been calming and cleansing. We'd all been in the dark and we'd all been sad, we'd all been overshadowed by this terrible loss.

I have tried to work this out therapeutically in other ways, but nothing has come close. In constellations I addressed each experience of trauma one by one. It was by a pure chance I found constellations, and suddenly the world opened up for me and I started to feel unburdened. I doubt I would have got there with any other modality. I might have got somewhere close with sand tray or art therapy – something may have emerged? I can only speculate, but I can tell you years of talking therapy got nowhere near close to it.

This is the reason a colleague and I got interested in constellations. We were working together, we had a good working relationship and knew one another's work, and we said, "Look, we're good therapists, we know we get good outcomes, we effect change, we've got clients who are doing all the right things, but some are not changing. What's going on?" At that time, I was working with Julian who was open to intergenerational trauma and my colleague, and I said, "Well, supposing these clients are grappling with intergenerational trauma." As soon as we opened that door, we started to see change in clients who had been stuck.

There needs to be a willingness to do the transgenerational cultural stuff, where it's possible to uncover the unspoken between parents and a child or between siblings. If someone were to consider using Family Constellations work I'd say, don't hesitate; be prepared to be surprised, and be kind to yourself; in other words, be patient. The overarching thing is finding personal peace and contentment. That supersedes everything else, and if the cost of that is to uncover things that one isn't supposed to know, well, it's a personal choice. For me, I have no hesitation whatsoever. It's absolutely fine. I would actually say to someone, "It's fine to choose not to follow this route, but if you do, then you may be choosing to stay with whatever pain you're carrying."

"Am I willing to pay the cost of what the truth might be?" It's a very personal choice. In my heart I'm always baffled that people choose to stay with secrets. I want to say, don't let the perpetrators ruin your life, because it's the perpetrators who don't want the truth to be out, and they may not even be alive anymore. Why would you let them dominate your life now? I don't quite get it, but I understand people are like that. I do think the unconscious is harder to push against than the known, but I don't regret a moment of doing it to find my sister Rose.

18 The ABC of grief

Aftermath

The impact of the loss of a child or sibling reverberates throughout all relationships. Some people may be more sensitive than they were to stimuli and feel that their resources are significantly diminished for quite some time, if not for the rest of their lives. The way someone views themselves and others may suddenly change in ways that are shocking for all concerned. Some people seem to switch overnight from being a kind, softly spoken person to someone who snaps and snarls or just walks off without a word, all of which can be rather unsettling. It is also important to realize that not only do the parents and siblings experience these processes, but others do too. A number of the participants referred to how sometimes other people's behaviour towards them was uncharacteristic and took them by surprise, and that for most, the relationships returned to some sort of equilibrium as the bonds were established again.

Understanding what may happen can help us appreciate the reactions of the bereaved person as well as those around them.

Alienation

When someone experiences a significant trauma or loss, their lives are irreversibly changed, and along with that, any trust previously held in life, other people, or any existing faith or belief may also temporarily go. Most will be in a state of shock, feeling alienated from all that was previously familiar. Some may experience symptoms of post-traumatic stress disorder (PTSD), such as:

- Intrusive distressing memories or dreams;
- Flashbacks;
- Feeling detached;
- Distorted thinking;
- Hypervigilance;
- Exaggerated startle response;
- Inability to concentrate or complete daily activities;
- Poor sleep.

This was certainly the case for many of the participants in the research.

When someone is in this place of utter turmoil, they feel so shaken up that they don't know who they are, what they are doing, or why. They may feel hopeless, ineffective, and helpless and are unsure of other people, turning away from them believing they cannot help. Some people may become withdrawn or monosyllabic, whilst others may appear obsessive and controlling, at times seeing the world in very black-and-white terms. They may appear insensitive or uncaring towards another and believe others are unfeeling and unresponsive towards them. Unable to self-soothe, they may resort to alcohol, drugs, or even quite extreme, risky, or even criminal behaviours to help numb or distract themselves from the pain. A few may believe that this awfulness will never end, and that either they may as well be dead, or they are going crazy.

Antagonistic

Sometimes someone may blame others for what has happened, even seeking restitution/legal action against them which may not be warranted by the reality of the situation. They can be irritable, aggressive, or dismissive, believing others are untrustworthy and unreliable. They may appear to self-soothe, and to be autonomous and self-reliant; however, this is a pseudo autonomy defending against their need for others. The grandiosity that some display covers underlying feelings of worthlessness and low self-esteem. Should you offer help without being asked, the person may take offence, believing that you consider them incapable.

Alone

At other times someone may want to get away from the situation or other people so that they can be on their own. They may blame themselves for anything bad that happened and, as a result, have low self-esteem and self-worth and can easily feel overwhelmed. They can be very sensitive to comments or remarks and easily assume that others are critical of them. They may frequently seek approval or reassurance. With others, they may be tentative in any requests for help and, because they expect rejection, do not express anger authentically, rarely confronting another's unhelpful or inappropriate behaviour. Should someone offer help without being asked, they may struggle to accept it as they consider themselves undeserving, but the fact that someone offered is very important.

Awareness

Once someone has begun to reach a place of equilibrium, where basic trust in themselves, others, and life is tentatively restored, then they regain their relational awareness. They begin to feel better about themselves, others, and the world. Their relationships with others may be restored and improved, and they are able to complete necessary tasks. They gain a meta perspective and can see the situation for what it is, making informed choices based on the facts before them. They ask for and accept help in a straightforward manner, expressing grief openly, seeking support and contact with others. They can stay present, expressing their sadness, anger, or distress in an authentic way. They're appreciative of another's help and support. If unhappy with something or someone, they will then confront in a respectful way seeking a win-win solution. They will request answers to their questions in a straightforward manner, and they can self-soothe in a way that is supportive of themselves and does not diminish their need for others.

The most important thing for someone to do after a trauma is to find a way to tell their story and for their narrative to be heard, either verbally or, if they prefer, they can write down their story in a journal or diary. Some people like to be creative and draw their experience or use other media to express themselves. Whatever someone chooses to do, the purpose is to help them find a way to understand what has happened and to begin to make sense of that experience. This will help them to begin to feel calm and with that, rational thinking usually returns, and they can then change how they view themselves and others.

Because someone can fluctuate through these processes, a bit like being in a pinball machine, at times they may wonder whether they are making any significant progress. This oscillation is normal because, as well as grieving for their deceased child or sibling, life is also happening, and each person is being impacted by those other events.

Bonds

When someone dies, the deep connection that others had with them will be broken, but that is not to say the bond has gone. It is clear from all the stories in this book that the bond each parent has with their child, or sibling with their brother/sister, continues, but in a different way. Neither 'move on' in their bereavement; they learn to live with their loss and to maintain a bond, however tentative. The bond that continues may well depend upon the relationship that the bereaved person had with their child or sibling and on their process of relating to themselves and others and is likely to change over time.

Rupture and reconnecting bonds

The rupture and cautious reconnecting of bonds happens as soon as someone dies. A number of the participants talk of the interactions they had with their child or sibling's body. For example, Claire talked of how important it was for her that others treated Emilie normally. She said that a few people held and talked about her as they would have had she been alive, discussing how beautiful she was and how she looked like Claire. The need for Claire at this moment was for other people to say 'hello' to Emilie, to welcome her into the world, as this enabled her to do the same, reconnecting with her daughter.

Edward talked of the moment Jacky died, that one minute he was alive and the next he was dead and how profoundly disorienting it was for him to be in the room with Jacky's body. How he didn't know what to do, how to be. How it felt wrong when strangers (undertakers) came and took Jacky's body away. Some of this experience is echoed in Julia's story. She talks of finding Pippa's body and of the moments afterwards, how she still cannot talk about it, yet the shock of the rupture, sense of incomprehension is almost palpable.

I can resonate with some of this too, finding Vikki dead. The shock of her cold skin, pale face, and blue lips. I felt uncomfortable touching her, which was so at odds with how we had been when she was alive. Sitting in the kitchen sometime later, the senior paramedic was asking questions and spoke of Vikki in the past tense. I remember how jarring that was, it felt like a slap across the face, that she (the paramedic) was okay with the fact that Vikki was dead, but I wasn't yet ready to acknowledge the full reality of what had happened. Later, when the undertakers came to take her away, I wanted to go with her. I didn't want her to be on her own. I struggled with her being away, and I even wanted to phone up the mortuary to ask if she was okay. After the post-mortem had been completed, all I wanted and needed was for her to be back in our hometown, to be close by. I needed to find a way to reconnect with her.

Joanne also spoke of how important it was that Rebecca was home as soon as possible. How she went to see her every day in the chapel of rest and that one day as she and her husband were "sitting with Rebecca's body, this beautiful light came through the window. Because it was January, it was grey, but this beautiful sunshine came through and just rested on the three of us . . . We felt that Rebecca went then." This is a gentler releasing of a bond with Rebecca whilst staying connected to her in a different way.

A few people were unable to see the body, and that added a different dimension to their experience. For example, Beth mentions that she couldn't see Jim's body, and as a result her mother then wondered if it was actually Jim's body, that maybe a mistake had been made; this could be seen as a need to keep the existing bond intact, or some may refer to it as denial. Beth was asked if tissue samples could be taken from Jim and what she wanted done with them once they were no longer needed. She was shocked how he had suddenly gone from being a brother, a person, to being a body; this could be seen as another rupture in the bond she had with Jim.

A number of people commented on how they dealt with their child's ashes. Joanne kept Rebecca's for six years and to begin with would take them on holiday with her if they went away. Claire and John held on to Emilie's ashes for seven years. Claire had a ring made with some of them, but when it arrived it was too big, and Claire felt like she had lost Emilie again, another rupture to the bond. They scattered the rest of them at the farm where they go on her anniversary and it was a family bonding process. Wilf and Kath have Michael's ashes; they say they cannot let them go yet.

The shock, distress, and trauma involved in the death of a child or sibling may tap into other beliefs about self, others, or life. Some people may struggle with the rupture and reconnection of any bond. Allowing a gradual adjustment of the bond with the person who died is important, the adaptation to not having them around takes time and needs to be done in a respectful and timely manner that honours the bond the person has with the child or sibling.

Hostage bonds

Hostage bonds are those that remain in a frozen or restricted state for a period of time. In the research there were a number of causes for the short-term development of these bonds. One unconscious purpose was to avoid the pain of the reality of the loss. One way to do this is through blame, guilt, and regret. It was common for a number of the participants to question their own behaviour or that of other people to understand the reason(s) for their child or sibling's death. This is normal and is a way of helping the bereaved person to make sense of what happened so that they can let go of the questions that can otherwise make a person feel like a hostage to the situation. George Kohlrieser in his book *Hostage at the Table* writes,

> all of us can be taken hostage metaphorically – that is, made to feel threatened, manipulated, and victimized – every day by bosses, colleagues, customers, family members, or virtually anyone with whom we interact. We can also become hostage to events or circumstances happening in our lives. We can even become hostages to ourselves, our own mind-sets, our emotions, and our habits.[1]

If the bereaved person can find answers to their questions, they will be more able to fully grieve for their loss. If not, then they may feel like a hostage. Carol talked about this when she referred to the driver of the car who was probably the last person to see David alive, the poor police investigation, and her experience at the inquest. For a time, she was consumed with a need to know what happened to enable her to make sense of those last crucial moments of David's life. After the inquest, she realized that she was not going to get the information that she needed, and although the knowledge was still hard for her, she was able to accept that she will never know. Had this not happened, then she may have stayed in this place for much longer.

Hostage bonds can also come about due to a lack of information needed to help someone process their loss. For example, John (Chapter 12) spoke of finding his brother Jamie in his cot, how he noticed his unusual colouring and realized something was wrong. He explains how, as a child himself, he was unable to fully comprehend what had happened, how hard he found it to deal with the intrusive image which was intensified by his mother's scream and horror. Something of the bonds between John, Jamie, and his mother were frozen in that moment and, because nothing was said directly to him to help him process what he had seen, it continued to remain in that frozen state for years.

Some of the hostage bonds can be caused by someone blaming themselves for what happened, "I should have done . . ." or "If only . . ." or "What if . . ." Although these questions are understandable and normal, if someone were to ruminate on them for a long period of time, then their bond with the deceased person is likely to be constrained in some way as the bond is with the blame, guilt, or regret rather than with the deceased person.

Challenging existing bonds

Many of the people spoke of how their lives had changed as a result of their experience. Generally, this was around how they viewed their connection with themselves, their family or others and life and how some bonds were broken.

A number of people spoke of a change in their ability to be with other people. For example, Elisa, Julia, and Rose talked of changes in their ability to tolerate or be around certain people. Here the emphasis is on discerning which bonds are positive and mutually beneficial and cultivating them and discarding those that are not.

Others talked of how particularly in the early years they struggled with their bond to continue their own life. For some this was in terms of day-to-day functioning. Steffy said that she didn't feel she could function in any way and felt partly shut down from the world. Carol talked of feeling like she had lead boots on: everything was an effort and in slow motion, music sounded like it was underwater, and she felt exhausted much of the time. She felt she was in a fog and couldn't concentrate; five years later, her concentration is better than it was, but she is still unable to read for pleasure. She said after three to three and a half years she decided to focus on her own health and getting fitter. The increased activity helped her to clear her head and to get a different perspective.

For John (Chapter 12) this was different in that the hostage bonds that he had with his mother and with Jamie were frozen and, because Jamie's death was never discussed, there was no one with whom he could get help. As a result, his bond with life was challenged, and he decided that in order to survive, he needed to look after and protect himself.

Others too found their bond with life challenged. For example, Julia said that in the early days she thought she should kill herself because she couldn't make it right after Pippa died. She talked of how she sometimes felt flat, depressed, and with no energy and at other times felt okay; now she has a sense of feeling settled. Susan also thought of suicide but didn't do anything because of her other children and grandchildren. Beth hasn't felt suicidal but has wanted to 'not exist' for a minute or two. For these participants it was the bonds, particularly with their other children, partners, or other significant relationships that prevented them from acting on their suicidal thoughts. In each of their stories there is something about hope and the future, for continued bonds with others.

Continuing bonds and developing resilience

For many people, continuing bonds are a normal and helpful experience. A continuing bond has been defined as 'the presence of an ongoing inner relationship with the deceased person by the bereaved individual.'[2] These continuing bonds can take many forms; some of those mentioned by the participants were:

1 Remembering and talking about the person who died;
2 Displaying photographs or creating and sharing photograph albums;
3 Acknowledging anniversaries and birthdays;
4 Going to favourite places previously enjoyed by both the bereaved and their child/sibling;
5 Having a grave to keep clean and replenish with fresh flowers;
6 Retaining some personal possessions and spending time with them;
7 Sharing their experience with others going through a similar grieving process;
8 Retaining letters and cards from friends/family after the death;
9 Talking with their child or sibling, and imagining conversations with them;
10 Being involved in school, community, or charitable projects.

Some of these things may not be possible or desirable for the individual, but that does not matter. What does matter is that they do what works for them.

These continuing bonds help the bereaved in retaining their connection with their child or sibling in a way that supports them in living their lives. Some may argue that having continuing bonds may prevent a person from realizing the full reality of the loss, but according to my research that is not the case. Rather, the bonds facilitate a process of gradually changing the relationship that the bereaved person has with their child or sibling. Some of the participants said in the early weeks/months after the death they might spend a lot of time with the deceased's possessions, holding them and being with them as a way of maintaining a connection; but as time has gone on the need to do this has reduced, so the occurrence is occasional rather than daily or weekly.

The use of continuing bonds is something that will be specific and unique to each individual and may well depend upon their attachment style, the relationship they had with the person who died, and the circumstances of their death.

Compassion

In many of the stories there was a lack of compassion shown by other people towards the bereaved. Most of those who commented said they thought this was because the other person did not know what to say. The lack of compassion shown could also be because the other person felt some belief or judgement of the bereaved or the person who died. For example, the lack of compassion towards John (Chapter 12) and his siblings might have been because their parents were so shocked themselves that they were incapable of showing any compassion to the children.

Several people mentioned that they thought others would be judgemental of their child/sibling. For example, Wilf and Kath, Steffy, Beth, Carol, and Nancy all felt at some point that others might be making judgements about their child/sibling's drug use and as a result may not have felt any compassion for the deceased person or for the bereaved. In the short term, for a few, this compounded their grief as they were reluctant to talk openly with others about what had happened. There's a sense of shame that they were in some way responsible, and this can be heard in their lack of self-compassion.

Others mentioned how they felt less able to be compassionate towards others; their tolerance of others changed. For some, over time, this changed again so they felt able to support other bereaved parents or siblings.

Those that were able to be self-compassionate were more able to continue healthy bonds with their child or sibling. Self-compassion can often be achieved by listening to others' stories of loss, being able to resonate with different people's experiences, and taking comfort in knowing that others have survived and are living well. This links with phase four of transformational loss (see Chapter 20).

Chapter 25 contains some compassion and mindfulness exercises.

Notes

1 G. Kohlrieser (2006). *Hostage at the Table*. San Francisco, CA: Jossey-Bass, p. 1.
2 M. Stroebe and H. Schut (2005). To Continue or Relinquish Bonds: A Review of Consequences for the Bereaved. *Death Studies*, 29, p. 477. Reprinted by permission of the publisher (Taylor & Francis Ltd, www.tandfonline.com)

19 Living with loss

After experiencing the loss of a child or sibling, it would be understandable that someone may believe they will never be happy again. But it may be possible. The challenge is to find something to engage in, to take pleasure from, and to make meaning for their life from now on.[1] For some people this may be focussing on surviving children, parents, or grandparents. For others it might be offering a listening ear, raising money for a particular cause. Some may concentrate on challenging attitudes, behaviours, procedures, or systems that they encountered. The most important aspect of this is for someone to be true to themselves. To listen to what their heart and mind is really saying underneath all the detritus of the should, ought, and must messages, often self or other imposed. Reaching a point of acceptance – of themselves, others, and life and all that it entails.

When considering how someone can live with their loss, I think it's useful to have a framework on which to consider what someone may need at a particular time; one such framework is Maslow's Hierarchy of Needs.[2]

Maslow's Hierarchy of Needs

According to Maslow:

> Human needs arrange themselves in hierarchies of pre-potency. That is to say, the appearance of one need usually rests on the prior satisfaction of another, more pre-potent need. Man is a perpetually wanting animal. Also no need or drive can be treated as if it were isolated or discrete; every drive is related to the state of satisfaction or dissatisfaction of other drives.[3]

Maslow developed these needs into a pyramid; see Figure 19.1.

Physiological needs

Looking at the diagram, someone's basic necessities concern their physiological needs, and these need to be met first. One of the most important

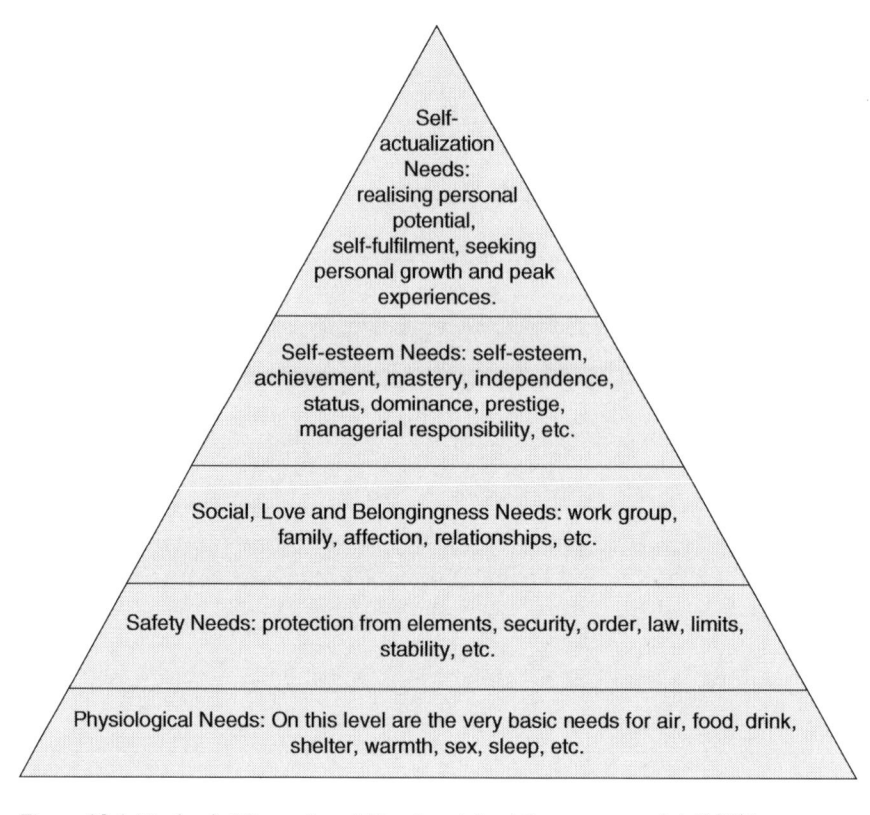

Figure 19.1 Maslow's Hierarchy of Needs original five-stage model (1987)

in the research was food. Each person has a specific relationship with food. Some people really enjoy their meals and savour each bite. Others eat quickly and barely taste what they are eating. Several may graze enjoying a variety of flavours and textures. A few may eat for comfort, and a handful may be disinterested in food. At a time of significant distress, food may help to soothe someone or could be purely a means of survival, or anything in between. A person's resources will be limited. They may lose their appetite and struggle to find the energy and enthusiasm, not only in terms of preparing and cooking food but also going shopping and buying the ingredients in the first place.

This is where friends and family can be a huge support. A meal or dish prepared with love can be consoling and may help to calm frayed nerves. Even if little is eaten, what is left can be put in the fridge or freezer for another day. This can also act as a reminder to the bereaved person or family that they are not forgotten; that someone else does care about them. The significance of food being prepared by others is evident in almost all of the stories in this book. For example, Claire and John had an evening meal provided for them every night for five weeks. Julia talked of meals being prepared by friends and family, with them all sitting around the table talking. Steffy mentioned how a friend came around with some food every day. Carol also said that family members made sure she was eating, and they would have meals together. Beth spoke of a couple of friends who travelled to them on the day of Jim's funeral and made a meal for them for afterwards. These acts of love can be so welcome, especially when someone has no appetite or little energy for shopping and cooking.

Sleep too can be a significant problem for many bereaved parents and siblings. Difficulties such as ruminating, intrusive thoughts/images, or nightmares may lead to an inability to fall or stay asleep at night. Others may prefer to sleep during the day and be awake at night because it's quieter. One person may seek sleeping tablets to help getting to sleep. Another may drink alcohol or take other drugs to help them to sleep, or to fall into a stupor that numbs them from their pain. Sleeping in a routine with a regular bedtime, avoiding caffeine, and bright light (especially from computers or mobile phones) can reduce stress and help someone to get to sleep.

A desire for sex can diminish or become very significant. One partner may find it difficult to initiate sex because they don't want to intrude upon the grief of their partner or to be insensitive. Another may be disinterested in sex, but they do want intimacy and togetherness. It is important then that couples find a way to talk to one another about what they need and want, to negotiate, cooperate, and compromise so that each gets what they need, but not at the expense of the other.

Safety needs

Order, limits, and stability are often things that go by the wayside after a traumatic event. Particularly when referring to the death of a child or sibling, the normal order of things has gone, although this is a more contemporary and Western belief. Particular limits that someone may lose could be their food or alcohol intake and any drug use (prescribed or otherwise), as mentioned by Susan and Rose. Tolerance of others can be reduced as discovered by Carol, Julia, Rose, and Elisa. In this stage some parents may feel overprotective of their surviving children and put in stringent curfews or rules. Others may become forgetful or neglectful, for instance, by saying nothing about what has happened either because of their own trauma or because they don't want to upset their surviving children, as experienced by John (Chapter 12).

Some people may feel scared at their lack of control. Any behaviours or actions could be seen as a way of attempting to regain some equilibrium. If they are able to bring back some structure, they and those around them are likely to begin to feel increasingly stable and secure. Structure can be very basic to begin with – choosing a time to get out of bed in the morning, a time to eat meals, and a time to go to bed can all help. Every person needs some structure, and some like more structure than others. Once someone has a basic structure in place, they can begin to add in more activity, such as making phone calls, writing letters/emails, or shopping for food. Others may wish to resume some of their usual activities which might be sport or fitness training, social events, or meeting friends. Some may prefer the structure that going back to work, school, or college brings, whilst others may feel this is too much. Getting an appropriate balance for the individual and as a family is the key.

Social, love, and belongingness needs

These needs can be very tricky for people who are grieving the loss of a child or sibling. Few in their social circle may be able to stay with the pain of their grief. Any feelings of isolation can increase or be reduced by the words and actions of others. A family may feel blown apart by what has happened. Each may blame themselves or one another for the events that led up to the death. If these fears or fantasies are shared, whether within the family or with friends, this can lead to new insights or greater understanding, as well as a sense of relief for having spoken their truth and been heard. The wider social context can also help or hinder here, this is when the few kind words from strangers can mean the most.

Kindness and generosity of time can make a huge difference to those who are grieving. A willingness to listen without judgement and to offer love and care, a hug, a caress, an invitation to a meal or other social event – to know that they are not forgotten and are still welcome and accepted in their social circle or in another's family or group – can all help.

Thinking in a positive way can help with increasing mood and energy to complete tasks and to be in relationships with others. This may also increase social support.[4] This may seem like an odd activity after the death of a child or sibling, but expressing gratitude can be one way of thinking positively. One simple exercise that I find works well is to write down three things for which you are grateful every day. They can be anything from being able to breathe without pain; having somewhere safe to live; having caring friends or family; watching the sunrise each morning; having rain to water the plants; or the sunshine to warm cold, tired, and aching bones. I realize when someone has just lost their child or sibling, they may be unlikely to want to feel any gratitude for a while. But even during that horrible time, there is likely to be something to appreciate.

One of the things that I, and some of the research participants, struggled with was laughing. I found this to be true when I was working with clients too. When they found something funny, they might initially laugh but then felt guilty or even bad about doing so. Saying such things as "I shouldn't be laughing," "If I laugh, does that mean I've forgotten what's happened?" I remember the day before Vikki's funeral, I was sitting with some of my oldest friends. Over cups of tea we sat together telling funny stories and laughing. Part way through our reminiscing, the doorbell rang, I answered the door to see a close family member standing there with a solemn expression on their face. I then suddenly remembered why we were all meeting together. I felt so bad for laughing and even enjoying myself when my daughter was dead. Sometime later, I decided that happiness is as much a part of life as sadness; they are two sides of the same coin. Since then I have continued to laugh at funny events, and I no longer scold myself for doing so. I have and do still sometimes use humour to cope with difficult emotions or events; sometimes this may be appropriate, or at other times it may be an expression of anxiety, which is sometimes called gallows humour.

This type of laughter is also mentioned by Steffy. She said that when she went with a friend to pick up Jason's belongings from the police station, they had fits of laughter that was so incongruent to the seriousness of what she was doing. She attributes some of her laughter to being anxious and also to the manner of the police officer she dealt with and, the lack of respect she experienced. On another occasion she experienced some odd looks from someone she knew when she was laughing with a friend. She felt the looks were saying, "Why is she laughing? She shouldn't be laughing. She should be mourning." However, some of Steffy's colleagues sent her messages that they thought would make her laugh as they thought she'd appreciate them.

Being able to laugh, as well as cry, or be angry or scared, is a valuable asset in coping with life and all that it brings.

Self-esteem needs

When someone loses a son or daughter, brother or sister, their self-esteem is likely to take a significant battering. They are likely to question whether they were a good enough parent or sibling. Whether they are still a parent or sibling. Whether they contributed to the death in any way, either by doing or not doing something, or by saying or not saying something. At work someone may feel unable to do some or all of their job, as experienced by Nancy. Others may feel the need to be at work, school, or college, to continue with doing something that allows them to feel normal. The task of colleagues/teachers is to support the person, to enable them to do what they can or to stay at home if that would be better for them. If they do stay at home, it is important that someone acts as the main contact for anything work or course related. That can then free up other friends, teachers, and colleagues to send messages of support.

A younger person may feel like they've lost some of the gains they had made in terms of growing independence. Some may revert back to behaviours from when they were younger. Others may feel ostracized at school or become a 'celebrity' with fellow students wanting to be their best friend to get the full story, as experienced by Rose. Some people may use social media to send messages of support or offers of help. Others may turn it into their own personal drama with them as the centre of attention. A few may be cruel by ridiculing, belittling or making jokes. Schools/colleges can make a big difference here. If the child or young person who died is known to them, they could, for example, run a drop-in session whereby students can go to talk about their friend; have a classroom session where the circumstances of the death are shared and discussed in an age-appropriate way. So the other children or young people have clear factual information to help them to understand what has happened; creative workshops can help some express their feelings (for some ideas, see Chapter 25), or there could be a sponsored event to raise money for a charity that supports or researches the issues that contributed towards the student's death.

Teachers can be a source of help and support for bereaved siblings. Perhaps offering a quiet and safe place where they can go to be on their own if things are getting too much for them. Offering a listening ear if they want to talk about what has happened or even give information. To provide space for them to express themselves in a more creative or physical way, for example: art; planting something in the school garden; making use of the punch bag in the gym, if there is one; or spending time with the class rabbit or any other animal. Just stroking a cat or playing with a dog can soothe someone's frayed nerves. Indeed, for some people being around animals is more beneficial that being with people.

Speaking with another interested person can help someone transform their emotional experiences into a coherent narrative.[5] The very act of talking can help to restructure someone's thinking, reduce the emotional intensity of their memories, and move away from a depressive or ruminative thinking position.[6,7] This in turn can help to re-build someone's self-esteem, especially if the person who is listening is able to be with their pain and distress and to normalize their experience.

Self-actualization needs

The top stage refers to someone being able to realize their full potential, achieve self-fulfilment, and seek personal growth and peak experiences. This is likely to take some time to recover for bereaved parents and siblings. For some, this may feel impossible. It is a time when someone can convert what has been a truly terrible experience into something that gives them, their life, and that of their deceased child or sibling meaning, significance, and a purpose.

Self-care

Self-care, like self-compassion, seems to be something that many people struggle with especially after a traumatic loss. For some people, it is far easier said than done. Activities such as yoga can help reduce stress levels and build resilience.[8,9] Going for a walk to get some exercise and fresh air or connecting in some way with nature can help. Even a short five-minute walk can increase a feeling of well-being.[10] Many of the participants found that being in nature or gardening was helpful to them.

Other interests might include reading a book; watching a favourite programme or film; listening to music; catching up with a friend; having a massage or a soak in the bath. Others may choose art or craft activities; fitness pursuits, e.g. fishing, Pilates, going to the gym, or attending a running club; others may prefer more social activities such as going to a concert or a comedy club; or reminiscing and laughing about happier times. It does not matter what you do so long as it works for you and fits in with your beliefs, values, and attitudes. For some ideas on developing a self-care strategy, see Chapter 24. For some other therapeutic activities, see Chapter 25.

Living well after the death of a child or sibling can, at times, be challenging. Annual reminders can trigger someone back into the depths of their grief. How to manage anniversaries and birthdays is often a question that arises from bereaved people, and there is no simple straightforward answer.

Anniversaries

Some time ago I attended a workshop on dealing with anniversaries. One of the options was to think of the favourite food, film, and music of the person who had died and what behaviour they had that most annoyed us. The suggestion was that on the anniversary, we eat that food, watch that film, listen to that music, and enact that behaviour. Some in the room thought this might be a good idea, and I could see others were not convinced. I was horrified. I thought, "Why on earth would I want to do that?"– my daughter and I had totally different tastes in music/films and indeed food. I couldn't think of anything worse. Once I got over my aversion at this suggestion, I thought about whether there was anything in this proposal that I could use.

I know that what is important to me is the relationships I have with the people I care about and who care about me and my family. Thus, what works for me on anniversaries and other life events is having a connection with those people in some way. Whether that is face to face, over the phone, or even via a text. What supports me is some acknowledgement from another of the significance of that particular day. To know that Vikki is not forgotten just because she is no longer here. That they too continue to have a bond with her and us. To know that another is also holding us in mind as we cope with her loss. I cannot yet imagine a time when I will not value such an acknowledgement.

A bereaved parent or sibling's task when it comes to anniversaries or special events is to work out what suits them and their family best. What suits one person may not work for someone else, and so compromises may need to be made. Anniversaries and/or birthdays were specifically mentioned by many of the people I interviewed. Some had rituals around anniversaries.

For example, Claire and John and their children go to a working farm each year, something that they all enjoy and look forward to visiting. Joanne said that on Rebecca's birthday they go out as a family, and at Christmas she lights candles. On the anniversary of her death, they initially let off balloons, but that changed and now she and her husband go off for a long walk. Steffy lights a candle on Jason's birthday. Wilf and Kath go to a special picnic area on Michael's birthday. John (Chapter 12) said that his parents would put flowers on Jamie's grave on Christmas Day.

It's not just the deceased person's birthday that can be difficult, as Rose commented. She feels her birthday is now ruined after the death of her sister. Each year is a constant reminder of what Lizzie hasn't been able to do. I find Mothering Sunday something of a challenge. I realize that the original meaning of this day seems to have long been forgotten and it is now more of a commercial event. To me, this day, along with Christmas and Father's Day, is advertised as a harmonious day full of family fun; no tears are to be shed. It is probably fair to say that there are many people who do not buy into the Christmas fantasy, and this is usually, if grudgingly, accepted. For bereaved parents and siblings, as well as those who no longer have access to a parent or child, Mother's Day and Father's Day can be just as difficult, if not more so because there seems to be little acknowledgement that these days can be a struggle for some.

The lack of acknowledgement of the significance of an anniversary/event was a cause of some distress to a number of people. Most commonly, this lack of recognition was from family members. Coupling that with the fact that someone in their family did not comment or acknowledge the event made it more difficult for those who were grieving. There seemed to be a lack of recognition and understanding of the continuing bond that still exists. See Chapter 18 for more on continuing bonds.

The days leading up to anniversaries can bring their own challenges. John (Chapter 3), and Beth said that they found the period just before the anniversary is often more challenging than the day itself. Beth said that she found the first-year anniversary worse than when Jim died. During the lead-up to the anniversary, she was wondering what had been happening for Jim that resulted in his deciding to kill himself. Elisa said that she found the tenth anniversary of Ellen's death harder than the ones previously.

What is clear from the stories is that anniversaries, birthdays, and other events are important milestones. They need to be acknowledged in some way with friends and family members, in particular, having an important role in recognizing the significance of the bond the bereaved still have for those who have died.

Acceptance

An important aspect of dealing with the loss of a child or sibling is to find a way of being in the world that focusses on what is, rather than what it should or shouldn't be. It is about reconnecting with our true, authentic self, of living in the here and now, accepting all that happens without blame, or the need to change or control.

Martin Wells writes:

> Many of us suffer under the illusion that we can control our lives, that we can become the authors of our destinies and "put a new show on the road." We tend to ignore the fact that we do not know what will happen next, what life will bring us. We prefer to remain attached to the story, the drama, the hope, the search, the promise of a better place.[11]

Further, "By practicing ongoing deep acceptance of our own contracted responses, our own stories, and those of our clients, we help both ourselves and our clients to open up to a field of spacious acceptance."[12] In addition, Jung said, "We cannot change anything unless we accept it. Condemnation does not liberate, it oppresses. I am the oppressor of the person I condemn, not his friend and fellow-sufferer."[13]

When someone's son or daughter, brother or sister dies, whatever the circumstances, I think it is natural for someone to wonder whether they could have done something differently. This is where hindsight can seem unforgiving or punishing. Had someone had sufficient warning beforehand of what was going to happen, I think it likely that they would have done something to prevent the death. This is where the 'what if' and 'if only' roundabout can tie someone up in knots, leading to a downward spiral into blame of self or another, where nothing is resolved because it cannot be fixed. The challenge to stay with what is; to accept that mistakes may have been made; to acknowledge and give space to the excruciating physical and emotional pain of being bereaved, the loss of someone dear; as well as the agony of knowing that something different might have happened; can all feel too much. But it is in this place that it is possible to honour that pain, with compassion, and to find peace within ourselves.

How someone manages their life after the death of their child or sibling is a personal process. Some may need certain types of support, while others may need something completely different. Family, friends, colleagues, and professionals, if they are courageous enough, can all play their part in accompanying the bereaved parent or sibling on this journey to a new normal – where living well means embracing the reality of what has happened and finding a way to transform their loss into something that gives their life, and that of their child or sibling, meaning and purpose. (See Chapter 20 for more on transformational loss.)

Notes

1 A. Lee Duckworth, T.A. Steen and M.E.P. Seligman (2005). Positive Psychology in Clinical Practice. *Annual Review of Clinical Psychology*, 1, pp. 629–651. DOI: 10.1146/annurev.clinpsy.1.102803.144154.
2 A. Maslow (1943). A Theory of Human Motivation. *Psychological Review*, 50, pp. 370–396. APA. Content now in the public domain. DOI: 10.1037/h0054346.

3 Ibid., p. 370.
4 S. Lyubomirsky, L. King and E. Diener (2005). The Benefits of Frequent Positive Affect: Does Happiness Lead to Success? *Psychological Bulletin*, 131(6), pp. 803–855. DOI: 10.1037/0033-2909.131.6.803.
5 J.M. Smyth, N. True and J. Souto (2001). Effects of Writing about Traumatic Experiences: The Necessity for Narrative Structuring. *Journal of Social and Clinical Psychology*, 20, pp. 161–172. DOI: 10.1521/jscp.20.2.161.22266.
6 A. Neumann and P. Philippot (2007). Specifying What Makes a Personal Memory Unique Enhances Emotion Regulation. *Emotion*, 7, pp. 566–578. DOI: 10.1037/1528-3542.7.3.566.
7 J.M.G. Williams, T. Barnhofer, C. Crane, D. Hermans, F. Raes, E. Watkins, et al. (2007). Autobiographical Memory Specificity and Emotional Disorder. *Psychological Bulletin*, 133, pp. 122–148. DOI: 10.1037/0033-2909.133.1.122.
8 J. Thirthalli, G.H. Naveen, M.G. Rao, S. Varambally, R. Christopher and B.N. Gangadhar (2013). Cortisol and Antidepressant Effects of Yoga. *Indian Journal of Psychiatry*, 55(Suppl 3), pp. S405–S408. DOI: 10.4103/0019-5545.116315.
9 S.C. Chung, M.M. Brooks, M Rai, J.L. Balk and S. Rai (2012). Effect of Sahaja Yoga Meditation on Quality of Life, Anxiety, and Blood Pressure Control. *Journal of Alternative and Complementary Medicine*, 18, pp. 589–596. DOI: 10.1089/acm.2011.0038.
10 A.E. Van den Berg, T. Hartig and H. Staats (2007). Preference for Nature in Urbanized Societies: Stress, Restoration, and the Pursuit of Sustainability. *Journal of Social Issues*, 63, pp. 79–96. DOI: 10.1111/j.1540-4560.2007.00497.x.
11 M. Wells (2012). From Fiction to Freedom: Our True Nature Beyond Life Script. *Transactional Analysis Journal*, 42(2), p. 147. DOI: 10.1177/036215371204200208. Reprinted by permission of the publisher (Taylor & Francis Ltd, www.tandfonline.com).
12 Ibid., p. 148.
13 Copyright 1933 from *Modern Man in Search of a Soul* by C.G. Jung, Harcourt, Brace, pp. 234–235. Reproduced by permission of Taylor and Francis Group, LLC, a division of Informa plc. Permission conveyed through Copyright Clearance Center, Inc.

20 Transformational loss

As I listened to stories and read and re-read the transcripts, I was struck by how the participants experienced the days, weeks, months, and years following their loss. I noticed that their experiences, and mine, showed a process of transformation that is described in transformational learning theories.[1] Mezirow talks about how an incident can set off a whole chain of events that may help to make meaning, to change a perspective and frame of reference. In other words, after such experiences as a traumatic loss, a person can change their frame of reference, or way of thinking about the world, and make meaning of their life and their experience. He describes the frame of reference as:

> the structures of assumptions through which we understand our experiences. They selectively shape and delimit expectations, perceptions, cognition, and feelings. They set "our line of action."[2]

He writes that through transformational learning:

> We transform our taken-for-granted frames of reference (meaning perspectives, habits of mind, mind-sets) to make them more inclusive, discriminating, open, emotionally capable of change, and reflective so that they may generate beliefs and opinions that will prove more true or justified to guide action.[3]

Mezirow suggested there are ten phases of transformational learning which can be applied to grief, making it a transformational grief process:[4]

1. A disorienting dilemma

At the loss of a child or sibling, the parent/sibling's world turns upside down, and their frame of reference is shaken and forever changed. They can experience shock, denial, trauma. They may feel unsure of themselves or others, bonds are ruptured, compassion can disappear. Edward talked of the moment Jacky died, how profoundly disorienting it was for him to be in the room with Jacky's body. He didn't know what to do, how to be. He said that he felt no emotion but numbness, that he wanted to feel but he couldn't. He spoke of how he struggled with putting the pieces together and felt empty. Some of this experience is echoed in Julia's story. She talks of seeing Pippa's body and of the moments afterwards, how she still cannot talk about it. Yet, the shock of the rupture – the sense of incomprehension – is almost palpable.

Nancy talked of how she was in shock for about a year, as does Carol. Carol also goes on to say that it was during the second year after David's death that the full reality of what had happened impacted her. Before then, she hadn't realized she had been in shock. Rose said that she wondered if she'd cope without her older sister. She also spoke of how unnerving it was when she saw her dad crying.

2. Self-examination with feelings of guilt or shame

This is likely to include reassessing one's ability or identity as a parent or sibling in light of the death, questioning self – what did I do wrong? What could I have done to prevent this happening? The 'what if' and 'if only' roundabout. Some may worry about surviving children/siblings or be fearful of their own future; there is often little self-compassion. Bonds with others are challenged. Many may feel completely overwhelmed by their thoughts and feelings. Claire initially blamed herself and would spend hours online reading up on anything that she could have possibly done. Steffy refers to feeling guilt, blaming herself for being a bad mother. At times this was reinforced when others spoke to her; for example, when someone said "Yes, it's a shame. A shame what happened to him really, but you did have a bad history, didn't you?" Steffy also refers to a sense of guilt when her brother Matthew died. Kath refers to feelings of guilt for her and Wilf having different parenting styles. Wilf feels guilt for working so much when Michael was young, how he believes he was a poor father and cannot see a time when he can forgive himself.

There is an implicit sense of shame too that comes across in some of the narratives. Kath said that she didn't want to see anybody that knew what had happened. Susan refers to not wanting the other volunteers where she worked to know about Michael's death. John (Chapter 12) also picked up on a sense of shame in terms of what the neighbours would think when Jamie died – how there was a dislike of being the centre of attention. This was echoed by Rose too, especially with regard to what was published in the local newspaper about Lizzie. For others the implicit nature of shame or blame comes from others being unwilling to talk about the person who died. Nancy mentions that some people avoid her or are unwilling to talk about Angel which she finds very hard. Wilf and Kath also experienced some people avoiding them, believing that they did not know what to say. John (Chapter 12) said other people avoiding the subject of his loss was really difficult for him. He was aware that some people seemed to be treating him differently, but nothing was actually said.

3. A critical assessment of epistemic, socio-cultural, or psychic assumptions

The loss of a child is an uncommon event and therefore 'shouldn't' happen, giving rise to the questions "Why me?" "Why my child/sibling?" Thoughts and feelings about family and friends arise, questioning relationships. There can be a lack of compassion towards other people, some bonds may be ruptured or changed, and others strengthened. Previously held beliefs may be shaken or reinforced. Some may be blaming others for the death, seeking answers to their questions. If they are stuck in this phase, they may continue to blame another to the point of persecution. Others contemplate the meaning of life, reviewing their own existence. There may be a realization that their way of living has not been fulfilling or indeed healthy for them. They question what's important in life and may feel frustrated at another's inability to see the bigger picture.

The reaction and behaviour of family members was significant for almost all of the participants. Claire and John (Chapter 3) spoke of how their respective parents were unable to provide any comfort or support. Joanne talked of how she felt abandoned by her family. Shireen and Beth both mention how their respective mothers were unable to help them. Julia, on the other hand, felt supported by family members, and although Steffy felt some members of her family were hopeless, she did get support from two of her brothers.

This phase can be incredibly painful for all involved as the bereaved seek answers, apologies, or acceptance of responsibility. For example, Nancy sought answers and apologies from the mental health services who had been looking after Angel. Carol sought answers from the police and the car driver about the final minutes of David's life.

Some began to question their life's purpose. Carol talked of how she felt she'd lost her life's purpose as she primarily identified as being a mum, and Nancy said that she'd lost her purpose, that she felt she was in limbo, just marking time until she died.

A number of participants felt that their basic trust in life was challenged. Claire wondered if Sam would be alive in the morning. Elisa commented that when she had another baby, she would frequently need to check on them to make sure they were still alive. Joanne mentioned how she was fearful if someone was late home and scared that she might lose another child. John (Chapter 12) commented on how, many years after Jamie's death, he felt the need to check on his own children when they were asleep.

A year after Jacky died, Edward was shocked to realize that Jacky had been his number one security person, and that was scary as he also realized he was all alone in terms of his biological family. This sense of aloneness was also felt by John (Chapter 12), who talked of the archaic sense of loneliness he had and how this was reinforced after Jamie's death, as he realized he was on his own and needed to deal with what had happened and to toughen up.

A number of the participants had religious or spiritual beliefs, and these influenced their experience. Claire and John both refer to how their belief and trust in God was reinforced by their experiences. Elisa also mentions how her faith was important to her in coping with what had happened to Ellen. Joanne says that her faith shifted and that she now feels more restored in nature than in church. Nancy said that she felt she lost her faith, and Carol said she stopped going to church after David died as she found it too difficult.

4. Recognition that one's discontent and the process of transformation are shared and that others have negotiated a similar change

During this phase some people may be talking with or reading of others who have lost a child or sibling, seeking reassurance that they have survived this event and are continuing to live and live well. Someone may begin to feel some hope. New bonds are formed and ideas about continuing bonds with their loved one can form. Compassion for self and others can return. Sometimes they may speak with people who are not living well, and this may cause them to recycle an earlier phase.

John (Chapter 3) spoke of a couple who had also experienced a stillbirth, and although what the couple said was hard to hear, he felt it was useful to know. Julia said that she had a visitor who was from Compassionate Friends. She found it useful knowing that the person in front of her had experienced the loss of a child 12 years previously. She also received some cards/letters from people who had lost a child, and she had found that helpful. She in turn did this for a few other people and has developed some good friendships as a result. Susan had a letter from someone she knew who had lost a son which was welcome. Wilf and Kath too refer to valuing support from friends whose son had killed himself. I experienced a huge amount of support from some friends, one of whom had lost her daughter some 15 years beforehand and another couple whose daughter had died just two years earlier. I found it invaluable having more immediate as well as longer-term experiences to draw upon.

A few people mentioned the use of support groups. Joanne and her family used the camps offered by Winston's Wish that they all found very effective. Kath considered going to a support group but decided not to because she didn't want to hear others' stories, as she felt she had enough of her own grief to deal with.

5. Exploration of options for new roles, relationships, and actions

In this stage the bereaved parents/sibling may be questioning their role. Am I still a mother/father/brother/sister? This is particularly hard for those for who do not have any surviving children or siblings. Relationships with others may change, and their beliefs may no longer be compatible. Some relationships may end, and others start. Some bonds break beyond repair, others are challenged or changed, and new ones can form. During this phase someone can feel a little chaotic and unsettled to begin with, and compassion for self and others fluctuates until a sense of purpose or meaning starts to form. What do I want from my life? What is my legacy? Some may review their own mortality and that of those to whom they are close.

A number of participants referred to changes in relationships. Carol spoke of finding some people draining and so became disciplined about who she would permit herself to be around. She also spoke of how her tolerance of other people has changed and that she prefers to be with people who have a level of emotional intelligence. This was echoed by Rose, and Claire also spoke of how some previously close friends were unable to support them. Julia, although she had some people back away from her and the family, spoke of how she felt supported by her community, both in terms of family members and also in terms of Pippa's friends and people who lived nearby.

Some participants were prompted to make other changes, Nancy said that after what happened to Angel, she took a role at work where she no longer worked on the front line. Shireen felt a sense of urgency, a wish to make meaningful contributions. She attributed this to getting older which, along with Tariq's death, focussed her mind.

Julia talked of how her parenting style changed. She felt that she needed to make sure everyone stayed alive and that she found it hard to be a mother. She says she became overprotective of her other children in a 'policeman' way, and that her youngest daughter pushed her away, telling her not to interfere. She found this difficult to cope with but knows it was the right thing to do for her daughter. Julia said how desperate she was to know her youngest daughter, in particular, would be safe.

6. Planning of a course of action

At this stage people may return to previously held plans that were put on hold. New plans may be prompted by the realization that life is finite. Alternatively, some may feel they have lost 'their way' and want to reinvest in a life that is more meaningful and fulfilling. Bonds can be strengthened, compassion for self begins to increase, compassion for others may still fluctuate, and ideas for continuing bonds with the deceased person begin to form.

Susan had been waiting to start a bereavement support group that was put on hold when Michael died. She was almost at the point of being able to fulfil this wish when her sister died, which would have meant a move back to phase one. She waited four years in all before she could complete her plan. Joanne, Steffy, and Julia all thought about getting involved in local projects to help others. Carol decided after about three years that she needed to get fitter. I began to think about undertaking this research project, spoke with others about what I wanted to do, and tentatively began to explore my options.

7. Acquisition of knowledge and skills for implementing one's plans

Some examples of this would be reading books, going for therapy, attending courses, meeting new people, and getting a taste of what life might be like in the future. Self-esteem may start to increase as does compassion for self, new bonds may start to form, and compassion for others may continue to fluctuate.

Julia said she found some books useful. Carol also mentioned reading a lot, both books and articles. Beth talks of a tide-based language she and her brother Baz created and called emocean (a combination of emotion and ocean), which they used as a way to talk with one another. They applied this way of communicating to talk deeply of their feelings.

A number of the participants received some form of counselling or therapy. For example, John (Chapter 3) had some counselling from the hospital a few months after Emilie died and some psychotherapy a few years later, all of which he found useful. Julia says her youngest daughter had some counselling early on, but that wasn't useful for her. She considered it was too early in the grieving process for her to make use of it. Julia had a counselling friend who would call every day, and they would talk which she found helpful. Steffy said that therapy helped her, as did Shireen and Edward. Susan also had some counselling with mixed results. She said she wanted to speak with someone who had some life experience and had children of their own, although she didn't think it necessary that they had had a similar experience in order to be helpful.

8. Provisional trying of new roles

This can be an exciting and scary time. Exciting because it is new and life affirming. Scary because some may feel concerned that by undertaking this new role, they may 'forget' their child/sibling or are being disloyal to them in some way. If they are able to stick with their new roles, their self-confidence may grow, and they can feel more hopeful for their future without their child/sibling. Many may need a lot of support at this time to enable them to complete this stage. If they are unable to complete this phase, they are likely to lose confidence, self-esteem, and motivation and may well revert to an earlier phase. Compassion for self and others can also fluctuate depending upon how this stage develops, and bonds can be strengthened or challenged.

Joanne talked of how she began working with an organization running courses for parents supporting children through change and loss, and how that has given her purpose, as did raising money for charity and later becoming a counsellor and helping others. Julia talked of how she got actively involved with Papyrus (a charity involved in the prevention of young suicide) and working with schools in talking about mental health issues for adolescents. Steffy got involved in a college project and the local drug and alcohol agency in their campaign against drugs, and a poster was made in honour of Jason.

I began this research project. I sent out emails to colleagues and some bereavement organizations asking them to let their clients know of this project and inviting prospective participants to contact me and started undertaking some interviews.

9. Building of competence and self-confidence in new roles and relationships

As people practise their new role, they will build faith and trust in themselves, others, and life. This can be a very life-affirming time. Compassion for self and others increase and bonds develop.

A number of the participants changed their work role as a result of their experience. An example is Joanne, who after her experience with the parenting groups decided to train to be a counsellor. Carol spoke of how she changed her role at work and, as her confidence grew, began to feel more able to talk about David with work colleagues. Julia continued in her work as a therapist. Steffy re-trained to be a psychotherapist and uses her experience to help other bereaved parents. For me, as I continued to interview participants, the shape of the research changed, I became increasingly interested in the uniqueness of each story and how each person was managing their grief.

10. A reintegration into one's life on the basis of conditions dictated by one's new perspective

At this point/in this stage, people are ready to accept life without their child/sibling. They recognize their child or sibling's continued importance in their current life. They are able to feel compassion for themselves and others. The bonds they have with friends/family will be reinforced, for good or ill, and new bonds are welcomed and cherished. There's a sense of knowing how the bonds with their child or sibling will continue in a way that honours and celebrates their life, whilst allowing the bereaved person to continue with their own life, in a way that they find fulfilling and rewarding.

A number of participants refer to how their lives have changed as a result of their experience and what they have learned. For example, Steffy has used her experience to change her life. She referred to her realization about how tenuous life is. She commented that she's learned a lot about herself, about what is important in life and what is not. Consequently, she believes she is more positive, her life has changed a lot, and she sees Jason's death as a gift.

Shireen talked of her connection in nature and in gardening which helps her to appreciate her time on the planet. The need to be in nature is echoed by Susan, Julia, and Carol. Joanne also said that as a family they go on more holidays and spend time together, as memories are more important than things.

Elisa mentions how they put together a photobook for Ellen, as they have with each of their children. She describes how the book tells the story of Ellen's life and what happened to her, and how it is often brought out by her children and used to talk about her in a way that normalizes and validates her life. I too created a photobook. Although putting it together brought up a whole range of feelings and emotions, I can now cherish the happier times in Vikki's life, something I hadn't been able to do before.

These phases are not linear in their occurrence. Certain stages may be experienced multiple times within the transformation process, plus events can happen that pull someone back to an earlier phase, rather like the snakes on a snakes and ladders board. A visual representation of the snakes and arrows of transformational grief are shown in Figure 20.1.

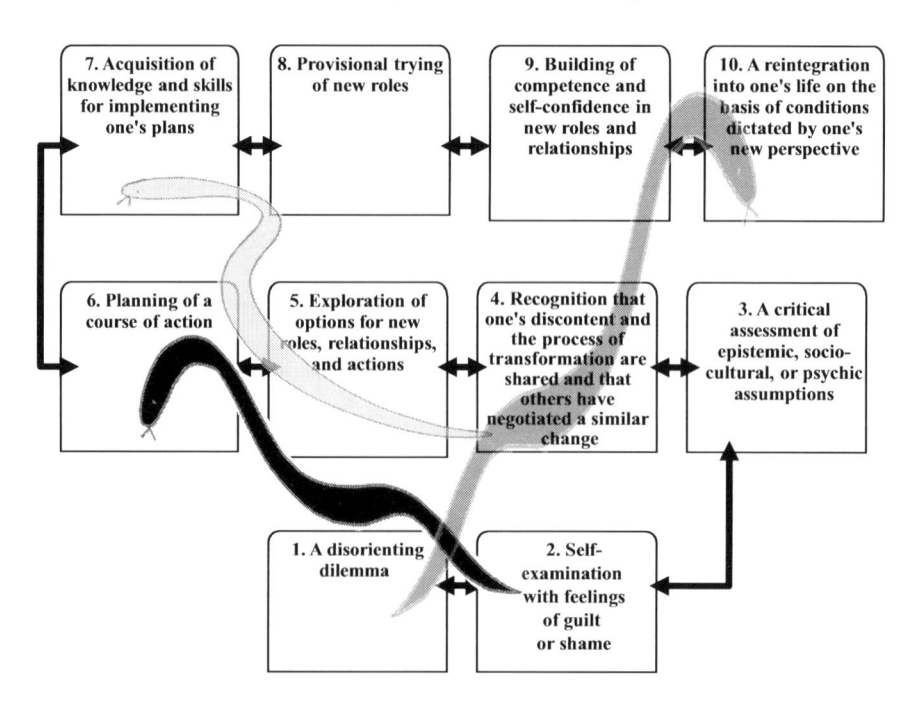

Figure 20.1 The snakes and arrows of transformational grief

This is not to say that all loss must be transformed into a beautiful new package, neatly tied up with a bow. Rather, this research indicates that loss is messy, turbulent, and challenging. Each phase interacts with the others in a dynamic process. It is possible that some people can get stuck in any one of those phases. They may feel so stuck in the story of what happened to their child or sibling that their identity is lost. The narrative may be all-consuming and so overwhelming that the person is unable to see themselves as separate. They may feel like a hostage to the events of what happened, to their own thoughts, feelings, and behaviours, or to those of others. The challenge is to separate from the story, to make meaning from the experience and to recover one's authentic self, which is the consciousness that comes before the story.[5]

I believe with sufficient and appropriate help and support, it is possible for someone to transform their loss into something that honours the life of those who have died, alongside finding a way to live well and to even thrive whilst all the time respecting their ongoing grief, continuing an appropriate bond with their child or sibling, and developing resilience.

Notes

1 J. Mezirow and Associates. (1990). *Fostering Critical Reflection in Adulthood*. San Francisco, CA: Jossey-Bass.
2 J. Mezirow (2000). Learning to Think Like an Adult: Core Concepts in Transformation Theory. In: J. Mezirow, ed., *Learning in Transformation: Critical Perspectives on a Theory in Progress*. San Francisco, CA: Jossey-Bass, p. 16. Republished with permission of John Wiley & Sons. Permission conveyed through Copyright Clearance Center, Inc.
3 Ibid., pp. 7–8.
4 J. Mezirow (1991). *Transformative Dimensions in Adult Learning*. San Francisco, CA: Jossey-Bass, pp. 168–169. Republished with permission of John Wiley & Sons. Permission conveyed through Copyright Clearance Center, Inc.
5 J. Bernie (2010). *Ordinary Freedom*. Salisbury, England: Non-Duality Press, p. 30.

Part II

21 Models of grief and bereavement

Although transformational learning can be used as a model for understanding the phases of grief over a longer period of time (see Chapter 20), there are other specific grief models that are used to understand the processes of bereavement. It does not matter which model someone uses so long as what they use is helpful to those who wish to make sense of their own or another's grief. Some of these models are outlined in this chapter; other models are available, and you may have your own preferred model that is not mentioned here.

Staged models

Some people may prefer to think about their grief in terms of stages such as Kübler-Ross's five-stage model[1] and Bowlby and Parkes's four phases of grief.[2] This latter model integrates the Kübler-Ross model into four phases.

Bowlby and Parkes's four-phases-of-grief model

1. *Shock and numbness.* This equates to the denial stage of the Kübler-Ross model. Many of the participants refer to feeling numb or being in shock; this is a normal reaction to a trauma. When in this phase, someone may feel they are on autopilot, and having some structure can help. Concentration is usually impaired, and any significant decisions are best delayed until the bereaved are able to think more clearly. Some of the participants also spoke of feeling foggy-headed or absent-minded and said that they felt they were in shock for about a year. Someone in this phase may withdraw from others or the world in general or may immerse themselves in work – anything to avoid the pain of what has happened.
2. *Yearning and searching.* This encompasses the anger and bargaining stages of the Kübler-Ross model. During this phase, anger can be an important feature, whether that is aimed at the bereaved person themselves, the person who died, someone involved in their care or who contributed to their death, or the world in general. The bereaved may have thoughts such as, "Why me, my child, my sibling?" "Who's to blame?"

"Why are you happy when I'm so sad?" Anyone who gets in the way may feel the full force of the person's anger. In this stage someone might be bargaining with God or a higher power, requesting a change in the situation in exchange for a commitment to change their own behaviour. The bargaining is irrational, and the person usually knows that is the case. This is also the stage of the 'what if' and 'if only' questions and comments – a time when they look for and 'see' they deceased person in the street or elsewhere. This may accompany a longing to be with the deceased which can be experienced as a physical pain. Some may feel restless and be constantly asking questions in an attempt to make sense of their loss. The grief that is experienced can mean that the bereaved person has little time or patience with other people.

3   *Disorientation and despair.* This is a phase of uncertainty for those who are bereaved and links with the depression stage outlined in the Kūbler-Ross model. The reality of their loss is now accepted, and the bereaved person may feel anxious, depressed, hopeless, helpless, or uncertain. They may struggle to function in their usual way, or they can no longer see any point in what they do or even why they live. A number of the participants spoke of their feelings of despair and depression. Some experienced suicidal thoughts.

4   *Reorganization and recovery.* During this phase, the bereaved person begins to put their life back together incorporating the acceptance stages of the Kūbler-Ross model, and the finding-meaning stage that was added later.[3] The bereaved person begins to come to terms with the reality of the loss, realizing that there is a desire to continue living without the person who died. The person may start to feel a bit better, has more energy for life and other people, has 'good days' and 'bad days.' There may be an increase in energy, cognitive functioning may improve, and self-esteem and confidence increase. They may begin to feel enjoyment in life again. Some of the participants referred to feeling increasingly able to go out to places where they had previously gone with the bereaved person and could experience some enjoyment. During this time the bereaved may begin to transform their grief into a more peaceful and even hopeful experience.

There is no time laid out for the accomplishment of each of these phases. I find that these models can be useful in the early days/weeks after a bereavement. They can help someone to realize that their feelings are normal and that they will change over time.

Visual models

Some people may prefer to have a visual model to understand their experience, such as the Waterfall of Bereavement, sometimes referred to as the Whirlpool of Grief.[4]

The Waterfall of Bereavement

The Waterfall of Bereavement was developed by Richard Wilson and is a pictorial representation of the nature of grief (see Figure 21.1).[5] This model may also appeal to those who prefer a kinaesthetic or even auditory way of experiencing the world.

The beauty of the model is that it depicts the turbulent nature of grief and how someone may feel 'on the rocks' whether that is through a sense of disorganization or through pain or other physical symptoms. It is clear to see that the river of life does not run smoothly through the journey of grief. Another advantage of this model is that it can help someone to talk about their experience by way of metaphor. For some people this can feel safer. It can also be easier for those supporting them to appreciate what the other person is undergoing, because although they may not be able

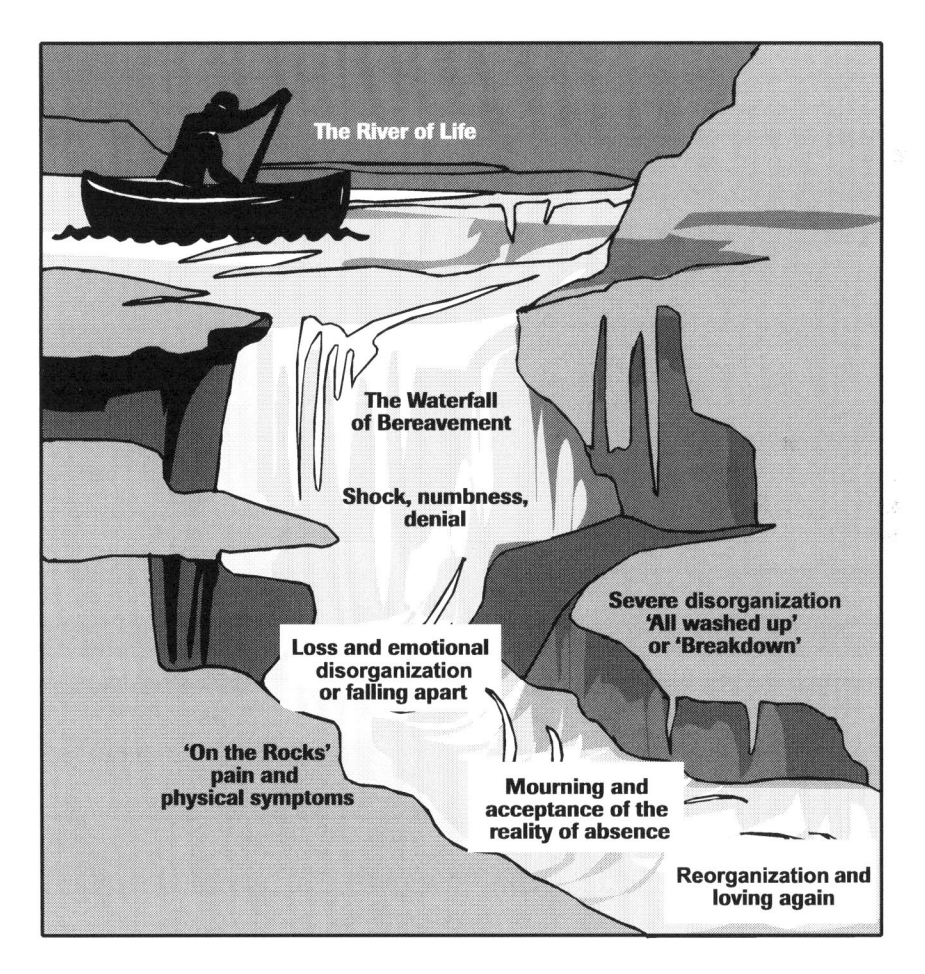

Figure 21.1 The Waterfall of Bereavement

218 *Part II*

to relate to the other's actual situation, they may be able to relate to the metaphor.

Task models

I find Worden's tasks of mourning with associated mediators,[6] and the Dual Process Model,[7] useful as they explain what someone may need to focus on in order to adjust to their loss.

Worden's tasks of mourning

Worden identifies four tasks of mourning and includes what he calls mediators; I think of these as mitigating factors. This leads to a complex model which I think fits with the nature of grief and is worth some explanation. Each task contains elements of all the stages or phases mentioned earlier. The model is summarized in Table 21.1.

Task I: to accept the reality of the loss

The acceptance of the loss is on both an intellectual and emotional basis. The intellectual acceptance of the loss is usually achieved first. The emotional acceptance can take a long time, particularly if the physical contact between the bereaved person and their loved one was intermittent.

Task II: to process the pain of grief

The anguish experienced by some people can feel overwhelming, and they attempt to avoid it by rationalizing or distracting themselves. This can be exacerbated by others bestowing platitudes such as "everything happens for a reason," "they wouldn't want you to be so upset," or "they're at peace now." These phrases deny the reality of the heartache and make it clear that the speaker is not emotionally available to provide help. This task can be delayed if the person has minimal support or if they are focussed on supporting others. When they are ready to work through their own grief, others may not be understanding, believing that they are seeking attention or 'should be over it by now.'

Task III: to adjust to a world without the deceased

There are three areas of adjustment:

a   *External adjustments* – adjusting to life without the deceased person. Edward spoke of how he's adjusting to going for walks without Jacky, something they regularly did when Jacky was well.
b   *Internal adjustments* – this involves the bereaved person adjusting their sense of self. Being a parent is for some their core identity, and when

Table 21.1 Summary of Worden's Task/Mediator Model

Mediator Task	1. Kinship: Who Died?	2. The Nature of Attachment	3. How the Person Died	4. Historical Antecedents	5. Personality Variables	6. Social Variables	7. Concurrent Stresses
I: To Accept the Reality of the Loss	Child	a. The strength of the attachment	Natural, Accidental, Suicidal or Homicidal	Resilience or trauma from past events that need to be taken into account.	a. The age and gender	a. Support availability	Other agencies involved: relationship, employment, financial, or health difficulties
II: To Process the Pain of Grief	Sibling	b. The security of the attachment			b. The person's coping style	b. Support satisfaction	
	Grandchild		a. Proximity		c. Attachment style	c. Social role involvements	
III: To Adjust to a World Without the Deceased: Internal, External, and Spiritual Adjustments	Half or Step Sibling	c. The ambivalence in the relationship	b. Suddenness or expectedness		d. Cognitive style	d. Religious resources and ethnic expectations	
	Parent	d. Conflict with the deceased	c. Violent/ traumatic deaths		e. Ego strength: self-esteem and self-efficacy		
	Stepparent	e. Dependent relationships.	d. Multiple losses		f. Assumptive world (beliefs and values)		
	Grandparent		e. Preventable deaths				
	Aunt		f. Ambiguous deaths				
IV: To Find a Way to Remember the Deceased While Embarking on the Rest of One's Journey Through Life	Uncle		g. Stigmatized deaths				
	Cousin						
	Niece						
	Nephew						
	Spouse						
	Partner						
	Friend						

their child dies, this role is called into question; it is also more difficult for those who do not have any other children. A sibling may have to adjust to now being an only child; or a middle child suddenly becomes the oldest or youngest.

c   *Spiritual adjustments* – previously held beliefs, values, and attitudes may be challenged and some changed after a death. Many of the participants lost their trust in the world as previously held beliefs about order were confronted. A child is not supposed to die. In addition, there is a loss of the imagined future. Some in the research noted that their belief in their faith/church was wobbled; others ceased believing.

Task IV: to find a way to remember the deceased while embarking on the rest of one's journey through life

Remembering can be achieved through talking, dreaming, writing, and sharing. Some people may find this stage the most challenging, preferring to hold on to their existing attachment or bond with the deceased person in such a way that they are not able to form new relationships, and they appear to others to be stuck in their grief.

Mediators

There are seven mediators:

Mediator 1: kinship (who died?)

As all the participants lost either a child or sibling, their grief would have been greater than if the person had been a distant relation. Further, as the death was out of the normal order of life, this too had a greater impact on them.

Mediator 2: the nature of attachment

Most of the participants had strong bonds with their child or sibling. Some experienced ambivalence related to their behaviour which in a few cases caused some conflict. None were dependent on the person who died, but for many, part of their identity was about being a parent or a sibling.

Mediator 3: how the person died

Some of the participants were present when their child or sibling died, others were in fairly close proximity. All the deaths, except Jacky, were unexpected, and all were experienced as traumatic for different reasons. Many were preventable, and some involved substance misuse or suicide. All of these factors hindered the completion of various tasks for the participants.

Mediator 4: historical antecedents

Someone's resilience from past events will influence their reaction to a new loss. This is evident for some of the participants and people in their support systems as unresolved or transgenerational losses complicated the grieving process. For more on this see Chapter 22.

Mediator 5: personality variables

John (Chapter 12) was only eight years old when his brother Jamie died, and Rose was 16 when her sister Lizzie died. Both had little life experience to help them cope with what was happening to them and those around them. Many of the participants had a secure attachment style and tended to have an optimistic view of life. After the initial shock had decreased, this supported them in their relationships with others. Some were able to revise initial grandiose thinking, such as "I'll never recover from this," "No one can possibly help me," or "My life is over now," into something that acknowledged their loss whilst adjusting to their new life. Others had a belief that suggested a reunion in death or a sense that the person is still present in their life in some way, which helped them.

Mediator 6: social variables

The greater and more appropriate support the participants had, the less they suffered significant complications in their grieving. Actions rather than words tended to be more useful and satisfying. What is clear is that a parent or sibling's grief remains throughout their life. Even those who have been bereaved for over 20 years are still sometimes taken by surprise at the enduring pain of their loss. Most of the participants had other roles in their life, other than being a parent or sibling. These other roles supported them as they adjusted to their loss. Others changed those roles because of their experience. A number had religious, cultural, or spiritual rituals or beliefs that challenged or sustained them.

Mediator 7: concurrent stresses

Other factors that may impact on someone's grief might include the involvement of the police or other external agency, as referred to by a number of the participants. Some, like Nancy, may no longer feel able to do their job because their role creates too much additional stress on top of their grief. For a few, the financial impact of a funeral caused additional strain, as mentioned by Steffy who had to borrow money for Jason's funeral.

This very comprehensive model includes many of the extenuating factors experienced by the participants. It can be used to help someone consider what task they may be dealing with at any specific time and what mediators may also need to be taken into account. This helps them feel more in charge of their own process, whilst appreciating the uniqueness of their experience.

This model illustrates why bereaved parents and siblings have so much to contend with as many of the mediators complicate each task, extending their mourning process. Therapists might consider using Table 21.1 as a template, adding in details of each mediator as appropriate. This may help identify whether any mediator has not been taken into account or needs further exploration, especially if they or their clients perceive themselves as stuck.

Dual Process Model

I like two things about the Dual Process Model. First, this model visually illustrates the oscillating nature of grief that I and all of the participants experienced. Second, it can help someone to see whether they have a tendency to avoid their grief or stay away from making necessary changes so they can continue with their life.

The authors of this model suggest that people undertake what they call loss-oriented coping and restoration-oriented coping in unique ways.

Loss-orientation coping means focussing on and managing some aspect of the loss experience itself. This may include, for example, feeling the impact of their grief, reminiscing, ruminating, remembering, as well as yearning for the person who died, and avoiding tasks that need to be done.

Restoration-oriented coping focusses on the secondary sources of stress that accompany the loss. These may include having to make life changes, such as changing a job, moving to a new house, learning how to do something that was previously undertaken by the person who died. In terms of a bereaved parent it could mean having to come to terms with no longer fulfilling a parenting role and finding something else to do to occupy their time. For a sibling it could be having to cope with going back to school, or no longer having their brother or sister to talk to and seek help from, so they need to find support elsewhere. During this phase the bereaved person may need to develop new skills or establish different roles and relationships.

During the grieving process the person oscillates between the two styles of coping, as show in Figure 21.2.[8]

This model could also be used to show how someone is managing the mediators and tasks of mourning mentioned earlier. In many ways this model depicts more accurately the reality of the grief process. The earlier staged models seem to suggest a move from one stage to the next. This model shows how someone moves in and out of their grief and of making necessary life adjustments, both of which are needed in order to manage their loss. Many of the participants refer to the powerful nature

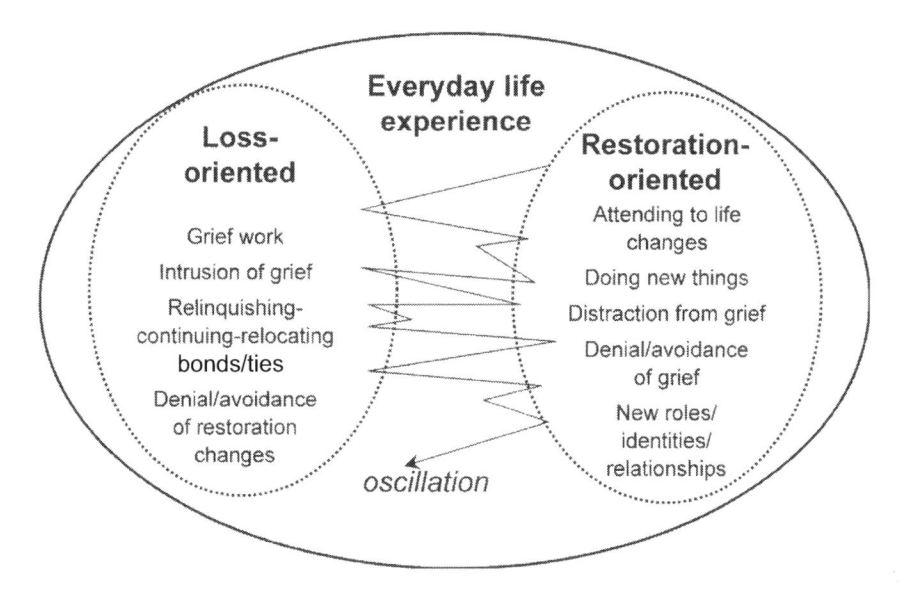

[Figure: The Dual Process Model diagram showing two overlapping circles labeled "Loss-oriented" (containing: Grief work, Intrusion of grief, Relinquishing-continuing-relocating bonds/ties, Denial/avoidance of restoration changes) and "Restoration-oriented" (containing: Attending to life changes, Doing new things, Distraction from grief, Denial/avoidance of grief, New roles/identities/relationships), within an "Everyday life experience" oval, with "oscillation" arrows between them.]

Figure 21.2 The Dual Process Model

of their grief, how sometimes they felt as though they were getting on with some aspect of their life (restoration coping) when something would trigger them back into their grief (loss coping). Others refer to the need for work or other tasks to give them some temporary respite from their grief. This model can help to appreciate how sometimes someone may just want to stare into space, watch the television, or get lost in a book but the next day feel able to go to work, spend time looking through photograph albums, or want to talk about the person who died. Many fluctuate and have what the participants experienced as 'good days' and 'bad days,' and that all of this is normal and indeed necessary in order to cope with their loss.

Although I like both of these task-focussed models, two further aspects that I think are worthy of closer attention are that of continuing bonds (see Chapter 18)[9] and meaning making.[10]

Meaning making

It is now widely accepted that in order to restore an attachment to the person who died, bereaved people need to find meaning in their loved one's life and death. This certainly seems to be my own experience as well as those of the participants. Robert Neimeyer, referring to the importance of meaning making after grief, states, "Viewed in a constructivist perspective, grieving entails as a central process the *attempt to reaffirm or reconstruct a world of meaning that has been challenged by loss.*"[11] This is achieved by a bereaved person concentrating on:

1 Processing the 'event story' of the death, and its implications for their ongoing lives;
2 Accessing the 'back story' of their life with the deceased loved one.

Both of these need to be done in such a way that it re-establishes some attachment or bond with the person who died.[12]

Processing the 'event story' of the death, and its implications for their ongoing lives

This includes the bereaved asking themselves a range of questions, some of which focus on the death itself and any events leading up to the death. These may include what role they played in these events, if any; how they feel about what has happened; what they want and need. They may also examine previously held beliefs and values; changes in self-concept; how the loss changes their life view and how they can make meaning from their loss. These questions can be facilitated by what is called a restorative retelling of the event story of the death.[13]

Restorative retelling of the event story of the death

This includes the person describing all aspects of the story, including those that they might usually avoid sharing. This can be achieved in different ways, each of which needs to be done in a safe and secure environment.

One way is to tell and retell the story with another person. In order for this to have the maximum effect, the listener would ideally have sufficient context for the story. For instance, that they know the background to the relationship, the philosophical or spiritual beliefs that help the bereaved person, and any other support systems that they can use. The process is a gentle one that takes place over a number of sessions; each time the person adds in more detail until the full story is revealed. The goal is to help the bereaved person to integrate all aspects of the story in such a way that provides them with a greater meaning of the death.

This explains why someone may have a need to keep telling their story over and over again. I found this useful and, although at times I felt that I was just repeating myself, what I realized was that each time, I would make another connection or add in a little more detail that I had not mentioned before. This also may explain why some people seem to go 'around the houses' in telling their story; there are so many twists and turns that as a listener it can be difficult to maintain focus and get a clear picture of what happened.

Directed journaling[14]

This involves someone writing down what they are thinking, feeling, and experiencing, using words, images, photographs, or drawings, that help them to make sense of their experience. What makes directed journaling different from freewriting is that the bereaved person is invited to focus on a specific topic or aspect of their loss. This could be how the loss occurred; the impact of the loss on them in terms of their role as a parent or sibling; or the nature of the responses from those around them. Directed journaling can be used to help the bereaved person to explore what they have learned from their loss; to express any gratitude for any changes in their beliefs or perceived gifts that occurred as a result of the loss.

This can be a useful way of working, particularly for people who feel reluctant to talk about what has happened or who wish to express themselves or explore their experience in a more creative way. For other creative ways of working with loss, see Chapter 25.

Behavioural activation[15]

Behavioural activation is another option, whereby the bereaved person uses activity to increase behaviours that lead to rewarding or pleasurable experiences. A number of the participants found satisfaction in nature, gardening, going for walks, or smashing bottles at the bottle bank. This process can be very useful, particularly if someone feels as though they are stuck in a negative cycle in their grief, perhaps spending a lot of time ruminating which may lead to feelings of depression. If this is happening, then the person can schedule a 'rumination slot' into their day whereby they allow themselves to reflect on the issue(s) only for that period of time. If these thoughts arise at other times of the day, then they use pleasurable or rewarding activities as a distraction, whilst also reassuring themselves that they can return to the topic the next day.

Accessing the 'back story' of their life with the deceased loved one

This involves the bereaved person reconstructing their self-narrative after their loss and reframing their bond with their loved one. Themes might include:

1 Establishing how they want to manage a connection with the person who died;
2 Reflecting on memories of their relationship and whether there is a need for any reparation or forgiveness;
3 Thinking about what memories give them happiness and pleasure and encourage a celebration of the person's life and achievements;
4 Assessing what they have learned from their relationship and what will help them to build resilience.[16]

This reconstruction can be achieved through imagined dialogues and legacy work.

Imagined dialogues

These can be facilitated by the use of two-chair work. Originally devised by Moreno and later adapted by numerous other therapeutic modalities, these imagined dialogues can be an effective way of resolving 'unfinished business' that someone may have with a deceased person.[17] This technique involves symbolically placing the person who died on an empty chair in front of the bereaved person (client). The client speaks to the chair as if the deceased person were sitting there. They may express their anger, sadness, or dismay at the death; tell them how they are feeling; and disclose any regrets, wishes, or expressions of gratitude. Then, when they have finished, the client moves to sit in the other chair and responds as the deceased person. This technique can be incredibly powerful and lead to resolutions and even a new understanding of what happened.

Legacy work[18]

This refers to the bereaved finding a way to recognize and honour the life of the deceased person. This can be done via scrapbooking; creating photograph albums, like those mentioned by Elisa; montages or collages; storytelling – writing their own book; or making a film or documentary. It could be setting up a charity or undertaking charitable work; contributing to research (as all the participants for this project have done) or raising awareness of specific issues. This was done by Steffy concerning drug use and by Julia regarding mental health in schools. This legacy work can be incredibly rewarding and usually has a lifespan of its own.

Completion of these aspects can help someone to make or take some meaning about the life and death of their child or sibling, leaving them free to get on with their own life whilst remembering, honouring and continuing a bond with the person who died. For more information on continuing bonds, see Chapter 18.

Notes

1 E. Kübler-Ross (1969). *On Death and Dying*. New York: Macmillan Publishing.
2 J. Bowlby and C.M. Parkes (1970). Separation and Loss within the Family. In: E.J. Anthony and C. Koupernik, eds., *The Child and His Family*. New York: Wiley, pp. 197–216. Republished with permission of John Wiley and Sons, permission conveyed through Copyright Clearance Center, Inc.
3 D. Kessler (2019). *Finding Meaning: The Sixth Stage of Grief*. New York: Scribner.
4 C. Hindmarch (2000). *On the Death of a Child*. Oxon: Radcliffe Medical Press.
5 Copyright (2000) from *On the Death of a Child* by C. Hindmarch. Reproduced by permission of Taylor and Francis Group, LLC, a division of Informa plc.

6 J.W. Worden (2018). *Grief Counselling and Grief Therapy. A Handbook for the Mental Health Practitioner*. 5th ed. New York: Springer Publishing, pp. 41–76. Republished with permission of Springer Publishing; permission conveyed through Copyright Clearance Center, Inc.
7 M. Stroebe and H. Schut (1999). The Dual Process Model of Coping with Bereavement: Rationale and Description. *Death Studies*, 23(3), pp. 197–224. DOI: 10.1080/074811899201046.
8 M.S. Stroebe, H.A.W. Schut and W. Stroebe (2005). Attachment in Coping with Bereavement: A Theoretical Integration. *Review of General Psychology*, 9(1), p. 51. DOI: 10.1037/1089-2680.9.1.48. APA, reprinted with permission.
9 D. Klass, P.R. Silverman and S.L. Nickman (1996). *Continuing Bonds: New Understandings of Grief*. Washington, DC: Taylor & Francis.
10 R.A. Neimeyer (2016). Helping Clients Find Meaning in Grief and Loss. In: M. Cooper and W. Dryden, eds., *The Handbook of Pluralistic Counseling and Psychotherapy*. Thousand Oaks, CA: Sage, pp. 211–222.
11 Ibid. Emphasis in original.
12 Copyright 2014 from Meaning Making and the Art of Grief Therapy. In: B.E. Thompson and R.A. Neimeyer, eds., *Grief and the Expressive Arts: Practices for Creating Meaning*. Reproduced by permission of Taylor and Francis Group, LLC, a division of Informa plc. Permission conveyed through Copyright Clearance Center, Inc.
13 E.K. Rynearson and A. Salloum (2011). Restorative Retelling: Revisiting the Narrative of Violent Death. In: R.A. Neimeyer, D. Harris, H. Winokuer and G. Thornton, eds., *Grief and Bereavement in Contemporary Society: Bridging Research and Practice*. New York: Routledge, pp. 177–188.
14 W.G. Lichtenthal and R.A. Neimeyer (2012). Directed Journaling to Facilitate Meaning Making. In: R.A. Neimeyer, ed., *Techniques of Grief Therapy*. New York: Routledge, pp. 161–164.
15 C.R. Martell, M.E. Addis and N.S. Jacobson (2001). *Depression in Context: Strategies for Guided Action*. New York: W.W. Norton & Company.
16 R.A. Neimeyer and B.E. Thompson (2014). Meaning Making and the Art of Grief Therapy. In: B.E. Thompson and R.A. Neimeyer, eds., *Grief and the Expressive Arts: Practices for Creating Meaning*. New York: Routledge, p. 216.
17 J.D. Moreno (2014). *Impromptu Man: J.L. Moreno and the Origins of Psychodrama, Encounter Culture, and the Social Network*. New York: Bellevue Literary Press.
18 R.A. Neimeyer and B.E. Thompson (2014). Meaning Making and the Art of Grief Therapy. In: B.E. Thompson and R.A. Neimeyer, eds., *Grief and the Expressive Arts: Practices for Creating Meaning*. New York: Routledge, p. 219.

22 Transgenerational loss and Family Constellations

Transgenerational trauma and epigenetics

I am including this chapter on 'unknown loss' to give readers a context to Sally's story (Chapter 17). She used Family Constellations to validate the existence of her older sister, Rose, whose life and death had been concealed. The situation was more painful because Rose was a child of incest, and Sally's grandfather, the perpetrator of the incest, was invested in secrecy. Rose, however, could not be denied because she had a place in the system, and the symptoms were picked up by Sally. Working with a systemic therapist enabled Sally to move through the grieving process and find a resolution that gave her some peace. I hope this chapter will encourage readers to incorporate in their understanding of grief the possibility that unresolved traumas from previous generations may reverberate through the family system and show up in the form of grief without any clear explanation. These traumas will include the untimely losses of siblings and children that have not been fully integrated into the family narrative.

Recent research confirms that later generations do have responses such as fear and terror to memories of trauma that are not in their experience. It also confirms that such traumatic experiences can have a long-lasting impact on the physical or mental health, and on the behaviour, of subsequent generations.[1,2,3] Research into the survivors of the Holocaust found that their children, and sometimes grandchildren, displayed high levels of anxiety, depression, and PTSD.[4] Some of the children felt overly protective of their parents, had an elevated need for control or increased childlike dependency and a preoccupation with the Holocaust.[5]

Some researchers have studied the mechanism by which trauma is passed down the generations genetically. It seems that not only those directly impacted by trauma develop lower cortisol levels, but this is carried on in their children and later generations, as if the whole genetic makeup is changed. The children of Holocaust survivors showed lower cortisol levels and changes in a stress-related gene linked to PTSD and depression.[6,7,8] Other research into epigenetics, mainly using mice, show that trauma or stress experienced before conception, as well as during pregnancy or after birth, may influence the reactions or behaviour of the offspring and later generations.[9,10,11,12,13] In one experiment using mice, the adult mouse was subjected to the smell of cherry blossom and at the same time received a small electric shock to its foot. Understandably, the mouse developed a fear response to the smell of cherry blossom even without the electric shocks. Subsequent descendants demonstrated alarm when they smelt cherry blossom even though they had not been part of the experiment; this included mice born through IVF.[14]

Although the research into epigenetics in humans is still early in its development, many psychotherapists and others who work in the mental health field have known, or suspected, that significant events in the lives of previous generations can impact later generations. This emerges in family dysfunction that cannot easily be tracked to its origins. There are some people who are sceptical about the idea of trauma being passed down through the genes. The whole nature/nurture debate will continue and, as the research evolves, more will be discovered.

Systemic Family Constellations and the Orders of Love[15]

Sally used this approach to find the source of the disorder in her family and the source of her pervasive feelings of loss and fear. Bert Hellinger identified certain features, which he called the "Orders of Love," which are present in a healthy family system:

Precedence

Those who were there first have priority over those who came later. This does not depend on their merit. However, where someone misuses their position and causes trauma, the system is disturbed. Sally's grandfather betrayed his responsibility by abusing his daughters. He then appears to have caused Rose's death and left Sally's mother traumatized.

Inclusion

Everyone has their place in the family, including stillborn children or people who have died. This was affirmed constantly in my research, where participants passionately wanted their dead child or sibling to be acknowledged. Where attempts are made to deny a member their place (as was done to Rose), some other family member will, out of awareness, experience symptoms that belonged to the dead member. It is as if the person sacrifices themselves for the sake of restoring wholeness to the greater family system. Entanglements can show up in many forms, including illness, disorders, depression, or other mental health problems, suicide, or self-sabotaging behaviours. Sally had nightmares in which she seems to have identified at times with Rose and at others with her mother. A number of the participants spoke of how they keep their child/sibling's place in the family and of how they sometimes struggle to do that when asked how many children they have or if they have brothers or sisters.

Personal fate

No one can take the fate from another, however much they wish to do so. Sally could not change Rose's fate, but she was able to affirm Rose's place in the family and acknowledge her fate. She was also able to acknowledge her mother's trauma.

Balance

Human beings seek to maintain a balance between giving and receiving. Hellinger and other systemic therapists linked this to a sense of rightness.[16,17] He also noted that where giving and receiving is out of balance, harmony is disturbed. The need for balance is present when later family members seek to get justice for a wronged family member, maybe generations before. It is also relevant to this research, in the discomfort of those who have not lost a child or sibling and may feel guilty because of that.

The method

Hellinger evolved a way of working with a group to uncover these sources of disturbance in the family system. Representatives are chosen for family members who seem relevant to the issue. The representatives then follow the responses in their bodies. People are amazed to hear representatives talk 'just like Uncle Jack.' As the process evolves, the facilitator aims to re-establish movement and restore existing but previously denied connections. This way of working was very helpful to Sally, who found what she felt was the truth about Rose. She also felt less alone and eventually felt able to take her rightful place as her mother's second child, with her 'big sister' Rose, who could manage her own fate.

The systemic approach is gradually being acknowledged and has a lot to teach us about healthy families and the impact of previous losses on the health of the family system. When one loss is unresolved, any subsequent losses can feel more intense. When Rebecca died, Joanne's mother's grief triggered the unresolved loss of her own sister who'd died many years beforehand.

The prevention of such transgenerational trauma is achieved through other people being able to be with a bereaved parent or sibling's loss. Sheila McCarthy Dodd says,

> For the people that I've worked with who have had children who've died, there aren't that many places where they'd felt met and understood.

> Those sacred spaces are so important. The capacity to be with that kind of tremendous pain and loss, and with people who are living with the death of their child, as a culture, we're not so skilled in it.
>
> I think that the narrative that children shouldn't die isn't helpful. It's not that I think children should die, either. There's something about the death of a child as being unnatural and that it shouldn't happen that just stokes fear and phobia around it and stops people from being with the death in an ordinary way. I think that's just terrible for people who've lost a child. Family constellations is a place where it's not shied away from, so that those involved can learn how to be with their loss and grief, to be in the thick of it. Not knowing what to say is about not knowing how to be with death and with those who are grieving. It is important for everyone that this changes.[18]

Healing in Constellations comes from acknowledging the reality of what happened, without judgement, separating out the different elements so that each is given its rightful place, using these orders of love. Once done, and once the family is now 'straight' again, any symptoms the entangled person was experiencing will stop.

As Enid Welford writes,

> The healing that appears to occur in a constellation does not change the past. It reveals a clearer narrative that helps some individuals to find resolution and to take their place confident in their identity. For some, that is enough; for others, a constellation brings them face to face with the compromises they made as children and still continue to make.[19]

The constellation process can also be useful in helping someone to feel connected to someone from a past generation that has experienced something similar and survived. This links with phase four of transformational loss (see Chapter 20).

Sally's story is an example of how her mother's unspeakable and unprocessed loss was passed down to her and how she used the constellations as a way of identifying the existence of her sister and the likely cause of her death. This acknowledgement of Rose – even giving her a name – is significant, and honouring her place in the family system has been deeply healing for Sally and for her son.

Other options

This way of working may not suit everyone and requires considerable skill by the facilitator. Similar results can be achieved in individual work by therapists experienced in this field. Using such techniques as imagined dialogues or two-chair work, as mentioned in Chapter 21, and creating a timeline to plot events whether from the client's own life or the life of their transgenerational family can also be useful. Other creative ways of working are mentioned in Chapter 25. What seems important is that both the bereaved and those helping them allow for the possibility that some of the current difficulties may have their roots in previous generations.

For those who would like to know more about Systemic Family Constellations, some key texts may be worth looking at, for example: *Love's Hidden Symmetry*;[20] *Even if It Costs Me My Life*;[21] *Acknowledging What Is: Conversations with Bert Hellinger*;[22] *No Waves Without an Ocean*;[23] and *To the Heart of the Matter*.[24] Other good reads are: *Family and Systems Constellation: In the Company of Good People*;[25] *Connecting to Our Ancestral Past: Healing Through Family Constellations, Ceremony, and Ritual*;[26] and *The Tears of the Ancestors: Victims and Perpetrators in the Tribal Soul*.[27]

Anyone interested in training in Systemic Family Constellations can find more information from the Centre for Systemic Constellations. Their website address is www.thecsc.net.

Notes

1 B. Bezo and S. Maggi (2018). Intergenerational Perceptions of Mass Trauma's Impact on Physical Health and Well-being. *Psychological Trauma: Theory, Research, Practice, and Policy*, 10(1), pp. 87–94. DOI: 10.1037/tra0000284.
2 A. Lehrner and R. Yehuda (2018). Cultural Trauma and Epigenetic Inheritance. *Development and Psychopathology*, 30(5), pp. 1763–1777. DOI: 10.1017/S0954579418001153.
3 Y. Danieli (1998). *International Handbook of Multigenerational Legacies of Trauma*. New York: Plenum Press.
4 J.J. Sigal and V. Rakoff (1971). Concentration Camp Survival: A Pilot Study of Effects on the Second Generation. *Canadian Psychiatric Association Journal*, 16(5), pp. 393–397. DOI: 10.1177/070674377101600503.
5 Y. Danieli, F.H. Norris, J. Lindert, et al. (2015). The Danieli Inventory of Multigenerational Legacies of Trauma, Part II: Reparative Adaptational Impacts. *American Journal of Orthopsychiatry*, 85(3), pp. 229–237. DOI: 10.1037/ort0000055.
6 R. Yehuda and L.M. Bierer (2008). Transgenerational Transmission of Cortisol and PTSD Risk. *Progress in Brain Research*, pp. 121–135. DOI: 10.1016/S0079-6123(07)67009-5.
7 S.T. Yahyavi, M. Zarghami, F. Naghshvar, et al. (2015). Relationship of Cortisol, Norepinephrine, and Epinephrine Levels with War-induced Posttraumatic Stress Disorder in Fathers and Their Offspring. *Revista Brasileira de Psiquiatria*, 37, pp. 93–98. DOI: 10.1590/1516-4446-2014-1414.
8 R. Yehuda, N.P. Daskalakis, L.M. Bierer, et al. (2016). Holocaust Exposure Induced Intergenerational Effects on FKBP5 Methylation. *Biological Psychiatry*, 80(5), pp. 372–380. DOI: 10.1016/j.biopsych.2015.08.005.
9 J.C. Chan, B.M. Nugent and T.L. Bale (2018). Parental Advisory: Maternal and Paternal Stress Can Impact Offspring Neurodevelopment. *Biological Psychiatry*, 83, pp. 886–894. DOI: 10.1016/j.biopsych.2017.10.005.
10 H.J. Clarke and K.F. Vieux (2015). Epigenetic Inheritance through the Female Germ-line: The Known, the Unknown, and the Possible. *Seminars in Cell Developmental Biology*, 43, pp. 106–116. DOI: 10.1016/j.semcdb.2015.07.003.
11 J. Bohacek and I.M. Mansuy (2015). Molecular Insights into Transgenerational Non-genetic Inheritance of Acquired Behaviours. *National Review Genetics*, 16, pp. 641–652. DOI: 10.1038/nrg3964.

12 L. Ly, D. Chan and J.M. Trasler (2015). Developmental Windows of Susceptibility for Epigenetic Inheritance through the Male Germline. *Seminars in Cell Developmental Biology*, 43, pp. 96–105. DOI: 10.1016/j.semcdb.2015.07.006.
13 A.C. Ferguson-Smith (2011). Genomic Imprinting: The Emergence of an Epigenetic Paradigm. *National Reviews Genetics*, 12, pp. 565–575. DOI: 10.1038/nrg3032.
14 B. Dias and K. Kessler (2014). Parental Olfactory Experience Influences Behavior and Neural Structure in Subsequent Generations. *Nature Neuroscience*, 17, pp. 89–96. DOI: 10.1038/nn.3594.
15 B. Hellinger, G. Weber and H. Beaumont (1998). *Love's Hidden Symmetry: What Makes Love Work in Relationships*. Phoenix AZ: Zeig, Tucker & Theisen Inc.
16 I. Boszormenyi-Nagy and B.R. Krasner (1986). *Between Give and Take: A Clinical Guide to Contextual Therapy*. New York: Brunner/Mazel.
17 I. Boszormenyi-Nagy (1986). Transgenerational Solidarity: The Expanding Context of Therapy and Prevention. *American Journal of Family Therapy*, 14, pp. 195–212. DOI: 10.1080/01926188608250641.
18 S. McCarthy-Dodd (2020). Private Communication, 5 March 2020.
19 E. Welford (2019). Healing the Fallout from Transgenerational Trauma: Supporting Clients in Making Peace with Their History. *Transactional Analysis Journal*, 49(4), p. 335. Taylor & Francis, DOI: 10.1080/03621537.2019.1650233. Reprinted by permission of Taylor & Francis Ltd, www.tandfonline.com.
20 B. Hellinger, G. Weber and H. Beaumont (1998). *Love's Hidden Symmetry: What Makes Love Work in Relationships*. Phoenix, AZ: Zeig, Tucker & Theisen Inc.
21 S. Hausner (2011). *Even if It Costs Me My Life*. Santa Cruz: Gestalt Press.
22 B. Hellinger (1999). *Acknowledging What Is: Conversations with Bert Hellinger*. Phoenix, AZ: Zeig, Tucker & Theisen Inc.
23 B. Hellinger (2006). *No Waves Without an Ocean*. Heidelberg: Carl Auer International.
24 B. Hellinger (2003). *To the Heart of the Matter*. Phoenix, AZ: Zeig, Tucker & Theisen Inc.
25 F. Mason Boring (2018). *Family and Systems Constellation: In the Company of Good People*. Scotts Valley: CreateSpace Independent Publishing Platform.
26 F. Mason Boring (2012). *Connecting to Our Ancestral Past: Healing Through Family Constellations, Ceremony, and Ritual*. Berkeley, CA: North Atlantic Books.
27 D. van Kampenhout (2008). *The Tears of the Ancestors: Victims and Perpetrators in the Tribal Soul*. Phoenix, AZ: Zeig, Tucker & Theisen Inc.

23 Resilience, grief, and grief disorder

I have worked with many people who have experienced trauma. Some people appear to recover sooner than others. Since Vikki died, I have become more curious about this. One way of understanding how someone responds to grief is to consider how resilient they are and what can be done to protect and promote resilience.

What is resilience?

Resilience has been defined by a number of different researchers as:
"the ability to bounce back from adversity, frustration, and misfortune";[1] or "the positive psychological capacity to rebound, to 'bounce back' from adversity, uncertainty, conflict, failure or even positive change, progress, and increased responsibility."[2] I have not witnessed very much 'bouncing back' from the participants in this project, certainly not in the lively way that this term suggests. Rather, their resilience has been a steadier and at times slow process. It seems more akin to that described as "a stable trajectory of healthy functioning after a highly adverse event";[3] and as "as the capacity of a dynamic system to adapt successfully to disturbances that threaten system function, viability, or development."[4]

Factors that affect resilience

Some factors that may affect someone's resilience are:

A secure attachment style

Someone who has a secure attachment style, whether that is with family or friends, are likely to be more resilient than those who do not. This is partly because they have stable relationships; they tend to be compassionate both towards themselves and other people; and they are able to ask for and accept help from others. Furthermore, they are able to plan and complete tasks, as well as take time to relax and enjoy themselves. For more information on attachment styles, see Chapter 24.

Personality

If someone is easy-going, then they may not take themselves too seriously, and they are more likely to be able to deal with the ups and downs of life.[5] Similarly, if they are an optimist or have an enquiring mind, they are more likely to think, problem-solve, and understand what has happened. Some people can self-regulate, controlling their thoughts, feelings, and behaviour. This means that they tend to be more grounded and composed and are less prone to anxiety.

Life history

If a person has successfully recovered from previous loss or trauma, this may give them confidence that they will recover again. However, if there is unprocessed trauma or if the person has other current stressors, e.g. problems at work or in relationships, this can hinder their capacity to deal with the new incident.

Economic resources, etc.[6]

Access to enough money, housing, food, and safety will all help someone meet their basic physiological needs which are the building blocks of resilience. See Maslow's Hierarchy of Needs in Chapter 19.

A number of these factors are similar to some of the extenuating considerations or mediators suggested by Worden in Chapter 21.

Measuring resilience

The grief models in Chapter 21 can help the bereaved to measure their resilience. The Dual Process Model, for example, can indicate whether someone is able to oscillate between loss-oriented and restoration-oriented coping in a natural and fluid way. If they predominantly use one domain, it might suggest they lack resilience. Transformational learning (see Chapter 20) can be used to establish what someone may need at any specific step; to find and develop skills, thereby promoting resilience, as well as identifying what may hinder the person from completing a particular phase.

Nietzsche said, "*From life's military school.* – What doesn't kill me makes me stronger."[7] I've heard similar quotes from time to time, and I think of them as a way of encouraging resilience. I also know that some people find this a rather glib statement that detracts from or minimizes the distress someone is feeling, suggesting there should always be a positive outcome. I believe that when someone experiences something distressing or stressful, it is possible to learn something from that event that they may be able to use again in the future, whether that is for a similar event or something completely different. This can help someone to build resilience that will enable them to bounce back or adapt when things don't go according to plan.

The death of a child or sibling is certainly something that does not go according to plan. What follows are ideas about how grief impacts on a person and what they can do to help themselves and build their resilience.

The physiological impact of grief

Grief can manifest itself in many different ways. For many people there are a range of emotional responses such as feelings of anger, rage, sadness, fear, depression, numbness, and even relief. Any or all of these may be expressed or internalized.

Grief also causes physiological changes in the body. From my research and experience of working with people who have been bereaved, many of them had a number of physical reactions such as:

- Initially feeling shaky;
- Unable to complete daily tasks;
- Loss of appetite or overeating;
- Unable to focus or concentrate;
- Lethargy;
- Headaches;
- Chest pain;
- Difficulty in getting to sleep or waking in the early hours;
- Feelings of depression;
- Anxiety;
- Panic attacks;
- Heart problems;
- Weight gain;
- Diabetes.

Many of these responses are common, and some people experienced a number of them over the course of the days, weeks, months, and even years following the death.

These responses are caused by changes in the body that occur in times of stress and trauma. For instance, when someone has a shock, they often feel shaky, their heartrate and blood pressure rise, and they may sweat. These responses are caused by cortisol being released by the adrenal glands. Cortisol is used by the body to control blood pressure, blood sugar levels, and metabolism and to reduce inflammation. This extra surge of cortisol gives the person the energy to react to the situation, which is sometimes called the fight, flight, or freeze response. Once the initial event has passed, the person's cortisol levels will reduce and their heartrate and blood pressure will return to normal.

Two other hormones, serotonin and dopamine, also need consideration. They are important for someone's mental health and sense of well-being. These hormones act as neurotransmitters and work in a number of ways, including regulating someone's mood, their emotions, their sleep/wake cycle, their ability to think and concentrate, as well as their metabolism and appetite. When someone has a pleasurable experience, dopamine is released, and this may lead them to feeling more alert, focussed, motivated, and happy. If someone is in a stressful situation, the cortisol that is released reduces the amount of serotonin and dopamine. This explains why someone can feel so lethargic, unable to control their emotions, or to sleep properly. They may feel as though they've lost the ability to think clearly or concentrate on anything for more than a few minutes.

For some people, the aftermath of that trauma is such that feelings of apprehension, helplessness, and fear of something else going wrong persist. As a result, the person's body continues to react to the perceived threat, releasing additional cortisol which, if continued for a sustained period, result in the difficulties mentioned earlier. Any of these issues may decrease someone's self-esteem and confidence and affect their memory and brain function, hindering their normal effectiveness in activity and relationships.[8]

If someone has appropriate support coupled with a healthy way of managing their stress, they are unlikely to experience these significant health issues for long, and this will protect and promote their resilience. How long the initial symptoms take to subside will depend upon the person, what support they have, and what other stressors they have in their life. If they are unable to get the support that they need, this can aggravate any health problems which can, if left untreated, become chronic.

What appears to be very important is that other people accept the person. Telling them that they "should be over it by now" or that they "need to move on" is not beneficial and often causes further distress. Neither is it useful to have time limits on grieving as this can put pressure on the person to appear to have 'got over it' which, in the case of bereaved parents or siblings, is not actually possible.

When does normal grief turn into a disorder?

There is some controversy over the potential pathologizing of grief. It is such a unique process influenced by numerous and varied factors, such as those described by Worden as mediators (see Chapter 21), by the nature of the bonds the bereaved has with the deceased (see Chapter 18), their attachment styles (see Chapter 24), and the physiological responses mentioned previously.

Two diagnostic manuals provide criteria that need to be met for someone to be diagnosed with a mental health disorder. The books are called the

International Statistical Classification of Diseases and Related Health Problems, 11th Edition (ICD-11) and the *Diagnostic and Statistical Manual of Mental Disorders, Fifth Edition* (DSM5). Each book contains a grief disorder called either Prolonged Grief Disorder (ICD-11), the diagnostic criteria for which are summarized in Table 23.1,[9] or Persistent Complex Bereavement-Related Disorder (DSM5), the diagnostic criteria of which are similar.[10]

Most of the measures given for these disorders were experienced by many of the participants. According to Table 23.1, these indicators need to be present in excess of either 6 (ICD-11) or 12 (DSM5) months for the person to be considered as suffering from a disorder. In other words, the symptoms experienced by the participants are seen as normal and become 'disordered' only if they are still suffering after these stated timelines. But there is an added stipulation that the person's symptoms should be in excess of the cultural or religious norms.

This raises a very important question: what are the cultural norms when dealing with a loss of a child or sibling? I'm not sure that there is a norm, there are so many factors that influence someone's grief; moreover, the death of a child or sibling is still a relatively taboo subject, so that it is not easy to establish a cultural norm. However, I would suggest that many of the participants experienced the criteria mentioned in sections A and B

Table 23.1 Diagnostic criteria for ICD-11 Prolonged Grief Disorder

ICD-11 Prolonged Grief Disorder

A. At least one of the following
    1. Persistent and pervasive longing for the deceased;
or
    2. A persistent and pervasive preoccupation with the deceased.

B. Examples of intense emotional pain
Accompanied by intense emotional pain e.g. sadness, guilt, anger, denial, blame; Difficulty accepting the death; Feeling one has lost a part of one's self; An inability to experience positive mood; Emotional numbness; Difficulty in engaging with social or other activities.
C. Time and impairment criterion
Persisted for an abnormally long period of time (more than six months at a minimum): following the loss, clearly exceeding expected social, cultural, or religious norms for the individual's culture and context. Grief reactions that have persisted for longer periods that are within a normative period of grieving given the person's cultural and religious context are viewed as normal bereavement responses and are not assigned a diagnosis.
The disturbance causes significant impairment in personal, family, social, educational, occupational, or other important areas of functioning.

for a minimum of five years, and some will never go away completely. Examples are:

- Persistent and pervasive longing or yearning for the deceased;
- Feeling one has lost a part of one's self;
- Anger, sadness, guilt, blame related to the death;
- Feeling isolated from family, social, or occupational areas of functioning;
- Loss of identity and/or purpose or meaning in life.

All these markers are likely to remain to some degree or another. How someone experiences them does change over time, but that doesn't necessarily mean the intensity is continually decreasing. As a number of participants pointed out, various triggers can evoke very painful feelings and thoughts years after the initial loss.

Medication or therapy

Many of the participants experienced some form of low mood or depression after the death of their child or sibling. A few sought professional help with medication or counselling. It is a very personal choice whether someone needs medication or some form of therapy. There are pros and cons to each. Some people may prefer to opt for prescribed medication to help them cope in the short term with their distress, and any associated symptoms as mentioned earlier, until they feel able to deal with the reality of their loss. Some may need help getting to sleep, so a short course of sleeping tablets can be beneficial. Others may feel so low that they are unable to get out of bed; therefore, a course of antidepressants can be useful to take 'the edge off,' enabling them to complete basic functions such as washing, getting dressed, cooking and eating, maybe even looking after other children. The challenge with using medication as a coping strategy is to take it only for the shortest time necessary.

It may seem odd for me as a psychotherapist to say that counselling or psychotherapy is not necessarily an easier or even appropriate option for someone in the early stages of grief. Counselling may involve someone recounting, reliving, or re-experiencing the events that led up to their loss and can feel overwhelming if attempted too early on in their grieving process. Trauma is not something that can be tackled 'head on'; rather, it is something that needs to be managed slowly, one bite at a time, allowing the person to gently digest what has happened and to slowly adjust to their new normal. Therapy at the wrong time could unwittingly re-traumatize the client, leading to increased symptoms as described earlier and dissatisfaction with the service offered.[11,12,13]

Some of the participants sought counselling or psychotherapy to deal with a specific issue. For example, Carol wanted to speak with someone about her anger but didn't want to do this with family or friends. Edward,

Steffy, and Shireen referred to really valuing the therapy they'd received sometime after their initial loss. Others mentioned speaking with someone who had been through a similar experience or joining a group. It would appear that those people who gained something from this did so because they were able to see that their terrible loss was survivable.

It seems that because the majority of the participants had good support systems whether they were within their family, friends or community they did not seem to develop significant mental health problems. This may have been because they were able to talk about what had happened with people who were interested, cared and were able to listen. Those that had negative social interactions or relationships tended to have an increased risk of anxiety, depression and suicidal ideation.[14,15,16]

Younger people may also have other added complications that can influence their ability to cope with their loss. Some may not understand what has happened, or why as in the case of John (Chapter 12). For others, the increased levels of cortisol, mentioned previously, can have a greater impact on their physiology and may lead to mental health problems later in life.[17,18] It is important, therefore, that particularly younger people experiencing a traumatic event, such as the death of a sibling, are offered appropriate help and support. This will help them through their grieving process and reduce the likelihood of developing mental health problems later on.

Assessment tools

Some professionals may find it useful to use the tools and criteria that follows in this section to ascertain if someone needs professional help in dealing with their grief, whether that is medication or some form of therapy. A number of well-known scales or tools are used to assess the impact of events or how someone is coping with their grief. The ones I have chosen to include here are freely and easily available.

Adult attitude to grief, and child or young person's attitude to grief[19]

These are useful forms for measuring an adult's or child/young person's attitude to grief. The answers from these forms can help in identifying someone's core grief reactions and coping responses. For more information, visit https://mapping-grief.care/home/.

Core bereavement items[20]

This a questionnaire that specifically focusses on three core items: (1) images and thoughts; (2) acute separation; and (3) grief. This form is available from https://core.ac.uk/reader/10893217.

The grief intensity scale[21]

This is produced by Weill Cornell Medicine: The Centre for Research on End of Life Care. This scale assesses someone's thoughts, feelings, and behaviours and the intensity of their response to the death. It assesses someone's risk of developing Prolonged Grief Disorder. The scale is available to complete online from https://endoflife.weill.cornell.edu/research/grief-intensity-scale.

The prolonged grief disorder questionnaire (PG-13)[22]

This is used to assess whether someone may be experiencing prolonged grief as outlined earlier. A number of questionnaires are available, one for adults, one for children, and in numerous languages. This questionnaire can be found at https://endoflife.weill.cornell.edu/research/assessments_and_tools.

Revised impact of event scale[23]

This is used to evaluate the degree of distress someone feels in response to trauma. The form can assist professionals in determining if someone is suffering from post-traumatic stress disorder. A copy of the revised version is available from various websites online.

SIBAM model[24]

I find it helpful to see the loss of a child or sibling as a trauma. The SIBAM model is a different way of understanding recovery from trauma. It was created to conceptualize how the elements of phenomenological experience relate to one another, and need to be integrated, before the brain can let go of hypervigilance and place the trauma in the past. The model incorporates both implicit memories, e.g. any sensory images, physical sensations, feelings and automatic behaviours, and explicit memory such as facts, the sequence of events, and resolution, all of which help with creating meaning.

SIBAM is an acronym that stands for Sensation, Image, Behaviour, Affect and Meaning.

Sensation: meaning such things as pain, smells, nausea, heat, numbness, tension, heart rate, rest, etc.

Image: either internal, such as memories, dreams, symbols, or metaphors, or external, for example a dead body, crashed car, or a specific object.

Behaviour: this may include, actions, body posture, facial expressions, words, sounds, voluntary or involuntary body movements, eye movements, etc.

Affect: feelings and emotions, such as joy, sadness, fear, anger.

Meaning: beliefs, thoughts, attitudes, judgements, understanding, and narratives.[25]

When something happens, a person will have an image of what is going on; they will have feelings, sensations, and behavioural responses that are attached to their experience; and they will make some meaning that they then attribute to the event. For example, when I initially peered into Vikki's room, she appeared to be asleep in her bed (image), but I had a sense that something was wrong (sensation). I shouted to my husband to call for an ambulance (behavioural response). As I went further into her room, I could tell she wasn't breathing. I began to feel panic (feeling/affect). I touched her arm and was shocked by how cold it was (feeling/sensation), I then began to realize she might be dead. I stared at her unable to work out what had happened (image, searching for meaning). I pulled back the duvet, half expecting to see a wound, but all I could see was that her blood had pooled all along her back (image). I realized then that she had been dead for quite a while, and nothing I or anyone else could do could change that. I felt numb and cold (sensation, affect, and beginning to make meaning). I then ran to the door to call out that there was no point in calling an ambulance (behaviour). But I still couldn't work out what had happened, how had she died (struggling for meaning). I stayed with her, and after a while I saw the painkillers that she had taken, and I then grasped what must have happened (developing meaning). Each time another professional arrived, e.g. the paramedics, police, and undertakers, I was confronted with more images, sensations, feelings, behaviours.

When an event is traumatic, these elements become fragmented; for example, sensation separates from images, affect disconnects from meaning, behaviour detaches from affect. So, although the account is now clear and logical, at the time, and in the hours and days afterwards, all I had was an overload of images, feelings, sensations, and behavioural responses. My meaning making fluctuated with every additional piece of information.

Some people are unable to integrate these elements, and so they may dissociate, or detach, from some aspects of the experience whilst staying attached to other features. I've been told the weather was hot and sunny during the month Vikki died, but I have no recollection of that. Under normal circumstances I might have been sitting outside relaxing and reading a book or weeding the garden. Instead I focussed on tasks that needed to be completed, such as organizing her funeral, choosing her coffin, selecting music, and inviting people to speak. This was followed by booking a venue for a wake afterwards, ordering food, and finding photos for a slideshow. I was so consumed with all the practicalities and wanting to look after my family (behaviour), and trying to understand what had happened (meaning), that the beauty of a blue sky with the sun shining (image), and feeling its warmth (sensation), along with the usual desire to relax (affect), remains completely lost to me.

The SIBAM model can be used as a map to help someone make sense of the way they are responding to the trauma and making sense of what happened. Any of these tools can be used to assess how someone is managing their grief and to identify strategies that may help them to build their resilience.

Notes

1 J. Ledesma (2014). Conceptual Frameworks and Research Models on Resilience in Leadership. *SAGE Open.* DOI: 10.1177/2158244014545464.
2 F. Luthans (2002). The Need for and Meaning of Positive Organizational Behavior. *Journal of Organisational Behaviour*, 23, pp. 695–706. DOI: 10.1002/job.165. Republished with permission of John Wiley and Sons. Permission conveyed through Copyright Clearance Center, Inc. DOI: 10.1002/job.16.
3 S.M. Southwick, G.A. Bonanno, A.S. Masten, C. Panter-Brick and R. Yehuda (2014). Resilience Definitions, Theory, and Challenges: Interdisciplinary Perspectives. *European Journal of Psychotraumatology*, 5(1), p. 2. DOI: 10.3402/ejpt. v5.25338. This is an open-access article distributed under the terms of the Creative Commons Attribution 4.0 Unported (CC-BY 4.0) License (http://creative commons.org/licenses/by/4.0/).
4 A.S. Masten (2014). Global Perspectives on Resilience in Children and Youth. *Child Development*, 85(1), pp. 6–20. DOI: 10.1111/cdev.12205.
5 S. Chess (1989). Defying the Voice of Doom. In: T.F. Dugan and R. Coles, eds., *The Child in our Times: Studies in the Development of Resilience.* New York: Brunner and Mazel.
6 G.A. Bonanno and E.D. Diminich (2013). Annual Research Review: Positive Adjustment to Adversity – Trajectories of Minimal-Impact Resilience and Emergent Resilience. *Journal of Child Psychology and Psychiatry*, 54(4), p. 383. DOI: 10.1111/jcpp.12021.
7 F. Nietzsche and R.F.H. Polt (1997). *Twilight of the Idols or, How to Philosophize with the Hammer.* Indianapolis, IN: Hackett Publishing, p. 6. Emphasis in original.
8 J.B. Echouffo-Tcheugui, S.C. Conner, J.J. Himali, P. Maillard, C.S. DeCarli, A.S. Beiser, et al. (2018). Circulating Cortisol and Cognitive and Structural Brain Measures: The Framingham Heart Study. *Neurology*, 91(21), pp. e.1961–e.1970. DOI: 10.1212/WNL.0000000000006549.
9 Reproduced from World Health Organization. (2019). *International Statistical Classification of Diseases and Related Health Problems*, 11th ed. (ICD-11), https://icd.who.int/browse11/l-m/en#/http://id.who.int/icd/entity/1183832314
10 American Psychiatric Association. (2013). *Diagnostic and Statistical Manual of Mental Disorders*, 5th ed. (DSM5), Arlington, VA: American Psychiatric Association. DOI: 10.1176/appi.books.9780890425596.
11 H. Schut, M.S. Stroebe, J. van den Bout and M. Terheggen (2001). The Efficacy of Bereavement Interventions: Determining Who Benefits. In: M.S. Stroebe, R.O. Hansson, W. Stroebe, and H. Schut, eds., *Handbook of Bereavement Research: Consequences, Coping and Care*, 3rd ed. Washington, DC. American Psychological Association, pp. 705–737.
12 G.A. Bonanno (2005). Resilience in the Face of Potential Trauma. *Current Directions in Psychological Science*, 14(3), pp. 135–138. DOI: 10.1111/j.0963-7214.2005.00347.x.
13 J.M. Currier, R.A. Neimeyer and J.S. Berman (2008). The Effectiveness of Psychotherapeutic Interventions for Bereaved Persons: A Comprehensive Quantitative

Review. *Psychological Bulletin*, 134(5), pp. 648–661. DOI: 10.1037/0033-2909. 134.5.648.
14 D. Fone, J. White, D. Farewell, M. Kelly, G. John, K. Lloyd and F. Dunstan (2014). Effect of Neighbourhood Deprivation and Social Cohesion on Mental Health Inequality: A Multilevel Population-based Longitudinal Study. *Psychological Medicine*, 44(11), pp. 2449–2460. DOI: 10.1017/S0033291713003255.
15 A.R. Teo, H. Choi and M. Valenstein (2013). Social Relationships and Depression: Ten-Year Follow-up from a Nationally Representative Study. *PloS One*, 8(4), e62396. DOI: 10.1371/journal.pone.0062396.
16 Z.I. Santini, A. Koyanagi, S. Tyrovolas and J.M. Haro (2015). The Association of Relationship Quality and Social Networks with Depression, Anxiety, and Suicidal Ideation among Older Married Adults: Findings from a Cross-sectional Analysis of the Irish Longitudinal Study on Ageing (TILDA). *Journal of Affective Disorders*, 179, pp. 134–141. DOI: 10.1016/j.jad.2015.03.015.
17 E.F. Walker, P.A. Brennan, M. Esterberg, J. Brasfield, B. Pearce and M.T. Compton (2010). Longitudinal Changes in Cortisol Secretion and Conversion to Psychosis in At-risk Youth. *Journal of Abnormal Psychology*, 119, pp. 401–408. DOI: 10.1037/a0018399.
18 R.C. Kessler, P. Berglund, O. Demler, R. Jin, K.R. Merikangas and E.E. Walters (2005). Lifetime Prevalence and Age-of-onset Distributions of DSM-IV Disorders in the National Comorbidity Survey Replication. *Archives Of General Psychiatry*, 62, pp. 593–602. DOI: 10.1001/archpsyc.62.6.593.
19 L. Machin (2014). *Working with Loss and Grief*. 2nd ed. London: Sage.
20 P.C. Burnett, W. Middleton, B. Raphael and N. Martinek (1997). Measuring Core Bereavement Phenomena. *Psychological Medicine*, 27, pp. 49–57. DOI: 10.1017/S0033291796004151.
21 Weill Cornell Medicine Center for Research on End-of-Life Care, New York. Available from: https://endoflife.weill.cornell.edu/research/grief-intensity-scale [Accessed 9 September 2020].
22 H. Prigerson and P.K. Maciejewski (2009). *Prolonged Grief Disorder PG-13*. Boston, MA: Centre for Psycho-oncology and Palliative Care Research.
23 D.S. Weiss and C.R. Marmar (2004). The Impact of Event Scale-Revised. In: J.P. Wilson and T.M. Kean, eds., *Assessing Psychological Trauma and PTSD*. 2nd ed. New York. Guildford Press, pp. 186–187.
24 P.A. Levine (2010). *In an Unspoken Voice: How the Body Releases Trauma and Restores Goodness*. Berkeley, CA: North Atlantic Books.
25 P.A. Levine (2015). *Trauma and Memory: Brain and Body in a Search for the Living Past: A Practical Guide for Understanding and Working with Traumatic Memory*. Berkeley, CA: North Atlantic Books, pp. 66–70.

24 Protection and self-knowledge

This chapter provides information and activities on topics that I think are important to consider when working with those who are grieving. The first section looks at how you as a professional can protect yourself and your clients and includes topics such as boundaries, assertiveness, self-care, compassion, and compassion fatigue. The second section invites you to identify your own personal processes so you can understand why you may find it easier or more difficult to work with certain people. There are a number of activities that you may wish to use; if not, feel free to skip on to the next section. Additional questions and activities are in Appendix 1.

Protection

Working with parents and siblings who are bereaved can be challenging, and there can be a risk of vicarious, or second-hand trauma. Protection is therefore essential for yourself and your clients; without it, you may end up developing compassion fatigue and burnout. This might leave your clients feeling unsafe, unsupported, and potentially re-traumatized. If you have suitable systems in place, these can help you to feel empowered as a professional. Your clients will then feel secure and more trusting in the work you are doing together.

Boundaries

Boundaries are in some ways the easiest and yet sometimes the most challenging of requirements. They are the building blocks of protection and may include procedures for how you or others may behave, and what may be done if someone breaches those guidelines or limits. One significant boundary is that of time. In the professional world specifically, a great deal is made about starting and ending a meeting on time, whether that is for a consultation, supervision, or training session. The purpose of adhering to these time boundaries is to provide protection to the professional and the client. If the professional does not keep to the set time, then the client may begin to feel unsafe; they no longer feel held in the therapeutic space. The session can then take on a quality that is more akin to an informal conversation that someone may have with a friend and moves away from the professional space, leaving the client feeling more vulnerable. Clients benefit from knowing that if they wish to explore sensitive personal history or a specific experience, there is only a limited amount of time for them to be in that painful place before needing to prepare to re-enter the world outside of the session. Sticking to time boundaries shows respect to all involved, that once the session is finished, each can get on with other meetings/sessions or activities for that day. Boundaries are protective of bereaved people, for example, in choosing when and with whom they wish to express their feelings, or to keep their own counsel.

If you are running a group for bereaved people, another important boundary is the amount of time each person may have to talk. You may choose to divide the time up equally, or you may choose to have a more fluid process, allowing those who wish to speak the opportunity to do so. The former idea can feel a bit prescriptive, but each person then knows they will have their own space to talk. The second idea may feel more natural; however, it's important that the group is facilitated rather than letting one or two people dominate. I had this experience a while ago. Although the person running the group asked the participants not to take up too much time, three people dominated the whole session. Although I could appreciate that these people wanted to speak, as a participant I wanted to hear from other people about their experience. I remember looking at my watch towards the end of the workshop and was relieved to see that there was only ten minutes left. However, the session then over-ran for another 15 minutes. My experience was that the boundaries were stated but not adhered to, leaving me doubting the potency of the facilitators.

One of my favourite concepts, the Drama Triangle, can be used to illustrate what happens when boundaries are blurred or broken.[1]

The Drama Triangle[2,3]

Each corner contains one of three positions, or roles: Persecutor, Rescuer, and Victim (see Figure 24.1).

It is important to say that these roles are played out of awareness; few people avoid getting into such processes, but sometimes they can be very destructive. When someone is in the Persecutor role, they tend to view themselves as being better than other people in some way. Instead of being assertive, they can be rather forthright and can be experienced as antagonistic, aggressive, intimidating, bullying, or controlling. They may be quite unaware of the impact they have on the other person.

Someone in the Rescuer role may also see themselves as being better than others, but they are more caring than the Persecutor. They may see their role in life as helping others and tend to jump in to solve others' problems before waiting to be asked. Instead of being assertive, they can appear to be too agreeable and not stand up for themselves, preferring to put the other person first; but this can lead to their feeling alone and isolated.

```
Persecutor  ←——————————→  Rescuer
         ↖  ↘          ↙  ↗
           ↘          ↙
             ↘      ↙
               Victim
```

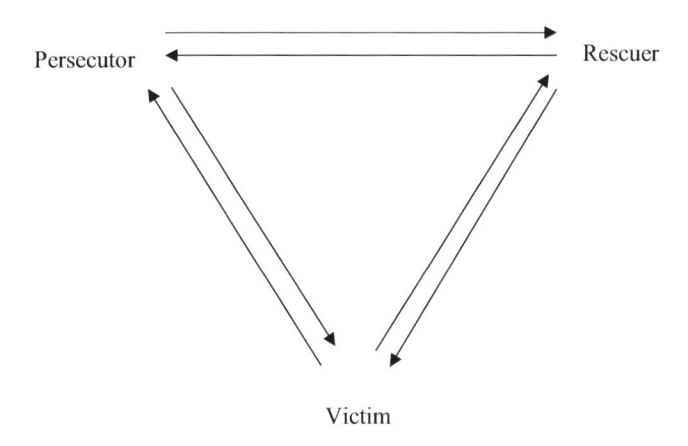

Figure 24.1 The Drama Triangle

If someone is in the Victim role, they are unlikely to be doing anything to solve their problems. They may see other people as being better than themselves or as equally incapable. Instead of being assertive, they are passive and may complain or withdraw. They may be feeling alienated, as described in Chapter 18.

An important point to make here is that not everyone who is feeling that they are helpless, wants to help another, or wants to confront another's behaviour is on the Drama Triangle. In order to be on the Drama Triangle, the person needs to be disregarding or undervaluing some aspect of themselves, the other person or reality of the situation.

Imagine this scenario: Keith has recently been bereaved, his brother having died. Keith lives on his own and feels alone and isolated. He wants other members of his family to phone him up, but they do not. He doesn't want to phone them because he believes they don't really care about him or are too busy with their own lives. During a conversation with Harriet, a social worker, Keith complains about the lack of contact from his family (Victim). Harriet remembers her own sense of isolation when her own sister died a few years beforehand and her family did not contact her. She feels very angry about this apparent neglect of Keith. Harriet knows Keith's sister, Joanne, as she is a work colleague in another department, so she decides to phone her up (Rescuer). Harriet angrily tells Joanne of Keith's unhappiness and demands that she phones up her brother (Persecutor). Joanne initially feels bad for not phoning her brother (Victim). Then she feels incensed by Harriet's interfering. She phones up her brother and tells him off for complaining, saying, "The phone goes both ways, you know" (Persecutor). Keith now feels bad (Victim), he phones Harriet and is angry with her for getting involved, and says, "You should mind your own business" (Persecutor). Harriet now feels bad and says, "But I was only trying to help you" (Victim).

Using this example, it is easy to see how someone can move from one position to another when faced with certain situations. One thing to remember about the Drama Triangle is that any response is an instinctual reaction. Once someone becomes aware of the roles they take and how that affects them, they are then able to respond in a different way and respond within the Awareness ARENA.

The Awareness ARENA

Someone stepping into the Awareness ARENA functions with greater authenticity, autonomy, and assertiveness. It requires the person to take a step back from the situation, something that is sometimes much easier said than done. They can assess what is going on and decide what their response will be in a way that retains respect for themselves and the other person, while acknowledging the rights, abilities, and responsibilities of both parties (see Figure 24.2).

ARENA stands for Acknowledge, Respond, Express, Name, and Attune.

Acknowledge

Acknowledge own potency and presence – remaining focussed and present, a person will use thinking based on the situation and state their wants or

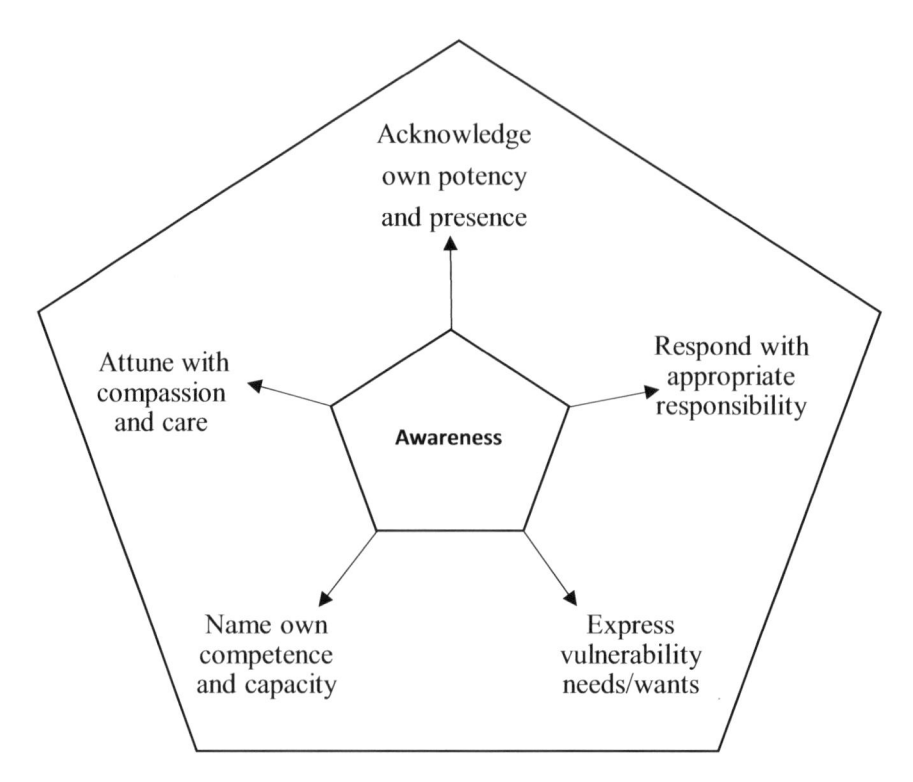

Figure 24.2 The Awareness ARENA

needs, seeking a solution that works for all. They will manage their own thinking, feelings, and behaviours.

Keith may realize that although he believes his family are busy, he needs to have some contact with them, and he will phone Joanne and ask for help.

Harriet may listen to Keith, support him in making contact with Joanne, and ask him what, if anything, he needs/wants from her.

Respond

Respond with appropriate responsibility – a person will consider what options they have for dealing with the situation, including whether they have any responsibility for the final outcome. They will use their listening skills and wait for a specific request for help before acting.

Harriet may decide that her options now are to help Keith find his own solution as she is not responsible for his problems.

Keith will make the phone call to Joanne to ask her for her help.

Express

Express fears, wishes, and concerns whilst owning, acknowledging, and voicing any feelings of vulnerability.

Harriet would acknowledge that the anger she felt was related to her own personal story.

Keith may admit that he hadn't let Joanne know of his need for support because he felt guilty about an argument he had with her a year ago.

Joanne may concede that she was still feeling hurt by comments Keith had made a year ago.

Name

Name own competence and capacity – this involves a person stating whether they have the skills, ability, and time to deal with their own problems or to help another.

Joanne, on receiving Keith's phone call, may offer immediate help, or she may decline to speak to Keith then but offer to visit him the following weekend.

Harriet may draw on her previous experience to give information to Keith about what sources of help and support worked for her.

Attune

Attune with compassion and care – using compassion, both for themselves and others, a person will be able to attend to the problem with care for all concerned.

Harriet may express her care for Keith by words or therapeutic touch. She may feel compassion towards herself remembering her own grief.

Keith may acknowledge Harriet's care and begin to find some self-compassion.

Joanne may feel some compassion for Keith and acknowledge how much she cares for him.

It's worth bearing in mind that using the Awareness ARENA may not necessarily be easy for those who are bereaved. Their behaviours may be more akin to the Alienation, Antagonistic, or Alone responses mentioned in Chapter 18. A number of the participants wished that others had done or said something, but as they themselves didn't really know what it was that they needed or wanted, they were unable to potently ask for their needs to be met. This is where professionals can really help: by being aware of the differences between the Drama Triangle and the Awareness ARENA, they can utilize the most appropriate and effective response for themselves and their client.

Assertiveness

Being assertive is a key skill needed for keeping boundaries, for valuing yourself and other people, and for helping you to make decisions. It is also an important element for the Awareness ARENA. One way to think about this is to consider someone's roles and responsibilities. I like the following list adapted from one created by Anne Dickson:[4]

1 Each of us has the right to be treated with respect, care and compassion, to make our own decisions and to change our mind at any time;
2 Each of us has the right to say what we want and need – to ask for and accept help, whilst taking responsibility for our own thoughts, feelings, and behaviours;
3 Each of us has the right to be treated as a potent person, sharing our unique intelligence, knowledge, and skills;
4 Each of us has the right to express our emotions and vulnerabilities in any way that does not cause harm;
5 Each of us has the right to say what we think, based on our own principles, beliefs, and values;
6 Each of us has the right to have faults and made mistakes;
7 Each of us has the right to ask for more information or say "I don't know";
8 Each of us has the right to be a free, independent person, unconstrained by others' approval.

Some people struggle with being assertive, especially if their early life experience told them that they were not important or had to please other people. It's worth bearing in mind that many bereaved people feel unable to ask for what they want, usually because what they want is not possible and they are probably unaware of what they might need. Some may also change their minds as they go through the grieving process, which can be confusing for those supporting them. The potency of the professional in using these rights and responsibilities can enable them to avoid the Drama Triangle roles, protecting themselves and their clients.

Self-care

Self-care is essential for being effective and reducing the possibility of excessive stress or burnout. Many professionals in the helping professions are very good at supporting other people but may not be so good at looking after themselves. Bereaved people can also be at risk of burnout if they are looking after others in the family and neglecting their own needs. Here are some activities to consider for yourself or to use with clients. If you consider you already have a good self-care strategy, move on to the next section on compassion and compassion fatigue.

Activity 1

1 Take a large piece of paper. In the centre, draw a circle and inside write the words 'self-care.' Now around the outside of the circle, write down all the ways that you look after yourself. It can be anything that works for you, from eating healthily, going for a long walk, making sure you have enough sleep, catching up with friends, to practising yoga, mindfulness, or any other fitness activities that promote your well-being.
2 Once you have written down all your ideas, what do you notice? Is there any pattern to what you have written? For example, are most of your activities similar, or is there a broad spectrum? If there are any other people in your self-care strategy, are they people who are generally supportive of you, or do you end up doing more of the support?
3 Is there anything you'd like to add or change to your diagram? If so, what would your diagram look like once it was revised? Consider using different-coloured pens to add in new ideas and then write down how you will make time to complete them.

A key process in maintaining self-care is to think about what beliefs, values, and attitudes are important in your life.

Activity 2

1 Take a piece of paper and draw three columns. At the top of the first column, write Beliefs; the middle column, Values; and the final column, Attitudes.
2 In the Belief column, write down the things you hold to be true about life, that you truly believe for yourself. This may include any faith, spiritual or religious beliefs, beliefs from your culture, your experiences in life, from people you hold as mentors, from books or articles you have read.

3   In the Values column, add in what is really important to you. This might include your family, friends, happiness, money, property, job/career, nature, animals, politics, etc.
4   In the Attitudes column, write in what influences your actions, including how you treat other people and manage problems. This may include things like treating others with respect, complying to peer or organizational pressure, being professional, having integrity, being reliable, following the rules, or taking shortcuts to save time/money. You may want to split this column in two – one based on your home life and another based on your work life – and see if there are any differences.
5   Looking at your lists of beliefs, values, and attitudes, think about how they influence your role(s). For example, do your personal beliefs and values mirror those where you work or with others in your family? If they do not, how do you manage that tension or conflict? How do you look after your own needs? Do you need/want to make any changes? If so, what do you need to make them?

One way of making any changes is by using simple aims and SMART objectives. SMART is an acronym that means Specific, Measurable, Achievable, Relevant, and Time-specific.

Imagine that one of my beliefs is that people should take responsibility for their own health and well-being. I value my husband and children and want to live as long as possible to be able to spend time with them. My attitude could be that because I work hard, at the end of each day I'd rather go home, cook the dinner, and relax during the evening; I'm too tired to do any exercise. On reviewing my self-care list, compiled in Activity 2, I realize that I'm not paying enough attention to my fitness. My attitudes and actions do not fit in with my beliefs and values. I decide that in order to be more congruent with my belief, I need to lose weight and get fit.

My objectives might be:

- Specific: I want to lose 6 kilos of weight and to run in the local 10k marathon next year.
- Measurable: on Monday I will join the local slimming club and follow their dietary advice. Starting next Tuesday, I will go for a run three days a week, starting off with five-minute sessions. I will increase my running time by five minutes each week, reaching 40-minute sessions by week eight and hour-long sessions by week 12.
- Achievable: I can schedule the slimming club and runs into my diary. The club meets on a Monday evening and I will go for a run on Sunday morning and straight after work on Tuesday and Thursday.
- Relevant: Following the slimming club advice will help me to lose weight and going for a regular run that increases weekly will build my stamina and will help me run the marathon.
- Time bound: I will achieve my objective within six months.

Activity 3

1 Think about your overall aim(s): what do you want to get from your self-care strategy?
2 Once you have an aim, then consider how you are going to achieve it using SMART objectives.

It may be useful to share your aims and objectives with another person who will support and encourage you.

Compassion and compassion fatigue

Being able to have compassion is an essential for being with bereaved parents and siblings. Some people can get a lot of pleasure and fulfilment from their role, whether they are a parent supporting their surviving children, a social worker who is working with a grieving family, or a counsellor working with a bereaved couple or young person. This compassion satisfaction can reduce the likelihood of developing compassion fatigue and increase resilience.[5,6,7] For more information on compassion, see Chapter 18, and for a compassion meditation, see Chapter 25.

If someone doesn't have a good self-care strategy, or if they are overloaded at work, they can develop compassion fatigue. They may feel physically and mentally exhausted, unable to cope with their everyday life. This can result in their responding with apathy or indifference towards the suffering of others, which is usually at odds with their usual behaviour.[8]

The symptoms of compassion fatigue include:

- Sleep disturbance;
- Increase in emotional intensity;
- Cognitive impairment, unable to concentrate or feeling woolly headed;
- Unable to make clear decisions;
- Withdrawal from others;
- Loss of confidence and drive;
- Low mood;
- Loss of appetite or overeating;
- Low self-esteem;
- Unable to self-regulate emotions;
- Feelings of lethargy or apathy;
- Feelings of despair;
- Feelings of fear about going to work or performing one's role.

Compassion fatigue is debilitating, and it can take quite a long time to recover. Some people may need to take a significant amount of time off work, others may prefer to switch their role to one that is less demanding of them for a time.

Activity 4

1. Complete the Professional Quality of Life Scale which measures your compassion fatigue and compassion satisfaction levels and is available from https://proqol.org/uploads/ProQOL_5_English_Self-Score.pdf.[9]
2. What do you notice about your scores? Is there anything you need to do to reduce the likelihood of your developing compassion fatigue?
3. Looking back at the self-care picture you made earlier, is there anything else you'd now like to add?
4. Consider your caseload. Are there any people with whom you work that may be better helped by someone else, for example, if the issues they are bringing are too close to home?
5. Reflect on the information about Maslow's Hierarchy of Needs in Chapter 18. What do you notice about your own needs?
6. What changes would you like to make, and how will you make them?

If you have completed all the activities from this section, you will now have a clear self-care strategy that you can revise on a regular basis.

Identifying personal processes

Understanding how your own thinking, feeling, and experiences may influence your view of yourself, and your interactions or relationships with other people, is important. The activities in this section may help you to uncover your own internal process and discover why you may find it easier or more difficult to be with certain people.

Attachment styles

Each person has attachment patterns that may differ according to where they are and the person/people they are with at that time. For instance, someone may feel content with themselves and others at work, but not at home. Alternatively, they may feel secure with their partner but unsure of themselves with their boss. Some may feel secure at home and at work, but not when they go home to visit parents. Knowing how you might move from one style to another can be useful in identifying whether you may take up positions on the Drama Triangle as described earlier in this chapter.

An attachment style is the way that someone has an emotional bond with another person. A number of names are given to the different attachment styles, and for the purposes of this chapter I'm drawing on the work of Bowlby, Ainsworth, and Main.

Bowlby and Ainsworth originally identified three styles, called secure, insecure ambivalent, and insecure avoidant.[10] Main later added a fourth style, disorganized.[11]

Secure attachment style

Someone with this style has basic trust in themselves, others, and life. They tend to be optimistic and get on with other people and with the tasks they need to complete, making informed choices based on the facts before them. They will ask for, receive, and offer help in a straightforward manner. They express their thoughts and feelings in an authentic way and are appreciative of another's support. If unhappy with something or someone, they will then confront in a respectful way seeking a win-win solution. With others, they are emotionally available and respond appropriately using the Awareness ARENA.

Insecure ambivalent style

If someone has this style of attachment, they tend to believe that others are better, worth more, and are more successful. They may feel like running away when things get tough, blaming themselves for anything bad that happens. They are caring of others and usually complete tasks, often jumping in to help, rather like the Rescuer on the Drama Triangle. Although very capable, they often don't recognize or celebrate their achievements. They want to be close to other people but either feel they don't deserve their love or care or may believe that sooner or later, the other will leave. Due to their fear of rejection, they can be anxious, frequently seeking reassurance or approval.

Insecure avoidant style

If someone has this style of attachment, they tend to believe that they are better than others. They may blame others if anything bad happens, putting the other down or undermining them in order to get rid of them. They may take up the Persecutor role on the Drama Triangle. They consider that others are untrustworthy and unreliable and as a result find it hard to delegate. Some can appear aloof, defensive, and unfriendly, suppressing their feelings. Their preference is to be on their own, and they pride themselves on being self-sufficient.

Disorganized

If someone has this style of attachment, they tend to feel down on others and themselves. They may feel hopeless, ineffective, and helpless and tend to not get on with other people or with any tasks they may need to perform. Others may experience them as negative, complaining, passive, unpredictable, or chaotic, and as a result are unsure how to respond to them. Whatever response they give to the other may appear to be wrong; this reinforces their belief that others are unreliable and confirms their place as a Victim on the Drama Triangle.

Attunement

Someone's ability to get alongside another who is grieving can be influenced by several factors, whether they have experienced grief or loss themselves and if they have how they managed that experience. For example, if they have had a similar loss, had sufficient support and space to tell their story, or been able to make meaning and transform their loss, then the resilience they built up will protect them and help them to support those who are grieving. On the other hand, if they have not experienced loss, they may feel bewildered by another's grief and unsure what to say, think, feel, or do, as it is so alien to them. They have nothing to base this new experience on. If they have had a loss but did not receive enough support, or if others were critical or withdrew from them, then they may feel overwhelmed by the other's grief as they have so much of their own unprocessed grief to manage.

Another way of thinking about this is to consider how someone responds to another's distress. Certain people prefer to think about the problems and seek a solution. Consequently, they may struggle with someone who is expressing their feelings as they are not in a position to problem-solve. Others may wish to express their feelings about the situation first, and they may feel ignored if the person they are speaking with starts telling them what to do. Some people may prefer to do something practical to help and struggle if there is no task for them to perform. As a professional, you may achieve a greater rapport or sense of attunement with your client if you can match their preference, whether that is thinking, feelings, or action. It is easy to find out what someone's preference is by asking a simple question such as "How are you today?" A thinking person may respond with "I think I'm doing okay," a feelings person with "I feel so sad," or an action person with "I'm busy watering the plants." If you can get onto the other's wavelength, then they are more likely to feel seen, heard, and understood, and any conversation will be more effective.

There is no right or wrong with any of this. Knowing your own preferences can be useful in understanding why your approach may work really well for some people but perhaps not for others.

Notes

1 S. Karpman (1968). Fairy Tales and Script Drama Analysis. *Transactional Analysis Bulletin*, 7(26), pp. 39–43. Available from: https://karpmandramatriangle.com/pdf/DramaTriangle.pdf
2 S. Karpman (2014). *A Game Free Life: The New Transactional Analysis of Intimacy, Openness, and Happiness*. San Francisco, CA: Drama Triangle Publications.
3 S. Karpman (2019). *Collected Papers in Transactional Analysis*. San Francisco, CA: Drama Triangle Publications.

4 A. Dickson (2019). *A Woman in Your Own Right*. London: Quartet Books, pp. 59–69.
5 B.H. Stamm (2002). Measuring Compassion Satisfaction as Well as Fatigue: Developmental History of the Compassion Satisfaction and Fatigue Test. In: C.R. Figley, ed., *Treating Compassion Fatigue*. New York: Brunner-Routledge, pp. 107–119.
6 S.C. Voss Horrell, D.R. Holohan, L.M. Didion and G.T. Vance (2011). Treating Traumatized OEF/OIF Veterans: How Does Trauma Treatment Affect the Clinician? *Professional Psychology: Research and Practice*, 42, pp. 79–86. DOI: 10.1037/a0024163.
7 H.J. Burnett Jr. and K. Wahl (2015). The Compassion Fatigue and Resilience Connection: A Survey of Resilience, Compassion Fatigue, Burnout, and Compassion Satisfaction among Trauma Responders. *International Journal of Emergency Mental Health and Human Resilience*, 17, pp. 318–326. DOI: 10.4172/1522-4821. 1000165.
8 F. Cocker and N. Joss (2016). Compassion Fatigue among Healthcare, Emergency and Community Service Workers: A Systematic Review. *International Journal of Environmental Research and Public Health*, 13, p. 618. DOI: 10.3390/ijerph13060618.
9 B.H. Stamm (2009). *Professional Quality of Life: Compassion Satisfaction and Fatigue Version 5 (ProQOL)*. Available from: https://proqol.org/uploads/ProQOL_5_English_Self-Score.pdf [Accessed 9 September 2020].
10 M.D.S. Ainsworth (1973). The Development of Infant-mother Attachment. In: B. Cardwell and H. Ricciuti, eds., *Review of Child Development Research*, Vol. 3. Chicago: University of Chicago Press, pp. 1–94.
11 M. Main and J. Solomon (1990). Procedures for Identifying Infants as Disorganized/Disoriented during the Ainsworth Strange Situation. In: M.T. Greenberg, D. Cicchetti and E.M. Cummings, eds., *Attachment in the Preschool Years: Theory, Research, and Intervention*. Chicago: University of Chicago Press, pp. 121–160.

25 Creative ways of working with loss

There are numerous creative ways of working with loss. Being open to different options benefits both the client and the professional. You may have your own preferences, or your client may have their individual ideas. These are some of my favourites.

ATTEND[1]

ATTEND is an acronym which stands for Attunement, Trust, Therapeutic Touch, Egalitarianism, Nuance, and Death education. I rather like this model, as it focusses on the process of what needs to occur between the client and the professional. Each element is practised within a mindfulness framework, see the following.

Attunement

Being attuned with someone means being able to use all your senses to fully understand what another person is experiencing, to resonate with them, to be 'in the moment' with empathy and self-awareness. For more on attunement see Chapter 24.

Trust

Trust is key, particularly when someone's trust has been shaken by traumatic loss. The practitioner needs to trust that basic core listening skills and non-verbal communication through eye contact, facial expressions, and appropriate body language will convey a willingness to support, as well as being mindful of any tone of voice, pitch, as well as the words used. Simply sitting with another can be more powerful than any words or actions. As Sheila McCarthy Dodd said in Chapter 22, being able to be in those sacred spaces, to honour and accept the pain and distress of another, is one of the greatest gifts that can be given. Accepting the person as they are, and the situation as it is, means that the other person can also begin to accept the reality of what has happened.[2] That acceptance coupled with compassion builds trust in the relationship.

Therapeutic touch

This can be very powerful and also controversial as it may not be appropriate for some people, whether that is the professional, or the client, or both. As a professional, it's best to be mindful of your own process first. What do you think or feel about touching your client? Would it be an authentic gesture, or would you feel awkward or uncomfortable? If the latter, then I would suggest no touch would be sensible. If you are comfortable with touch, what would be in the best interests of your client? I suggest sensitive enquiry about their response to the idea of any touch. This could be gentle pressure on the uppermost part of the client's hand, or their shoulder or back. Some authors suggest that touching is essential in the development of attunement and intimacy in the therapeutic undertaking.[34] I'm not so sure, as touch may be experienced as positive or negative depending upon the frame of reference of the receiver. Some professionals may also have ethical codes or frameworks that specifically mention whether touch between the professional and the client is permitted.

Egalitarianism

The development of an equal relationship between the professional and the client requires the professional to have an open mind, so that the client can decide their desired focus or outcome. In regard to the death of a child/sibling, this could be exploring how the client can be active in any funeral plans or memorial service – making sure that their needs or wishes are met, or of finding their own way to say goodbye. Later, this equality of relationship could be about helping the bereaved work out how to deal with anniversaries and other milestone events. Alternatively, it could involve reassuring the client as they struggle with the changing bonds and supporting them as they begin to make meaning of their loss. For more on the different types of bonds and meaning making, see Chapters 18 and 21 respectively.

Nuance

Refers to the professional being attentive to any familial or cultural preferences which may be different from their own frame of reference. In terms of grief, this could be something as simple as the type or style of clothing worn to a funeral, whether there is a coffin and what it looks like, or even whether there is a funeral at all in any traditional sense. There are some amazing options available these days, with designs ranging from a Dr Who Tardis to a guitar or a popcorn box. They can be made out of various materials from bamboo to banana leaves, cardboard to wicker or wood. Other decisions could include whether there will be a burial or cremation; if the latter, how and where the ashes will be stored or when and where they will be scattered. Also to be considered is how the life of the person who has died is remembered, whether there is a wake or not, whether the bereaved wish to have visitors to call on them, or whether they would prefer their own privacy. There are so many nuances that neither the professional nor the bereaved may be aware of any prejudices they may hold or of all the options available to them.

Death education

Death education is in two parts. The first part concerns the bereaved person, and the second part refers to the professional.

Part 1

This part concerns answering any questions the parents or siblings may have regarding the end-of-life care or death of their child/sibling. For example, if there is a specific cause of death; how that came about; what was done to help save their life; whether the death was peaceful, quick, or painful, etc.; whether there is to be a post-mortem, and if there is to be one, what happens; and how will their loved one be cared for by the pathologist. There may be concerns about any tissues or fluids that might be removed and what will happen to them afterwards. Some may have questions about seeing the body of their dead child/sibling; whether they can spend time with them, hold them, etc. Questions may also relate to any funeral options, whether there will be an inquest or police enquiry, and what involvement there will be of other agencies and why.

Part 2

This part relates to the continuing training and development of the professional in dealing with death and grief in all its forms, including the impact this has on them as individuals as well as in their work role. Reading this book, answering the questions and completing any of the activities in Appendix 1 and the previous chapter, as well as considering the theories and research, will help the individual to appreciate the impact of loss on themselves; to understand with compassion their own reactions and responses; to consider how they might work with the bereaved; all of which will enable them to deal with the aftermath of the death of a child or sibling.

Creative techniques

Sand tray

If you haven't already got one, they are easy to put together. I use a fairly large tray; something like a cat litter tray is good. Fill it halfway up with clean and dry sand. Collect numerous and varied objects, they can be natural items such as shells, marbles, and small pieces of stone or wood. You can also use other objects such as action figures, miniature animals, insects, toys, and containers. Charity shops can be a great place to get these if you don't already have them. I find a camera can be useful too in recording the work as it creates a visual account of the work undertaken by the client. Using a sand tray is a great way of working symbolically and is especially good for people who are visual or kinaesthetic. Feeling the sand and the objects in their hands can trigger all sorts of processes that might otherwise not come to the fore.

Using sand tray work to understand someone's grief can be very revealing. Clients can choose objects to represent themselves, the person who died, other family members, and friends. Once they have chosen an item, you may wish to ask them to identify the qualities of the object they have chosen that characterizes, for them, each person. Then ask the client to position the chosen objects in the sand, each in relation to the others, and to say why they have put the objects where they are placed. This is a really good way of understanding the dynamics at play between all those involved in the client's story. For some clients, this may be enough, for them to have a visual image of the subtleties involved in the narrative of their grief. Otherwise, you may wish to ask the client if there is anything they would like to change; for example, moving one object closer or further away from another or putting a new object between two other objects. It may even be taking one object out altogether.

As well as understanding the relational dynamics mentioned earlier, the objects could be used to explore how someone feels about their grief – whether they are close to or detached from it, if there are barriers which could be other people or issues that are getting in the way of their processing their grief. Consider inviting the person to imagine that the sand represents their grief and ask them to place themselves and the other people in their life, including the person who died. The sand and any other objects can symbolize any blocks or restrictions. I had a client who moved all the sand up to one end of the tray and put himself at the other end. Then he tipped the tray so that the sand completely covered him and those around him. We explored what he needed to stop him from 'drowning' in the sand. By the end, the sand was moved so that the tops of the objects were above the level of the sand, and there were pieces of string tied between the object that represented the client and something he experienced as secure and solid. This enabled him to see that although he was immersed in his grief, he was not going to sink below the surface and die, which had been his fear, and that there were still people and things in his life that were reliable and stable that would support him.

Sand tray work can be used to identify and process feelings after a loss. Again, the client chooses objects that represent the various conflicts or struggles that they are experiencing. Some clients, for example, find it difficult to express anger towards the person who died; or they may feel conflicted, especially if they had an ambivalent relationship with them. As before, they can choose an object that represents each thought or feeling. As the professional observing the client, you may wish to ask questions about the objects or the positions. Alternatively, you may simply make comments regarding what you notice as the client chooses, places, and moves the objects. I tend to find that younger clients are more at ease with this way of working and usually need minimal input. Adult clients may initially feel a bit awkward and 'silly,' but as they gain confidence, this decreases. That said, sand tray work may not appeal to all clients. There needs to be a sense of trust in the relationship between the professional and the client in order for them to feel safe enough to work in this way.

Buttons

I love buttons; they come in so many shapes, sizes, and colours. Buttons can be used in a similar way to the sand tray mentioned earlier and be placed on a table or on the floor. Again, charity shops can be a good place to get buttons. Having a variety, including misshapen and broken buttons, is useful.

Art and pictures

Art therapy is a modality in its own right and needs specific training.[5] The art I am suggesting here is not art therapy, but it may well be therapeutic. I had a client whose daughter had died. As my client described her experience, I sometimes struggled to follow or fully appreciate the ramifications of her pain and distress. So, she created a picture illustrating the turmoil she was in and brought it with her to her next session. I was blown away by what she brought, I could immediately see and understand the rawness of what she had been trying to tell me. In the centre of the chaos shown in the picture, there was a gaping hole symbolizing the impact of the loss of her child. From then on, we used the picture in our work together, perhaps focussing on one aspect or another, and over time she created a 'patch' with embroidery to cover and protect the hole.

For some people, pictures and images can tell their story far more effectively than words. I keep a stack of postcards, pictures, and photos that can be used by a client to 'paint a picture' of their experience. Sometimes they may choose one to represent what they want for the future and keep it as a sort of transitional object.[6]

Salt bottles

For this activity you need a clean, wide-necked glass or plastic bottle or jar, with a lid, some salt, large coloured chalks, an A3 sheet of paper, and a small piece of card, something like an index or postcard or a small greetings card is good.

Invite the client to think about what characteristics they valued most in the person who died and write them down on the piece of card. For each characteristic, they choose a colour from the available chalk and note it on the card. Next, pour some of the salt onto the A3 piece of paper and rub over it with one of the chosen chalks so the salt changes colour. When complete, pour it into the bottle or jar. Repeat this for all of the characteristics so that at the end they have a full jar with layers of coloured salt. The bottle and card can be a lovely visual reminder of the person who died.

Journaling

There are different ways of journaling. Some people like to use their journal to write down all their thoughts and feelings; they may draw pictures in with the text. This way of using a journal can help someone to write about successes they have had; to clarify their thinking of particular topics or issues;[7] to write about their beliefs and values; to keep a list of things, people, aspects of their life for which they are grateful; to gain perspective on the issues that are troubling them; to develop a plan of action; to reduce stress; and to act as a resource for when the going gets tough, thereby protecting resilience.[8]

It is possible to use journaling without words, purely with images, pictures, diagrams, collages, etc. This may suit someone who finds it hard to write down what they are experiencing or feel so overwhelmed by their thoughts or feelings. Others may struggle with the informal or creative nature of this way of expressing themselves, perhaps because they consider that they are not artistic or cannot draw. The beauty of this way of processing events or issues is that it can tap into inner resources that the person is not even aware they possess.

Letter writing

Letter writing can be very useful in helping someone to manage unfinished business with someone who has died. There is no formula or specific way to structure such a letter; rather, that the person writes down all the things they would like to say to the deceased. Once the letter is complete, there are various options. One is to destroy the letter. This could be by burning it; ripping it up into tiny pieces and throwing it away; posting it in a blank envelope; putting the letter into the coffin before a funeral; or, if the funeral has already happened and they still have the ashes, burn the letter and carefully collect the cool ashes and add to the ashes container. Alternatively, bury the letter in the garden or other special place. Use the letter as a starting point for the 'imagined dialogues' or any two-chair work, as described in Chapter 21. This can be incredibly powerful as well as insightful and rewarding.

Mindfulness

Mindfulness can help someone develop their capacity to be with their emotional responses and to increase their ability to self-regulate. This means that the person may then be more available for other relationships, personal or professional. Mindfulness can also be useful for dealing with other situations such as anniversaries and other significant family or life events as well as for health issues.[9]

Although mindfulness is an ancient Buddhist practice, it has relevance for our lives today. According to Kabat Zinn, it has all to do with really awakening, and existing in congruence with oneself and with the world. He goes on to say that, mindfulness concerns intentionally listening carefully in a specific manner, in the here and now, and without judgement. This kind of attentiveness creates a greater consciousness, clearness, and agreement of here-and-now reality.[10]

Using mindfulness can help individuals to "work with the universal vulnerabilities and challenges that are an inherent part of being human."[11] In other words, it can help anyone to deal with life and death and all that that entails.

When someone suffers from a trauma such as the death of a child or sibling, they are in many ways very awake. Some may even argue too much so, as they may be feeling completely exposed and raw, vulnerable to every sensation, and hypervigilant in all that is going on around them. They are, however, unlikely to be living in harmony with themselves or the world. The challenge with mindfulness is to stay in the moment, in the here and now.

Mindfulness exercises

The internet is awash with mindfulness exercises that anyone can use. This is one of my favourites, learned years ago, that I find very useful.

Find somewhere where you won't be disturbed for at least five minutes, a place that is warm and where you feel safe. Sit on a chair, with both of your feet resting on the floor, or you can lie down. Put your hands in your lap or rest them on your legs or on the ground. Close your eyes and focus on your breathing. Take a deep breath in through your nose to a count of five, hold to a count of five, and then breathe out through your mouth, also to a count of five. Repeat this three times. Then allow your breathing to return to its usual rhythm. Notice when you inhale how you can feel the air filling your lungs, and then as you exhale how it leaves your body through your mouth. As you sit quietly, notice what is going on inside your body. Bring a soft attention to any areas where you feel any tension, aches, or pains. Feel free to move to alleviate any discomfort. Once you have briefly scanned your body, bring your attention to your feet or body, resting on the floor, and feel the floor supporting you. Move your attention up through your ankles, calves, and knees, then continue to your thighs and hips. Pay gentle attention to your pelvic area, genitals, bottom, and back as you lean into the chair or floor and allow it to support you. Now bring a delicate awareness to your abdomen and chest, noticing your ribcage expanding and contracting with each breath. Move on up to your shoulders and neck, then down through your arms to your wrists, hands, and fingers. Next, gradually notice your head and face, your eyes, nose, and mouth, relax your jaw, and pay attention to any feeling in your ears, forehead, and scalp.

Notice where your clothes touch your body, what the clothes feel like – whether they are comfortable and well fitting, soft or rough – and whether your feet feel supported by any footwear. Become aware to the air around you and where it touches your body. Is it warm or cool, a breeze or still? Then focus on what you can smell, followed by what you can taste, if anything, and then what you can hear. Pay detailed attention to each smell, flavour, or sound. Then, when you are ready, open your eyes and notice, as if for the first time, all you can see around you, the wallpaper, paint, or pictures on the wall, any carpet or rug on the floor – observe all the colours and textures. Pay attention to the furniture and any ornaments or objects in the room. Allow yourself some time to feel at one with yourself and your surroundings.

A whole range of mindfulness courses are available, some online, others at local centres, some through the NHS. There are books, some with CDs that make mindfulness easily accessible. As with many things, any success with mindfulness is achieved by practising it. If you can incorporate it into your daily routine, so much the better.

The CIRCLE of compassion

I have found the CIRCLE of Compassion, adapted from the RAIN of compassion,[12] a useful tool in developing compassion for self or others, and that is best done when in a quiet and peaceful space with no interruptions. The CIRCLE of Compassion can help someone to become aware of any unconscious paralysis or stuckness that may be causing them internal torment and suffering. CIRCLE stands for Connect, Inhabit, Research, Cherish, Linger, and Embrace.

Connect

Connect with what is going on. Consciously acknowledge your thoughts, feelings, bodily sensations, and behaviours regarding anything that is happening in or around you. Fully embrace all that you are experiencing, notice every nuance, and broaden your awareness of your experience.

Inhabit

Fully occupy this experience by simply noticing your thoughts/feelings and behaviours without trying to problem-solve or fix them. If you feel judgemental or have an internal critical voice, notice that too; allow yourself to be with your experience. It does not mean you agree with the judgements; rather, by staying with and focussing on your process, this allows you to pause, to be fully in the moment, and to let any painful feelings to arise.

Research

This is a time when you can use your curiosity to wonder about what you are experiencing. Notice how you may hold yourself hostage to any negative internal voices that are causing you a sense of paralysis or stuckness; see if you can identify where they come from. As you wonder, see if you can locate the issue(s) in your body and identify your felt sense. Pay detailed attention to each sensation. Allow yourself to truly feel what you are feeling without judgement, in a kind way that will allow you to own any vulnerable feelings of shame, hurt, sadness, anger, or fear.

Cherish

Cherish yourself; see if you can identify what it is that the frightened, angry, sad, hurting, or vulnerable part of you really needs. Do you need to do something, or to say something kind to yourself? Do you need forgiveness, to get support or love from another? What affirmations do you need? Can you give them to yourself, or get them from another? What can you say to yourself that would be most helpful or useful at this time? If you struggle with this, think about a person you know and admire, imagine what they may say to themselves if they were in the same situation and then say that to yourself. Alternatively, imagine your younger self in front of you – standing in front of a mirror can help with this. What do you notice? What does that part of you need? What advice, care, or support can your adult self say to your younger self?

Linger

Allow yourself to stay in this forgiving, mindful, tender, and aware place. Your increased awareness and nurturing your younger self, being kind and compassionate, can release you from previously held and unhelpful beliefs, attitudes, or hostage bonds.

Embrace

Welcome your developing compassionate self. Allow yourself to be more compassionate with others and embrace your authentic self.

Many people find self-compassion rather challenging to achieve. If you believe you have done something wrong or neglected to do something, see if you can find a way to talk to yourself with compassion. Living with self-compassion will enable you to find a way to live more fully and to be more available for the people with whom you work. You may even wish to share this meditation with your clients, to help them be more compassionate with themselves in their grief. As with mindfulness, a number of radical compassion meditations and resources are available online.[13]

Do remember, the more you can practise, the easier you will find it to use and heal aspects of yourself that are currently hurting, fearful, or in distress.

Notes

1. J. Cacciatore and M. Flint (2012). Attend: Toward a Mindfulness-based Bereavement Care Model. *Death Studies*, 36, pp. 61–82. DOI: 10.1080/07481187.2011.591275. Reprinted by permission of the publisher Taylor & Francis Ltd, www.tandfonline.com.
2. J. Bernie (2010). *Ordinary Freedom.* Oakland, CA: Non-Duality Press.
3. A. Montagu (1986). *Touching: The Human Significance of the Skin.* 3rd ed. New York: Harper & Row Publishing, p. 282.
4. G. Heuer (2005). 'In My Flesh I Shall See God' Jungian Body Psychotherapy. In: N. Totton, ed., *New Dimensions in Body Psychotherapy.* Maidenhead, UK: Open University Press, p. 108.
5. www.hcpc-uk.org/standards/standards-of-proficiency/arts-therapists/
6. D.W. Winnicott (1953). Transitional Objects and Transitional Phenomena. *International Journal of Psychoanalysis*, 34, pp. 89–97.
7. K.A. Baikie and K. Wilhelm (2005). Emotional and Physical Health Benefits of Expressive Writing. *Advances in Psychiatric Treatment*, 11(5), pp. 338–346. DOI: 10.1192/apt.11.5.338.
8. J.M. Smyth, J.A. Johnson, B.J. Auer, E. Lehman, G. Talamo and C.N. Sciamanna (2018). Online Positive Affect Journaling in the Improvement of Mental Distress and Well-Being in General Medical Patients with Elevated Anxiety Symptoms: A Preliminary Randomized Controlled Trial. *JMIR Mental Health*, 5(4), p. e11290. DOI: 10.2196/11290.
9. P. Grossman, L. Niemann, S. Schmidt and H. Walach (2004). Mindfulness-based Stress Reduction and Health Benefits: A Meta-analysis. *Journal of Psychosomatic Research*, 57(1), pp. 35–43. DOI: 10.1016/S0022-3999(03)00573-7.
10. J. Kabat-Zinn (2004). *Wherever You Go, There You Are: Mindfulness Meditation for Everyday Life.* London. Piatkus, pp. 3–4.
11. R. Crane (2009). *Mindfulness-based Cognitive Therapy.* New York: Routledge, p. 3. Reproduced with permission of the Licensor through PLSclear.
12. T. Brach (2020). *Radical Compassion: Learning to Love Yourself and Your World with the Practice of RAIN.* London: Ebury Publishing.
13. www.tarabrach.com/meditation-rain-compassion/

Appendix 1
Questions and activities

These questions are aimed at trainees or those who are learning or wish to develop their self-reflective practice.

Chapter 18: the ABC of grief

1. If you have experienced bereavement, do you recall showing a wish to push people away, antagonizing anyone, or wishing to be alone? If so, what was that experience like for you?
2. What options do you have when working with a client who may be behaving in any of these ways?
3. Which types of bonds do you have in your life? How do they work for you?
4. If you have any hostage bonds, how might they restrict you in your work?
5. How do you manage any continuing bonds?
6. How can you use knowledge of these different bonds with your clients?

Chapter 19: living with loss

Maslow's Hierarchy of Needs

Look at Maslow's Hierarchy of Needs.

1. What do you notice about your own needs?
2. Which would you consider met, and which are unfulfilled?
3. What options do you have to satisfy those currently unmet needs?
4. How might you work with this model with your clients?

Self-care

5. What self-care strategies does your client have? How might you introduce self-care to them?
6. What options are available to them locally in terms of classes or groups?
7. How might you use any of the activities in Chapter 24 with your clients?

Anniversaries

8   What do anniversaries mean to you?
9   How do you manage anniversaries?
10 How might you support your client with anniversaries?
11 What is your own view of acceptance?
12 How might you help facilitate acceptance in your client?
13 What might hinder you in doing so?

Chapter 20: transformational loss

1   Think of a bereavement you have had. How did you manage each phase of transformational loss? What helped or hindered you?
2   Think of a client; how are they managing the different phases?
3   What options do you have to support them?

Chapter 21: models of grief and bereavement

1   Which models in Chapter 21 appeal to you personally?
2   What other models of grief do you know about and like to use with clients?
3   If you are working or have worked with a bereaved person, as you reflect on the work you did together, describe how you understand your work using either one of the models in Chapter 21 or your own preferred model.

Chapter 22: transgenerational loss and Family Constellations

1   How do you think about transgenerational loss?
2   What techniques might you use to explore such a loss?
3   What additional safety/protection systems would you put in place?
4   What additional training might you need to feel competent and confident to work in this way?

Chapter 23: resilience, grief, and grief disorder

1   How would you describe your own resilience?
2   What factors affect your resilience?
3   Thinking about one of your bereaved clients, how would you describe their resilience?
4   What options do you have to support yourself and your client in protecting or developing resilience?
5   Use any of the assessment tools and decide which ones might work for you with your clients.

Chapter 24: protection and self-knowledge

Protection and boundaries

1 How do you think about protection for yourself and your clients?
2 What are your strengths or limitations in terms of time boundaries?
3 What additional resources or support do you need in terms of protection?

Drama Triangle

Recall a time when you have used one of the Drama Triangle positions and answer the following questions:

1 What role were you in to begin with?
2 What was it about being in that role that is familiar to you?
3 What role did you end up in?
4 What was it about being in that role that is familiar to you?

The Awareness ARENA

Now using the Awareness ARENA, ask yourself the following questions:

1 What is the problem?
2 What is it about this problem or person's behaviour that is causing me difficulties?
3 What resolution am I hoping to achieve?
4 How much am I willing to negotiate with the other person?
5 How do I feel about this problem?
6 What am I willing to do?
7 What am I not willing to do?
8 How can I leave this situation in a way that maintains respect for all parties involved?
9 What is the main problem?
10 What have I done already to sort this out?
11 What happened?
12 What worked, and what did not?
13 Why might that be?
14 What other experiences have I had that may be similar to this one?
15 What can I take from previous experiences to help myself now?
16 What do I need so that I am feeling compassion/care towards myself and the other?
17 What skills and abilities do I have to help with this problem?
18 Do I have the time to be involved with resolving this problem? If not now, when?
19 What are options are open to me?
20 How do I feel about asking for help/support?

Assertiveness

1 What is it that may stop you from being assertive?
2 Which of the rights and responsibilities mentioned in the chapter do you feel comfortable accepting, and which ones cause you a struggle?
3 When you contemplate being assertive, what do you think about yourself?
4 What messages do you hear in your mind?
5 What options do you have to help you to be more assertive?

Attachment styles

1 Which attachment style(s) do you notice you tend to use at work, or at home?
2 Do you notice any of these styles in terms of the Drama Triangle roles or Awareness ARENA attitudes for your own behaviour or those with whom you work?
3 What changes would you like to make so that you are predominately in the Awareness ARENA? How will you make those changes?

Chapter 25: creative ways of working with loss

ATTEND model

1 Which elements of the ATTEND model do you like, and which ones would you struggle with in your work?
2 What other ethical codes or professional practice frameworks do you have that you can use alongside this model?
3 What training needs have you identified that would help you in your work with bereaved parents and siblings?
4 How will you fulfil those training needs?

Creative techniques

1 Which, if any, of the creative techniques in Chapter 25 appeals to you as a way of you processing your own material?
2 How might you use any of these ideas with your clients?
3 What additional safety/protection issues might you need to consider when working in this way?

Mindfulness and compassion

1 What mindfulness or compassion exercises can you incorporate into your life and work?
2 What other techniques might you use for yourself and with your clients?

Understanding personal reactions to death

Read any of the stories contained in Part I and then answer the following questions.

1. How does the narrative impact on you? What are your thinking, feeling, and behavioural responses?
2. Did you notice whether you felt drawn to any positions on the Drama Triangle?
3. How would you use the Awareness ARENA if you were working with this person?
4. What aspects of the narrator's experience resonate with any of your experiences of grief and loss?
5. What would be a difficult conversation for you to have with the narrator if they were your client?
6. How would you broach such a conversation?
7. How would you work with them if they were your client?
8. How would you manage your own shock or distress?
9. What would you normally say to a bereaved person? Do you opt for thinking or feelings, or go into problem-solving or wanting to do something practical?
10. How might you use any of the theories, grief models, or resources in this book with this person?
11. How do you or would you like to be able to talk with others about death? What are your own dying wishes?
12. What do all these answers tell you about yourself?

For those who are counsellors and psychotherapists, some additional questions to answer would be:

13. What do you notice in terms of transference and counter transference?
14. What else does that tell you about yourself?
15. What other models or concepts come to mind?
16. How might you collude with a client who appears to be avoiding aspects of their grief process?
17. How might your own process get in the way of the client expressing themselves?
18. What issues might you take to supervision?
19. What would be the learning for you in working with this client?
20. How would you protect yourself and your client in the work?

Appendix 2
Sources of help and support

Continuing to live after the death of a child or sibling is not straightforward, and a number of organizations can offer help and support.

After a Suicide

This booklet can be read online at: https://supportaftersuicide.org.uk/wp-content/uploads/2016/09/Scotland-after-a-suicide.pdf. Printed copies can be ordered by contacting the Scottish Association for Mental Health (SAMH) Information Service or calling 0800 9173466.

Bereaved Through Suicide

This booklet can be read online at: http://supportaftersuicide.org.uk/wp-content/uploads/2016/09/NI-bereaved-by-suicide.pdf or by contacting Northern Ireland Public Health Agency on 0300 5550114.

CALM (Campaign Against Living Miserably; www.thecalmzone.net)

CALM is a registered charity which exists to prevent male suicide in the UK. The helpline and webchat service is free and confidential.

A helpline at 0800 585858 and a webchat at www.thecalmzone.net/help/webchat/ are both open seven days a week, 5 p.m.–midnight.

Child Bereavement UK (https://www.childbereavementuk.org)

Child Bereavement UK supports children, young people (up to 25 years old), parents, and families to rebuild their life after death. The charity also offers training for professionals to assist them in supporting bereaved families. The service includes a telephone helpline, an online chat service, and support groups for parents, families, and young people. The website also offers useful resources for schools and professionals.

Helpline: 0800 02 888 40; open Monday to Friday 9 a.m. to 5 p.m.

Childhood Bereavement Network (www.childhood bereavementnetwork.org.uk/)

This online only service signposts bereaved people to help and support available in their area. The website also contains a number of resources for schools.

Compassionate Friends (www.tcf.org.uk)

Compassionate Friends run a helpline and online support service for bereaved parents and their families. They also have a comprehensive list of leaflets and factsheets that can be read or downloaded from www.tcf.org.uk/content/support-resources/.

Helpline: 0345 123 2304, open daily 10 a.m.–4 p.m. and 7 p.m.–10 p.m.

Cruse Bereavement Care (www.cruse.org.uk)

Cruse is a national charity for bereaved people in England, Wales, and Northern Ireland. There is a freephone helpline and online chat service for bereaved children, young people, and adults. The website also contains a wealth of information on bereavement and loss.

Helpline: 0808 808 1677; open Monday and Friday, 9:30 a.m.–5 p.m.; Tuesday, Wednesday, and Thursday, 9.30 a.m.–8 p.m. and weekends 10 a.m.–2 p.m.

The webchat service is available Monday to Friday 9am-9pm.

Cruse Bereavement Care Isle of Man (www.cruseisleofman.org)

Cruse Isle of Man is affiliated to Cruse Bereavement Care. They offer a helpline, one-to-one support and groups for adults, children, and young people. They also provide information for schools and organizations.

Helpline: 01624 668191 for new enquiries available 9 a.m.–12 noon, or email info@cruseisleofman.org

Cruse Bereavement Care Scotland (www.crusescotland.org.uk)

Cruse Scotland is a charity for bereaved people in Scotland. There is a freephone helpline and online chat service for bereaved children, young people, and adults. The website also contains a wealth of information on bereavement and loss.

Helpline: 0845 600 2227, open Monday to Friday, 10 a.m.–8 p.m. (4 p.m. on Friday)

The Good Grief Trust (www.thegoodgrieftrust.org)

The charity is run by bereaved people and offers emotional and practical support, and information on other services available in the UK.

Sudden bereavement helpline 0800 2600 400 open 10 a.m.–4 p.m.
National bereavement partnership helpline 0800 4480 800 open 7 a.m.–10 p.m.

Grief Encounter (www.griefencounter.org.uk)

Offers a range of services for adults, children, and young people.
   Helpline: 0808 802 0111, webchat service open Monday to Friday, 9 a.m.–9 p.m.
   Ecounselling is available via ecounselling@griefencounter.org.uk

Help Is at Hand

Produced by the Department of Health, this is an excellent resource for people bereaved by suicide and other sudden, traumatic death in England and Wales. The booklet can be read online at: https://supportaftersuicide.org.uk/resource. Printed copies can be ordered by phoning 0300 123 1002, quoting 2901502/Help is at Hand.

Hope Again (www.hopeagain.org.uk)

Hope Again is the youth section of Cruse Bereavement Care and is specifically for children and young people. The service offers a listening ear with another young person, information and advice, and short videos from bereaved young people.
   Helpline: 0808 808 1677 open Monday to Friday 9:30 a.m.–5 p.m.

National Bereavement Partnership Covid-19 Hub

The National Bereavement Partnership Covid-19 Hub provides practical advice, support, and information to all those affected by the Covid-19 pandemic.
   Helpline: 0800 448 0800; SMS Helpline: 0786 002 2814; both open Monday to Sunday 7 a.m.–10 p.m.

PAPYRUS Prevention of Young Suicide (https://papyrus-uk.org)

PAPYRUS Prevention of Young Suicide offers support and advice to children and young people (under 35) who may be at risk of suicide and to those concerned that a young person could be thinking of suicide.
   Helpline: 0800 068 4141, text service 07860 039967, and email pat@papyrus-uk.org; open Monday to Friday 9 a.m.–10 p.m., weekends and bank holidays 2 p.m.–10 p.m.

RoadPeace (www.roadpeace.org)

A national charity for those who are bereaved and injured through road traffic accidents. They provide information and support, via literature,

local groups, and contact with people who have suffered a similar experience.
Helpline: 0845 4500 355 9 a.m.–9 p.m. daily

Samaritans (www.samaritans.org)

Samaritans provide emotional support to anyone who is struggling to cope and needs someone to listen. Local branches can be visited during the day.
Helpline: 116 123; text service 07725 909 090, open daily 24 hours
Welsh language line: 0808 164 0123
Email: jo@samaritans.org, response time 24 hours.

Sudden (www.suddendeath.org)

Sudden is an initiative that is run by the road safety charity Brake. Brake provides a case-management service for people suddenly bereaved by road crashes in the UK. Sudden provides free advice, information, webinars, and seminars on coping with a sudden death for the bereaved adults and children, carers, and professionals.
Helpline: 0800 121 6510, open Monday to Friday 10 a.m.–3 p.m.

Support After Murder and Manslaughter (www.samm.org.uk)

SAMMS offers a confidential helpline where a person can talk to someone who has been bereaved through homicide. SAMMS also offers training to professionals.
Helpline: 0121 472 2912 or 0845 872 3440
Email: samm.national@gmail.com

Survivors of Bereavement by Suicide (SOBS; https://uksobs.org)

SOBS offers support for those bereaved or affected by suicide through a helpline answered by trained volunteers who have been bereaved by suicide and a network of local support groups. This service is for people over the age of 18.
Helpline: 0300 111 5065, open daily 9 a.m.–9 p.m.
Email: email.support@uksobs.org

Support After Suicide Partnership (www.supportaftersuicide.org.uk)

This website provides information on local support systems.

Winston's Wish (https://www.winstonswish.org)

Winston's Wish is a leading charity providing specialist child bereavement support services across the UK. Services include a national helpline, an email service, a crisis service for young people, training for professionals, and specialist publications.

Helpline: 08088 020 021, open Monday to Friday 9 a.m.–5 p.m. and Wednesday evening 7 p.m.–9:30 p.m.

If in crisis, text WW to 85258; open daily 24 hours, this is a free service.

Young Minds (https://youngminds.org.uk)

The helpline provides advice and support to those concerned about the emotional well-being or behaviour of a young person. The charity offers training for professionals working with young people.

Helpline: 0808 802 5544, Monday to Friday 9:30 a.m.–4 p.m.

Young Minds Crisis Messenger service for young people in urgent need: text YM to 85258.

Index

A&E *see* hospital
abandonment 59, 172, 219
absent minded 111
acceptance 37, 44–5, 49, 51, 68, 101, 193, 200–1, 205, 216, 218, 258, 269
accident 113–14, 117, 163, 219, 276
acknowledgement 23, 39, 53, 57, 59, 166, 188, 199–201, 221, 230–1, 248–50
adjustments 189, 218–22, 239
adoption 36, 48, 52, 152, 181
aftermath 1, 18, 185, 237, 260
aggression 168, 246
Ainsworth, M. 254
alcohol 50, 56, 85, 88–9, 93, 117, 122, 139–40, 157–8, 179, 186, 195, 209
Alder Centre 26, 32
alienation 185–6, 250
alone 38, 63, 96, 111, 136, 148, 150, 178, 186, 206, 230, 246, 250
ambulance 55, 72, 94, 119, 126, 131, 242
anger 25, 51, 64, 91, 96, 110, 141, 146, 167, 186–7, 215–16, 226, 236, 238–9, 241, 249, 261, 266
anniversaries 14–15, 24, 26, 37, 39, 43, 47, 58–9, 62, 65, 86, 128, 134, 166, 189, 191, 199–200, 259, 264, 269; *see also* birthdays
antagonistic 186, 250
anxiety xii, 84, 102, 105, 146, 182, 197, 216, 228, 235–6, 240, 255
appetite 139, 143, 194–5, 236–7, 253
ashes 24, 26, 37, 62, 65, 83, 97, 128, 188–9, 259
assertiveness 245–8, 250, 271
attachment 14, 16, 25, 37, 149, 172, 178, 191, 219–21, 223–4, 234–5, 237, 254–5, 271

ATTEND 258–60
attention 10, 133, 139, 141, 198, 204, 218
attunement 13, 136, *248*, 249, 256, 258–9
authenticity 84, 98, 186–7, 200, 211, 248, 255, 259, 266
avoidance 13, 57–9, 84, 87, 97, 125, 178–9, 189, 204–5, 215, 218, 222, 272
awareness 186–7, 258, 266
Awareness ARENA 248–50, 255, 270–2
awkwardness 42–3, 48, 139, 141, 143, 262

barrier 83, 146, 158, 261
behaviour change 185–7
belongings 84, 86, 117, 159, 166, 175–6, 182, 191
bereavement *see* grief
bipolar disorder 126, 135, 156–7
birth stories 23, 181
birthdays 37, 39, 57, 59; *see also* anniversaries
blame 20, 22, 34, 46, 56, 70, 77, 87, 91, 106, 110, 114, 124, 127, 144, 151, 186, 189–90, 196, 204–5, 215, 238–9, 255
blended family 149
blood pressure 117, 236–7
body 42, 56, 61, 83, 108, 160, 187–8, 204, 260; decomposing 161; finding 9, 72, 96, 107–8, 130–1, 150, 160; laying out 97; *see also* ashes; grave
bonds 4, 14, 23, 33, 56, 150, 173–4, 178–9, 185, 187–92, 199–200, 203–9, 211, 220, 223–6, 237, 254, 259, 266, 268; *see also* continuing bonds; hostage bonds

borderline personality disorder 96, 126, 135, 156, 158; *see also* mental health
boundaries 245–6, 250, 270
Bowlby, J. 215, 254
brain aneurysm 89–90
breast cancer xii, 115, 135
bullied 92–3, 97, 246
butterflies *see* symbols

candles 65, 91, 200
cannabis *see* drugs
cards xii, 24, 55–6, 58–9, 77, 82, 86–7, 117, 162, 164, 191, 206
cause of death: absent end-diastolic flow 17; brain aneurysm 89; drug overdose 9, 80, 92, 120, 138, 156; hanging 67; Leukaemia 54; miscarriage 17, 28; motor neurone disease 169; pneumonia 40; reaction to medication 148; road traffic accident 113; stillbirth 17, 28; Sudden Infant Death Syndrome 41, 130; suicide 67, 120, 138, 156
change 9, 16, 83–4, 154, 203–10, 221–2; in world view 22, 26, 42, 49, 220, 224–5
chapel *see* faith
charities *see* Compassionate Friends; Gloucestershire Sunflowers; Papyrus; Winston's Wish
chasm *see* void
church *see* faith
cocaine *see* drugs
coffin 61, 82–3, 97, 126, 160–1, 163–4, 242, 259, 263
community 47, 56, 74, 115, 158, 191, 207, 240
compassion 109, 112, 152, 192, 198, 203–9, 234, *248*, 249–51, 253–4, 258, 260, 265–7, 270, 271; CIRCLE of 265–7
Compassionate Friends 63, 77, 116, 274
compassion fatigue 245, 251, 253–4
concentration 10–1, 105, 111, 215, 253
contentment 184, 254
continuing bonds 14, 83, 128, 166, 191–2, 198, 200, 206–7, 211, 223, 268; *see also* anniversaries; bonds; hostage bonds
control 75, 96, 143–4, 186, 201, 228, 235, 246; lack of 56, 64, 142, 195, 237
coping strategies 9, 35, 37–9, 59, 62, 64–5, 77–8, 85, 91, 112, 119, 125, 128, 143, 154, 162, 197–200, 206, 210, **219**, 225, 239, 251; *see also* sharing experience; talking with others; therapy
coroner *see* inquest
cortisol levels 228, 236–7, 240
cot death *see* Sudden Infant Death Syndrome
counselling *see* therapy
couples 52, 64, 127; differences in grieving 38, 51, 58, 64, 78, 80, 109, 125; *see also* relationships
creative ways of working 260–4
cultural context 42–4, 153, 177, 184, 205, 221, 231, 238, 251, 259

decisions: difficulty making 72–3, 143, 215, 253
denial 51, 188, 203, 215, **238**
depression 15, 36, 117, 216, 225, 227–9, 236, 240
Diagnostic and Statistical Manual of Mental Disorders Fifth Edition 238
directed journaling 225, 227
disorientation 175, 186, 216
dopamine 237
dragonflies *see* symbols
Drama Triangle 246–8, 250–1, 255–6, 270–2
dreams 62, 116, 181–2, 185, 241
drug overdose 9, 80, 92, 120, 138, 156
drugs 81, 85, 88–90, 93–6, 100–3, 106, 108–9, 113, 120–3, 126–7, 129, 143–4, 149–50, 152, 157–9, 186, 192, 195
DSM5 *see* Diagnostic and Statistical Manual of Mental Disorders Fifth Edition
Dual Process Model 13–14, 222–3, 235

embarrassment 141; *see also* shame
emocean 167, 208; *see also* metaphor
emotional 11, 31, 47, 56, 59, 61, 64, 74, 79, 116, 124, 126, 128, 201, 216–18, 229, **238**, 241–2
emotional intelligence 69, 109, 154, 207, 255
emotions *see* reactions
empathy 38, 258; *see also* attunement
energy 37, 87–8, 162, 196, 216, 236; lack of 13–15, 105, 111–12, 142, 190, 194–5

epigenetics 228–9
equilibrium 185–6, 195
expectations 27, 31, 203, **219**

Facebook *see* social media
faith 24, 33–4, 44–7, 50–1, 58, 62, 64, 66, 87, 97, 105, 111, 154, 162, 185, 206, 209, 220, 251; *see also* spiritual belief
Family Constellations 180–4, 228–32, 269; *see also* unconscious knowing
Father's Day 200
fault *see* blame
fear 25, 76, 97, 101, 132, 132–4, 136, 196, 204–5, 228–9, 231, 236–7, 241, 249, 253, 261, 266–7; *see also* scare
feathers *see* symbols
feelings: detached from 13–14, 43, 97, 185, 242, 261; managing others 86, 167, 249; *see also* reactions
fight, flight, freeze 236
fingerprint 126
flashbacks 185
flowers 47, 57, 65, 114, 132, 164, 191, 200
foggy headed *see* concentration
food 31–2, 73, 82, 110, 140, 143, *194*, 194–6, 235, 242
forgiveness 83–4, 125, 152, 204, 225, 266
Four-Phases of Grief Model 215–16
frame of reference 25, 203–4, 259
friends 21–6, 31–2, 34–5, 37, 39, 41, 44, 47–9, 52, 56, 58–9, 61, 63–4, 69, 73–7, 82–90, 109–12, 115, 117, 125, 127, 139–41, 144–5, 153, 162, 164, 177, 179, 194–200, 205–9, 240
funeral 35, 42–3, 61, 66, 82–3, 87, 89–90, 115, 118, 132, 136, 140, 142, 150–2, 161, 164, 221, 242, 259, 260; *see also* undertaker
funeral director *see* undertaker
future: loss of 13, 49, 126, 220

Gloucestershire Sunflowers 98
grandparents 3, 56, 64, 134, 154, 193, **219**
gratitude 196, 225–6
grave 45, 65, 91, 132–3, 191, 200
grief: ABC 185–92; assessment tools 240–3; disorder 237–9, 241; messy 26, 53, 211; oscillating nature 13–14, 187, 222, 235; *see also* cultural context; living with loss; pain; Persistent Complex Bereavement-Related Disorder; physiological impact; Prolonged Grief Disorder; reactions; support; what helped; what hindered
guilt 46, 48, 60, 87, 89, 124–5, 152, 158, 166, 189–90, 196, 204, *210*, **238**, 239; *see also* blame; regret

hair 126, 164
hanging: death by 72
Hellinger, B. 229–30
help *see* sources of help and support; what helped
helpless 4, 69, 123, 173, 186, 216, 237, 255
heroin *see* drugs
hole *see* void
hope 26, 51, 142, 191, 201, 206, 208, 216
hopeless 82, 85, 186, 205, 216, 255
horror 10, 18, 23, 25, 131, 133–4, 136–7, 178, 190
hospital 17–19, 22, 29–30, 40–2, 55, 57, 90, 94–6, 113–14
hostage bonds 189–90, 211, 266, 268; *see also* if only; what if roundabout
humour 52, 145, 164, 197
Hunniford, G. xii

ICD-11 *see* International Statistical Classification of Diseases and Related Health Problems 11th Edition
identity 9, 58, 149, 152–3, 204, 211, 218, 220, 231, 239; *see also* life purpose
if only 46, 190, 201, 204, 216; *see also* hostage bonds; what if roundabout
imagined dialogues 226, 231, 263
impact of loss *see* loss
impatient 48, 142
inclusion 229
innocence: loss of 25, 27
inquest 75, 84, 96, 106, 107–9, 115, 125, 141, 150, 163, 189, 260; verdict 75, 84, 96, 125, 163
insensitive comments 10, 53, 56–7, 87, 139, 165, 186
intensive care unit 40–1, 45, 57, 89
International Statistical Classification of Diseases and Related Health Problems 11th Edition 238
intrusion 56–7, 132

intrusive images or thoughts 10, 136, 182–3, 185, 190, 195, 225, 240–2
isolation 44, 63, 107, 132, 134, 196, 239, 246
ITU *see* intensive care unit

jigsaw puzzle 14, 107, 110, 125, 183
journal 187; *see also* directed journaling
journalist 115, 141; *see also* publicity
judgement 142, 192, 196, 231, 242, 266
Jung, C.G. 201
justice 115, 230

Kohlrieser, G. 189
Kübler-Ross, E. 215–16

laughter 19, 31, 82, 84, 86, 91, 118, 141, 145, 196–7, 199
legacy work 52, 63, 74–5, 85–6, 226; *see also* Transformational Loss
legal action 186
lethargy 236–7, 253; *see also* energy
letters *see* cards
Leukaemia 54–5
life: beginning to live again 59, 64, 88, 164, 178, 182, 193–9, 216, 224
life changes 24, 50, 52, 88, 119, 190, 224–5
life purpose 14, 86, 88, 109, 189, 198, 201, 205, 207, 209, 239
living in here and now 58, 76, 182, 201, 264
living with loss xii, 4, 35, 51–2, 64–5, 86, 107, 116, 123–4, 127–9, 187, 193–9
limbo 97, 205
loneliness 118, 136, 206
longing *see* yearning
looking after others 10, 31, 56, 72, 239, 251
loss: distraction from 31–2, 39, 51, 225; of potential 9, 49, 165; previous 56, 228–31, 235; of self 109; *see also* attachment; concentration; coping strategies; cultural context; fears; future; grief; intrusive images or thoughts; living with loss; meaning making; memory; pain; sleep; sharing experience; suicidal thoughts; talking with others; therapy; transformational loss; transgenerational loss; unprocessed loss or trauma; working with loss

managing parent's grief 166; *see also* parents
Maslow, A. 193
Maslow's Hierarchy of Needs *194*
McCarthy Dodd, S. 230, 258
meal *see* food
meaning making 58, 63, 87–8, 106–8, 111, 119, 131–2, 135–6, 144, 152, 154, 175, 180–3, 187, 189, 216, 225, 242–3; *see also* continuing bonds; transformational loss
medication 239–40
memory: box 23, 26; impaired 144, 237, 241
mental health 229, 237, 240; *see also* bipolar disorder; borderline personality disorder; psychotic episode
metaphor 167, 178, 208, 217, 241
Mezirow, J. 203
mindfulness 264–5
miscarriage 18, 20, 24, 32–4, 138
missing *see* yearning
Mitchell, J. 172
MND *see* motor neurone disease
money 47–8, 82, 89, 235
mortality: own 60, 97, 147, 154–5, 162; parents 147
Mother's Day 200
motivation 31, 237, 142; lack of 76, 112, 118, 208; *see also* energy, lethargy
motor neurone disease 169
mourn *see* grief
Moustakas, C.E. 12
moving on *see* living with loss
music 105, 119, 140, 190, 199, 242

nature *see* coping strategies
need to understand 76, 97, 105–7, 110, 131, 133, 137, 155; *see also* meaning making
Neimeyer, R.A. 223
new normal 32, 37, 117, 173, 201, 239
newspaper *see* publicity
Nietzsche, F. 178, 235
nightmares 181, 195, 229
normality 42, 58, 75, 183
numbness 55, 139, 175, 179, 186, 195, 204, 215, 236, 241–2

Orders of Love 229–31
overprotective *see* protection
overwhelm 31, 186, 204, 211, 218, 239, 256, 263

pain 43, 50, 144, 196; avoid 76, 116, 178–9, 186, 189, 195, 215; enduring 221; expressing 76; tolerate 42, 178–9, 198, 201; *see also* emotional pain, physical pain
panic 25, 59, 75, 242; attack 21, 25, 29, 58, 182, 235
Papyrus 74–5, 209, 275
paramedics 55, 72, 107, 131, 188
parents: experience of 18, 21, 35–6, 59, 75–6, 82, 89, 91, 131–2, 135–6, 138–9, 143–4, 151–2, 159–61, 163, 166–8; *see also* grandparents
Parkes, C.M. 215
patience *see* tolerance
peace 76, 184, 201, 217, 228
Persistent Complex Bereavement-Related Disorder 238
personal process 215, 254–6
perspective: changed 24–5, 42, 190, 203, 210; external 24, 153; regained 112, 187, 263
pets 31, 39, 65, 140, 198
photobook 49–50, 210
photographs 61–2, 91, 116, 161, 163, 166, 191, 225–6, 242
physical pain 10, 50, 175, 201, 216–18, 236, 241–2
physiological impact of grief 114, 119, 236–40
physiological needs 193–4, *194*, 235
platitudes 23, 218
pneumonia 40
poems 115, 161–2, 164, 182
police 72–3, 81, 84, 90, 93–4, 96, 104–6, 114, 126, 131, 139, 160, 221, 260
positivity 32, 52, 84, 88, 190, 196, 210, 234–5
possessions *see* belongings
post-mortem 19, 75, 105, 188, 260; report 105
post-traumatic stress disorder 9, 45, 133, 139, 185–6, 241; *see also* intrusive images or thoughts; sleep
pot *see* drugs
potency 246, 248, *248*, 251
prayer 33–4, 41, 162
privacy 10, 64, 163, 166, 260

Prolonged Grief Disorder 238, 241; diagnostic criteria **238**
prosecute 114
protection 9, 23, 30, 60, 75, 190, *194*, 195, 207, 228, 241–56; *see also* safety
psychiatric problems *see* mental health
psychotherapy *see* therapy
psychotic episode 103–4
PTSD *see* post-traumatic stress disorder
publicity 75, 85, 97, 108, 115, 125, 141, 204

questions: answering 18, 25, 32, 37–8, 49, 53, 144, 188, 260; asking 50, 52–3, 107–9, 216, 260; unanswered 20, 24, 97, 105–7, 158, 163, 189–90, 204–5; *see also* unfinished business

rational thinking 45, 187
reactions *see* acceptance; anger; blame; denial; depression; disorientation; friends; guilt; hope; horror; numbness; panic attack; regret; relief; sadness; shock; support; what helped; what hindered
reaction to medication 148
reality: need for 26–7
reassurance 38, 41–2, 44, 46, 62, 64, 75, 77, 186, 206, 225, 255, 259
registering death 18–19
regret 66, 104, 153, 176, 189–90, 226
relationships: lost 16, 22, 80, 109, 207; strengthened 107, 109, 166, 175, 187, 209; *see also* couples
relief 123–5, 168, 196, 236
religion *see* faith; spiritual belief
reliving 182, 239; *see also* flashbacks
remembering *see* continuing bonds
reporter *see* journalist; publicity
resilience: definitions 23; developing 191–2, 198–9, 225, 236–7; factors affecting **219**, 221, 234–5; measuring 235–6; *see also* grief models; Maslow's Hierarchy of Needs; transformational loss
respect 160, 163, 189, 246, 248, 250, 252; lack of 19, 85, 107, 197; lost 47
responsibility: acceptance of 205, *248*, 249–50; sense of 78; *see also* blame; guilt
retaining ties *see* bonds; continuing bonds; hostage bonds; meaning making
re-traumatize 239, 245

reunion 24, 88, 98, 111, 163, 221
road traffic accident 113
rupture and reconnecting bonds 187–9, 203, 205

sadness 44, 50, 65–6, 84–6, 89, 127–8, 141, 154–5, 160–1, 165, 167, 178, 182–3, 187, 197, 216, 226, 236, **238**, 239, 241, 266
safety *194*, 195, 235, 269, 271; *see also* control; protection
sand tray 183–4, 260–2
scare 43–4, 105, 133, 136–7, 178, 195, 205; *see also* fear
self-actualization needs *194*, 198
self-care 198–9, 251–4
self-esteem needs *194*, 197–8
selfish grief xii, 119, 133
self-knowledge 245–55
self-reflective practice 253–6, 268–72
self-soothe 186–7
sensationalize 10–11, 19
sensitivity 87, 145, 165, 185–6
serotonin 237
shame 109, 133, 183, 192, 204–5, *210*, 266
sharing experience 76, 86, 88, 136, 177, 191, 200, 224–5; *see also* talking with others; transformational loss
shock 56, 72, 74, 97, 105, 111, 133–4, 159, 175, 185–6, 188–9, 203–4, 215, 236
SIBAM Model 241–3
siblings: attitude towards 131–4; involvement in funeral 61, 66, 83, 89–90, 115, 118, 132, 140, 142, 150–2, 161, 164; separation 19, 25; *see also* grandparents; isolation; parents; telling siblings; therapy
sleep 185–6, 195, 236–7
snakes and arrows of transformational grief 210; diagram *210*
social, love and belongingness needs *194*, 196
social media 10–11, 91, 108, 139, 141, 197–8
songs *see* music
sources of help and support 273–7
spiritual 47, 62, 72, 77, 87, 119, 154, 162, 206, **219**, 220–1, 224, 251; *see also* faith
statistics 1–3
stillbirth 17, 28

stuckness 116, 184, 205, 211, 220, 222, 225, 265
Sudden Infant Death Syndrome 41, 130
suicidal thoughts 74–5, 115, 117, 143–4, 190–1, 216, **219**, 229, 240
suicide 67, 120, 138, 156
suicide note 69, 78, 158, 163
support: groups 23–4, 273–7; *see also* what helped; what hindered
surreal 9, 22, 42, 83, 104
surviving children *see* siblings
symbols 16, 62–3, 66
systemic family constellations *see* Family Constellations

taboo 3, 18, 23, 238
talking with others 11, 38, 44, 50–3, 56, 64, 73–4, 86, 99, 111, 116, 118, 134, 136, 165–6, 168, 177–9, 187, 191, 195, 198, 206, 220, 224, 256, 262
tasks and mediators of mourning 218–22, 235; summary **219**
teachers 134, 197–8
telling others 21, 30, 35, 56, 59–60, 73, 81–2, 128, 144
telling siblings 31, 73, 82, 105, 114, 138–9, 159–60
therapist 20, 180, 222, 228–31
therapy 208, 239–40; benefit of 32, 38–9, 59, 84, 87, 110, 119, 153, 239–40; creative techniques 260–3; experience of 25, 32, 36, 64, 90, 118, 133, 184; unsuitability 44, 64, 76, 118, 183–4, 239; *see also* working with loss
time off work 34, 41, 48, 58, 82, 164–5, 197, 253
tips from bereaved parents and siblings 51–2, 88, 98, 111–2, 119, 128–9, 135–6, 144, 168, 178–9
tissue samples 160, 188
tokens *see* fingerprint; hair
tolerance: changes in 48, 109, 111, 142, 145–6, 178, 190, 192, 195, 207, 216
transformational loss 203–13; phases 203–10; *see also* legacy work
transgenerational loss 221, 228–32, 269
transgenerational trauma 184, 228–30; *see also* cultural context; transgenerational loss
triggers 51–2, 86, 118, 126, 133–4, 176, 199–200, 223, 230, 239
trust: lost 59, 185–6, 205–6, 220; rebuilding 209, 245, 258; reinforced 206

turmoil 15, 186, 262
twin 148–53
two-chair work *see* imagined dialogues

unconscious knowing 46, 134, 180, 184; *see also* Family Constellations
undertaker 126, 163–4, 188; *see also* funeral
unfinished business 226, 263; *see also* questions, unanswered
unprocessed loss or trauma 56, 97, 132–3, 149, 154, 221, 228, 340, 235, 256

validation 180, 183, 210, 228
values 35–6, 134, 199, **219**, 220, 224, 250–2, 263
vicar 58, 61–2, 73
vicarious trauma 245
visualization 77
void 86, 91, 109, 116–17, 160, 262

wake *see* funeral
walking *see* coping strategies
Waterfall of Bereavement 216–7, *217*
Welford, E. 231
well-being *see* self-care
Wells, M. 201

what helped 9, 21–2, 24, 32, 34–5, 37–8, 41–2, 44–7, 58–9, 61–5, 74, 77–8, 86–7, 110, 119, 127–8, 134, 136, 140, 143–4, 152–3, 161, 163, 177, 179, 190, 208, 221, 256
what if roundabout 19, 105, 163, 190, 201, 204, 216
what hindered 19, 21, 23–4, 37–8, 45, 47, 51–2, 56–7, 75, 77, 82, 84–5, 87, 106–7, 122–6, 132, 134, 136, 139–41, 145–7, 160, 166–7, 196, 220, 235, 237
Whirlpool of Grief *see* Waterfall of Bereavement
Winnicott, D.W. 70
Winston's Wish 64, 277
withdraw 92–3, 186, 215, 247, 253
Worden, W. 175, 218–20
working with loss: art 262; buttons 262; letter writing 263; mindfulness 264–5; salt bottles 262–3; sand tray 260–1; *see also* ATTEND; compassion, CIRCLE of; compassion fatigue; directed journaling; Family Constellations; imagined dialogues
wreath 83, 164

yearning 64, 81, 153, 174–6, 215–16, 236, 252–3